The Foreign Corrupt Practices Act in a New Era

To various people throughout my life who had confidence in me and gave me an opportunity to succeed. Because sometimes all one needs is an opportunity. Thank you.

The Foreign Corrupt Practices Act in a New Era

Mike Koehler

Founder and Editor of FCPA Professor and Law Professor, Southern Illinois University School of Law, USA

Edward Elgar

Cheltenham, UK • Northampton, MA, USA

Published by
Edward Elgar Publishing Limited
The Lypiatts
15 Lansdown Road
Cheltenham
Glos GL50 2JA
UK

Edward Elgar Publishing, Inc.
William Pratt House
9 Dewey Court
Northampton
Massachusetts 01060
USA

A catalogue record for this book
is available from the British Library

Library of Congress Control Number: 2013957784

This book is available electronically in the ElgarOnline.com Law Subject Collection, E-ISBN 978 1 78195 441 6

MIX
Paper from responsible sources
FSC www.fsc.org FSC® C013056

ISBN 978 1 78195 440 9

Typeset by Columns Design XML Ltd, Reading
Printed and bound in Great Britain by T.J. International Ltd, Padstow

Contents

About the author

Professor Mike Koehler is a leading expert on the FCPA and other anti-corruption laws and initiatives. He has testified before Congress on the FCPA and is also a frequent speaker before business and academic audiences. Leading law reviews and journals have published Professor Koehler's scholarship; his work has been cited in legal briefs, judicial decisions, policy papers, and Congressional testimony; and he is a frequent featured source on the FCPA and related topics in various national and international media.

Professor Koehler founded and edits the award-winning FCPA Professor website (www.fcpaprofessor.com). Described as the '*Wall Street Journal* concerning all things FCPA-related,' FCPA Professor is read by a world-wide audience of attorneys, business and compliance professionals, scholars and students, journalists and other interested persons.

Prior to academia, Professor Koehler was an FCPA attorney in private practice and conducted FCPA investigations around the world, negotiated resolutions to FCPA enforcement actions with government enforcement agencies, and advised clients on FCPA compliance and risk assessment. Professor Koehler's FCPA insights are further informed by having read and analyzed: the FCPA's entire legislative history, every FCPA enforcement action, and every FCPA judicial decision.

Professor Koehler is a law professor at Southern Illinois University School of Law and was previously a law professor in the College of Business at Butler University.

Prologue

The year was 2000 and I was a first year attorney in a big law firm. The firm's listing of new matters was circulated to attorneys via the 'green sheet' – literally a green sheet of paper listing the new matters brought into the firm, the engagement attorney, and a brief description of the matter.

There it was, the Foreign Corrupt Practices Act.

I had never heard of the law, but I was instantly intrigued. At the time, I had extensive international travel experience largely the result of a unique mentoring relationship I benefited from as a student and the thought of focusing on international issues was a goal of mine as I began my legal career.

I set out to learn as much as I could about this law called the FCPA and took the brave step, for a first year attorney in a big law firm, of contacting the Washington D.C. engagement partner to express my interest in the FCPA and my willingness to assist on the matter. Time passed and the phone did not ring, but I was persistent. Several months later, an opportunity arrived and before I knew it, I was flying around the world to places like Indonesia, India, and China investigating corporate conduct that could implicate the FCPA. The work was fascinating and it opened my eyes to the complexities of doing business in the global marketplace. I was like an FCPA sponge and the international trips provided me an opportunity to read everything FCPA-related I could find.

I succeeded in my private practice career and grew as an FCPA practitioner. I conducted FCPA investigations around the world, negotiated resolutions to FCPA enforcement actions with government enforcement agencies, and advised clients on FCPA compliance and risk assessment.

However, the more I learned about the FCPA, its enforcement, and the reasons why Congress enacted this pioneering statute in 1977, the more questions I had. I soon realized that many in the industry I have come to call FCPA Inc. were singing from the same sheet of music and few of the pressing 'why questions' raised by this new era of FCPA enforcement were being asked.

I became motivated to ask the why questions, but knew that my position at a big law firm did not provide the best platform. As many attorneys do after spending several years at a big law firm, I began to reevaluate my career and asked myself what about the law, and the FCPA in particular, I enjoyed the most. For me, it was research and writing, asking the why questions, and injecting a candid and informed scholarly voice into the issues. I began doing so in 2009 when I launched my FCPA Professor website as I transitioned to my current academic career. This book is the culmination of my work thus far and I hope you find value in the pages that follow.

Introduction and overview

This book is about the Foreign Corrupt Practices Act ('FCPA'), and the FCPA is about bribery, at least a certain type of bribery – bribery of 'foreign officials.' Bribery of course is bad, and all would agree that providing a suitcase full of cash to a foreign government official to secure a foreign government contract is bribery.

You may be asking, 'how can an entire book be devoted to this topic and how can enforcement of the FCPA be controversial?' It is a good question to ask early in this book, but perhaps at the risk of over-simplication, the above scenario is where the consensus often stops.

Payments to incentivize a low-ranking foreign official with ministerial or clerical duties to do something that the official ought to do anyway – is this bribery? In passing the FCPA Congress said no, but FCPA enforcement actions in this new era seem to suggest otherwise.

Is it bribery when a corrupt foreign tax official threatens to assess penalties and shut down a company's offices unless a cash payment is made and the company acquiesces so that it can continue to do business in the country? In the eyes of the FCPA's dual enforcers (the Department of Justice and the Securities and Exchange Commission), the answer seems to be yes.

If person 'x' is the recipient of a corporate gift or entertainment or other things of value why might we call it effective sales and marketing and maintaining good will with a customer, yet if person 'y' is the recipient why might we call it bribery?

You will learn in this book that in 1977 Congress passed the FCPA. The FCPA was a pioneering statute – the first-ever law governing the conduct of domestic companies in their interactions with *foreign* government officials in *foreign* markets. Yet in passing the FCPA, Congress was confronted with many difficult and complex questions. In short, Congress quickly learned, as the above questions highlight, that corporate bribery was not the 'simple, safe issue it seemed at first blush.' The FCPA's legislative history detailed in this book teaches that:

> Trying to define exactly what bribery is is a real problem. You and I would have no trouble saying what a bribe is and what isn't. However, having said that, it's very difficult to put it down on paper in statutory language that

> would not be damaging to some legitimate things that happen on the periphery … In certain instances, we have a gray area when it comes to this bribery question.

The FCPA's legislative history further instructs that there will be 'countless situations' in which fair-minded individuals 'will be hard-put to determine whether a particular payment or practice is a legitimate and permissible business activity or a means of improper influence.' It was noted that reasonable persons 'and even angels will differ on the answers … [and] such distinctions should make us less sweeping in our judgments and less confident in our solutions.'

This is particularly true, as Congress acknowledged, given the foreign business conditions and barriers that often funnel well-intentioned businesses into an arbitrary world where harassment bribery flourishes and is condoned. Indeed, a former Chief of the DOJ's FCPA unit observed:

> In my almost 40 years of experience, I have rarely seen American companies affirmatively offering bribes in the first instance; rather they are typically reacting to a world not of their making. It is a fact that corruption in government remains endemic worldwide and that is not likely to change. As the world shrinks companies who seek to do the right thing can't help but confront corrupt officials – as customers, regulators, and adjudicators – and confront them often.'

There are many other difficult and complex questions relevant to this new era of FCPA enforcement.

Who decides what bribery is? Under our legal system, Congress passes laws, enforcement agencies enforce the laws, and courts oversee an adversarial system in which mitigating facts and potential defenses are weighed to determine if the enforcement agency has met its high burden of proof as to each element of the law that Congress passed. Yet, as detailed in this book, FCPA enforcement in this new era has largely bypassed this system that has served our country well since its founding.

Are business organizations that resolve FCPA enforcement actions or subject to FCPA scrutiny 'bad' or 'unethical.'? The enforcement agencies often link FCPA enforcement to classical notions of bribery such as roads not being built, schools lying in ruins, and basic public services going unprovided. However, many companies that resolve FCPA enforcement actions are otherwise viewed as industry leaders that sell the best products for the best prices. Some of these companies have been recognized as being among the 'world's most ethical companies' during the same general time period relevant to an FCPA enforcement action or instance of FCPA scrutiny. How is it that a 'world's most ethical company' can also be the subject of FCPA enforcement? Moreover, can it truly be said that the sole reason such companies obtained or retained the business was because of the alleged improper payments?

Is it bribery if the conduct was engaged in with the knowledge and support of the highest levels of the U.S. government? Are there two tiers of justice when it comes to FCPA enforcement in which certain companies that sell certain products to certain customers are treated differently than other companies?

If bribery – however defined – is bad, does that mean that all attempts to punish bribery and deter future misconduct are good? Why has FCPA enforcement increased such that it is now a top legal and compliance concern for companies doing business in the global marketplace? Is more FCPA enforcement an inherent good, regardless of resolution vehicles used, regardless of enforcement theories, and regardless of actual outcomes? Has the quantity of FCPA enforcement actions become a higher priority for the enforcement agencies than the quality of the enforcement actions?

A former DOJ Assistant Chief for FCPA enforcement candidly stated, 'the government sees a profitable program, and it's going to ride that horse until it can't ride it anymore.' However, should return on investment be a consideration in law enforcement or should enforcement agencies only enforce a law consistent with Congressional intent in the context of an adversarial system with appropriate checks and balances and judicial scrutiny? Indeed, one of the greatest challenges in this new era is how to enforce the FCPA consistent with the rule of law, and its demand for transparency and consistency, and in a way that inspires public confidence that enforcement is fair and actually effective in achieving the laudable objectives of the FCPA.

What have been the effects of this new era of FCPA enforcement? In response to this new era, more business organizations have implemented in good faith, pro-active compliance policies and procedures designed to minimize FCPA risk. Yet, why does FCPA compliance remain difficult for even the most well-managed and well-intentioned companies and why are so many companies the subject of FCPA scrutiny?

Has this new era of FCPA enforcement resulted in wasteful over-compliance, with companies viewing every foreign business partner with irrational suspicion and companies deploying teams of lawyers and specialists around the world spending millions of dollars to uncover every potential questionable or unethical corporate payment? Indeed, one of the effects of this new era of FCPA enforcement has been the emergence of a 'thriving and lucrative anti-bribery complex' that, in the words of a former Chief of the DOJ's FCPA unit, has been 'good business for law firms, [...] good business for accounting firms, [...] good business for consulting firms, the media – and Justice Department lawyers who create the marketplace and then get [themselves] a job.' For many FCPA Inc. participants, the new era of FCPA enforcement has been a desirable boom.

Yet is the status quo in fact desirable from a legal or policy perspective? Has this new era of FCPA enforcement been successful in actually reducing bribery? If not, can the FCPA be improved through amendment and can certain enforcement agency policies and procedures be revised to better achieve the original aims of the FCPA? As the FCPA's legislative history instructs, 'just because the FCPA spotlights a sensitive subject [...] some people turn a blind eye to its shortcomings rather than risk being accused of being soft on bribery.'

It is these questions, and many more, which make the FCPA a worthwhile and controversial topic capable of filling the pages of an entire book.

This book begins the same way I began my testimony before a Senate committee that was examining FCPA enforcement.

> The FCPA is a fundamentally sound statute that was passed by Congress in 1977 for a specific reason. [...] In enacting the FCPA in 1977, Congress specifically intended for its anti-bribery provisions to be narrow in scope and Congress further recognized and accepted that the FCPA would not cover every type of questionable payment uncovered or disclosed during the mid-1970's. [...] That the FCPA is a fundamentally sound statute does not mean that FCPA enforcement is always fundamentally sound.

That is what this book is about – the FCPA and its enforcement in a new era.

In 2010, the DOJ Assistant Attorney General proclaimed, 'we are in a new era of [FCPA] enforcement; and we are here to stay.' While much of what defines this new era began sprouting years prior, the formal declaration of the new era was a significant milestone. Indeed, of the nearly 900 federal statutes the DOJ criminal division enforces, the FCPA is one of the DOJ's 'top priorities' and the DOJ has stated that its 'focus and resolve in the FCPA area will not abate.' Likewise, in 2010 the SEC created a specialized FCPA Unit and declared that the FCPA would be a 'vital part' of its overall enforcement program. The SEC stated that the FCPA Unit would be 'more proactive' in its enforcement of the FCPA including through 'targeted sweeps and sector-wide investigations.'

For these reasons, the FCPA has emerged as a top legal and compliance concern for companies – both public and private and across a variety of industry sectors – doing business in the global marketplace.

Understanding the FCPA's new era is thus a fundamental skill-set for a diverse group of professionals navigating this marketplace. Simply put, if you are a professional doing business in the global marketplace, the FCPA needs to be part of your vocabulary.

Yet the declaration of the FCPA's new era in 2010 was also a curious milestone. Not one word of the FCPA has changed since 1998, and it was not obvious why a new era of FCPA should be declared or why FCPA enforcement has materially and dramatically changed over the past decade.

This book dissects the FCPA's new era, and readers from the classroom, to the courtroom, to the boardroom will benefit from the chapters that follow which place the FCPA's new era in context and provide a practical and provocative analysis of the FCPA, its enforcement, and related topics.

In dissecting the FCPA's new era, you will confront the FCPA statutory text, legislative history, and judicial decisions. Much of this legal authority is presented in depth in its original source format because what a law says, what Congress intended the law to mean, and how courts have interpreted the law is what matters most in this new era of FCPA enforcement. However, you will learn that what seems to matter most in this new era is not such legal authority, but non-legal sources of information such as enforcement agency guidance and resolved FCPA enforcement actions known as prosecutorial common law.

From these various sources of authority and information, you will understand how many instances of corporate FCPA scrutiny in this new era raise two distinct questions. The first is whether Congress, in passing the FCPA, intended to capture the conduct at issue. The second is whether the conduct at issue can expose a company to an FCPA enforcement action given the current enforcement theories of the DOJ and SEC.

This book injects innovative and provocative concepts to the study of the FCPA and its enforcement such as the 'world's most ethical FCPA violators,' 'the façade of enforcement,' the 'three buckets' of FCPA financial exposure, 'FCPA Inc. and the business of bribery' and the 'offensive use' of the FCPA. Useful tables and charts will better instruct you on various aspects of the FCPA's new era and its legal and policy implications. In addition, throughout this book you will assemble a pair of 'FCPA goggles' and learn compliance pointers and risk-assessment strategies that can lessen the likelihood of FCPA violations from occurring when doing business in the global marketplace. In this way, the book provides a toolkit that you can use in your profession to better understand the FCPA, its enforcement, and the many legal and policy issues present in this new era.

This book places an emphasis on learning FCPA issues incrementally in the belief that foundational knowledge introduced early will best enhance understanding and comprehension of specific FCPA topics that follow. Consistent with this objective, the nine chapters of this book are organized as follows.

CHAPTER 1

In this new era of FCPA enforcement, it may seem odd to begin by rewinding the clock back to a different era. However, to best understand and appreciate the FCPA's new era, it is first necessary to understand and appreciate why the FCPA became a law. As with most new laws, the FCPA did not appear out of thin air. Rather you will learn of the real events and real policy reasons that motivated Congress to act and pass the FCPA.

Chapter 1 tells the FCPA's story through original voices of actual participants who shaped the pioneering law signed by President Jimmy Carter in 1977. This chapter will also highlight early FCPA enforcement and how the FCPA matured through its 1988 and 1998 amendments into its modern form. By the end of Chapter 1, you will possess a firm understanding for why Congress enacted the FCPA, what conduct Congress sought to capture in enacting the law, and how the FCPA was enforced prior to this new era. Knowledge of this FCPA history is critical to understanding the FCPA's new era and addressing the FCPA's future.

CHAPTER 2

This book, of course, focuses on a particular statute, but it is important to understand from the beginning that other general legal principles, as well as general DOJ and SEC enforcement policies and resolution vehicles, impact FCPA enforcement. Chapter 2 highlights such general foundational knowledge to best enhance your understanding and comprehension of the specific FCPA topics that follow.

The first general legal principle is *respondeat superior*. Business organizations operating in the global marketplace act through employees and agents, and pursuant to *respondeat superior*, employee and agent conduct can expose a business organization to legal liability, both criminal and civil, even if the employee or agent acts contrary to the organization's pre-existing compliance policies. Understanding this key legal principle, as well as the realities of the global marketplace that are also highlighted, instruct how companies often become the subject of FCPA scrutiny. Because of *respondeat superior*, and the realities of the global marketplace, not all companies that resolve FCPA enforcement action are 'bad' or 'unethical,' and this chapter introduces you to the term 'world's most ethical FCPA violators.'

Next, general DOJ and SEC enforcement policies are introduced and the 'carrots' and 'sticks' relevant to resolving a corporate FCPA enforcement action are highlighted. Mindful of these 'carrots' and 'sticks,' business organizations are often motivated to resolve FCPA enforcement actions for reasons of risk aversion, and not necessarily because the enforcement agency has a superior legal position. Discussion will next turn to the typical resolution vehicles used to enforce the FCPA in this new era – DOJ non-prosecution agreements ('NPAs') and deferred prosecution agreements ('DPAs') and SEC 'neither admit nor deny' settlements. You will confront the controversial aspects of these resolution vehicles and can decide whether they are in the public interest or facilitate a 'façade' of FCPA enforcement. Against the backdrop of several general enforcement agency policies that impact FCPA enforcement is also a specific DOJ policy that has resulted in the FCPA being enforced differently than most other federal criminal statutes.

Prior to diving into the specific elements of the FCPA's anti-bribery and books and records and internal controls provisions in Chapters 3 and 4, it is useful to first address the question of what the FCPA actually means. Chapter 2 thus concludes by setting forth a hierarchy of FCPA legal authority and other information and you will discover that much of what defines this new era of FCPA enforcement is non-binding, non-legal sources of FCPA information including so-called prosecutorial common law.

With the foundational knowledge acquired in Chapter 2, a comprehensive analysis of the FCPA's provisions can proceed in a more informed and sophisticated manner.

CHAPTER 3

Chapter 3 provides a comprehensive analysis of the FCPA's anti-bribery provisions and its general elements: offering or paying money or anything of value, to a foreign official, to obtain or retain business, with a corrupt intent. For each element, legal sources of authority as well as non-legal sources of information will be discussed.

To state the obvious, providing a suitcase full of cash to a foreign government official to obtain a foreign government contract satisfies the elements of the anti-bribery provisions. However, you will learn that FCPA enforcement actions seldom involve such scenarios and the proper scope of the anti-bribery provisions is subject to much dispute in this new era as legal development of these elements is still in its infancy.

You will also learn that the FCPA's anti-bribery provisions prohibit not only direct payments to 'foreign officials' to 'obtain or retain business,' but also payments to 'any person' 'while knowing' that the payments will be provided to a 'foreign official.' Given the prevalence of foreign third parties, the FCPA's third-party payment provisions often present the greatest source of FCPA risk for companies competing in the global marketplace. In addition to the substantive elements of the anti-bribery provisions, jurisdictional issues will also be discussed including extra-territorial jurisdiction as to U.S. actors as well as the expansive jurisdictional theories advanced by the enforcement agencies in bringing FCPA enforcement actions against foreign actors.

Even if all of the substantive elements of the anti-bribery provisions have been met and there is jurisdiction over the actor, the final step in analyzing the anti-bribery provisions is determining whether the FCPA's facilitating payment exception or the FCPA's affirmative defenses apply. After highlighting legal authority and non-legal sources of information relevant to the exception and affirmative defenses, the question is posed whether the FCPA's facilitating payment exception has any real meaning in the new era or whether the enforcement agencies have essentially repealed this exception through its enforcement theories.

Chapter 3 will conclude by highlighting other legal issues also relevant to FCPA enforcement in this new era, including statute of limitations issues and how the FCPA is a supply-side statute targeting only one actor in a bribery scheme.

CHAPTER 4

The FCPA is a law much broader than its name suggests. Indeed, most FCPA enforcement actions are not foreign in nature and do not involve allegations of bribery. This odd dynamic is the result of the FCPA's books and records and internal controls provisions which are among the most generic substantive legal provisions one can find.

In Chapter 4, you will learn that Congress intended for the FCPA's more glamorous anti-bribery provisions to operate in tandem with these generic provisions to reduce instances of corporate bribery and other misconduct. Although allegations of foreign bribery are not necessary for the FCPA's books and records and internal controls provisions to be implicated, these provisions, which apply only to so-called issuers under the FCPA, are nearly always charged in issuer FCPA anti-bribery violations. The enforcement theory giving rise to books and records and internal controls violations in nearly every instance is that the alleged improper payments were misrecorded on the issuer's books and records and insufficient internal controls allowed the improper payments to occur.

While a dull read, the FCPA's books and records and internal controls provisions are nevertheless potent provisions particularly because they operate independently of the FCPA's anti-bribery provisions and can be charged even if all the elements of an FCPA anti-bribery violation are not met. Even though potent, you will nevertheless learn from the FCPA's legislative history that Congress specifically qualified these provisions through concepts of reasonableness and good faith.

Against the backdrop of generic statutory language, Chapter 4 will also highlight legal authority and enforcement agency guidance concerning the books and records and internal controls provisions. From there, enforcement agency theories are introduced through actual FCPA enforcement actions, and the question is posed whether certain theories are in fact consistent with relevant legal authority or even enforcement agency guidance.

CHAPTER 5

Chapters 3 and 4 will provide a comprehensive analysis of the FCPA's anti-bribery and books and records and internal controls provisions. Yet just because these provisions may be violated does not mean that an FCPA enforcement action will result. To state the obvious, the enforcement agencies must first learn of the improper conduct. Chapter 5 begins by highlighting the typical origins of FCPA enforcement actions including the prominent, yet controversial, role voluntary disclosures play in serving as the basis for most FCPA enforcement actions.

Next, Chapter 5 introduces you to the 'three buckets' of FCPA financial exposure. The first bucket is pre-enforcement action professional fees and expenses, and you will learn how long FCPA scrutiny typically lasts and why. The second bucket is fine, penalty and disgorgement amounts in an actual FCPA enforcement action, and you will learn how such amounts are calculated by the enforcement agencies as well as certain controversial aspects regarding these amounts. The third bucket is post-enforcement action professional fees and expenses, and you will learn that a company's financial exposure rarely ends with an FCPA enforcement action. Of these 'three buckets,' while settlement amounts in an actual FCPA enforcement action tend to get the most attention, pre-enforcement action professional fees and expenses are often the most expensive aspect of FCPA scrutiny and enforcement.

Chapter 5 will then analyze and compare the FCPA's two enforcement regimes: corporate enforcement actions and individual enforcement actions.

After highlighting various facts and figures from corporate FCPA enforcement actions, certain uncomfortable truths regarding corporate FCPA enforcement will be discussed including how certain companies in certain industries appear to be immune from FCPA anti-bribery charges and how the general fight against bribery and corruption suffers from several double standards.

After highlighting various facts and figures from individual FCPA enforcement actions, discussion will focus on how, despite enforcement agency rhetoric to the contrary, FCPA enforcement in this new era is largely corporate enforcement only. However, on occasion individuals are also charged with FCPA offenses and this chapter will also discuss dynamics relevant to resolving FCPA individual enforcement actions. Unlike business organizations subject to FCPA scrutiny, individuals are often more motivated to put the enforcement agencies to its burden of proof at trial and this chapter will also highlight how the enforcement agencies have generally struggled when put to its burden of proof in individual FCPA enforcement actions.

Chapter 5 concludes with a discussion of sentencing issues in individual enforcement actions and how sentencing judges often see shades of gray in FCPA enforcement actions that the DOJ portrays to be black and white.

CHAPTER 6

That FCPA enforcement has increased in this new era begs the question why? Chapter 6 offers several practical and provocative reasons for the increase in FCPA enforcement.

Practical reasons include that there is more international business, the introduction of NPAs and DPAs to the FCPA context, and the impact another law – Sarbanes Oxley – has had on FCPA enforcement.

Provocative reasons highlighted include the belief by many that FCPA enforcement has increased because it is lucrative for the government. In addition, one of the effects of this new era of FCPA enforcement has been the emergence of a thriving and vibrant anti-bribery complex called FCPA Inc. and the issue will be explored whether FCPA Inc. itself is one of the reasons for the increase in FCPA enforcement and scrutiny.

Even though FCPA enforcement has trended upward during this new era, enforcement statistics need to be viewed in the proper context. Chapter 6 concludes by placing FCPA enforcement statistics in the proper perspective and demonstrating that the FCPA is not nearly the boogeyman it is often portrayed to be.

CHAPTER 7

Chapter 7 explores the FCPA's long tentacles and demonstrates how actual FCPA enforcement actions brought by the DOJ and/or SEC are often just one consequence of FCPA scrutiny in this new era.

Indeed, when the dust settles on a corporate FCPA enforcement action a company may become the subject of a foreign law enforcement investigation or enforcement action based on the same core conduct alleged in the FCPA enforcement action. After all, the U.S. action was based on allegations that the company, or someone on its behalf, made payments to a foreign official to obtain or retain business. It is thus understandable why foreign law enforcement agencies may also investigate the conduct and seek monetary fines and penalties.

Next, Chapter 7 focuses on the business effects of FCPA scrutiny and enforcement. You will learn from various case studies how FCPA scrutiny can impact a company's business operations and strategy in a variety of ways from market capitalization, to cost of capital, to merger and acquisition activity, to impeding or distracting a company from achieving other business objectives. For these reasons, FCPA scrutiny and exposure is not just a legal issue, but a business issue as well that needs to be on the radar screen of business leaders operating in the global marketplace.

FCPA scrutiny and enforcement can also expose corporate directors and executives to private FCPA-related civil suits. Although courts have held that the FCPA does not provide a private right of action, in this new era, plaintiff's lawyers representing shareholders often target corporate leaders with civil suits alleging, among other things, breach of fiduciary duty or that the company engaged in securities fraud, in connection with the company's FCPA scrutiny. Chapter 7 highlights FCPA-related shareholder litigation and explores whether such suits serve a purpose or are merely parasitic actions which feed off FCPA scrutiny and enforcement in this new era.

Chapter 7 next discusses an emerging trend. Ordinarily, companies are in a defensive posture when it comes to the FCPA. However, in this new era the FCPA is increasingly being used 'offensively' to achieve a business objective or to further advance litigating positions.

In short, the FCPA has long tentacles and there are many reasons to comply with the FCPA in addition to the obvious reason that non-compliance can expose a company and culpable individuals to an FCPA enforcement action. At the same time, because of the FCPA's long tentacles and the feeding frenzy that often follows FCPA scrutiny or enforcement actions, it is important that FCPA enforcement be subjected to meaningful judicial scrutiny and that enforcement actions represent legitimate instances of provable FCPA violations, not merely settlements entered into for reasons of risk aversion.

CHAPTER 8

Chapter 8 is devoted to FCPA compliance. However, before diving into the specifics of this topic, it is important to recognize that FCPA compliance is difficult for even the most well-managed and well-intentioned business organization. This is due to *respondeat superior*, the realities of doing business in the global marketplace, and the shifting and often conflicting messages by the enforcement agencies. Because of these difficulties, and the fact that rogue employees exist and no compliance program can ever prevent all misconduct, FCPA risk can't be eliminated.

However, FCPA risk can be effectively managed and minimized, and one positive result of the increase in FCPA enforcement in this new era has been the related increase in 'soft' enforcement of the FCPA through compliance policies and procedures. Certain FCPA enforcement actions provide an opportunity to learn and Chapter 8 will showcase various teachable moments from compliance failures in actual enforcement actions.

FCPA compliance however is not a one-size-fits-all proposition. Rather effective and cost-efficient FCPA compliance is best achieved through conducting a risk assessment, and you will learn the basic fundamentals of conducting a risk assessment so that compliance can be uniquely tailored to a company's FCPA risk profile.

Chapter 8 also highlights various FCPA compliance best practices – from high-level commitment to third-party due diligence and oversight, to review and monitoring of compliance programs – designed to manage and minimize FCPA risk. A component of FCPA best practices is ensuring that compliance is not viewed strictly as a legal function but rather holistically throughout a business organization. This requires not only active engagement and participation by legal personnel, but also training of other personnel such as finance and audit professionals so that they can approach their job functions with FCPA goggles on and recognize FCPA risk and report it to appropriate experts within the organization.

Even though more FCPA compliance is one positive result of this new era, Chapter 8 concludes by examining whether certain aspects of FCPA enforcement have resulted in wasteful overcompliance and whether too much FCPA compliance and training have resulted in compliance fatigue and its unintended consequence of numbing individuals to the FCPA.

CHAPTER 9

This book concludes by returning to an opening thesis – while the FCPA is a fundamentally sound statute, this does not mean that the FCPA could not be improved or that FCPA enforcement is always fundamentally sound. Indeed, one of the greatest challenges in this new era is how to enforce the FCPA consistent with the rule of law, and its demand for transparency and consistency, and in a way that inspires public confidence that enforcement is fair and actually effective in achieving the FCPA's objectives.

Reforming a law called the 'Foreign Corrupt Practices Act' has always been a political hot potato and a substantive, issue-based discussion has always been difficult. However, declaration of the FCPA's new era and wider recognition of the enforcement theories and policies which have come to define this era have resulted in the positive development of greater attention to the FCPA and its enforcement on Capitol Hill and among other policy makers and interested observers.

Chapter 9 focuses on FCPA reform and, among others things, highlights recent reform proposals and related Congressional hearings. As history instructs, the mere discussion of FCPA reform has once again been opposed by some who have advanced the simplistic – either you are against bribery or for bribery – position. The implicit position of those opposing FCPA reform would seem to be that the FCPA is a perfect statute and that the current FCPA enforcement policies are best achieving the laudable objectives of the FCPA.

This is not the position advanced in Chapter 9. Rather, FCPA reforms are suggested that are designed to ensure that the FCPA is best achieving the original goals of the law and that FCPA enforcement is transparent and otherwise consistent with the rule of law. Using the knowledge base acquired throughout this book, you can analyze this new era of FCPA enforcement and determine for yourself whether FCPA reform is warranted.

1. Before the new era: the story of the FCPA and its early enforcement

In a book titled 'The Foreign Corrupt Practices Act in a New Era', it may seem odd to begin by rewinding the clock back to a different era. However, to best understand and appreciate the FCPA's new era, it is first necessary to understand and appreciate why the FCPA became a law in 1977. As with most new laws, the FCPA did not appear out of thin air. Rather, real events and real policy reasons motivated Congress to act and pass the FCPA, and this chapter begins by telling the FCPA's story.

In this chapter, you will also be introduced to early FCPA enforcement and understand how the FCPA matured through its 1988 and 1998 amendments into its modern form.

A. THE IMPORTANCE OF THE FCPA'S LEGISLATIVE HISTORY

Why Congress enacted the FCPA and what conduct Congress sought to capture by the law are topics that are often overlooked in this new era. However, the FCPA's legislative history is important and the Supreme Court has noted that the legislative history of a statute is frequently the most fruitful source of instruction as to its proper interpretation.[1] In the FCPA context, an appellate court explained:

> Our task in interpreting the FCPA 'is to construe the language so as to give effect to the intent of Congress.' To do so, we look primarily to the language of the statute and secondarily to its legislative history, which includes 'the purpose the original enactment served, the discussion of statutory meaning in committee reports … and the remarks in debate preceding passage.'[2]

Another appellate court noted: 'As the [FCPA's] language itself is amenable to more than one reasonable interpretation, it is ambiguous as a matter of law. We turn therefore to legislative history in our effort to ascertain Congress's true intentions.'[3]

Indeed, a statute's legislative history is all the more important when it contains vague and ambiguous terms and it has been noted that 'vagueness and ambiguity are the DNA of the FCPA.'[4] Although you will learn that judicial scrutiny of FCPA enforcement is rare, in the few instances in which the FCPA has been subjected to judicial scrutiny judges have frequently found that the FCPA's elements are ambiguous and thus resorted to the legislative history.[5] Sources of FCPA legislative history that judges have consulted include committee reports; statements by legislators in debates, particularly those sponsoring legislation; testimony at congressional hearings; facts and circumstances Congress was aware of when considering the law; and bills considered but rejected by Congress.[6]

Understanding the FCPA's legislative history is thus not merely an interesting history lesson or an academic exercise. Rather, the rule of law demands an analysis of the legislative history in giving meaning to the FCPA. For this reason, Chapter 1 begins by highlighting the FCPA's extensive legislative history.

B. THE STORY OF THE FCPA

In the mid-1970s, Congress journeyed into uncharted territory. After more than two years of investigation, deliberation and consideration, what emerged in 1977 was the FCPA. The FCPA was a pioneering statute and the first law in the world governing domestic business conduct with *foreign* government officials in *foreign* markets.

In this section, the FCPA's story is told largely through original voices of actual participants who shaped the pioneering and controversial law signed by President Jimmy Carter in 1977.

Among other issues, you will learn in this section:

- how the foreign corporate payments problem was discovered, specific events that prompted congressional concern, and the policy ramifications of those events – most notably foreign policy – which motivated Congress to act;
- that upon discovery of the foreign corporate payments problem, Congress's first task was to determine if the payments were adequately captured by existing law;
- how seeking new legislative remedies to the foreign corporate payments problem was far from a consensus view of the U.S. government and the divergent views as to a solution;

- how Congress sought to address the foreign corporate payments problem from a variety of angles and the resulting two main competing legislative responses to the problem – a disclosure approach as to a broad category of payments and a criminalization approach as to a narrow category of payments; and
- how the FCPA was intended to be a limited statute in that even though Congress learned of a variety of foreign corporate payments to a variety of recipients and for a variety of reasons, Congress accepted in passing the FCPA to capture only a narrow category of such payments.

The Foreign Payments Problem

Discovery of the foreign corporate payments problem in the mid-1970s resulted from a combination of work by the Office of the Watergate Special Prosecutor, including related follow-up work and investigations by the SEC, and Senator Frank Church's Subcommittee on Multinational Corporations (Church Committee).

The Report of the SEC on Questionable and Illegal Corporate Payments and Practices (SEC Report) stated:

> In 1973, as a result of the work of the [Watergate Prosecutor] several corporations and executive officers were charged with using corporate funds for illegal domestic political contributions. The Commission recognized that these activities involved matters of possible significance to public investors, the nondisclosure of which might entail violations of the federal securities laws. ... The Commission's inquiry into the circumstances surrounding alleged illegal political campaign contributions revealed that violations of the federal securities laws had indeed occurred. The staff discovered falsifications of corporate financial records, designed to disguise or conceal the source and application of corporate funds misused for illegal purposes, as well as the existence of secret 'slush funds' disbursed outside the normal financial accountability system. These secret funds were used for a number of purposes, including in some instances, questionable or illegal foreign payments.[7]

Along with the SEC's work, the Church Committee also helped shine a light on questionable foreign corporate payments. In 1975, the Church Committee held the first of several hearings generally dealing with U.S. corporate political contributions to foreign governments. Senator Church opened the hearings as follows:

> In the course of the Watergate Committee hearings and the investigation by the Special Prosecutor, it became apparent that major American corporations

> had made illegal political contributions in the United States. More recently, the [SEC] has revealed that several multinational corporations had failed to report to their shareholders millions of dollars of offshore payments in violation of the Securities laws of the United States. … The [SEC] is understandably concerned that the disclosure requirements of U.S. laws are complied with. This subcommittee is concerned with the foreign policy consequences of these payments by U.S.-based multinational corporations. This is not a pleasant or easy subject for the corporations involved or U.S. Government officials to discuss in a public forum. This subcommittee deliberated long and hard as to whether it should pursue this matter, and, if so, in what fashion. It decided by a unanimous vote to initiate this investigation and to do so in open public hearings. For what we are concerned with is not a question of private or public morality. What concerns us here is a major issue of foreign policy for the United States.[8]

The Church Committee held separate hearings regarding Gulf Oil, Northrop, Mobil Oil, and Lockheed. Each of these corporations was the subject of allegations, or had already made admissions, concerning questionable payments made directly or indirectly to foreign government officials or foreign political parties. For instance, Gulf Oil principally involved contributions to the political campaign of the President of the Republic of Korea. Northrop principally involved payments to a Saudi Arabian general. Exxon and Mobil Oil principally involved contributions to Italian political parties. Lockheed principally involved payments to Japanese Prime Minister Tanaka, Prince Bernhard (the Inspector General of the Dutch Armed Forces and the husband of Queen Juliana of the Netherlands), and Italian political parties. In addition, foreign payments by United Brands and Ashland Oil also concerned Congress. United Brands principally involved payments to Oswaldo Lopez Arellano, the President of Honduras and Ashland Oil principally involved payments to Albert Bernard Bongo, the President of Gabon.

Even though the problematic corporate payments unearthed in the mid-1970s were extensive and significant, efforts were made to place the conduct in the proper context. For instance, a Department of the Treasury official stated during a 1976 House hearing:

> Although I do not wish to minimize the seriousness of the problem, the situation can be put in the proper light by noting that the approximately 200 firms [the subject of questionable payment inquiries] come from a total of more than 9,000 that regularly file with the Commission. … Only a relatively few firms appear to have engaged in making questionable payments abroad. The vast bulk of our firms conduct their businesses ethically and completely in accord with the laws of the United States. We should not let the activities of a minority of U.S. firms operating abroad cast doubts on the nature or conduct of U.S. business generally.[9]

Even as to the companies implicated in the questionable conduct, the SEC Report noted that '[t]he conduct reported varies significantly, and the companies included can by no means universally be characterized as wrongdoers.' In a 1975 speech included in the legislative record, the SEC Chairman stated:

> All improper foreign payments, of course, are not big bribes. Many of them are small and in the foreign community where made possibly not really regarded as improper at all. If the local plant manager in a foreign country has to slip a weekly mordita of modest amount to the postman in order to get regular mail deliveries, or to the customs inspector, the fire inspector or the tax collector, is that something for us to get excited about? In our public statements, individual members of the Commission have said no, at least where these payments conform to custom and usage. Similar payments, at the local level, anyway, are not unknown in the United States.[10]

Likewise, the SEC Chairman stated:

> It is, of course, important … to make distinctions among these companies. It is quite true that in some cases the payments were cynically and arrogantly made by top corporate officials who knew they were acting contrary to existing laws and regulations and without the authority of their board of directors. Indeed, many went to great lengths to conceal their conduct from the outside auditors, outside directors, and of course, the shareholders. But it is equally true that in a very large number of cases, the sums of money that have been involved are relatively small and were made by persons at a much lower level of management who went to great pains to conceal their own activities from their superiors. Unfortunately, the distinctions between these different types of corporate misconduct have not been made sufficiently clear to the public.[11]

Indeed, some resented that U.S. companies were being unjustly pilloried for a worldwide problem. Senator Abraham Ribicoff was the most passionate in his views. During a 1975 Senate hearing in the early stage of Congress's investigation of the problem, he described a recent trip to world capitals to discuss various trade issues and stated:

> What disturbed me as I traveled around the world was the realization that American business was being internationally blamed for activities which are very obvious to me were a very common practice throughout the entire world. […] And I sort of resented American companies being pilloried for what was a common practice throughout the world. … American corporations have been pilloried on the front pages and the television of not only the United States but throughout the entire world. And the world and the American people have been given to believe that American corporations are the only malefactors of this practice. And, yet, anybody who knows what is going on

> worldwide knows this is a worldwide phenomenon; that business houses and business corporations in every nation of the world are paying under the table and are guilty of bribes but none of them paint them this way.[12]

Foreign policy was the primary policy concern from the discovered foreign corporate payments which motivated Congress to act. Representative Robert Nix, who chaired a series of House hearings in 1975 as to the foreign corporate payments, stated:

> There has been a negative impact on our foreign policy already because of these revelations. Peru has expropriated property of the Gulf Corp. in that country. Costa Rica is considering expropriation legislation and other countries in Latin America may be considering such steps. The interference in democratic elections with corporate gifts undermines everything we are trying to do as a leader of the free world … In Italy the Communist party is using the fact of multinational bribery in Italy against the political friends of the United States.[13]

In chairing another 1975 Senate hearing regarding the foreign payments, Senator Church again expressed that foreign policy was his chief concern:

> There is also little doubt that widespread corruption serves to undermine those moderate democratic and pro-free-enterprise governments which the United States has traditionally sought to foster and support. Several oil companies testified before the subcommittee that they had made huge political contributions in Italy and Korea, for example. They claimed to be supporting the democratic forces who are friendly to foreign capital in those countries, but in fact, they were subverting the basic democratic processes of those two countries by making illegal contributions and were, at the same time, providing the radical left with its strongest election issue. The large and steady gains made by the Italian Communist Party in recent elections are due in no small part to the fact that it is believed to be the only non-corrupt political force in the country, while the other parties are seen as the handmaidens of foreign and domestic financial interests. So that while bribes and kickbacks may bolster sales in the short run, the open participation of American firms in such practices can, in the long run, only serve to discredit them and the United States. Ultimately, they create the conditions which bring to power political forces that are no friends of ours … I have focused on the foreign policy aspects of this issue because that is the chief concern of my subcommittee.[14]

Senator Church further stated:

> These very practices have extremely serious consequences both for the conduct of U.S. foreign policy and the reception U.S. business receives

> abroad. U.S.-based corporations should not be allowed to weaken a friendly government through bribery and corruption while the United States is relying on that government as a stable sure friend in supporting our policies. U.S.-based corporations should not be supporting political factions antithetical to those supported by the U.S. Government. Nor do we want, as was revealed in Multinational Subcommittee hearings, the defense priorities of our allies distorted by corporate bribery.
>
> Further, when these payments become known, and they will and do, whether it be through revelations by Senate subcommittees or through the common knowledge that leads to revolution and the downfall of such governments …, the repercussions are often international and the foreign policy implications for the United States severe. Payments by Lockheed alone may very well advance the communists in Italy. In Japan, a mainstay of our foreign policy in the Far East, the government is reeling as a consequence of payments by Lockheed. Inquiries have begun in many other countries. The Communist bloc chortles with glee at the sight of corrupt capitalism.[15]

Representative Solarz, who emerged as a leader in the House as to the foreign payments problem, stated during a House hearing:

> What is at stake is much more than the individual interests of corporations which are competing for a share of foreign markets. What is in fact at stake is the foreign policy and national interest of the United States. It is clearly in our interest to put a stop to these pernicious practices. […] We simply cannot permit activity which so damages U.S. foreign policy.[16]

Even though foreign policy was the primary policy concern motivating Congress to act, it was not the sole concern. Congressional motivation was also sparked by a post-Watergate morality, economic perceptions including a sense that prohibiting foreign corporate payments would give U.S. companies a comparative advantage and actually help companies resist foreign payment demands, as well as global leadership.

Representative Solarz stated during a 1975 House hearing:

> Simple business ethics would seem to dictate the standards on which firms would conduct their affairs, and it is truly a sad commentary that the excuse put forward by most of the corporations is that other nations engage in bribery and massive political contributions as well. The conduct of commercial operations by foreign nations in a morally shabby manner is no excuse for American citizens to engage in such scandalous activities as well. To the extent that international bribery is characteristic of business dealings in other parts of the world, the participation of American firms in it warrants prompt and effective elimination. … What is at stake here is really, in a number of significant respects, the reputation of our own country, and I think that we have an obligation to set a standard of honesty and integrity in our business

> dealings not only at home but also abroad which will be a beacon for the light of integrity for the rest of the world.[17]

Even though many of the foreign corporate payments presented a moral quandary, not all participants in the legislative debate were prepared to offer a firm response. For instance, during a Senate hearing in 1975 focused on the Lockheed scandal, Senator John Tower stated: 'A central question is raised here and that is, is it morally right for an American company to operate within the mores and folkways of the society in which they are trying to do business? I'm not prepared to give a snap answer to that myself.'[18]

The above statement hinted at the many difficult and complex issues Congress encountered in addressing the foreign corporate payments problem as well as the many difficult and complex issues that remain in this new era.

As to economic perceptions being a factor motivating Congress to act, Senator Proxmire stated:

> Consider the argument against corporate bribery as a policy. The payoff may cost a lot of money and still not work. You are paying off people who are dishonorable or they won't accept the payoff. You may be double crossed. The payoffs, while deferring the pressure for a time, may cause bigger problems later on for obvious reasons because of the illegality involved … It is not a matter of being a Sunday School advocate of morality, although that is important, but it is a matter of having hard, practical sense. Once you go down the road of bribery, you are likely to be in serious trouble. It is bad economics as well as bad morality.[19]

A Senate Report stated as follows: 'There is a broad consensus that the payment of bribes to influence business decisions corrodes the free-enterprise system. Bribery short-circuits the marketplace. Where bribes are paid, business is directed not to the most efficient producer, but to the most corrupt. This misallocates resources and reduces economic efficiency.'[20]

The view was also expressed that prohibiting payments to foreign government officials could give U.S. companies a comparative advantage and actually help companies resist foreign payment demands. During a Senate hearing, the Chairman of the Board of Gulf Corporation, stated:

> You can help us and many other multinational companies which are confronted with this problem by enacting legislation which would outlaw any foreign contributions by an American company. Such a statute on our books would make it easier to resist the very intense pressures which are placed upon us from time to time.[21]

This observation was repeated often by congressional leaders who favored a direct payment prohibition. Senator Proxmire stated during a Senate hearing:

> I just conclude by pointing out how widespread the desire in the business community is for this kind of legislation. [The Chairman of Gulf Corporation] … indicated how helpful this kind of a law would have been for him. He said, such a statute on our books would make it easier to resist the very intense pressures which are placed on corporate officials from time to time. If they could cite our law which says we just may not do it, they would be in a better position to resist these pressures and refuse these requests.[22]

The perception that a direct payment prohibition could actually help U.S. companies resist foreign payment demands was also shared by others who testified during congressional hearings. For instance, an SEC Commissioner stated:

> I think that, if you could devise a workable mechanism for making these payments illegal, you could then give the American executive a degree of bargaining power. He could say: No. I would like to do it, but I can't because it is illegal,' so that I would be disposed to think that might be a good idea.[23]

Notably, a Senate Report stated as follows: 'A strong anti-bribery law would help U.S. multinational companies resist corrupt demands, and would enhance the reputation of U.S. business abroad.'[24]

A final factor evidenced in the legislative record motivating Congress to act was a recognition that U.S. companies were part of a world-wide problem, and that if the U.S. took a leadership position other countries would soon follow in enacting laws governing business conduct with foreign government officials in foreign markets.

For instance, Senator Proxmire stated:

> … It's to the great interest of every country that the people who sell to them don't bribe. Now if we have a reputation of being the one country that enforces the law and everything that we sell is sold on the basis of merit and competition and not on the basis of bribery, it seems to me that's an enormous advantage that shouldn't be overlooked. I would think unilateral action wouldn't isolate us. It would give us a great advantage and other countries would per force be constrained to follow.[25]

Deficiencies in Existing Law

Upon discovery of the foreign corporate payments problem, Congress's first task was to determine if the payments were adequately captured by existing law. While certain existing laws did indirectly deal with various aspects of the problem, you will learn in this section that the prevailing view was that existing laws were deficient and that a new and direct legislative remedy was needed.

In 1975 the House held a series of hearings largely focused on whether the discovered payments were already a violation of U.S. law. In opening the hearing, Representative Nix stated:

> Such payments to foreign officials are not a violation of American law at present, although they are very often a violation of foreign law. However, it is a requirement of the United States Code that American corporations make full disclosure of their assets and liabilities to the Securities and Exchange Commission, the Civil Aeronautics Board, and the Internal Revenue Service. It is also true that if the purpose of the payments was anticompetitive in intent, the Antitrust Division of the Department of Justice would have a basis to begin legal proceedings … We may need improvements in our law. There is always room for improvement. … Our hearing will continue until we can answer positively whether our present legal system can meet the challenge of foreign slush funds maintained by the foreign operations of American-based companies. Of course, that does not confine the operations of this subcommittee; it seeks to explore, to examine and to suggest legislation that will meet the needs of the problem that we face.[26]

Likewise, in opening a 1976 hearing, Senator Proxmire stated:

> By now, close to 100 publicly-held corporations have made disclosures to the [SEC] under the SEC's so-called voluntary program, of literally hundreds of millions of dollars paid over the years as bribes to foreign officials and political parties. This bloodletting, unfortunately, is continuing. It is the disgrace of our free enterprise system. In turn, the practice of bribing foreign officials has corrupted those paying the bribes, and has corrupted the free market system, under which the most efficient producers with the best products are supposed to prevail. There was a time when defenders of corporate bribery argued that you had to make under-the-table payments in order to compete in certain parts of the world. By now, I think, no responsible person would make that claim. … Yet, I fear, even though the issue is settled in theory, that many companies will continue paying bribes if they can get away with it, because the potential rewards are so great and the risks are minimal. Nobody has gone to jail. Only three corporations have fired their chief executive officers. At most, there has been some unfortunate publicity. Even Lockheed is reporting increased profits. And so we come to the need for a remedy. In my view, U.S. corporations should be prohibited from paying bribes anywhere in the world. They are already prohibited from paying bribes at home.[27]

During the hearing, Senator Proxmire further stated:

> What we are concerned about is the kind of payment that Lockheed, for example, engaged in and admits where a payment is made to a foreign official indirectly for the purpose of selling what that corporation has to sell to that country. It is a bribe. Now that kind of payment is not outlawed at the present time in our law and while it is outlawed in many foreign countries … it's very hard for those countries to prosecute because they don't have the facts. We may have the facts but we don't prosecute because it's not against the law. We are trying to bridge that situation and provide a provision in the law that would make this illegal so we have the basis for action.[28]

The primary focus of Congress's investigation was whether the existing securities laws, tax laws and/or antitrust laws adequately addressed the foreign corporate payments problem.

As to the securities laws, early in Congress's investigation of the problem, the SEC Chairman highlighted the potential deficiencies of the securities laws as a comprehensive solution to the problem. In a speech included in the legislative record he stated:

> The significance of this illegality and immorality is far from clear in all instances. Are we saying that every improper expenditure must be disclosed, as such, giving details, because it is improper regardless of other considerations? We are not saying that. At least we have not said it so far, and I, at least, do not propose that we should ever say it. … We are not concerned with corporate morality as such – just disclosure of material facts … . We do not regard ourselves as having a mandate to enforce, even indirectly, through compulsory disclosure, all of the world's laws and all of its perceptions of morality and right conduct. Some forbearance not only seems implicit in our governing statutes, but also may be essential to enable us to continue to do a competent job of investor protection … . As you can see, if we require disclosure of all violations of laws against bribery or political contributions on the ground that illegal payments are material per se, we may be hard pressed to explain that other illegal corporate acts are not equally material for the same reason … . If improper foreign expenditures are not to be regarded as material simply because they are improper, without more, what principles govern the separation of those that are material and those that are not? Is it the method by which payments are made, the size of the payments, the purpose for which they are made, or the hazards to the business for exposure of the payments? It is, I believe, all of these, in different proportions in different situations.[29]

An SEC Commissioner further indicated that 'the mere fact that a foreign payment has been made, particularly in a relatively small amount, is not necessarily a material fact to investors,' and 'there is a significant question as to the extent to which information about foreign payments, even if illegal under foreign law or our law, or regarded as being improper, is material to an investor in appraising investment in a very large corporation.'[30]

The SEC Commissioner further stated:

> While it is true that we have and have exercised authority to deal with the problem of companies that have maintained false books and records, there is no explicit requirement under the Federal securities laws dealing with that problem or, more to the point, requiring that corporations establish and maintain adequate systems of internal controls.[31]

Regarding the key concept of materiality under the securities laws, the SEC Commissioner stated:

> The problem is that the payment has to be disclosed only if it is material for purposes of our disclosure requirements. A company that is doing business abroad makes payments of numerous amounts for numerous purposes. They don't have to itemize each one of them in their disclosure documents with us, so that the mere fact that they made a payment would not necessarily have to be disclosed under our existing requirements.[32]

Senator Proxmire, in particular, was unconvinced that the existing securities law requirement of material disclosures, applicable only to publicly-held companies, was an effective remedy to the problem. Noting the SEC's position 'that disclosure of the identity of a recipient of a bribe is probably unnecessary because it may be of little significance to the investor,' Senator Proxmire stated:

> That is precisely the problem with tying it to materiality. It may indeed be immaterial to the investor. There is nonetheless a very good justification for a public policy requiring disclosure of the recipient of a bribe. The purpose is simply to inhibit the bribe in the first place. But by tying it to materiality in every case it becomes necessary to disclose a different defense which is really not material to our purpose here.[33]

As to whether existing tax laws adequately captured the discovered payments, an Internal Revenue Service official stated during a House hearing:

> In plain language, the Internal Revenue Code prohibits the allowance of any deduction for moneys paid to a foreign official if a similar payment would have been unlawful under the Federal statutes of the United States, whether or not the payment is lawful under the laws of the particular country employing the foreign official who receives the payment or the benefit of the payment.[34]

Thus, under the tax laws, the improper conduct was not in making the payment, but rather deducting the payment for tax purposes.

As to whether existing antitrust laws adequately captured the discovered payments, during a House hearing a DOJ antitrust official set forth various different 'hypothetical situations involving payments to foreign officials which might raise problems' under existing antitrust laws and stated:

> The kind of bribe, about which we have been reading a good deal recently, would most certainly not be, in itself, an antitrust violation. The reason is that such bribes are unlikely to have any direct and identifiable effect on U.S. foreign commerce. The bribe is not intended to harm a U.S. competitor's export opportunities. In sum, neither payment nor the withholding of payment can be directly related to the flow of imports into or exports from U.S. markets.[35]

The official concluded his testimony as follows:

> I am not sure I feel fully qualified to comment on the whole question of whether we ought to have a specific foreign bribery law. ... If the Congress feels – and I hear you very clearly as saying that this is an important problem we have got to do something about, then I think you had better look to a criminal law dealing specifically with the international bribery situation or expanding the scope of it and not look to the antitrust laws as the way of dealing with it in a general way.[36]

As to whether a new legislative remedy was needed to capture the discovered foreign payments, the following statement by the Chairman of the Board of Lockheed best sums up the then-existing landscape.

> So it is true that we knew about the practice of payments on some occasions to foreign officials. But so did everyone else who was at all knowledgeable about foreign sales. There were no U.S. rules or laws which banned the practice or made it illegal ... . No effort was made to condone such payments except to say ... that it was thought that it appeared to be necessary to make such payments in order to compete successfully in many parts of the world. ... If Congress passes laws dealing with commissions and direct or indirect payments to foreign officials in other countries, Lockheed, of course, will fully comply with them.[37]

Divergent Views within the Government as to a Solution and the Difficult and Complex Issues Encountered

Seeking new legislative remedies to the foreign corporate payments problem was far from a consensus view of the government, and the payments discovered were not the simple and safe issue they appeared to be at first blush. As Representative Eckhardt stated, 'despite the clear consensus at our hearings that foreign bribery is a reprehensible activity and effective remedial legislation is required, there were some differences in approach to this problem.'[38]

Numerous government agencies participated in congressional hearings and all expressed universal condemnation of the discovered payments. However, beyond such unsurprising statements, you will learn in this section of the deep divisions within the government as to the solution. Moreover, certain segments of the government were viewed by congressional leaders as being participants in, or at least enablers of, the very problem Congress was seeking to address.

For instance, while the State Department condemned the payments, it opposed unilateral U.S. legislation governing the conduct of U.S. citizens abroad in their relations with foreign government officials. During a House hearing, a State Department official stated:

> What, then, should be done? … We need to move carefully. Some have suggested that we should enact legislation making it a criminal act for U.S. companies to engage abroad in what we regard as improper activities here at home, such as corporate political contributions. Although investors operating in foreign lands would be wise to avoid even the appearance of impropriety in those countries, we believe it would not be advisable for the United States to try to legislate the limits of permissible conduct by our firms abroad. It would be not only presumptuous but counterproductive to seek to impose our specific standards in countries with differing histories and cultures. Moreover, enforcement of such legislation – and I think this is the most important point – would involve surveillance of the activities of foreign officials as well as U.S. businessmen and would be widely resented abroad. Extraterritorial application of U.S. law – which is what such legislation would entail – has often been viewed by other governments as a sign of U.S. arrogance or even as interference in their internal affairs. U.S. penal laws are normally based on territorial jurisdiction and, with rare exceptions, we believe that is sound policy. […] Corruption of friendly foreign governments can undermine the most important objectives of our foreign policy. But experience shows the United States cannot police the internal affairs of foreign states. In the final analysis the only solution to corruption lies in the societies concerned.[39]

Congressional leaders were troubled that the State Department was perhaps a participant in, or at least enabler of, the very problem Congress was seeking to address. The following exchange between Senator Jesse Helms and Lockheed's Chairman during a Senate hearing highlights this issue:

> *Helms*: 'Do you feel that these bribes or whatever name may be applied to them came as any surprise to the Government of the United States, specifically of the State Department?'
>
> [...]
>
> *Chairman*: 'I don't believe they came as any surprise to the State Department or to other branches of the U.S. Government.'[40]

Senator Helms directed the following statement to State Department officials during a hearing:

> I certainly don't want to even have the appearance of badgering you, and I don't want to belabor the point, but I am somewhat mystified in the light of all the reports that have come to me, sir, that apparently at the State Department during all of these years when these things were alleged to have occurred, that there was a complete 'hear no evil and see no evil.' Now, just tell me this one more time. Nobody at the State Department ever dreamed anything of this sort was going on at any time?[41]

On the Senate floor, Senator Church stated as follows regarding the State Department's perceived role in the problem:

> In all the months that we have investigated the practices of multi-million-dollar bribes and payoffs all over the world, we have yet to find any evidence of State Department concern or State Department initiative taken at any time to deal with the problem. When these bribes were finally exposed, they delayed for months even taking token action. So I really do not think the State Department wants any legislation in this field. I believe their attitude fairly could be characterized as one of indifference or perhaps benign neglect.[42]

Like the State Department, the Defense Department was also viewed by congressional leaders as being a participant in, or at least enablers of, the very problem Congress was seeking to address. Certain of the discovered foreign corporate payments involved defense contractor use of foreign agents in connection with foreign government business and among the series of House hearings in 1975 was one focused on the role of agents in foreign military sales. In opening the hearing, Representative Nix stated:

> The specific issue we are considering today is the part played in military sales contracts by foreign sales agents and the fees paid to them. [...] The Defense Department has at its disposal immense amounts of information on this very issue. No interest has been shown by the Department in this issue, in that its mission appears to be the promotion of arms sales.[43]

As to the Defense Department's role in the problem, Representative Solarz stated as follows: 'There were some recent revelations to the effect that the Defense Department had advised American arms people doing business to the effect that payoffs were a traditional way in that part of the world of facilitating the kind of transactions which they were interested in.'[44]

Likewise, Senator Proxmire noted during a Senate hearing:

> One of the most disturbing aspects of this is the role the Defense Department has played, especially with respect to defense contractors who sold abroad. We have a document which indicates that at one point a top official in the Defense Department had counseled defense contractors on paying bribes and urged them to do so under circumstances where it was necessary.[45]

The clear divisions within the government concerning the foreign corporate payments problem, as well as a lack of concern by certain segments of the government, were summarized by Senator Church as follows:

> Our Government has initiated no real concern with this problem. Rather, aside from some statements of a cosmetic nature, it prefers to stick its head in the sand and hear no evil, see no evil, and pretend there is no problem. But there is a problem, a problem of cancerous dimensions which is eating away at the vitals of democratic society. So there is a need for action, and action now.[46]

Despite Senator Church's call for action, many difficult and complex issues emerged as Congress considered solutions, and the payments discovered were not the simple and safe issue they appeared to be at first blush. The following exchange between Senator Proxmire and the Secretary of Commerce best captures this dynamic. Senator Proxmire stated during a Senate hearing:

> For more than a year now the [SEC] and the [Church Committee] have been generating reams of evidence on foreign bribery. [...] Yet it seems as if some, who rhetorically condemn bribery as roundly as the rest, want Congress to delay a remedy until the entire Fortune 500 have been investigated. I recall the story of an agency in the bureaucracy that was short on bureaucrats. They hired a talking parrot. [...] They taught him to say only one phrase: 'Very complex, very complex.' Sometimes I get the feeling that the parrot, that very complex parrot, is in charge of the Federal Government's groping, grasping policy on bribery. Certainly, there are subtleties and complexities in the foreign bribery issue, but we should be able to agree after more than a year of investigation the time has come to provide a remedy for an act as simple and outrageous as bribery.[47]

In response, the Secretary of Commerce stated:

> Even a parrot must occasionally be right … What I am saying … is that in the bribery area we are moving into uncharted national and international waters in which legislative remedies may be capable of achieving only part of the objectives we seek. As part of the process of considering specific legislative remedies, we should be certain that we have a clear understanding of the scope and magnitude of the problems to be addressed, a thorough assessment of the costs and benefits of the legislative remedies being advanced, and a reasonably precise plan for moving from where we are now to where we wish to be.[48]

As to the foreign business conditions giving rise to many of the discovered payments, an SEC Commissioner stated during a House hearing:

> These questionable payments by American corporations in foreign countries present a number of difficult problems for us, and for you in your deliberations … . For one thing, the exact purpose of such payments is often difficult to determine. It is normal and understandable that American corporations seeking to do business abroad will employ or retain sales agents, business consultants and others who are on the scene and familiar with local ways of doing business. Payments made to such intermediaries are often entirely proper, but may not always be so. Once the money is in the hands of a foreign agent, it may be difficult to determine exactly what he does with it. Of course, suspicions are always raised where large sums are paid for unexplained services and it is hard to determine exactly what the company is receiving for its money. We are told that in many countries it is almost customary to distribute various gratuities to persons in strategic positions in order to obtain favorable treatment. Indeed, such practices are not wholly unknown in the United States. These payments may or may not violate the laws of the country involved, and in countries having entirely different legal systems from the United States, local law on the subject may be quite obscure. But, even where a payment does not violate the law of the country involved, it is to be expected that foreign officials and governments would be sensitive to publicity about such payments and, therefore, such publicity may jeopardize the position of a company in foreign countries. Thus, while I am sure we can all agree that American companies should not, as a matter of principle, make payments to officials of foreign governments in return for favored treatment, it is often difficult to determine whether or not this has occurred. Moreover, we are not insensitive either to the difficulties American companies experience in doing business abroad, or to the fact that our lawsuits might create an impression in some minds of United States interference in the affairs of foreign countries.[49]

Highlighting many of these same issues, a representative of the New York City Bar who testified at a House hearing stated:

> Without in any way excusing the failures of U.S. business that have been exposed over the last 2 years – and I don't think they can be excused – the problem goes beyond those failures. It is not really addressing the whole problem to say that we need only look at the failure of U.S. business and not look at the context in which those failures occurred. We know from the evidence that has been exposed so far that in many cases the bribes were solicited, not volunteered. We know that there were cases of extortion. [...] We know, beyond that, from some of the filings with the SEC and from other sources, that it wasn't just U.S. business that was involved, and we certainly have reason to say that perhaps these practices in other countries were tolerated there.[50]

Yet just because foreign business conditions presented difficult issues for U.S. companies, all were not persuaded that this made the payments any less problematic. For instance, Senator Church stated during a Senate hearing:

> While such methods may be common practice abroad, I am skeptical of the argument that it is perfectly all right because everyone does it. I know of no country where bribes and kickbacks are either legal or publicly accepted. And the fact that the corporations, by their own admission, go to such lengths to disguise these practices, through the use of double bookkeeping, numbered Swiss bank accounts, and a system of code names that would do credit to the CIA, puts the lie to the argument that it is accepted practice.[51]

In addition to the issues Congress encountered regarding foreign business conditions, there was also concern that U.S. companies might be placed in a competitive disadvantage if Congress passed a unilateral law governing business interaction with foreign government officials. Despite such concerns, a certain degree of competitive disadvantage was accepted by Congress. For instance, Representative Moss stated during a House hearing:

> To think that no loss of business would occur in every instance would be unrealistic. Can we allow this to occur? Yes, if that is the small price we must pay to return morality to corporate practice. Yes, if that is the small price we pay to show that U.S. firms compete in terms of price, quality, and service and not in terms of the size of a bribe. Real competition works. The vast majority of American companies have operated successfully in foreign countries without the need to resort to bribery.[52]

Likewise, the Treasury Secretary stated during the same hearing: 'To the very, very small extent a particular company may lose a particular contract because it refuses to engage in this practice, I would be willing to say, all right, we will be at a slight competitive disadvantage and we will all sleep the better for it.'[53]

Foreign business conditions and competitive disadvantage issues aside, Congress also encountered the basic issue of defining bribery. The Treasury Secretary stated during a Senate Hearing:

> You know that trying to define exactly what bribery is is a real problem. You and I would have no trouble saying what a bribe is and what isn't. However, having said that, it's very difficult to put it down on paper in statutory language that would not be damaging to some legitimate things that happen on the periphery, such as payments of commissions. It's almost like the Justice who said that he can't define pornography, but he knows what it is when he sees it. In certain instances, we have a gray area when it comes to this bribery question. Outright payment to secure a particular contract to an official of a foreign government, fine, we have no trouble with defining that as a bribe. Payment of commissions to agent, which is an accepted practice throughout the world, is another matter.[54]

Legislative Proposals Leading to Enactment of the FCPA

Notwithstanding the many difficult and complex issues encountered, Congress proceeded to seek legislative remedies to the foreign corporate payments problem. Between 1975 and 1977, approximately twenty bills were introduced in the Senate or the House to address the foreign corporate payments problem. Although Congress sought to address the problem from a variety of angles (such as through amendments to the Internal Revenue Code, termination of Overseas Private Investment Corporation insurance and disclosure of foreign agent fees), this section details the two main competing legislative responses that emerged: a disclosure approach as to a broad category of payments and a criminalization approach as to a narrow category of payments.

As described in more detail below in a general chronology, the Ford administration favored a disclosure approach as to a broad category of payments. However, key congressional leaders, as well as the Carter administration, which took office in early 1977, favored a criminalization approach as a narrow category of payments. Despite significant minority concern, the FCPA adopted a criminalization approach as it was viewed as more effective in deterring improper payments and less burdensome on business.

In early 1976, with legislative activity intensifying and after being viewed as exhibiting indifference to Congress's nearly year-long investigation of the problem, President Gerald Ford issued a memorandum to various federal agencies establishing a 'Task Force on Questionable Corporate Payments Abroad' (the 'Task Force'). The memorandum stated:

> This is to advise you of my decision to appoint you to a Cabinet-level Task Force which I am establishing to examine the policy aspects of recent disclosures of questionable payments to foreign agents and officials by U.S. companies in conjunction with their overseas business operations. [...] Although the Federal Government is currently taking a number of international and domestic steps in an attempt to deal with this problem, I believe that a coordinated program to review these efforts and to explore additional avenues should be undertaken in the interest of ethical conduct in the international marketplace and the continued vitality of our free enterprise system. The full dimensions of this problem are not yet known but it is clear that a substantial number of U.S. corporations have been involved in questionable payments to foreign officials, political organizations or business agents. The possibility exists that more can be done by our government. There would also appear to be some interest in guidance as to what standards should be applied to the foreign sales activities of the overwhelming majority of American businessmen who are deeply concerned about the propriety of their business operations. The Task Force should explore all aspects of this problem and seek to obtain the views of the broadest base of interested groups and individuals. While the problems are complex and do not lend themselves to simple solutions, I am confident that your labors will contribute to a better international and domestic climate in which American business continues to play a vital and respected role.[55]

In a 1976 letter to Senator Proxmire, the Secretary of Commerce set forth the views of the Task Force on 'proposed legislation concerning questionable corporate payments abroad.' The letter stated:

> There are two principal competing general legislative approaches – a disclosure approach or a criminal approach. While it is possible to design legislation [...] which requires disclosure of foreign payments and makes certain payments criminal under U.S. law, the Task Force has unanimously rejected this approach. The disclosure-plus-criminalization scheme would, by its very ambition, be ineffective. The existence of criminal penalties for certain questionable payments would deter their disclosure and thus the positive value of the disclosure provisions would be reduced. In our opinion the two approaches cannot be compatibly joined. The Task Force has given considerable scrutiny to the option of 'criminalizing' under U.S. law improper payments made to foreign officials by U.S. corporations. Such legislation would represent the most forceful possible rhetorical assertion by the President and the Congress of our abhorrence of such conduct. It would place business executives on clear and unequivocal notice that such practices should stop. It would make it easier for some corporations to resist pressures to make questionable payments. The Task Force has concluded, however, that the

> criminalization approach would represent little more than a policy assertion, for the enforcement of such a law would be very difficult it not impossible. Successful prosecution of offenses would typically depend upon witnesses and information beyond the reach of U.S. judicial process. Other nations, rather than assisting in such prosecutions, might resist cooperation because of considerations of national preference or sovereignty. Other nations might be especially offended if we sought to apply criminal sanctions to foreign-incorporated and/or foreign-managed subsidiaries of American corporations. The Task Force has concluded that unless reasonably enforceable criminal sanctions were devised, the criminal approach would represent poor public policy. The Task Force has similarly analyzed the desirability of new legislation to require more systematic and informative reporting and disclosure than is provided by current law. The Task Force recognized that additional disclosure requirements could expand the paperwork burden of American businesses … and that they might, in some cases, result in foreign relations problems – to the extent the systematic reporting and disclosure failed to deter questionable payments and their publication proved embarrassing to friendly governments. At the same time the Task Force perceived several very positive attributes of systematic disclosure. First, it deemed such disclosure necessary to supplement current SEC disclosure, which as noted already covers only issuers of securities making 'material' payments, and does not normally include the name of the payee. Such disclosure would provide protection for U.S. businessmen from extortion and other improper pressures, since would-be extorters would have to be willing to risk the pressures which would result from disclosure of their actions to the U.S. public and to their own governments. It would avoid the difficult problems of defining and proving 'bribery.' It would offer a means to give public reassurance of the essential accountability of multinational corporations … . The President has decided to recommend that the Congress enact legislation providing for full and systematic reporting and disclosure of payments made by American businesses with the intent of influencing, directly or indirectly, the conduct of foreign governmental officials. At the same time, the President has decided to oppose, as essentially unenforceable, legislation which would seek broad criminal proscription of improper payments made in foreign jurisdictions.[56]

Shortly thereafter, President Ford announced 'three new initiatives' based on the findings of the Task Force. In the announcement, President Ford stated: 'As a deterrent to bribery by American-controlled industries, I am directing the task force to prepare legislation that would require corporate disclosure of all payments made with the intention of influencing foreign government officials. Failure to comply with the new disclosure laws would lead to civil and criminal penalties.'[57]

President Ford also urged enactment of the proposed legislation and stated:

> I am transmitting to the Congress my specific proposal for a Foreign Payments Disclosure Act. This proposal will contribute significantly to the deterrence of future improper practices and to the restoration of confidence in American business standards. This legislation represents a measured but effective approach to the problem of questionable corporate payments abroad: It will help deter improper payments in international commerce by American corporations and their officers. It will help reverse the trend toward allegations or assumptions of guilt-by-association impugning the integrity of American business generally. It will help deter would-be foreign extorters from seeking improper payments from American businessmen. It will allow the United States to set a forceful example to our trading partners and competitors regarding the imperative need to end improper business practices. It does not attempt to apply directly United States criminal statutes in foreign states and thus does not promise more than can be enforced. Finally, it will help restore the confidence of the American people and our trading partners in the ethical standards of the American business community.[58]

Bills based on the Task Force's recommendations were soon introduced and at Congressional hearings that ensued, a Department of Commerce official stated as follows in advocating the Ford administration position:

> The existence of the criminal prosecution would be of some value to an American businessman in resisting improper requests for payments abroad. I don't believe, however, that it would have as much value as the disclosure requirements, for the following reasons. A would-be foreign extorter who asks for $50,000 to do something of importance to the American company, on the one hand would be told, 'I can't give you that money because if I do I might have to go to jail,' and the extorter says, 'That is your problem, bud, but there is no way, your law can reach me.' If you have a disclosure provision and the American businessman says, 'If I give you that money, I am going to have to report the payment to the Department of Commerce, possibly to the SEC, and it will therefore be in the public record, and your name will be in the public record.' If we are right that every other country in the world, virtually every other country, has laws against public bribery and extortion, then it is our guess that the extorter will be substantially deterred. We believe that a combination of sunlight and encouragement of other nations to enforce their own laws represents a much more effective way to end corrupt payments than does direct, unilateral criminalization by this country of actions taking place in foreign jurisdictions. We urge the Congress not to substitute tokenism for real action to deal with the questionable payments problem. The danger in such tokenism is that it will create complacency. Congress will wash its hands of an important problem without having taken meaningful, enforceable action.[59]

However, many were not convinced that the Task Force-inspired disclosure legislation was an adequate response to the problem. In a passionate statement which speaks to the political context of Congress's deliberations, a witness stated during a 1976 House hearing:

> The principal policy issue raised … of course, is whether [the bill] should prohibit the bribery of foreign officials at all. The Ford administration … prefers to rely solely upon the offending corporation notifying the Department of Commerce of its misdeed, with the Department not making that fact known until as much as a year later, and then only if our national interest would not be adversely affected. What a pitifully pallid response to a major moral crisis. Have we learned nothing from the attempted coverup of Watergate? Have we no shame, no decent respect for the opinions of mankind? How could this country continue to preach abroad the virtues of the free competitive market system and continue to call for economic justice and political integrity, how could we hope to avoid unreasonable restrictions and attacks on American corporations abroad, if we are unwilling to specially and directly prohibit and penalize this wasteful, corrosive, shabby practice? Do we really wish to align ourselves around the world with the cynical and the corrupt, with those who profit from bribery or wink at it as customary and unavoidable, or should we not instead align ourselves with those business and government officials who have stoutly resisted all pressures and temptations, and who would be vastly relieved today if a U.S. criminal statute said loudly and clearly that all U.S.-based enterprises continuing to engage in such practices did so at their own peril.[60]

The Task Force-inspired disclosure legislation did not gain traction in Congress, but a bill introduced by Senator Proxmire that sought to directly criminalize payments to foreign officials did. The bill was soon reported to the Senate and the Senate Report stated as follows:

> The Committee considered two approaches for curbing the kind of bribery payments to foreign officials … One approach would be to require that these bribes be publicly disclosed. The other approach would be to prohibit them by law with criminal penalties for those who violate the law. The disclosure approach was … recommended by the [Task Force]. The Task Force report to the Committee argued that disclosure would constitute an effective deterrent whereas an outright criminal prohibition would be difficult to enforce. The Committee carefully weighed these arguments and decided that a direct criminal prohibition is the better approach. As the Task Force itself pointed out, a direct criminal prohibition of foreign bribes 'would represent the most forceful possible rhetorical assertion by the President and the Congress to our abhorrence of such conduct. It would place business executives on clear and unequivocal notice that such practices should stop. It would make it easier for some corporations to resist pressures to make questionable payments.' On the other hand, merely requiring the disclosure of bribes would leave ambiguous whether such payments might be acceptable. Indeed, it would imply that bribery can be condoned as long as it is disclosed. The Committee considered whether a criminal prohibition might be more difficult to enforce than a

> disclosure requirement. The Committee concluded that an outright prohibition would be at least as feasible to enforce as any meaningful disclosure requirement. Under the disclosure approach … , all payments made to foreign officials for the purpose of 'obtaining or maintaining business with or influencing the conduct of a foreign government' would have to be disclosed. Clearly, in order to enforce such a disclosure requirement and apply sanctions for failure to file reports, it would be necessary to prove that an undisclosed payment was actually made, and that it was made with an improper purpose. Thus, the same evidence necessary to prove a violation of a direct prohibition would have to be marshaled in order to enforce a disclosure statute. Beyond that, there would be the additional burden of proving that an issuer willfully failed to file a report describing the bribe. Accordingly, the Committee concluded that a disclosure approach has at least the same enforcement problems inherent in the direct prohibition approach and none of its advantages. The bill, as reported, therefore, provides a direct criminal prohibition.[61]

The Senate unanimously passed the bill and it was referred to the House. However, House efforts to address the foreign corporate payments problem paused for the 1976 elections in which the Democratic candidate Jimmy Carter defeated Republican President Ford. During the campaign, Carter 'derided the [Ford] administration's … "proposal to allow corporations to engage in bribery so long as they report such illegal transactions to the Department of Commerce."'[62] As Representative Michael Harrington stated after Carter took office, 'we now have an administration whose prime foreign policy concern to date has been to restore morality and ethical principles to all of our international relations.'[63]

When Congress opened after the 1976 elections, legislative efforts to address the foreign corporate payments problem soon renewed, and focused on bills with criminal payment provisions. With President Ford out of office, the Task Force-inspired disclosure legislation fell by the wayside. In early 1977 Senator Proxmire introduced a bill similar to the one previously passed by the Senate and stated as follows.

> Last year this bill passed the Senate by a unanimous vote […] . Let's not kid ourselves. This bill is not home free. It was stopped last year in the House by the opposition of those objecting to the provisions of the bill. It will take strong support from the administration and those of us in Congress who believe in it to get the bill passed.[64]

The Senate Report stated:

> The committee … concluded that the criminalization approach was preferred over a disclosure approach. Direct criminalization entails no reporting burden on corporations and less of an enforcement burden on the Government. The

criminalization of foreign corporate bribery will to a significant extent act as a self-enforcing, preventative mechanism.[65]

In the House, Representative Eckhardt introduced a bill, which in compromise with the Senate bill, ultimately become the FCPA. The House Report stated:

The committee considered two possible approaches for curbing the type of bribery payments defined [in the bill]. One approach is to require that these payments be publicly disclosed and criminal penalties imposed for failure to disclose. The other approach, which the committee adopted [...] is to outlaw the payoffs with criminal sanctions.

The [House] received extensive testimony on both approaches ... There emerged a clear consensus that foreign bribery is a reprehensible activity and that action must be taken to proscribe it. After carefully considering all the testimony adduced, the committee concluded that it should be outlawed rather than legalized through disclosure. The committee believes the criminalization approach to be the most effective deterrent, the least burdensome on business, and no more difficult to enforce than disclosure.

The committee determined that disclosure can never be an effective deterrent because the anticipated benefit of making a bribe, such as winning a multimillion dollar contract, generally exceeds the adverse effect, if any, of disclosing one year later a lump sum figure without names, amounts or even countries. Criminalization, on the other hand, has proven an effective deterrent.

[...]

The committee also found that criminalization is no more difficult to enforce than disclosure. Both approaches involve proving beyond a reasonable doubt the same factual and legal elements. Most importantly, though, criminalization is far less burdensome on business. Most disclosure proposals would require U.S. corporations doing business abroad to report all foreign payments including perfectly legal payments such as for promotional purposes and for sales commissions. A disclosure scheme, unlike outright prohibition, would require U.S. corporations to contend not only with an additional bureaucratic overlay but also with massive paperwork requirements.[66]

As to a criminal prohibition of a narrow category of payments being less burdensome on business than a broader disclosure provision, Representative Eckhardt stated:

Disclosure legislation must embrace a wide range of activities, many of which appear perfectly legal and even ethical. And of course, if they must all be disclosed, along with that which is illegal, one may assume that the acts most readily disclosed will be those which are innocent acts. [...] A significant

> difference between the two approaches, often overlooked, is that criminalization is far less burdensome on business. Disclosure would require U.S. corporations doing business abroad to report all foreign payments including legal promotional payments and legitimate commissions to sales agents.[67]

In late 1977, all that remained was for Congressional conferees to iron out certain differences between a House bill and a Senate bill.

In short, the prevailing view was that the criminalization approach represented the best legislative response to the foreign corporate payments problem. In late 1977, after more than two years of investigation and consideration of the foreign corporate payments problem, and despite divergent views as to the problem and the difficult and complex issues presented, Congress completed its pioneering journey and passed the first law in the world governing domestic business conduct with foreign government officials in foreign markets. Speaking on the House floor, Representative Eckhardt summed up the journey and stated that the FCPA was 'one of the more important pieces of legislation to be considered by the Congress this year.'[68]

In December 1977, the FCPA became law as an amendment to the Securities Exchange Act of 1934. President Carter's signing statement stated:

> I am pleased to sign into law [...] the Foreign Corrupt Practices Act of 1977 and the Domestic and Foreign Investment Improved Disclosure Act of 1977. During my campaign for the Presidency, I repeatedly stressed the need for tough legislation to prohibit corporate bribery. [This bill] provides that necessary sanction. I share Congress' belief that bribery is ethically repugnant and competitively unnecessary. Corrupt practices between corporations and public officials overseas undermine the integrity and stability of governments and harm our relations with other countries. Recent revelations of widespread overseas bribery have eroded public confidence in our basic institutions. This law makes corrupt payments to foreign officials illegal under United States law. It requires publicly-held corporations to keep accurate books and records and establish accounting controls to prevent the use of 'off-the-books' devices, which have been used to disguise corporate bribes in the past. [...] These efforts, however, can only be fully successful in combating bribery and extortion if other countries and business itself take comparable action. Therefore, I hope progress will continue in the United Nations toward the negotiation of a treaty on illicit payments.[69]

The FCPA as a Limited Statute

Even though the FCPA was a pioneering statute, Congress intended for it to be a limited statute. In this section, you will learn that Congress was aware of a wide range of foreign corporate payments to a variety of recipients for a variety of reasons. However, Congress accepted in passing the FCPA to capture only a narrow category of such payments.

Among other things, you will learn in this section that Congress limited the FCPA's payment provisions to a narrow category of foreign recipients and further narrowed the range of actionable payments to those involving foreign government procurement or influencing foreign government legislation or regulations. In addition, Congress chose not to capture so-called facilitating payments given the difficult and complex business conditions encountered in many foreign markets.

During Congress's multi-year investigation of the foreign corporate payments problem, it learned of a wide range of foreign corporate payments to a variety of recipients for a variety of reasons. The SEC Report, which Congress placed great reliance on during its deliberation and consideration of the problem, contained an entire section titled 'Recipients of the Payments' and stated:

> The nature of the recipient often has been an important factor in determining that a corporate payment was a disclosable event. Various classes of recipients have presented these considerations, including but not limited to government officials, commission agents and consultants of the paying company, and recipients of commercial bribery.
>
> Government Officials: [...] The Commission has observed payments to government officials for four principal purposes. First, corporate payments have been made in an effort to procure special and unjustified favors or advantages in the enactment or administration of the tax or other laws of the country in question. ... Second, corporate payments may be made with the intent to assist the company in obtaining or retaining government contracts. It may be possible to distinguish payments intended to secure the favorable exercise of judgment or discretion on behalf of the governmental body from situations where the official, under applicable laws, regulations or customs, appears to have been permitted to act for suppliers in connection with government contracts and to be paid for such services. ... A third purpose for payments is to persuade low-level governmental officials to perform functions or services which they are obliged to perform as part of their governmental responsibilities, but which they may refuse or delay unless compensated. ... Another type of payment is the political contribution. Where these contributions are illegal under local law, they can be assimilated to bribery. ...
>
> Commercial Agents and Consultants: The Commission recognizes that corporations doing business abroad often engage the services of non-official nationals possessing specialized information with regard to business opportunities or relationships which are of assistance in securing or maintaining business. ...

> A variety of considerations, some legitimate and some questionable, may prompt the use of agents or consultants. … Commission or consultant payments substantially in excess of the going rate for such services may give rise to a disclosable event, depending upon the significance of the business involved. In many instances, this may suggest that a portion of the commission was, in fact, intended to be passed through to government officials or their designees to influence government action. …
>
> Commercial Bribery: The Commission also has observed payments made to improperly influence a non-governmental customer's use of a company's product or services.[70]

Congress could have legislated as to the wide range of foreign corporate payments discovered. Indeed, certain of the bills introduced during the legislative process captured a wide range of foreign corporate payments. Yet in passing the FCPA, Congress intended to capture only a narrow range of foreign corporate payments. Congress's intent on these issues would seem directly linked to the primary foreign policy motivation it had in investigating the foreign corporate payments as well as recognition of the difficult and complex business conditions encountered in many foreign markets.

Senators Church and Proxmire were clear as to the scope of the law they envisioned. Senator Church stated as follows:

> Let us be clear that we are not just talking about a little 'baksheesh' to grease the palm of some petty clerk in order to speed needed documents on their way through the bureaucratic labyrinth. What we are talking about is a concerted effort by the petroleum industry to buy favorable tax and energy legislation in a European country in which one U.S. company alone made over $50 million in contributions to the government parties and members of the cabinet over a 9 year period. What we are talking about is an arms industry campaign to flood the Middle East with weapons, in which a U.S. aircraft company paid over $100 million in agents' fees in one country to sell an airplane which has no competitor. A large part of that $100 million is known to have ended up in the Swiss bank accounts of high military and civilian defense officials of the purchasing country. I could go on with other examples, but it suffices to say that what is at issue here is a massive and widespread perversion of the free enterprise system.[71]

Senator Proxmire stated:

> I recognize it is hard [to define a bribe], but we are not concerned so much about the low level grease payments. What we are talking about is the payment, as I say, to make a sale … . What we are concerned about, as I say, and trying to get at … is bribery for the purpose of making sales abroad.

> [W]e define [a bribe] as a payment to an official of a foreign government for the purpose of inducing him to use his influence to secure business for the issuer or influence legislation or regulations of his government.[72]

Representatives Murphy and Eckhardt likewise stated during a House hearing: 'This bill is not concerned with so-called grease or facilitating payments, such as may be necessary to some petty clerk to speed documents through a bureaucracy. The bill does not address itself to "grease" or "facilitating" payments made to low-level clerical or ministerial government officials.'[73]

Senate and House Reports evidence the limited nature of the FCPA and that it would not capture all foreign corporate payments Congress learned of during its multi-year investigation.

A Senate Report stated:

> In drafting the bill … the Committee deliberately cast the language narrowly, in order to differentiate between such payments [to a foreign official corruptly intended to induce the recipient to use his influence to secure business, influence legislation or regulations] and low-level facilitating payments sometimes called 'grease payments.' Thus, [the bill] would not reach a small gratuity paid to expedite shipment through Customs or the placement of a trans-Atlantic telephone call, to secure required permits, or to ensure that a corporation's warehouses were not put to the torch. In other words, payments made to expedite the proper performance of duties may be reprehensible, but it does not appear feasible for the United States to attempt unilaterally to eradicate all such payments. However, where the payment is made to influence the placement of government contracts or to influence the formulation of legislation or regulations, such payment is prohibited … . The Committee fully recognizes that the proposed law will not reach all corrupt payments overseas.[74]

A House Report likewise stated:

> The scope … is limited by the requirement that the offer, promise, authorization, payment, or gift must have as a purpose inducing the recipient to use influence with the foreign government or instrumentality, or to refrain from performing any official responsibilities, so as to direct business to any person, maintain an established business opportunity with any person, divert any business opportunity from any person or influence the enactment or promulgation of legislation or regulations of that government or instrumentality. … The bill's coverage does not extend to so-called grease or facilitating payments. … The language of the bill is deliberately cast in terms which differentiate between such payments and facilitating payments, sometimes called 'grease payments'. In using the word 'corruptly', the committee intends to distinguish between payments which cause an official to exercise other than his free will in acting or deciding or influencing an act or decision and those

payments which merely move a particular matter toward an eventual act or decision or which do not involve any discretionary action. In defining 'foreign official', the committee emphasizes this crucial distinction by excluding from the definition of 'foreign official' government employees whose duties are essentially ministerial or clerical. For example, a gratuity paid to a customs official to speed the processing of a customs document would not be reached by the bill. Nor would it reach payments made to secure permits, licenses, or the expeditious performance of similar duties of an essentially ministerial or clerical nature which must of necessity by performed in any event. While payments made to assure or to speed the proper performance of a foreign official's duties may be reprehensible in the United States, the committee recognizes that they are not necessarily so viewed elsewhere in the world and that it is not feasible for the United States to attempt unilaterally to eradicate all such payments. As a result, the committee has not attempted to reach such payments. However, where the payment is made to influence the passage of law, regulations, the placement of government contracts, the formulation of policy or other discretionary governmental functions, such payments would be prohibited. The committee fully recognizes that the proposed law will not reach all corrupt payments overseas.[75]

As evident from the above legislative history, despite learning of a wide range of foreign corporate payments, Congress limited the FCPA's payment provisions to a narrow category of foreign recipients and further narrowed the range of actionable payments to those involving foreign government procurement or influencing foreign government legislation or regulations.

The FCPA also contained a limiting 'business purpose' test. The Conference Report stated:

The scope of the prohibition [in the Senate bill] was limited by the requirement that the offer, promise, authorization, payment, or gift must have as a purpose inducing the recipient to use his influence with the foreign government or instrumentality, influencing the enactment or promulgation of legislation or regulations of that government or instrumentality or refraining from performing any official responsibilities, so as to direct business to any person, maintain an established business opportunity with any person or divert a business opportunity from any person.

The House amendment was similar to the Senate bill; however, the scope of the House amendment was not limited by the 'business purpose' test [...] The conferees clarified the scope of the prohibition by requiring that the purpose of the payment must be to influence any act or decision of a foreign official (including a decision not to act) or to induce such official to use his influence to affect a government act or decision so as to assist an issuer in obtaining, retaining or directing business to any person.[76]

In short, despite learning of a wide range of foreign corporate payments to a variety of recipients and for a variety of reasons, Congress accepted in passing the FCPA to capture only a narrow range of such payments.

As discussed at the beginning of this chapter, the FCPA's legislative history is important in that it is a fruitful source of instruction as to the FCPA's proper interpretation. Understanding the FCPA's legislative history is thus not merely an interesting history lesson or academic exercise. Rather the rule of law demands an analysis of legislative history in giving meaning to the FCPA.

As you learn more about the FCPA's new era in the following chapters, your understanding of why Congress enacted the FCPA, and what Congress sought to capture in enacting the law, will give you an informed base to critically analyze this new era of enforcement. Your understanding of the FCPA's legislative history also highlights that many of the difficult and complex issues Congress confronted decades ago remain today.

C. ENFORCEMENT BEGINS AND THE FCPA MATURES

In analyzing this new era of FCPA enforcement, it is also important to understand how the FCPA was previously enforced and how the FCPA matured through its 1988 and 1998 amendments into its modern form.

This section profiles early FCPA enforcement actions and how certain of these actions foreshadowed difficult enforcement issues that remain in this new era. The level of enforcement for most of the FCPA's history was far less than it is today. In fact, the number of core corporate FCPA enforcement actions in a typical year in this new era exceeds the number of enforcement actions during a decade of early FCPA enforcement. This section will highlight various factors that explain this historical discrepancy including that the infant FCPA was widely viewed, even by the enforcement agencies, as an imprecise and confusing statute.

Despite its widely perceived deficiencies, reforming a law called the 'Foreign Corrupt Practices Act' was a political hot potato simply because of its name. Indeed early reform proposals included changing the name of the law so that a substantive, issue-based discussion could take place free from pro-bribery vs. anti-bribery rhetoric. This section will conclude by chronicling how the FCPA has matured as a statute into its modern form.

Early FCPA Enforcement

Given the SEC's active role in helping to uncover many of the foreign corporate payment issues leading to the FCPA's enactment, it was not surprising that the first FCPA case was brought by the SEC.

In 1978, the SEC filed a civil injunctive action against Page Airways, Inc. and certain of its officers and directors alleging that the company and the individual defendants 'engaged in a scheme to sell Gulfstream II aircraft and other aircraft, products and services, by directly and indirectly, making payments to foreign government officials and employees and other corrupt, illegal, improper or unaccountable payments.'[77] Foreshadowing an issue that remains today – the lack of transparency in many FCPA enforcement actions – the SEC release noted: 'In reaching settlement of this action, the Commission and Page considered concerns raised by another agency of the United States Government regarding matters of national interest.'

The DOJ's first criminal FCPA enforcement action soon followed and it was filled with intrigue. In 1979, the DOJ charged postage stamp distributor Kenny International Corporation with violating the FCPA's anti-bribery provisions for engaging in a scheme to influence the Government of the Cook Islands to renew a stamp distribution agreement.[78] The major players in the scheme were: Finbar Kenny (Chairman of the Board, President and majority shareholder of Kenny International); the Cook Islands Party (a foreign political party); and Sir Albert Henry (the Leader of the Cook Islands Party and the Premier of the Cook Islands).

The DOJ alleged that Kenny International could only be assured of renewal of the stamp distribution agreement by the continuation of the Cook Island Party's control of the Legislative Assembly and the retention of Sir Albert Henry as Premier. According to the DOJ, 'anticipating that the election would be closely contested, Sir Albert Henry and his fellow party officials determined that to guarantee their party's continued control in the Legislative Assembly it would be necessary to transport by air from New Zealand, a distance of approximately 1,800 miles, Cook Islands Party supporters to vote for them in the forthcoming election.'

Thereafter, the DOJ alleged that a personal representative of Sir Albert Henry and the Cook Islands Party solicited the financial assistance of Kenny and Kenny International to subsidize the air transportation costs of the Cook Island Party supporters. According to the DOJ, the defendants 'desiring the retention of Sir Albert Henry as Premier in order to insure the renewal of the stamp distribution agreement, agreed to provide the requested financial assistance upon the condition that Sir Albert Henry and the Cook Islands Party keep secret the source of the funds.'

A 1981 enforcement action against construction company Sam Wallace Company Inc. represented the first FCPA enforcement action involving both a DOJ and SEC component.[79] The conduct at issue involved payments to the Chairman of the Trinidad and Tobago Racing Authority to obtain and retain a contract to construct buildings at a racetrack in Trinidad. The DOJ alleged that the company, aided and abetted by certain of its officers and employees, caused a wholly-owned subsidiary company to 'create fictitious purchase orders to purported suppliers ... for the purpose of concealing the withdrawal of corporate funds' in order to make payments to the official. Based on the same core set of conduct, the SEC also brought civil charges against the company and certain of its executives. According to the SEC's complaint, the defendants 'disguised and concealed [the] payments on Wallace's book and records by utilizing, or causing to be utilized, certain false accounting entries which did not reflect the true nature and purpose of, and falsely described the expenditures used in the making' of the payments to the official.

In 1982, the first FCPA mega-case was brought and it involved five corporate defendants and twelve individual defendants. The DOJ indictment charged a conspiracy between the defendants (companies and individuals in the oil and gas services industry) to pay approximately $10 million to alleged Mexican foreign officials employed by Pemex, the national oil company wholly-owned by the Government of Mexico, and a third party 'knowing that all or a portion of such money' would be given to the official to induce the official to use his influence in order to assist the defendants in 'obtaining or retaining business with Pemex.'[80]

According to the DOJ, as part of the conspiracy various defendants arranged with a third party who held itself out as the Mexican agent of a defendant company 'while in truth acting primarily as the conduit for the bribe payments.' The DOJ alleged that the third party disguised the bribe payments as 'commissions' by providing various defendants 'false and fictitious' invoices for each payment received. The indictment further alleged that the defendants used the term 'folks' as a code word for the 'foreign officials' 'in order to conceal from others the true identities [of the] officials and the existence of the bribe scheme.'

The companies involved all ultimately pleaded guilty and were ordered to pay fines ranging from approximately $3.5 million to $5,000. The individuals all pleaded guilty or nolo contendere.

All individuals, that is, except for George McLean (the former Vice President of Solar Turbines International, a division of International Harvester Company). Even though International Harvester pleaded guilty to conspiracy to violate the FCPA, McLean won pre-trial dismissal of substantive FCPA charges against him based on the so-called Eckhardt Amendment (an original provision in the FCPA that is no longer part of the statute which generally required that in order to prosecute an employee for a substantive FCPA offense, the corporate employer must first be convicted of similarly violating the FCPA).[81] An appellate court, in rejecting the DOJ's appeal of the dismissal, concluded that 'both the language of the Act and its legislative history reveal a clear intent to impose criminal sanctions against the employee who acts at the behest of and for the benefit of his employer only where his employer has been convicted of similar FCPA violations.'[82]

Despite dismissal of substantive FCPA charges, McLean still faced prosecution on charges of conspiracy to violate the FCPA. On this charge, McLean exercised his constitutional right to a jury trial and put the DOJ, for the first time in FCPA history, to its high burden of proof at trial. He prevailed as the jury found him not guilty.[83] Even though McLean prevailed against the DOJ, his victory was not without costs. The thousands of hours he spent on his defense consumed his life and took him away from his young family, damaged his reputation, and changed his life forever.

In addition to the McLean matter, the DOJ also suffered FCPA defeats when put to its burden of proof in two other early FCPA enforcement actions.

In 1989, the DOJ criminally charged various individuals associated with AEA Aircraft Recovery (a company in the business of recovery of seized aircraft) including Alfredo Duran.[84] According to the charging documents, the various defendants conspired to make payments to officials of the Dominican Republic in order to obtain the release of two aircraft seized by the government. All of the defendants pleaded guilty except for Duran (a former Florida political leader) who pleaded not guilty and put the DOJ to its high burden of proof at trial. After the DOJ presented its evidence at trial, Duran filed a motion for judgment of acquittal and argued that 'no reasonable jury could find that the purpose of any of the alleged intended payments was to assist [...] in obtaining or retaining business' and that the government 'has failed to adduce sufficient evidence to prove any intended payments were not facilitating or expediting payments for the purpose of expediting or securing routine governmental action (i.e. grease payments).' The trial court judge granted a judgment of acquittal ending the case. According to media reports, in granting the acquittal, the judge said that 'the government failed to prove the charges against [Duran] were a crime under the FCPA.'

In 1990, the DOJ criminally charged Harris Corporation (a company that manufactured telephone switching systems) and two executives, John Iacobucci and Ronald Schultz, with conspiracy to violate the FCPA.[85] According to the charging documents, the defendants paid and authorized the payment of money to a third party 'while knowing that a portion of such money' would be offered or given, directly or indirectly, to officials of the Government of Colombia in order to influence the officials to award government telecommunications contracts to Harris. According to the indictment, pursuant to the conspiracy Harris retained an agent based upon representations that he had connections with officials in the government that he would use to assist Harris in obtaining telecommunications contracts.

Upon filing of the criminal charges, the Chairman and CEO of Harris stated: 'We believe that these charges are based upon a distorted view of the facts, and they represent a radical departure from existing enforcement policies. We have cooperated fully with the DOJ in its investigation of the allegations, providing clear evidence refuting the charges.'

The company, along with the individuals, put the DOJ to its high burden of proof at trial. In 1991, the trial court judge granted a motion for judgment of acquittal. Media reports stated:

> Shortly after the government rested its case, [the trial court judge] ruled from the bench that 'no reasonable jury' could convict the company nor its executives on any of the five bribery-related counts for which they were indicted. Citing insufficient evidence, [the judge] said the government had failed to show any intent by the defendants to enter into a criminal conspiracy. [The judge] also said it was the first time in his six years on the federal bench that he had dismissed a criminal case at mid-trial for lack of evidence.

After the judgment of acquittal, the Chairman and CEO of Harris stated:

> We're very pleased that [we] have been vindicated, but we believe the charges should never have been brought in the first place. The DOJ's case was based upon a distorted view of the facts and represented a radical departure from existing enforcement policies. As a result, American taxpayers have been burdened with unnecessary litigation costs, and Harris has incurred more than $3 million in legal fees, spent many hundreds of hours of our people's time, and suffered a substantial disruption of the corporation's business to prove an absence of wrongdoing that should have been apparent from the beginning. The case has also placed a heavy strain on our two employees named in the indictment.

The DOJ's early defeats when put to its high burden of proof in FCPA enforcement actions foreshadow an issue that remains in this new era of

FCPA enforcement as detailed in Chapter 5. That is, while enforcement agencies have had 'success' in exercising their leverage and securing large corporate FCPA settlements through resolution vehicles not subjected to any meaningful judicial scrutiny, when put to its burdens of proof in the context of an adversarial system, the enforcement agencies have substantially less success. In a legal system founded on the rule of law, this latter form of success is more meaningful than the former.

Regardless of wins and losses, early FCPA enforcement was less robust than in this new era of enforcement. Indeed, between 1977 and 1987, there were approximately ten core corporate FCPA enforcement actions and between 1988 and 1998 there were approximately fifteen core corporate actions. By comparison, in this new era of FCPA enforcement, when corporate compliance practices far exceed those of the past, there are approximately ten to fifteen core corporate FCPA enforcement actions *per year* and Chapter 6 will explore certain practical and provocative reasons for the increase in FCPA enforcement.

However, it is generally futile to draw many meaningful conclusions from early FCPA enforcement or compare it to enforcement in this new era. For starters, growing pains associated with a new law, and a pioneering one at that, were understandable as both business organizations and enforcement agencies alike were absorbing the law and its new expectations and challenges. For example, two years into enforcing the FCPA, the DOJ Assistant Attorney General stated: 'The interpretive questions arising under the Act depend on subtle judgments of fact and law. We're dealing with a new Act, where no one has much enforcement experience. It is an Act that presents questions there has never been occasion to address in domestic bribery law …'.[86]

Indeed, part of the reason for the general lack of early FCPA enforcement was that even the enforcement agencies viewed the FCPA as an imprecise and confusing statute. For instance, the new SEC Director of Enforcement stated in 1981 that he 'pledged to enforce, with discretion, the FCPA, which he criticized as being ambiguous.'[87] Among other ambiguities, the FCPA as originally enacted had an imprecise 'while knowing or having reason to know' standard applicable to liability for the conduct of third parties such as foreign agents. During FCPA reform hearings in the 1980s the DOJ Deputy Attorney General stated:

> The DOJ is sensitive to the unnecessary problems that the American business community has encountered in its attempts to interpret and apply the 'reason to know' standard. We also know it is difficult to define exactly what constitutes 'reason to know.' For that reason, the policy of the Department has been to prosecute only those cases where the evidence of awareness – whether

> direct or circumstantial – was so clear as to constitute actual knowledge of the bribe scheme.[88]

The DOJ Assistant Attorney General likewise stated during Congressional hearings that the then standard for third-party liability was akin to a 'simple negligence standard' and 'is plainly inappropriate and inconsistent with the general approach of modern criminal law to state-of-mind requirements.'[89] The U.S. Trade Representative was more blunt when describing this standard and said 'frankly, nobody knows what it means.'[90]

While Chapter 6 specifically discusses the reasons for the increase in FCPA enforcement in this new era, for present purposes it is useful to note that for much of the FCPA's history there were material differences in the law, enforcement agency policies, and the global business environment that all impacted early FCPA enforcement. For instance, fewer persons (both legal and natural) were subject to the FCPA for much of its history compared to now. When the FCPA became law in 1977 few foreign companies had shares listed on a U.S. exchange. As you will learn in Chapters 3 and 4, such a listing makes a company an 'issuer' and thus subject to the FCPA. By comparison, there are now approximately 1,000 foreign companies with shares listed on a U.S. exchange and thus subject to the FCPA.[91] In addition, in 1998 the FCPA was amended so that certain other foreign companies and foreign nationals could become subject to the FCPA under certain conditions. Furthermore, the resolution vehicles available to the enforcement agencies for much of the FCPA's history were materially different compared to today. For most of the FCPA's history, the DOJ only had two options upon learning of conduct that potentially violated the FCPA: charge the company or do not charge the company. As discussed in greater detail in Chapter 2, in 2004 the DOJ began using alternative resolution vehicles such as NPAs and DPAs to resolve FCPA enforcement actions, and use of these vehicles has unquestionably resulted in more FCPA enforcement actions.

Nor can any meaningful conclusions be drawn from comparing fine and penalty amounts in early FCPA enforcement actions to fine and penalty amounts in this new era. For starters, the FCPA's statutory fine and penalty amounts have changed over time. Perhaps more significantly, you will learn in Chapter 5 that criminal fine amounts in FCPA enforcement actions are rarely based on the statutory amounts, but rather based on the Alternative Fines Act, a statute passed in 2006, which can result in a fine amount up to twice the benefit the payer sought to obtain through the improper payment.[92] Moreover, it was not until 1990 that the SEC was given authority to assess civil monetary penalties in a wide variety of securities law enforcement actions including FCPA enforcement actions.[93] In addition, disgorgement, a central feature of most SEC FCPA enforcement actions in this new era, was not yet used in SEC enforcement actions.

Although certain historical comparisons of FCPA enforcement lack meaningful value, other comparisons are noteworthy. While one can question *how* the enforcement agencies held individuals accountable (i.e. criminal v. civil charges) during the early years of FCPA enforcement, the enforcement agencies *did* frequently hold individuals accountable when a company resolved an FCPA enforcement action. Indeed, during the FCPA's first decade, approximately 90 percent of corporate FCPA enforcements also resulted in related charges against company employees. This is a meaningful statistic and stands in stark contrast to this new era in which approximately 70 percent of corporate FCPA enforcement actions have not resulted in any charges against company employees. This FCPA enforcement statistic, as well as many others relevant to corporate and individual FCPA enforcement actions, are highlighted in greater detail in Chapter 5.

The FCPA's 1988 and 1998 Amendments

Against the background of early FCPA enforcement is perhaps the more important issue that while the FCPA was indeed a pioneering and valuable statute it was widely viewed as an imperfect statute. Indeed, almost as soon as the FCPA was passed in 1977 concerns were raised across a wide spectrum that the law was vague and ambiguous, and because of that, harmful to U.S. businesses seeking to compete in the global marketplace. The early 1980s saw much FCPA reform activity. In 1980, the Carter administration (recall that President Carter signed the FCPA into law in 1977) sent a report to Congress prepared by the Secretary of Commerce and the U.S. Trade Representative titled 'Report of the President on Export Promotion Functions and Potential Export Disincentives.'[94] In pertinent part, the report stated:

> The [FCPA] is identified by businessmen and attorneys as one of the most significant export disincentives. [...] The Act inhibits exporting because of uncertainty within the business community about the meaning and application of some of its key provisions.
>
> Uncertainty about the meaning of key provisions of the FCPA and how it will be applied is having a negative effect on U.S. exports. Many of the businessmen and attorneys consulted expressed the view that this uncertainty has a far greater impact than the actual prohibition against bribery. The problem described, in essence, is that what conduct is prohibited and what

> conduct is not prohibited under the Act is often unclear. In order to avoid possible violations of the Act, attorneys often give such cautious guidance that their clients simply forego any transactions where the FCPA could possibly become an issue.
>
> The effects of these uncertainties reportedly manifest themselves in various ways. Consultations with the private sector revealed instances in which U.S. companies: withdrew from joint ventures for fear they later could be held responsible for the acts of their foreign partners; incurred substantial legal and investigative costs to check the backgrounds of their sales agents abroad; were unable to obtain the services of effective sales agents; lost contracts simply because of the time needed to investigate sales agents abroad and institute safeguards; withdrew from existing markets; and declined to enter new markets.
>
> Finally, companies point out that the extent to which companies have been successfully prosecuted under the FCPA does not define the extent of the disincentive. Uncertainty can be a disincentive without any prosecutions and, moreover, exports are inhibited merely by the possibility of public charges and the adverse publicity surrounding them. Even where a company is totally convinced that a court would find that it had not violated the FCPA, it nonetheless may forego the export opportunity for fear that an enforcement agency could publicly charge it with a violation of the Act.

In 1981, the Government Accounting Office ('GAO'), the investigative arm of Congress, released a report titled 'Impact of Foreign Corrupt Practices Act on U.S. Business.'[95] The report was based in part on a GAO questionnaire survey of 250 companies randomly selected from the Fortune 1000 list of the largest industrial firms in the U.S. and the questionnaire addressed the FCPA's relationship to the following four areas: (1) corporate policies and/or codes of conduct; (2) corporate systems of accountability; (3) cost burdens, if any, incurred by management to comply with the FCPA; and (4) corporate opinions regarding the: (i) FCPA's effect on U.S. corporate foreign sales; (ii) the clarity of the FCPA's provisions; (iii) the potential effectiveness of an international anti-bribery agreement; and (iv) perceived effectiveness of the FCPA in reducing questionable payments.

The GAO found that while the FCPA 'has brought about efforts to strengthen corporate codes of conduct and systems of internal accounting control,' corporations reported that 'their efforts to comply with the [the FCPA] have resulted in costs that were greater than the benefits received' and that a substantial number of businesses 'reported that they had lost oversees business as a result' of the FCPA. The GAO report noted concerns that the FCPA's anti-bribery provisions were 'vague and ambiguous' and stated that while 'unambiguous requirements may be impractical and could provide a roadmap for corporate bribery' companies operating in the global marketplace 'should be subject to clear and consistent demands by the Government agencies for enforcing the act.'

Despite its widely perceived deficiencies, reforming a law called the 'Foreign *Corrupt* Practices Act' was a political hot potato simply because of the name of the law. Indeed early FCPA reform proposals included changing the name of the law so that a substantive, issue-based discussion could take place free from pro-bribery vs. anti-bribery rhetoric. For instance, among the first FCPA reform bills introduced in 1980 was the 'Business Accounting and Foreign Trade Simplification Act' which sought to change the name of the FCPA as well as other substantive changes.[96] The preamble of the bill stated, in pertinent part, as follows.

> The principal objectives of the [FCPA] are desirable, beneficial, and important to our Nation as well as to our relationships with our trading partners, and these objectives should remain the central intent of the [FCPA];
>
> exporters should not be subject to unclear, conflicting, and potentially damaging demands by diverse United States agencies responsible for enforcement of the [FCPA];
>
> legal interpretations and general compliance and enforcement practices associated with the [FCPA] should be developed in accordance with considerations underlying foreign policy relations, international trade, export promotion, international monetary policy, and other related civil and criminal statutes;

However, the mere discussion of FCPA reform was opposed by some who seemed to advance the simplistic – either you are against bribery or for bribery – position. Despite this political atmosphere, certain Congressional leaders demonstrated courage to reform the FCPA into a better, more useable statute for business and the enforcement agencies alike.

For instance, in 1981 Senator Alfonse D'Amato opened Senate hearings on an FCPA reform bill by stating:

> The discussion which takes place during these hearings is not a debate between those who oppose bribery and those who support it. I see the major issue before us to be whether the law, including both its anti-bribery and accounting provisions, is the best approach, or whether it has created unnecessary costs and burdens out of proportion to the purposes for which it was enacted, and whether it serves our national interests.[97]

Senator John Chafee stated:

> Critics have attempted to characterize my bill as a signal to U.S. companies that they can return to the 'bad old days' of foreign bribery. That is not my intent, nor should it be the signal. I abhor bribery, whether domestic or foreign, but I also dislike confusion. Thus, my bill will eliminate uncertainty while maintaining strong prohibitions against bribery. The ambiguities and murkiness of the bill's language have caused U.S. companies to withdraw from legitimate markets and contributed to the decline in the U.S. share of world exports. We need to end this confusion.[98]

During the hearing, Senator D'Amato also noted:

> The thing that bothers me about this kind of a debate is that we tend to posture this thing as if somebody were for or against bribery. I think it is important to state for the record that bribery of any foreign official by any U.S. concern is bad for our national health, and it is something that we have got to stop, we have got to deal with, and we have, I think, gone a long way with the FCPA. What we proposed to do is to simplify that law and to make it workable so that we can set that standard in concrete from now on and not have the abuses that occurred prior to 1977, but not by stopping exports, but by stopping bribery. That is the objective. [...] I think it is very important that in the committee's work that we not create the attitude that this committee is making it easier for businesses to engage in illegal activity. [...] I think that rather than hampering prosecution of illegal acts, [the reform bill at issue] would clarify and make possible just prosecution of those who engage in bribery. It would eliminate any 'gray area' by clearly spelling out the limits of the law.[99]

During the hearing, Senator John Heinz stated:

> There are many people that are extremist, and there are others who get carried away by their enthusiasm who are going to argue that even if we change the provisions in the present act, that are unnecessary or ambiguous or uncertain, that even though we are not doing so, we are legalizing bribery. That strikes me as the worst kind of demagoguery, because it implies that everything that Congress has done in the past is perfect. And does anybody believe that?[100]

As the U.S. Trade Representative stated:

> Just because the FCPA spotlights a sensitive subject, some people wish to turn a 'blind eye' to its shortcomings rather than risk being accused of being 'soft on bribery.' That is too easy a way out. Retreating from controversy will not cure the law's deficiencies. [...] Is there any U.S. law that ought to be above such review and clarification – especially one as complex as the FCPA?[101]

Indicative of the political challenges of reforming a law called the Foreign Corrupt Practices Act, FCPA reform took eight years and it is noteworthy how it occurred. In 1988 the FCPA was amended, not through a stand-alone bill, but through Title V, Subtitle A, Part I of the Omnibus Trade and Competiveness Act of 1988 signed into law by President Ronald Reagan.[102]

Principle changes to the FCPA in 1988 included: (i) amending the original 'reason to know' standard applicable to third-party liability; (ii) amending the FCPA to include certain affirmative defenses based on foreign law and reasonable and bona fide expenditures; and (iii) amending the FCPA to include an express facilitating payment exception. As to this later change, the FCPA's original definition of 'foreign official' contained an indirect facilitating payment exception by excluding from the definition of 'foreign official' 'any employee of a foreign government or any department, agency, or instrumentality thereof whose duties are essentially ministerial or clerical.' The effect of the 1988 amendments was to remove this indirect exception from the definition of foreign official in favor of an express stand-alone exception for 'routine governmental action.'

Issues related to third-party payments, the facilitating payments exception and the FCPA's affirmative defenses are discussed in greater detail in Chapter 3.

In 1998 the FCPA was further amended to incorporate certain aspects of the Organization for Economic Cooperation and Development ('OECD') Convention on Combating Bribery of Foreign Public Officials in International Business Transactions (the 'OECD Convention') signed by the U.S. and approximately thirty other countries in 1997.[103] Principle changes to the FCPA in 1998 included: (i) the creation of a new statutory provision applicable to certain foreign companies and foreign nationals; and (ii) expanded nationality jurisdiction as to U.S. companies and citizens by which the anti-bribery provisions can apply regardless of whether an improper payment scheme has a U.S. territorial nexus. These issues are likewise discussed in greater detail in Chapter 3.

NOTES

1. Flora v. U.S., 362 U.S. 145 (1960).
2. U.S. v. McLean, 738 F.2d 655 (5th Cir. 1984).
3. U.S. v. Kay, 359 F.3d 738 (5th Cir. 2004).
4. James Doty, 'Toward a Reg. FCPA: A Modest Proposal for Change in Administering the Foreign Corrupt Practices Act,' The Business Lawyer (Aug. 2007).
5. FCPA Professor, 'The FCPA as an Ambiguous Statute and the Importance of Legislative History' (Feb. 13, 2013).
6. See, e.g., Lewis v. Spork, 612 F.Supp. 1316 (N.D. Cal. 1985).

7. SEC, 'Report of the Securities and Exchange Commission on Questionable and Illegal Corporate Payments and Practices,' (1976), reprinted in Special Supplement, Sec. Reg. & L. Rep. (BNA) No. 353 (May 19, 1976).
8. Multinational Corporations and United States Foreign Policy: Hearings before the Subcomm. on Multinational Corps. of the S. Comm. on Foreign Relations, 94th Cong. 1 (1975).
9. Foreign Payments Disclosure: Hearings before the Subcomm. on Consumer Prot. and Fin. of the H. Comm. on Interstate and Foreign Commerce, 94th Cong. 2 (1976).
10. The Activities of American Multinational Corporations Abroad: Hearings before the Subcomm. on Int'l Econ. Policy of the H. Comm. on Int'l Relations, 94th Cong. (1975).
11. Foreign Payments Disclosure: Hearings before the Subcomm. on Consumer Prot. and Fin. of the H. Comm. on Interstate and Foreign Commerce, 94th Cong. (1976).
12. Protecting the Ability of the United States to Trade Abroad: Hearings before the Subcomm. on Int'l Trade of the S. Comm. on Fin., 94th Cong. (1975).
13. *Supra* note 10.
14. *Supra* note 12.
15. 122 Cong. Rec. S6515–16 (1976) (daily ed. May 5, 1976).
16. Unlawful Corporate Payments Act of 1977: Hearings before the Subcomm. of Consumer Prot. and Fin. of the H. Comm. on Interstate and Foreign Commerce, 95th Cong. (1977).
17. *Supra* note 10.
18. Lockheed Bribery: Hearings before the S. Comm on Banking, Housing, and Urban Affairs, 94th Cong. (1975).
19. Id.
20. S. Rep. No. 94-1031, at 3 (1976).
21. *Supra* note 12.
22. Foreign Corrupt Practices and Domestic and Foreign Investment Disclosure: Hearing before the S. Comm on Banking, Housing, and Urban Affairs, 95th Cong. (1977).
23. *Supra* note 10.
24. S. Rep. No. 94-1031, at 4 (1976).
25. Foreign and Corporate Bribes: Hearings before the S. Comm. on Banking, Housing, and Urban Affairs, 94th Cong. (1976).
26. *Supra* note 10.
27. *Supra* note 25.
28. Id.
29. *Supra* note 10.
30. Id.
31. Prohibiting Bribes to Foreign Officials: Hearing before the S. Comm. on Banking, Housing, and Urban Affairs, 94th Cong. (1976).
32. *Supra* note 10.
33. *Supra* note 31.
34. *Supra* note 10.
35. Id.
36. Id.
37. *Supra* note 18.
38. Corporate Business Practices and United States Foreign Policy: Hearing before the Subcomm. on Int'l Econ. Policy and Trade of the H. Comm. on Int'l Relations, 95th Cong.
(1977).
39. *Supra* note 10.

40. *Supra* note 18.
41. Abuses of Corporate Power: Hearings before the Subcomm. on Priorities and Econ. in Gov't of the Joint Econ. Comm., 94th Cong. (1976).
42. 122 Cong. Rec. S15857 (1976) (daily ed. Sept. 15, 1976).
43. *Supra* note 10.
44. Id.
45. *Supra* note 25.
46. 94 Cong. Rec. S6516 (1976).
47. *Supra* note 25.
48. Id.
49. *Supra* note 10.
50. *Supra* note 22.
51. *Supra* note 12.
52. *Supra* note 16.
53. Id.
54. *Supra* note 25.
55. Gerald R. Ford, 'Memorandum Establishing the Task Force on Questionable Corporate Payments Abroad' (Mar. 31, 1976).
56. *Supra* note 31.
57. Gerald R. Ford, Remarks Announcing New Initiatives for the Task Force on Questionable Corporate Payments Abroad (June 14, 1976).
58. Gerald R. Ford, Special Message to the Congress Transmitting Proposed Foreign Payments Disclosure Legislation (Aug. 3, 1976).
59. *Supra* note 22.
60. Id.
61. S. Rep. No. 94-103 (1976).
62. 122 Cong. Rec. 30,337 (1976) (daily ed. Sept. 14, 1976).
63. *Supra* note 16.
64. *Supra* note 22.
65. S. Rep. No. 93-114, at 10 (1977).
66. H.R. Rep. No. 95-640, at 6 (1977).
67. *Supra* note 38.
68. 123 Cong. Rec. 38,778 (1977).
69. Presidential Statement on Signing the Foreign Corrupt Practices and Investment Disclosure Bill, 13 Weekly Compilation of Presidential Documents 1909 (Dec. 20, 1977).
70. *Supra* note 7.
71. *Supra* note 12.
72. *Supra* note 25.
73. *Supra* note 22.
74. S. Rep. No. 94-1031 (1976).
75. H.R. Rep. No. 95-640 (1977).
76. H.R. Rep. No. 95-831 (1977).
77. FCPA Professor, 'The FCPA's First Compliance Monitor' (Aug. 26, 2011), containing links to original source documents.
78. FCPA Professor, 'Postage Stamps, Sir Albert Henry, Flying Voters, and the FCPA' (Aug. 24, 2011), containing links to original source documents.
79. FCPA Professor, 'Bribery at the Racetrack' (Nov. 11, 2011), containing links to original source documents.
80. FCPA Professor, 'The FCPA's First Mega Enforcement Action' (Mar. 18, 2013), containing links to original source documents.
81. FCPA Professor, 'Looking Back on the Eckhardt Amendment' (Mar. 19, 2013).
82. 738 F.2d 655 (5th Cir. 1984).

83. FCPA Professor, 'George McLean' (Mar. 20, 21, 2013).
84. FCPA Professor, 'An Important FCPA Case You've Likely Never Heard about' (May 7, 2012), containing links to original source documents.
85. FCPA Professor, 'One Win, One Loss' (May 16, 2011), containing links to original source documents.
86. 'Justice Outlines Priorities in Prosecuting Violations of For. Corrupt Practices Act,' The American Banker (Nov. 21, 1979).
87. Owen Ullmann, 'Corporate Lawyer Gets SEC Enforcement Post,' Associated Press (June 29, 1981).
88. Joint Hearing before the Subcommittee on International Finance and Monetary Policy and the Subcommittee on Banking, Housing, and Urban Affairs (June 10, 1986).
89. 'The Foreign Trade Practices Act,' Hearings before the Subcommittee on International Economic Policy and Trade of the Committee on Foreign Affairs, House of Representatives (1983).
90. Id.
91. SEC, 'Number of Foreign Companies Registered and Reporting with the U.S. Securities and Exchange Commission' (Dec. 31, 2010).
92. 18 U.S.C. § 3571.
93. Securities Enforcement Remedies and Penny Stock Reform Act of 1990. Pub. L. 101-429 (Oct. 15, 1990).
94. 'Report of the President on Export Promotion Functions and Potential Export Disincentives: Together with the Review of Executive Branch Export Promotion Functions and Potential Export Disincentives,' Transmitted to the Congress (Sept. 1980).
95. By the Comptroller General, Report to the Congress of the United States, 'Impact of the Foreign Corrupt Practices Act on U.S. Business,' (Mar. 1981).
96. S. 2763 (introduced May 28, 1980).
97. Joint Hearings before the Subcommittee on Securities and the Subcommittee on International Finance and Monetary Policy of the Committee on Banking, Housing, and Urban Affairs, U.S. Senate, 97th Cong. (May 20, 1981).
98. Id.
99. Id.
100. Id.
101. Id.
102. Public Law 100-418 (1988).
103. Public Law 105-366 (1998).

2. FCPA foundational knowledge

This book focuses on a particular statute, but it is important to understand from the beginning that other general legal principles as well as general DOJ and SEC enforcement policies and resolution vehicles impact FCPA enforcement. By highlighting such topics, this chapter provides general foundational knowledge to best enhance understanding and comprehension of the specific FCPA topics that follow.

The first general legal principle is *respondeat superior*. Business organizations operating in the global marketplace act through employees and agents. Pursuant to *respondeat superior*, employee and agent conduct can expose a business organization to legal liability, both criminal and civil, even if the employee or agent conduct is contrary to the organization's pre-existing compliance policies. Understanding this key legal principle, as well as the realities of the global marketplace, inform how companies often become the subject of FCPA scrutiny and why not all companies that resolve FCPA enforcement action are 'bad' or 'unethical.' Indeed, this chapter introduces you to the term 'world's most ethical FCPA violators.'

Next, general DOJ and SEC enforcement policies are introduced and the 'carrots' and 'sticks' relevant to resolving a corporate FCPA enforcement action are highlighted. Mindful of these 'carrots' and 'sticks,' business organizations are often motivated to resolve DOJ or SEC enforcement actions for reasons of risk aversion, and not necessarily because the enforcement agency has a superior legal position. Discussion will then turn to the typical resolution vehicles used to enforce the FCPA in this new era – namely DOJ NPAs and DPAs and SEC 'neither admit nor deny' settlements. The controversial aspects of these resolution vehicles will be confronted and you can decide whether they are in the public interest or facilitate a 'façade' of FCPA enforcement. Against the backdrop of several general enforcement agency policies that impact FCPA enforcement is also a specific DOJ policy that has resulted in the FCPA being enforced differently than most other federal criminal statutes.

Prior to diving into the specific elements of the FCPA's anti-bribery and books and records and internal controls provisions in Chapters 3 and

4, it is useful to first address the question of what the FCPA actually means. This chapter concludes by setting forth a hierarchy of FCPA legal authority and other information and you will discover that much of what defines this new era of FCPA enforcement is non-binding, non-legal sources of information including so-called prosecutorial common law. Mindful of this hierarchy, throughout this book much attention is focused on actual sources of legal authority because what matters most is what the FCPA says, what Congress intended the FCPA to mean, and how judges have interpreted the FCPA.

A. *RESPONDEAT SUPERIOR*

An important general legal principle that impacts FCPA enforcement is *respondeat superior*. Business organizations operating in the global marketplace act through employees and agents. Pursuant to *respondeat superior*, employee and agent conduct can expose a business organization to legal liability, both criminal and civil, even if the employee or agent conduct is contrary to the organization's pre-existing compliance policies.

The *respondeat superior* theory of corporate criminal liability is a common law construct that can be traced back to a 1909 Supreme Court case.[1] The issue before the court in *New York Central & Hudson River Railroad Company v. U.S.* was whether a railroad corporation could face criminal liability under a federal statute based on the acts of any officer, agent, or other person acting for or employed by the company. The company asserted that the statute at issue was unconstitutional because Congress had no authority to impute a criminal act not authorized by the board of directors to a corporation, due to the nature and character of the corporation as a legal person separate and distinct from its employees and agents.

While acknowledging common law tradition that a corporation could not commit a crime, the Supreme Court nevertheless stated that the 'modern authority, universally … is the other way.' Stating that it was well established in civil tort actions that a corporation may be held responsible for damages for the acts of its agent within the scope of his employment – even if the agent acted wantonly or recklessly or against the express orders of his employer – the Supreme Court held that 'the act of the agent, while exercising the authority delegated to him to make [business decisions] may be controlled, in the interest of public policy, by imputing his act to his employer and imposing penalties upon the corporation for which he is acting …'.

In short, the Supreme Court saw 'no good reason why corporations may not be held responsible for and charged with the knowledge and purposes of their agents, acting within the authority conferred upon them.' In so holding, the Supreme Court reasoned that the law 'cannot shut its eyes to the fact that the great majority of business transactions in modern times are conducted through [corporations], and particularly that interstate commerce is almost entirely in their hands, and to give them immunity from all punishment because of the old and exploded doctrine that a corporation cannot commit a crime would virtually take away the only means of effectually controlling the subject-matter and correcting the abuses aimed at.'

As to the scope of corporate criminal liability, Mary Jo White (the Chairman of the SEC) stated, while in private practice:

> [T]he sweep of corporate criminal liability could hardly be broader [and its] breathtaking scope always bears repeating: If a single employee, however low down in the corporate hierarchy, commits a crime in the course of his or her employment, even in part to benefit the corporation, the corporate employer is criminally liable for that employee's crime. It is essentially absolute liability.[2]

Respondeat superior corporate criminal liability has always been, and will likely always be, controversial particularly in an era of multinational corporations doing business around the globe in many difficult and challenging business environments and through the acts of tens of thousands of employees and agents.

Part of the controversy with this doctrine is due to the fact that many peer nations do not recognize corporate criminal liability. Moreover, in many countries that do – such as Canada, and Australia for instance – criminal liability can only be imputed to a business organization based on the conduct of so-called 'controlling minds' such as board of directors or executive officers.[3]

Despite its controversy, *respondeat superior* corporate criminal liability is the controlling standard in the U.S., and understanding this key legal principle is important in understanding FCPA enforcement. Set forth below is the relevant jury instruction in an enforcement action against Lindsey Manufacturing Company, the only time in FCPA history that a corporate FCPA charge was presented to a jury.

> To sustain the charge of conspiracy to violate the [FCPA] or violation of the FCPA against Lindsey Manufacturing Company ['Lindsey'], the government must prove the following propositions: first, the offense charged was committed by one or more agents or employees of Lindsey; second, in committing the offense, the agent or employee intended, at least in part, to benefit

> Lindsey; and third, the acts by the agent or employee were committed within the authority or scope of his employment. For an act to be within the authority of an agent or the scope of the employment of an employee, it must deal with a matter whose performance is generally entrusted to the agent or employee by Lindsey. It is not necessary that the particular act was itself authorized or directed by Lindsey. If an agent or an employee was acting within the authority or scope of his employment, Lindsey is not relieved of its responsibility because the act was illegal.[4]

While *respondeat superior* corporate criminal liability is broad, it does nevertheless have legal limitations. For instance, many multinational companies are organized for practical and legal reasons by distinct corporate entities such as a parent corporation and various subsidiary companies in foreign countries. It is black-letter law that the legal liability of each distinct corporate entity is to be contained within that entity absent a finding of abuse of corporate form such as insufficient capitalization, failure to hold annual meetings or the like. In short, legal liability does not ordinarily hop, skip and jump around a multinational company. However, in many FCPA enforcement actions in this new era, the enforcement agencies have advanced the theory that a parent corporation is legally responsible for the acts of subsidiary employees absent any allegation or suggestion that the parent company was aware of, or participated in, the alleged improper conduct.

Commenting on this trend in connection with an FCPA enforcement action against Ralph Lauren Corporation ('RLC'), Philip Urofsky, a former DOJ Assistant Chief of the Fraud Section, asked 'are there any limits to parent corporation liability' and stated.

> The facts of the case … point to the steady entrenchment of a more ominous prosecution theory: an approach that appears to approximate strict criminal and civil liability of parent corporations for their subsidiaries' corrupt acts. Although this disregard of corporate structures has been hinted at in previous SEC matters […] the RLC case puts both agencies firmly in the camp of this aggressive and unprecedented expansion of corporate liability. […] This approach, however, fails to honor the corporate form and the black-letter rule that to 'pierce the corporate veil' the government and other litigants must show that the parent operated the subsidiary as an alter ego, and itself paid no attention to the corporate form. Moreover, it is contrary to the language of the [FCPA's] original history. […] It is disquieting [that in the RLC case] the DOJ appears to have jumped on the charge-the-parent bandwagon, bringing a bribery case against a parent without alleging any involvement by the parent in those violations. One can only speculate that it did so because it had no jurisdiction over the foreign subsidiary itself, given that it also did not allege any act by the subsidiary in U.S. territory. However, as always, the maxim that bad facts make bad law applies, and evidentiary weaknesses cannot

> excuse the distortion of the statute's previously clear and reasonable allocation of responsibility.[5]

Like many corporate FCPA enforcement actions in this new era, the Ralph Lauren enforcement action was resolved via an NPA meaning, as discussed in more detail below, there was no judicial scrutiny of the enforcement action.

B. THE REALITIES OF THE GLOBAL MARKETPLACE

Respondeat superior, coupled with its broad application by the enforcement agencies, informs how companies often become the subject of FCPA scrutiny. Related to the issue of why companies often become the subject of FCPA scrutiny is pondering the following question, do companies subject to the FCPA do business in foreign markets: (i) intent on engaging in bribery as a business strategy and without a commitment to FCPA compliance; or (ii) with a commitment to FCPA compliance, yet subject to difficult and challenging business conditions?

To be sure there have been instances of the former; however Joseph Covington, a former DOJ FCPA Unit Chief, said that he has 'rarely seen American companies affirmatively offering bribes in the first instance.' Rather, he observed that companies doing business in global markets are 'reacting to a world not of their making' and that 'as the world shrinks companies who seek to do the right thing can't help but confront corrupt officials – as customers, regulator and adjudicators – and confront them often.'[6]

In many countries, companies subject to the FCPA must navigate difficult and challenging business conditions replete with trade barriers such as customs procedures; import documentation and inspection requirements; arcane and complex licensing and certification requirements; quality standards that require product testing and inspection visits; and foreign government procurement policies. These barriers are seldom transparent and local law often requires a third-party intermediary to navigate through them. As a result, companies seeking to do business in many foreign countries are often funneled into an arbitrary world of low-paying civil servants who frequently supplement their salaries through payments condoned in the host country.

For instance, if a company wants to allow public access to its buildings in China, it must obtain a fire safety certificate, and the process has been described as follows:

> To obtain a fire-safety certificate from a local fire department, a business owner must pass five 'checkpoints' in a complicated and lengthy administrative process. Each checkpoint is guarded by officials in charge of site inspections and reviewing construction blueprints, equipment and contingency plans. Bribes considerably expedite the process that officials might otherwise draw out for weeks, months or years. Bribes range from a few thousand yuan to hundreds of thousands, per official, depending on their rank and the size of the project. But money isn't everything – some officials must be wined and dined or given luxury cigarettes. Others request the services of prostitutes.[7]

Want to sell food in China? A practitioner shared the following communication.

> Got a call the other day from an American company wanting to sell its food products into China. And fast. The problem this company is facing is that one cannot 'just' sell food into China immediately. To sell food legally into China, foreign companies must first pass certification before China's General Administration of Quality Supervision, Inspection and Quarantine, better known as AQSIQ. The food company told me that its research had revealed that it typically takes around a year to secure this certification, but that someone in China was promising they could do it in 'around six to eight weeks.'[8]

In short, foreign trade barriers create bureaucracy, foreign bureaucracy creates interactions with foreign officials, and the more interactions with foreign officials, the greater a company's FCPA risk will be.

Such trade barriers and foreign business requirements often create the conditions in which harassment bribes flourish as demonstrated by the following FCPA enforcement actions.

- Helmerich & Payne, an oil and gas drilling company, resolved an FCPA enforcement action based on alleged payments made by second-tier subsidiaries to various officials and representatives of the Argentine and Venezuelan customs services in connection with the importation and exportation of goods and equipment related to company operations in those countries. As alleged, the payments were made through agents or customs brokers, involved low dollar amounts, and were 'made on an infrequent basis.'[9]
- Seed company Delta & Pine Land Company resolved an FCPA enforcement action based on alleged payments made or offered by a subsidiary to officials of the Turkish Ministry of Agricultural and Rural Affairs to obtain government reports and certifications such as farm field inspections that were necessary to operate in Turkey.[10]
- Tyson Foods, a poultry producer, resolved an FCPA enforcement action based on alleged payments made by a subsidiary to Mexican

veterinarians. As alleged, the veterinarians were required to be on-site at the company's facility to certify product for export and certain veterinarians were allowed to charge the facility for their work (to supplement their government salary) while certain other veterinarians were not. The resolution documents neither give any detail how the payments sought to influence the veterinarians nor suggest that the product at issue was not qualified for export.[11]

- Alliance International, a tobacco processor, resolved an FCPA enforcement action based, in part, on alleged payments made by a subsidiary to officials of a Kyrgyzstan government-purchasing agency with authority over the sale of tobacco by growers in the region. As alleged, the payments were demanded by the Kyrgyz officials to secure the company's continued ability to purchase tobacco from growers in the region the officials controlled.[12]

FCPA enforcement actions based on alleged conduct in high-growth markets like India and Nigeria further demonstrate how trade barriers and foreign business requirements often create the conditions in which harassment bribes flourish. According to Transparency International, 54 percent of Indians pay bribes to receive basic services and India's Chief Economic Advisor has acknowledged that 'harassment bribery is widespread in India.'[13] Recent FCPA enforcement actions concerning business conduct in India demonstrate that harassment bribery is common and that companies operating in India face – just as locals face – difficult conditions simply to get things done.

- Diageo, a spirits company, resolved an FCPA enforcement action based, in part, on alleged payments made by a subsidiary in connection with product label registration and securing favorable product placement and promotion at state-owned liquor stores.[14]
- Wabtec, a brake manufacturer, resolved an FCPA enforcement action based on alleged payments made by a subsidiary in connection with scheduling pre-shipping product inspections, issuance of product delivery certificates, and tax audits.[15]
- Dow Chemical resolved an FCPA enforcement action based on alleged payments made by a subsidiary in connection with registering products.[16]
- Baker Hughes, an oilfield services company, resolved an FCPA enforcement action based, in part, on alleged payments made by a subsidiary to obtain shipping permits.[17]

In addition to harassment bribes in India, several FCPA enforcement actions have involved business interactions with the Nigerian Customs Service (NCS). The NCS is a notoriously corrupt public institution, the process of clearing goods through Nigerian ports is bureaucratic and prone to corruption, and various customs laws and regulations are applied arbitrarily in order to solicit bribes.[18]

Business interactions with NCS officials have been the basis for several FCPA enforcement actions, including a coordinated FCPA enforcement action in 2010 involving several companies in the oil and gas industry.[19] The conduct at issue largely involved alleged payments to NCS officials in connection with securing temporary importation permits for oil drilling rigs. Other alleged conduct included indirect payments through a freight forwarder to NCS officials to expedite the importation of goods and equipment into Nigeria and payments to circumvent customs clearance processes with respect to importation of certain tools and materials.

As detailed in Chapter 1, in passing the FCPA Congress recognized the many difficult and challenging conditions companies often encounter in doing business in the global marketplace and exempted facilitating or so-called 'grease' payments from the FCPA. Yet given the soon-to-be discussed 'carrots' and 'sticks' relevant to resolving a corporate FCPA enforcement action, all of the companies in the above examples agreed to resolve the alleged FCPA scrutiny rather than put the enforcement agencies to their burdens of proof in establishing FCPA violations consistent with Congressional intent.

Another reality of the global marketplace is that engagement of foreign third parties is often required to understand the business landscape in many foreign markets; navigate the maze of foreign rules and regulations; and interact with the foreign officials who administer many entrenched bureaucracies. In fact, in many foreign countries engaging a local agent or having a local sponsor is a requirement of doing business in the country. In other countries, a company may be required to enter into a joint venture with a local entity as a condition of doing business in the country. In certain industries it is virtually guaranteed that a company will be required to have a foreign partner as a condition of doing business in the country.

These forced business relationships often result in FCPA scrutiny because of the FCPA's so-called third-party payment provisions discussed in more detail in Chapter 3. As explored in Chapter 8 in connection with FCPA compliance, to reduce FCPA risk and to negate knowledge under the third-party payment provisions, many companies devote considerable time and resources to conducting third-party due diligence and monitoring and supervising third-party conduct. However, it has been observed as follows.

> These measures will rarely provide firms with complete protection from liability. Agency costs within firms are never zero because agents' incentives are never perfectly aligned with the interests of their principals ... often caus[ing] agents to disregard internal firm policies and instructions if doing so will serve their own financial interests.[20]

Because of *respondeat superior* and the above realities of the global marketplace, not all companies that resolve FCPA enforcement action are 'bad' or 'unethical.' Indeed, one of the ironies of this new era of FCPA enforcement is that several companies have resolved FCPA enforcement actions, or have been subject to FCPA scrutiny, during the same general time period as being recognized as one of the 'world's most ethical companies.' Companies in this illogical group include: AstraZeneca, Deere & Company, General Electric, Hewlett-Packard, Novo Nordisk, Oracle Corporation, Rockwell Automation, Sempra Energy, and Statoil.[21]

Furthermore, because of *respondeat superior* and the realities of the global marketplace, FCPA compliance can be difficult for even the most well-managed and well-intentioned business organizations with a commitment to FCPA compliance. The current FCPA enforcement environment does not adequately recognize these dynamics or reward a company's investment in pro-active FCPA compliance, and amending the FCPA to include a compliance defense is one of the FCPA reform proposals discussed in Chapter 9 of this book.

In addition to understanding *respondeat superior* and the realities of the global marketplace, an informed and sophisticated analysis of this new era of FCPA enforcement also requires foundational knowledge of DOJ and SEC enforcement policies and resolution vehicles.

C. ENFORCEMENT AGENCY POLICIES RELEVANT TO FCPA ENFORCEMENT

As hinted at in Chapter 1 concerning early FCPA enforcement, the FCPA has dual enforcers – the DOJ and SEC. The DOJ, a criminal law enforcement agency, is the sole agency responsible for criminal enforcement of the FCPA – both the anti-bribery provisions and willful violations of the books and records and internal controls provisions. The SEC, a civil law enforcement agency, generally has jurisdiction only as to 'issuers' (a company, U.S. or foreign, that has a class of securities traded on a U.S. exchange or an entity that is otherwise required to file reports with the SEC) as well as 'issuer' employees and agents. The SEC can bring civil charges for violations of the anti-bribery provisions and books and records and internal controls provisions. Assuming both the DOJ and SEC have jurisdiction over a company or an individual, it is common for both agencies to be involved in the same core FCPA enforcement action and for both the DOJ and SEC enforcement actions to be announced and resolved on the same day. As discussed in Chapter 5, the FCPA's dual enforcement structure is controversial and in need of reform.

Unlike other provisions of the Securities Exchange Act which expressly provide for private causes of action (i.e. civil cases brought by parties other than government enforcement agencies), or in which courts have inferred a private right of action, courts have held that the FCPA does not contain a private cause of action.[22] This means that only the DOJ or SEC can bring an FCPA enforcement action. Accordingly, it is important to understand how general DOJ and SEC enforcement policies can impact FCPA enforcement.

This section introduces you to the 'carrots' and 'sticks' (policies offering a combination of rewards and punishment to induce behavior) relevant to resolving a corporate FCPA enforcement action. Business organizations, mindful of these 'carrots' and 'sticks,' are often motivated to resolve DOJ or SEC enforcement actions for reasons of risk aversion and not necessarily because the enforcement agencies have a superior legal position.

The 'carrots' and 'sticks' relevant to corporate enforcement actions – in the FCPA context or otherwise – include the DOJ's Principle of Federal Prosecution of Business Organizations ('Principles of Prosecution'), the U.S. Sentencing Guidelines ('Sentencing Guidelines'), and SEC resolution policy.

DOJ Principles of Prosecution

The Principles of Prosecution are found in the U.S. Attorneys' Manual and set forth the factors prosecutors 'should consider' in determining whether to bring criminal charges against a business organization or negotiate an agreement (such as an NPA or DPA) with the organization to resolve potential criminal charges.[23] Relevant factors include: 'the corporation's timely and voluntary disclosure of wrongdoing and its willingness to cooperate in the investigation of its agents.'

Under the heading 'Value of Cooperation,' the Principles of Prosecution state:

> In determining whether to charge a corporation and how to resolve corporate criminal cases, the corporation's timely and voluntary disclosure of wrongdoing and its cooperation with the government's investigation may be relevant factors. In gauging the extent of the corporation's cooperation, the prosecutor may consider, among other things, whether the corporation made a voluntary and timely disclosure, and the corporation's willingness to provide relevant information and evidence and identify relevant actors within and outside the corporation, including senior executives. Cooperation is a potential mitigating factor, by which a corporation [...] can gain credit in a case that otherwise is appropriate for indictment and prosecution. Of course, the decision not to cooperate by a corporation (or individual) is not itself evidence of misconduct, at least where the lack of cooperation does not involve criminal misconduct or demonstrate consciousness of guilt (e.g., suborning perjury or false statements, or refusing to comply with lawful discovery requests). Thus, failure to cooperate, in and of itself, does not support or require the filing of charges with respect to a corporation any more than with respect to an individual.

To demonstrate cooperation and avail itself of its mitigating potential, corporate defendants routinely agree to resolve FCPA enforcement actions. Simply stated, to challenge the DOJ's enforcement theories, its interpretation of facts, or to raise valid and legitimate FCPA defenses is not to cooperate with the investigation.

For instance, JGC Corporation of Japan was the subject of FCPA scrutiny given its participation in a joint venture operating in Nigeria. The joint venture operated through three Portuguese special purpose corporations and hired a U.K. citizen who, along with his Gibraltar corporation, allegedly paid bribes to Nigerian foreign officials. The FCPA could only apply to JGC to the extent the alleged bribery scheme had a U.S. nexus and, given the above general factual scenario, an obvious legal issue was whether the U.S. had jurisdiction over the Japanese company. However, the DOJ maintained that JGC was 'declining to cooperate' with its investigation 'based on jurisdictional arguments.'[24] Perhaps mindful of the adverse consequences of its perceived failure to cooperate (including the risk of an actual criminal indictment and associated business effects), JGC agreed to resolve its alleged FCPA scrutiny by paying approximately $218 million in criminal fines via a DPA not subjected to any meaningful judicial scrutiny.

Discussion of cooperation in the Principles of Prosecution focuses on issues such as identifying relevant actors and locating and disclosing relevant facts. However, the message DOJ sent in the JGC enforcement action would seem to be that merely raising bona fide legal arguments is not cooperating in an investigation and can expose a company under FCPA scrutiny to the 'sticks' the DOJ possesses.

Indeed, as Mary Jo White (the current Chairman of the SEC) stated while in private practice:

> Before making their decisions about charging companies, some prosecutors are exerting considerable – some say, extreme – pressure on corporate behavior under the not so subtle threat that if the company doesn't do as the government wishes, the company risks, at the end of the day, being indicted. [...] To ensure that a company does not become that 'rare' case resulting in a corporate indictment with all of its attendant negative consequences, a company must not poke the government in the eye by declining any of its requests or suggestion of how a cooperative, good corporate citizen is to behave in the government's criminal investigation. This template, in my view, can give prosecutors too much power.[25]

Sentencing Guidelines

The Principles of Prosecution are not the only 'carrot' nudging business organizations to resolve FCPA matters without mounting a defense and subjecting the enforcement theories to judicial scrutiny. When an FCPA enforcement action is resolved, the Sentencing Guidelines help determine a criminal penalty range. Application of the Sentencing Guidelines factors will result in a lower fine if the business organization 'reported the offense to appropriate governmental authorities, fully cooperated in the investigation, and clearly demonstrated recognition and affirmative acceptance of responsibility for its criminal conduct.'[26] In other words, challenging the DOJ and putting it to its burden of proof to establish factual evidence that supports the FCPA's legal elements is not 'affirmative acceptance of responsibility,' and such a challenge will result in an organization being treated more severely from a penalty perspective.

Largely due to the Principles of Prosecution and Sentencing Guidelines, as well as the many other negative business effects of FCPA scrutiny and enforcement discussed in Chapter 7, only two business organizations in FCPA history are believed to have put the DOJ to its burden of proof at trial. In both instances (the Harris Corporation enforcement action discussed in Chapter 1 and the Lindsey Manufacturing enforcement action referenced above and discussed in more detail in Chapter 6), the DOJ did not ultimately prevail.[27]

Against the backdrop of general DOJ enforcement policies that impact FCPA enforcement is also a specific DOJ policy that has resulted in the FCPA being enforced differently than most other federal criminal statutes.

Per DOJ policy:

> No investigation or prosecution of cases involving alleged violations of the [FCPA] shall be instituted without the express authorization of the Criminal Division. Any information relating to a possible violation of the FCPA should be brought immediately to the attention of the Fraud Section of the Criminal Division. Even when such information is developed during the course of an apparently unrelated investigation, the Fraud Section should be notified immediately.[28]

Commenting on this policy, William Jacobson, a former Assistant Chief of DOJ FCPA enforcement, rightly observed:

> [T]he FCPA has been recognized and treated as different by the U.S. government since its passage in 1977. [...] [The FCPA] is one of just a few, select statutes to be prosecuted centrally from one DOJ office. The overwhelming majority of federal criminal statutes may be brought by each of the country's U.S. Attorney's Offices, but FCPA actions may be brought only by the Fraud Section of the Criminal Division within Main Justice.[29]

The DOJ has also rightly observed that this policy 'distinguishes FCPA prosecutions from most other kinds of federal criminal cases.'[30] What this specific DOJ FCPA policy means is that FCPA enforcement is highly centralized and, from a supervisory and discretionary standpoint, very few individuals control FCPA enforcement. Because of the DOJ resolution vehicles typically used to resolve FCPA enforcement actions discussed below, these few individuals largely 'enforce' the FCPA behind closed doors in Washington D.C. often without any meaningful judicial scrutiny and in the general absence of case law setting the parameters of the FCPA.

It is these unique attributes of FCPA enforcement that warrant special rules, and among the FCPA reform proposals discussed in Chapter 9 is a prohibition on DOJ (or SEC) FCPA enforcement attorneys with supervisory and discretionary authority from providing FCPA defense or compliance services for five years upon leaving government service. As you will learn in Chapter 5, a typical career path of a DOJ or SEC FCPA enforcement attorney is to depart government service to a private law firm to provide FCPA investigative and compliance services to business organizations subject to the new era of FCPA enforcement they helped create.

While less tasty than the DOJ's 'carrots,' and less sharp than the DOJ's 'sticks,' the SEC also possesses similar 'carrots' and 'sticks' that impact FCPA enforcement.

SEC Policy

During this era of FCPA enforcement, the SEC's 'Seaboard Report' has guided companies subject to an SEC inquiry. In this report, the SEC listed criteria it will consider in determining how to resolve an enforcement action – from taking no enforcement action, to bringing reduced charges, to seeking lighter sanctions, to including mitigating language in documents to announce and resolve enforcement actions.[31]

Relevant criteria include whether the company 'cooperated completely with appropriate regulatory and law enforcement bodies and whether the company identified possible prohibited conduct and evidence with sufficient precision to facilitate prompt enforcement actions.'

SEC enforcement has become even more focused on cooperation as a result of SEC policy issued in 2010 that unveiled 'new cooperation tools.'[32] These tools include:

- Cooperation Agreements: Formal written agreements in which the cooperator may receive credit for cooperating in investigations or related enforcement actions if the cooperator provides substantial assistance such as full and truthful information and testimony;
- Deferred Prosecution Agreements: Formal written agreements in which the SEC agrees to forego an enforcement action against a cooperator if the individual or company agrees, among other things, to cooperate fully and truthfully and to comply with express prohibitions and undertakings during a period of deferred prosecution; and
- Non-prosecution Agreements: Formal written agreements, entered into under limited and appropriate circumstances, in which the SEC agrees not to pursue an enforcement action against a cooperator if the individual or company agrees, among other things, to cooperate fully and truthfully and comply with express undertakings.

This SEC policy, like the DOJ's Principles of Prosecution and the Sentencing Guidelines, often nudge companies subject to SEC regulation to resolve FCPA enforcement actions without mounting a defense and subjecting the enforcement theories to judicial scrutiny. Simply put, many companies choose to avoid a long, protracted legal dispute with its principal regulator.

According to Joseph Grundfest, a former SEC Commissioner, 'it is common practice in settled proceedings for the [SEC] to file complaints that cast defendants' actions in a harsh light and then to prohibit defendants from challenging the [SEC's] rendition of facts and law as articulated in the complaint.'[33] According to Grundfest, SEC complaints 'typically omit mention of valid defenses and of countervailing facts or mitigating circumstances' and therefore represent a 'one-sided record in which the [SEC] asserts its version of the facts and the law, and the settling defendants commit not to challenge that rendition.' Even the SEC itself has acknowledged that in its enforcement actions 'there is litigation risk on both sides, and that is why the parties choose to settle rather than litigate, and why the terms of a reasonable settlement do not necessarily reflect the triumph of one party's position over the other.'[34]

In short, the net effect of the above DOJ and SEC enforcement policies, and the 'carrots' and 'sticks' embedded in them, is often to induce business organizations subject to FCPA scrutiny to resolve enforcement actions for reasons of risk aversion and not necessarily because the enforcement agencies have a superior legal position. Business organizations are further motivated to resolve FCPA enforcement actions, including those based on aggressive enforcement theories, because the DOJ resolution vehicles typically used do not result in any actual prosecuted charges against the company and the SEC resolution vehicles typically used traditionally have not required the company to admit the allegations. These resolution vehicles are highlighted below.

D. RESOLUTION VEHICLES TYPICALLY USED TO ENFORCE THE FCPA

The typical resolution vehicles used to enforce the FCPA in this new era are DOJ Non-Prosecution Agreements (NPAs), Deferred Prosecution Agreements (DPAs) and SEC 'neither admit nor deny' settlements. The common thread in these resolution vehicles is the absence of any meaningful judicial scrutiny. After describing the attributes of these resolution vehicles, the controversial aspects of these vehicles will be examined and you can decide for yourself whether they, along with the enforcement agency policy discussed above, contribute to a 'façade' of FCPA enforcement.

DOJ Non-Prosecution and Deferred Prosecution Agreements

For most of the FCPA's history, the DOJ had two choices when faced with conduct that might implicate the FCPA: prosecute or do not prosecute. However, in 2004 the DOJ used for the first time in the FCPA context an NPA to resolve an enforcement action against InVision Technologies.[35] Since then, NPAs and related DPAs have been used to resolve approximately 85 percent of corporate FCPA enforcement actions and in 2012 NPAs or DPAs were used in connection with 100 percent of corporate FCPA enforcement actions.[36]

While NPAs and DPAs are also used to resolve other types of enforcement actions, the greatest use of these resolution vehicles is to resolve FCPA enforcement actions. For instance, in 2010 approximately 50 percent of all DOJ NPAs and DPAs were in FCPA enforcement actions; in 2011 approximately 40 percent were in FCPA enforcement actions, and in 2012 (a year that saw several trade sanctions and money laundering actions resolved with such vehicles) approximately 25 percent were in FCPA enforcement actions.[37] In short, to understand this new era of FCPA enforcement, it is necessary to understand NPAs and DPAs.[38]

The Principles of Prosecution state that 'in certain instances, it may be appropriate … to resolve a corporate criminal case by means other than indictment' and that NPAs and DPAs 'occupy an important middle ground between declining prosecution and obtaining the conviction of a corporation.' Per the Principles of Prosecution, NPAs and DPAs are intended to be a 'third option' between 'a criminal indictment, on the one hand, and a declination, on the other.' The Principles of Prosecution recognize that 'declining prosecution may allow a corporate criminal to escape without consequences' whereas 'obtaining a conviction may produce a result that seriously harms innocent third parties who played no role in the criminal conduct.' The Principles of Prosecution thus authorize DOJ prosecutors, 'under appropriate circumstances' to use NPAs and DPAs given that such vehicles 'can help restore the integrity of a company's operations and preserve the financial viability of a corporation that has engaged in criminal conduct' while still 'preserving the government's ability to prosecute a recalcitrant corporation that materially breaches the agreement.'

An NPA is not filed with a court, but instead is a privately negotiated agreement (often made public) between the DOJ and a business organization. These agreements often take the form of letter agreements from the DOJ to the organization's lawyer and generally include a brief, often bare-bones, statement of facts replete with legal conclusions that the company acknowledges responsibility for as well as a host of compliance undertakings that the company agrees to implement. Because an NPA is not filed with a court, there is absolutely no judicial scrutiny of these agreements including the statement of facts and legal conclusions that serve as the foundation of the agreement. In other words, there is no independent review of the statement of facts to determine if evidence exists to support the essential elements of the 'crime' not prosecuted or to determine whether valid and legitimate defenses are relevant to the alleged conduct.

A DPA, on the other hand, is filed with a court and thus has a look and feel much like a pleading, although the factual allegations are likewise often bare-bones and replete with legal conclusions. Like NPAs, DPAs are also the result of privately negotiated agreements between the DOJ and a business organization. In exchange for the DOJ agreeing to defer prosecution of the crime alleged (usually for a two- to four-year period), the company acknowledges responsibility for the conduct described in the allegations and agrees to implement a host of compliance undertakings.

Because a DPA is filed with a court, these agreements, at least in theory, could be subject to judicial scrutiny. However, a GAO report concluded that judicial scrutiny of DPAs was essentially nonexistent as well.[39] 'To assess what role the courts have played in the DPA process,' GAO 'obtained written responses to structured interview questions from judges who had overseen DPAs in federal courts.' Based on these responses, GAO found that 'judges reported that they were generally not involved' in the DPA process.

Thus, while DPAs could in theory be subjected to judicial scrutiny, the GAO report found that judges routinely 'rubber-stamp' DPAs without inquiring into whether factual evidence exists to support the essential elements of the crime alleged or to determine whether valid and legitimate defenses are relevant to the alleged conduct.

Credible evidence suggests that NPAs or DPAs are offered to companies even before the elements of a crime have been proven beyond a reasonable doubt. Practitioners have reported:

> We have heard from colleagues in the defense bar of prosecutors who, in their haste to compel the company's cooperation in pursuit of individuals, have pressed the entity to enter into an NPA or DPA before any particular's guilt could definitively be established. In such cases, the company is essentially forced to accept the filing of criminal charges (and all the related consequences, including negative publicity); to waive a host of its defenses; to admit to certain facts; to undertake costly remedial measure; and perhaps even to pay serious 'criminal' penalties all before the elements of the claim(s) against it can be proven beyond a reasonable doubt.[40]

Regarding NPAs and DPAs in the FCPA context, former DOJ Attorney General Alberto Gonzales observed 'two important truths' from his time as Attorney General.

> One, the FCPA gives prosecutors tremendous discretion in defining its scope, and, thus, tremendous leverage in charging decisions. Two, corporations do not like to be investigated by the Justice Department or the SEC for violations of the FCPA. It's bad for business. So, these cases often settled, charges were dropped in exchange for either NPAs or DPAs. In an ironic twist, the more that American companies elect to settle and not force the DOJ to defend its aggressive interpretation of the Act, the more aggressive DOJ has become in its interpretation of the law and its prosecution decisions.[41]

Given the lack of meaningful judicial scrutiny of NPAs and DPAs, some question whether these agreements are even agreements at all. A former DOJ prosecutor noted as follows.

> One of the problems with the process of negotiating a DPA is that it is not really a negotiation. Any push back by the company on a provision that the government requests is not only going to be shot down, but the government may see it as a reflection that the company's claimed contrition is not genuine. So, you don't even want to make the argument for fear that it will cause the government to look at you differently and decide that a deferral isn't appropriate.[42]

Others have argued that NPAs and DPAs, from a contract perspective, do not represent valid agreements because one party to the agreement is under duress.

> These agreements are made under duress. There is a threat of government indictment and resulting destruction of the entire business that induces the manifestation of assent to the DPA. But for the threat of possible prosecution by the government and its resulting consequences, these terms would not normally be agreed to by the corporation. [...] The economic reality is that if the corporation refuses to assent to the DPA, the result will likely be the death of the corporation or alternatively, severe financial consequences that will gravely injure the corporation. These consequences may result from an indictment even if the corporation is later declared innocent.[43]

Even though the Principles of Prosecution specifically state that NPAs and DPAs are intended to be a 'third option' between criminal indictment and declination, many observers believe that NPAs and DPAs have taken the place of declinations altogether and are simply a means for the DOJ to show results.

Indeed, in a 2012 policy speech devoted to NPAs and DPAs, the DOJ Assistant Attorney General stated: '[Companies] know that they will be answerable even for conduct that in years past would have resulted in a declination.'[44] The SEC Chairman, while in private practice, stated:

> [NPAs and DPAs are becoming] a semi-automatic response by the government in responding to corporate crime. [...] Prosecutors are thinking – before we close out this case that involves any kind of corporate crime, we should get something from the companies. [...] And prosecutors are like anybody else – when they devote a lot of time and effort to a case, they want something to show for it. And so I fear the deferred prosecution is becoming a vehicle to show results.[45]

Specifically in the FCPA context, former Attorney General Gonzales stated that FCPA enforcement actions resolved via NPAs and DPAs do not necessarily reflect instances of companies violating the FCPA, but rather companies feel compelled to agree to these vehicles. Equally problematic, Gonzales stated that enforcement actions resolved via NPAs or DPAs mean that 'legitimate wrongdoing is not being prosecuted as it should.'[46] He continued by saying that it is 'easy, much easier quite frankly' for the DOJ to resolve FCPA inquiries with NPAs and DPAs, that such resolution vehicles have 'less of a toll' on the DOJ's budget, and that such agreements 'provide revenue' to the DOJ. It is all 'unfortunate' the former Attorney General stated.

It is unfortunate, and there was nothing wrong with the 'prosecute or do not prosecute' criminal justice system that served our country well since its founding. Bringing criminal charges against a business organization or individual should not be easy. It should be difficult. Our founding fathers recognized this as a necessary bulwark against an all-powerful government. As a report from the Manhattan Institute for Policy Research states:

> 'Prosecutors' virtually unchecked powers under DPAs and NPAs threaten our constitutional framework. To be sure, prosecutors are acting upon duly enacted laws, but federal criminal provisions are often vague or ambiguous, and the fact that prosecutors and large corporations alike feel obliged to reach agreement, rather than follow an orderly regulatory process and litigate disagreements in court, denies the judiciary an opportunity to clarify the boundaries of such laws. Instead, the laws come to mean what the prosecutors say they mean – and companies do what the prosecutors say they must. Federal prosecutors are thus assuming the role of judge (interpreting the law) and of legislature (setting broad policy choices about industry conduct), substantially eroding the separation of powers.[47]

NPAs and DPAs are controversial because both agreements are privately negotiated behind closed doors, and thus lack transparency, and because both agreements are not subjected to any meaningful judicial scrutiny.

Further adding to the controversy is that the NPAs and DPAs contain so-called 'muzzle clauses' preventing the company from making any public statements, directly or indirectly through others (such as attorneys, etc.) contradicting the company's acceptance of responsibility for the conduct set forth in the agreements. Commenting on an NPA (outside the FCPA context), a *Wall Street Journal* opinion piece stated:

> In exchange for agreeing to read the government's script, [the company resolving its alleged legal scrutiny via an NPA] regained its ability to conduct business without a federal sword of Damocles dangling over its corporate head. This naked effort by federal prosecutors to control both news and outcomes, not to mention their own reputations, does not surprise those familiar with the modern federal criminal justice system. [...] Through these and myriad other techniques, federal investigators and prosecutors create an alternative reality that favors their own institutional interests, regardless of the truth or of justice. All citizens and companies become subject to the Justice Department's essentially unfettered power. Remedying this problem cannot be left to the victims of this governmental extortion, because their risks are too high if they fight; nor will their lawyers likely blow the whistle, since the bar makes a tidy living by playing the game. It is up to the rest of civil society to let the Justice Department emperor know that we see he is not wearing clothes.[48]

Should a company subject to an NPA or DPA make a public statement that the DOJ finds objectionable, the consequence can be actual prosecution of the conduct resolved via the NPA or DPA. For instance, in 2012 financial institution Standard Chartered agreed to resolve its alleged scrutiny for facilitating financial transactions with certain sanctioned countries such as Iran by paying approximately $230 million in criminal penalties pursuant to a DPA. While outside the FCPA context, the DPA contained a standard 'muzzle clause' found in FCPA resolution vehicles. A few months after the DPA, during an earnings call with investors, Standard Chartered's Chairman stated, in reference to the conduct at issue in the DPA, as follows. 'We had no willful act to avoid sanctions; you know, mistakes are made – clerical errors – and we talked about last year a number of transactions which clearly were clerical errors or mistakes that were made.'

According to a *Wall Street Journal* article, prosecutors 'pounced when they heard [the Chairman's] comments' and demanded a copy of the conference call transcript.[49] According to the article, '[the Chairman] and other top executives were [soon] in Washington to [apologize] before a room full of top prosecutors at the [DOJ], which threatened to bring criminal charges if [the Chairman] didn't recant.' According to the article, 'Standard Chartered officials and the U.S. prosecutors spent more than a week negotiating possible wording of the bank's retraction.' Standard Chartered ultimately issued a retraction stating that the Chairman's statement 'was wrong, and directly contradict[ed] [the company's] acceptance of responsibility in the DPA and accompanying factual statement.'

In short, the common features of resolving alleged instances of corporate criminal liability, in the FCPA context or otherwise, in this new era are as follows.

- The DOJ can use its leverage and the 'carrots' and 'sticks' it possesses to induce business organizations under scrutiny to resolve an enforcement action and pay a criminal fine.
- The DOJ can use an NPA or DPA to insulate its version of facts and enforcement theories from judicial scrutiny.
- In the resolution agreement, the DOJ can include a 'muzzle clause' prohibiting anyone associated with the company from making any statement inconsistent with the DOJ's version of the facts or its enforcement theories.
- If the DOJ believes, in its sole discretion, that a public statement has been made contradicting its version of the facts or its enforcement theories, the DOJ can 'pounce' and threaten to bring actual criminal charges.

Is this an effective system of justice? The answer is no, and among the FCPA reform proposals discussed in Chapter 9 is abolishing NPAs and DPAs in the FCPA context as these agreements both facilitate the under-prosecution of egregious instances of corporate bribery as well as the over-prosecution of corporate conduct.

DOJ NPAs and DPAs are not the only controversial resolution vehicles typically used to resolve FCPA enforcement actions.

SEC 'Neither Admit Nor Deny' Settlements

The typical method of resolving an SEC FCPA enforcement action also has a troubling feature in that corporate and individual defendants are generally able to resolve the enforcement action 'without admitting or denying' the SEC's allegations. In building FCPA foundational knowledge, it is also necessary to understand this central feature of SEC enforcement.[50]

The SEC's 'neither admit nor deny' settlement policy was adopted in 1972 and states:

> The Commission has adopted the policy that in any civil lawsuit brought by it or in any administrative proceeding of an accusatory nature pending before it,

> it is important to avoid creating, or permitting to be created, an impression that a decree is being entered or a sanction imposed, when the conduct alleged did not, in fact, occur. Accordingly, it hereby announces its policy not to permit a defendant or respondent to consent to a judgment or order that imposes a sanction while denying the allegations in the complaint or order for proceedings. In this regard, the Commission believes that a refusal to admit the allegations is equivalent to a denial, unless the defendant or respondent states that he neither admits nor denies the allegations.[51]

The SEC has announced certain revisions to its 'neither admit nor deny' settlement policy. For instance in 2012 the SEC announced that the settlement language would not be included in SEC enforcement actions involving parallel: (i) criminal convictions; or (ii) NPAs or DPAs that include admissions or acknowledgments of criminal conduct. In 2013 the SEC announced that it would no longer have a 'blanket policy' of permitting defendants to settle SEC cases without admitting to wrongdoing in certain cases involving

> misconduct that harmed large numbers of investors or placed investors or the market at risk of potentially serious harm; where admissions might safeguard against risks posed by the defendant to the investing public, particularly when the defendant engaged in egregious intentional misconduct; or when the defendant engaged in unlawful obstruction of the commission's investigative processes.[52]

Despite these revisions, the SEC's controversial 'neither admit nor deny' settlement policy remains in effect today and the SEC has vigorously defended the policy as allowing it 'to bring [a] matter to a speedy resolution, obtain compensation for victims in a timely manner, and allocate its limited resources to bringing additional enforcement actions for the protection of still more investors.'[53] Nevertheless, several federal court judges have expressed strong misgivings about this central feature of SEC enforcement. For instance, Judge Jed Rakoff in the influential U.S. District Court for the Southern District of New York has stated as follows in various cases:

- The SEC's practice of permitting defendants to neither admit nor deny the charges against them remains pervasive, presumably for no better reason than that it makes the settling of cases easier. This policy is 'a stew of confusion and hypocrisy unworthy of such a proud agency as the SEC.'[54]
- The SEC's policy is 'hallowed by history, but not by reason' and 'deprives the Court of even the most minimal assurance that the substantial injunctive relief it is being asked to impose has any

> basis in fact.' 'Purely private parties can settle a case without ever agreeing on the facts, for all that is required is that a plaintiff dismiss his complaint. But when a public agency asks a court to become its partner in enforcement by imposing wide-ranging injunctive remedies on a defendant, enforced by the formidable judicial power of contempt, the court, and the public, need some knowledge of what the underlying facts are: for otherwise, the court becomes a mere handmaiden to a settlement privately negotiated on the basis of unknown facts, while the public is deprived of ever knowing the truth in a matter of obvious public importance.'[55]

It is against this backdrop that the SEC enforces the FCPA and it is common for issuers to resolve FCPA enforcement actions without admitting or denying the SEC allegations.

As highlighted above, in 2010 the SEC announced new enforcement tools including NPAs and DPAs. At present, such resolution vehicles have been used to resolve only two SEC FCPA enforcement actions. However, with more such resolution vehicles expected in the future, SEC enforcement is likely to become even less transparent as SEC NPAs and DPAs, like those of the DOJ, result in even less judicial scrutiny of SEC enforcement theories.

The first four sections of this chapter have discussed general legal principles and general DOJ and SEC enforcement policies that impact FCPA enforcement as well as the typical resolution vehicles used in FCPA enforcement actions. These sections were not meant to suggest, or even imply, that all business organizations subject to the FCPA are law-abiding and ethical or that no company has ever violated the FCPA as intended by Congress and as interpreted by courts.

Rather, the goal of these sections was to provide a general foundational knowledge to best enhance understanding and comprehension of the specific FCPA topics that follow by demonstrating from the beginning that: (i) not all companies that resolve FCPA enforcement action are 'bad' or 'unethical'; (ii) business organizations, mindful of the 'carrots' and 'sticks' relevant to resolving an enforcement action, are often motivated to resolve FCPA enforcement actions, including those based on aggressive enforcement theories, for reasons of risk aversion and not necessarily because the enforcement agencies have a superior legal position; and (iii) the vast majority of FCPA enforcement occurs without meaningful judicial scrutiny.

Prior to diving into the specific elements of the FCPA's anti-bribery and books and records and internal controls provisions in Chapters 3 and 4, it is useful to first address the question of what the FCPA actually means. This chapter concludes by setting forth a hierarchy of FCPA legal authority and other information and you will discover that much of what defines this new era of FCPA enforcement is non-binding, non-legal sources of information including so-called prosecutorial common law.

E. FCPA LEGAL AUTHORITY AND NON-LEGAL SOURCES OF INFORMATION

What does the FCPA actually mean? To state the obvious, Congress declares the law, courts interpret the law, and enforcement agencies are obliged to enforce the law consistent with statutory language, congressional intent and judicial decisions. What happens however if courts are generally deprived of the opportunity to interpret the law? If an enforcement agency advances a legal theory without this check, does its enforcement theory represent the law if an FCPA defendant, mindful of the above 'carrots' and 'sticks,' agrees to resolve the enforcement action? What if, in the same context, the enforcement agency theory is inconsistent with the statutory language or congressional intent?

It is these difficult and thorny questions that often complicate an analysis of the FCPA, yet you will discover that much of what defines this new era of FCPA enforcement is non-binding, non-legal sources of information. To best assist in properly analyzing the FCPA in this new era, a hierarchy of FCPA legal authority and other information is set forth below.

Legal Authority

The best source of FCPA legal authority is the statute itself.[56]

Another source of FCPA legal authority is judicial decisions construing the FCPA's provisions. However, there is little substantive FCPA case law. As a judge stated in 2007 when put in the rare position of deciding an FCPA issue, there are 'surprisingly few decisions throughout the country on the FCPA.'[57] Similarly, in its 2010 review of FCPA enforcement, the OECD observed. 'Although enforcement under the FCPA is strong and increasing, there is relatively little jurisprudence that has developed since the FCPA was enacted.'[58]

Part of the reason for the general lack of FCPA case law is of course the 'carrots' and 'sticks' discussed above in resolving an enforcement action and the fact that NPAs and DPAs insulate enforcement agency theories from judicial scrutiny in all but the rarest of instances. Even as to the few substantive FCPA judicial decisions there are, you will notice in

Chapters 3 and 4 that most decisions are trial court decisions that lack precedential value and are not otherwise viewed as definitely resolving disputed legal issues.

A third source of FCPA legal authority is Congressional intent in enacting the law as represented in the legislative history. As discussed in Chapter 1, the legislative history of a statute is frequently the most fruitful source of instruction as to its proper interpretation. The FCPA's legislative history is particularly important as the statute itself contains several vague and ambiguous terms as has been noted several times in the rare instances in which the FCPA has been subjected to judicial scrutiny.

Even though the above legal authority sits atop the hierarchy of FCPA authority, much of what defines this new era of FCPA enforcement is non-binding, non-legal sources of information as detailed below.

Non-Legal Sources of Information

Non-binding, non-legal sources of information include resolved DOJ and SEC enforcement actions, DOJ and SEC guidance concerning the FCPA's provisions, and the DOJ's FCPA Opinion Procedure Releases. These non-legal sources of information are highlighted below and various sources of information are also discussed in Chapters 3 and 4 as relevant to the specific FCPA provisions.

Resolved enforcement actions

The increase in FCPA enforcement has resulted in more information in the public domain regarding the DOJ and SEC's enforcement theories including through publicly available resolution documents. In this way, a typical FCPA resolution vehicle provides insight into the DOJ and SEC's enforcement theories.

Indeed, the DOJ has stated: 'DPAs and NPAs benefit the public and industries by providing guidance on what constitutes improper conduct. [...] Because the agreements typically provide a recitation of the improper conduct at issue, the agreements can serve as an educational tool for other companies in a particular industry.'[59]

However, viewing these vehicles as a source of FCPA legal authority is not warranted. As discussed above, these agreements do not represent precedent, do not necessarily reflect the triumph of one party's legal position, and do not necessarily concern conduct that Congress sought to capture in enacting the FCPA. Rather, resolved FCPA enforcement actions represent a form of prosecutorial common law.

The dangers of prosecutorial common law have been well documented. Michael Levy, a former DOJ enforcement attorney and Supreme Court clerk, stated:

> Prosecutors don't set out deliberately to interpret criminal statutes in ways that convict hundreds of people on the basis of a standard that not a single Supreme Court Justice finds supportable, but it has happened already and may well happen again in the context of the FCPA because of a phenomenon I've referred to for a number of years as 'prosecutorial common law.'
>
> There are no law school classes or scholarly papers on prosecutorial common law, yet it governs, as a practical matter, an enormous amount of the daily life of the criminal justice system in white collar cases. Prosecutorial common law can be thought of as the 'common law of settlement.' In areas, such as complex white collar crime, in which prospective defendants either are highly unlikely to challenge the government in court (e.g., corporations) or highly unlikely to have both the fortitude and the personal wealth or strong support of another entity advancing fees to be able to challenge the government thoroughly and completely (e.g., most individuals), almost all cases are settled.
>
> But settling cases creates very different incentives for the two sides. The government has a long-term interest in developing the law because it is charged with enforcing that law not just against the settling party, but also against other parties in the future. Thus, the government has a strong institutional interest in pushing ever more aggressive interpretations of the governing criminal statute. On the other hand, the defendant, whether a corporation or an individual, is not particularly concerned about the scope of the statute as it might be applied to others in the future. The defendant wants the least possible punishment, right now.
>
> So, in many white collar cases, the government pushes hard for the defendant to plead guilty pursuant to expansive interpretations of a statute's jurisdiction and/or scope of liability, and defendants readily accept those interpretations in exchange for what they perceive to be the lowest available penalty.
>
> But what happens next?
>
> In the absence of much decided case law in the area – because so many defendants strike plea agreements rather than litigating their cases – prosecutors start to believe that the law means whatever they have been able to get defendants to agree to in earlier plea agreements. After all, they reason (ignoring the parties' different interests in settlements), 'Why would Global MegaCorp have agreed to plead guilty on this very same theory of liability if it didn't believe that (1) we had jurisdiction and (2) the conduct clearly violated the criminal statute?'
>
> And when the next case comes around, the government stretches the theory of liability or jurisdiction a little bit further. Again, nobody sets out to develop a statutory interpretation that goes beyond what any Supreme Court Justice would conclude was intended by Congress, but that is consistently what winds up happening because prosecutors (rather than judges) and settlements (rather

> than well-reasoned judicial opinions) wind up creating the 'common law' that prosecutors use to interpret these statutes.
>
> [...]
>
> [P]rosecutorial common law appears to be alive and well and indeed thriving in the FCPA context.
>
> [...]
>
> Because the stakes of corporate prosecution are so high, because the abilities of most individuals to challenge the government are so limited, and because DOJ and the SEC want to pursue ever more aggressive interpretations of the scope of both liability and jurisdiction, we see an enormous number of FCPA cases settled on grounds that are mutually beneficial to the government and the particular settling defendants. The defendants get certainty and what they perceive to be a lesser penalty; the government gets a major international corporation or other defendant to agree that the FCPA means what DOJ and the SEC want it to mean – and the government then can point to that agreement when negotiating with the next defendant.[60]

Another former DOJ enforcement attorney and Supreme Court clerk likewise stated:

> Most of [FCPA] cases have been settled. When that occurs, defendants have little incentive to refuse to agree to novel DOJ theories of prosecution or jurisdiction, so long as the penalty is acceptable. The department then cites its prior settlement as precedent when settling later ones. But no court approved the earlier settlement, and the prior settlement should have no precedential value in favor of the DOJ in later settlements.[61]

For obvious reasons, prosecutorial common law does not sit well with federal court judges and DOJ attempts to use its own prior charging decisions as evidence of FCPA legal authority have been soundly rejected. In two separate FCPA cases in the influential U.S. District Court for the Southern District of New York, judges have stated: 'the Government's charging decision, standing alone, does not establish the applicability of the statute' and DOJ's prior charging decisions is 'not the kind or quality of precedent this Court need consider.'[62]

Nevertheless, many citations in the 2012 FCPA Guidance discussed below are to the enforcement agencies own prosecutorial common law.

DOJ/SEC Guidance

Another form of non-legal FCPA information is guidance by the DOJ and SEC concerning the FCPA's provisions. Although Chapter 4 details SEC guidance prior to this new era concerning the FCPA's books and records and internal controls provisions, the most comprehensive form of FCPA enforcement agency guidance was jointly issued by the DOJ and SEC in 2012 and titled 'Resource Guide to the U.S. Foreign Corrupt Practices Act' (the 'Guidance'). The Guidance represents the DOJ and SEC's interpretations of the FCPA as well as its 'FCPA enforcement approach and priorities.' Among other things, the Guidance sets forth positions on the anti-bribery and books and records and internal controls provisions and is supplemented by various hypotheticals and vignettes ranging from gifts, travel and entertainment, to facilitating payments, to charitable donations.

Nevertheless, the guidance contains little new substantive information to those previously knowledgeable about the FCPA and its enforcement. Indeed, in a press conference introducing the Guidance, the DOJ Assistant Attorney General said that the Guidance 'does not represent a change in policy.'[63]

Moreover, the Guidance provides the following qualification.

> [The Guidance] is non-binding, informal, and summary in nature, and the information contained [in the Guidance] does not constitute rules or regulations. As such, it is not intended to, does not, and may not be relied upon to create any rights, substantive or procedural, that are enforceable at law by any party, in any criminal, civil, or administrative matter. [...] It does not in any way limit the enforcement intentions or litigating positions of [the DOJ, the SEC] or any other U.S. government agency.[64]

Indeed, while the Guidance lacks legal effect, it remains relevant to those subject to the FCPA for the simple reason that the enforcement agencies enforce the law. However, despite comments from the DOJ that one of its objectives in issuing the Guidance was to outline what the law is, the Guidance does not represent the law. Indeed, Steven Tyrell, the former Chief of the DOJ's Fraud Section during a period of FCPA enforcement escalation, stated that the Guidance is 'more of a scrapbook of past DOJ and SEC successes than a guide book for companies who care about playing by the rules.'[65]

Notwithstanding its lack of legal effect, the Guidance is undeniably a useful resource regarding the enforcement agencies' FCPA policies and positions. At the Guidance press conference, the SEC Enforcement Division Director stated that the Guidance provides a 'unique opportunity' for the enforcement agencies to 'communicate directly' with the business community regarding its FCPA enforcement policies and positions. Indeed, with the Guidance, any business person in the world can now print off a single document and read at their desk unfiltered information relevant to the enforcement agencies' positions and policies. In short, the Guidance is a useful resource as to enforcement agency

FCPA policies and positions because it collects in one document information that was previously scattered.

However, as described in Chapter 3, in certain instances what the enforcement agencies say in the Guidance has been rejected, in whole or in part, by courts. In this way, the Guidance is an advocacy piece and not a well-balanced portrayal of the FCPA as it is replete with selective information, half-truths, and worse, information that is demonstratively false.

FCPA Opinion Procedure Releases

Another form of non-legal FCPA information is the DOJ's FCPA Opinion Procedure Releases. The FCPA, when enacted, directed the DOJ Attorney General to establish a procedure to provide responses to specific inquiries by those subject to the FCPA concerning conformance of their conduct with the DOJ's 'present enforcement policy.'[66] Pursuant to the governing regulations of the so-called DOJ Opinion Procedure Release Program, only 'specified, prospective – not hypothetical – conduct' is subject to a DOJ opinion. While the DOJ's opinion has no precedential value, its opinion that contemplated conduct conforms with the FCPA is entitled to a rebuttable presumption should an FCPA enforcement action be brought as a result of the contemplated conduct. Since the program was enacted in 1980, the DOJ has issued approximately 60 releases on a wide range of issues from charitable contributions to gifts, travel and entertainment, to third parties.

Nevertheless, the Opinion Procedure Release Program is rarely utilized by business organizations subject to the FCPA and it is generally viewed as an ineffective source of FCPA information. For instance, in its 2010 review of FCPA enforcement, the OECD stated:

> So far, the FCPA Opinion Procedure has been used very little by the private sector to obtain DOJ advice on prospective transactions. [...] The non-governmental participants in the on-site meetings cited several reasons for the infrequent use of the Opinion Procedure. For instance, legal and private sector representatives felt that the Opinion Procedure is only useful in limited situations where the prospective fact situation is narrow and not going to change. They also find that the response time, which is 30 days after the request is complete, is too long in certain situations, such as entering joint ventures and mergers and acquisitions, where a company normally needs to make decisions relatively quickly. [...] The most pervasive concern of the private sector representatives was that availing themselves of the Opinion Procedure could expose them to potential enforcement actions by the DOJ, as well as provide competitors with information about their prospective international business activities.[67]

Returning to the question posed at the beginning of this section, what then does the FCPA actually mean? Given the above FCPA hierarchy of legal authority and other non-legal sources of information, this basic question is often anything but straightforward.

In many respects, those subject to the FCPA face a triple 'whammy' in trying to comply with the law in this new era of enforcement. The first 'whammy' is that several of the FCPA's key elements are vague and ambiguous. The second 'whammy' is the general lack of substantive FCPA case law. The third 'whammy' is that the gap filler is often non-binding, non-legal information such as resolved enforcement actions that are privately negotiated; entered into in the context of enforcement agencies possessing substantial 'carrots' and 'sticks'; often motivated by issues other than law and facts; and subject to no meaningful judicial scrutiny.

As a result, two questions can be asked about most instances of FCPA scrutiny in this new era. The first question, and the easiest, is whether, given the DOJ's and SEC's enforcement theories, the conduct at issue can expose a company to FCPA scrutiny and an FCPA enforcement action. The answer to this question is often yes. The second question, and more important one, is whether Congress in passing the FCPA intended to capture the alleged conduct at issue and whether a court would find the alleged conduct in violation of the FCPA. The answer to this question is often debatable.

FCPA practitioners have rightly noted:

> Although the [FCPA] was enacted [in 1977], there is little case law addressing many of the FCPA's most important elements. One of the problems with trying to nail down the requirements of the FCPA is that there is so little judicial precedent because most companies and individuals choose to avoid the embarrassment and expense of trial. Because of the dearth of adjudicated court decisions related to the FCPA, settlement agreements containing compromises that may be acceptable to both sides are also frequently cited as precedents, including by U.S. enforcement agencies. As a result, terms accepted as conditions of settlement become part of FCPA 'jurisprudence,' but may not always reflect how a court or jury would have decided the same issue. Unfortunately … some of the government's more interesting theories have been announced in settled cases, providing no opportunity to test the validity of those theories in court.[68]

Mindful of the above hierarchy of FCPA legal authority and information, throughout this book much attention is focused on actual sources of legal authority because what matters most is what the FCPA says, what Congress intended the FCPA to mean, and how judges have interpreted the FCPA.

Having built a solid foundation as to general legal principles and enforcement agency policies and resolution vehicles relevant to FCPA enforcement, a comprehensive analysis of the FCPA can now proceed in a more informed and sophisticated manner and Chapters 3 and 4 dissect the FCPA's anti-bribery provisions and books and records and internal controls provisions.

NOTES

1. N.Y. Central v. Hudson R.R., 212 U.S. 481 (1908).
2. Mary Jo White, 'Corporate Criminal Liability: What Has Gone Wrong?' 37th Annual Institute on Securities Regulation 815, 820 (PLI Corp. Law & Practice, Course Handbook Series No. B-1517, 2005).
3. See e.g., FCPA Professor, 'The Compliance Defense around the World' (June 28, 2011).
4. U.S. v. Enrique Faustino Aguilar Noriega, et al., Case 2:10-cr-01031-AHM (C.D. Cal.).
5. Philip Urofsky, 'The Ralph Lauren FCPA Case: Are There Any Limits to Parent Corporation Liability?' Bloomberg BNA Securities Regulation & Law Report (May 6, 2013).
6. FCPA Professor, 'Former DOJ FCPA Chief Supports FCPA Compliance Defense' (Oct. 4, 2011).
7. South China Morning Post, 'Fire Officials Put the Nation at Risk as They Rake in Bribes' (June 9, 2013).
8. Dan Harris, China Law Blog 'Doing Business in China. Do Not Pass Go. Do Not Go Directly to Jail' (Jan. 20, 2013).
9. Letter from Steven A. Tyrell, Chief, Fraud Section, U.S. Dep't of Justice (Criminal Div.), to Kimberly A. Parker, Attorney for Helmerich & Payne, Inc. (July 29, 2009).
10. Complaint, SEC v. Delta & Pine Land Co., No. 1:07-cv-01352 (D.D.C. July 25, 2007).
11. Information, U.S. v. Tyson Foods, Inc., No. 1:11-cr-00037-RWR (D.D.C. Feb. 10, 2011).
12. Letter from Denis J. McInerney, Chief, Fraud Section, U.S. Dep't of Justice (Criminal Div.), to Edward J. Fuhr, Attorney for Alliance One Int'l, Inc. (Aug. 6, 2010).
13. Transparency International, Global Corruption Barometer 2010; Kaushik Basu, 'Why, for a Class of Bribes, the Act of Giving a Bribe Should Be Treated as Legal' (Mar. 2011).
14. Diageo plc, Exchange Act Release No. 64978 (July 27, 2011).
15. Complaint, SEC v. Westinghouse Air Brake Techs. Corp., No. 08-cv-706 (E.D. Pa. Feb. 14, 2008).
16. Dow Chem. Co., Exchange Act Release No. 55287 (Feb. 13, 2007).
17. Information, U.S. v. Baker Hughes, Inc., No. 4:07-cr-00130 (S.D. Tex. Apr. 11, 2007).
18. Nigeria Country Profile, Business Anti-Corruption Portal.
19. Press Release, U.S. Dep't of Justice, 'Oil Services Companies and a Freight Forwarding Company Agree to Resolve Foreign Bribery Investigations and to Pay More than $156 Million in Criminal Penalties' (Nov. 4, 2010).

20. Joseph Yockey, 'Solicitation, Extortion, and the FCPA,' 87 Notre Dame Law Review 781 (2011).
21. FCPA Professor, 'Friday Roundup' (March 8, 2013).
22. Lamb v. Phillip Morris, Inc., 915 F.2d 1024 (6th Cir. 1980).
23. See DOJ, U.S. Attorney's Manual § 9-28.000.
24. Deferred Prosecution Agreement, U.S. v. JGC Corp., Case 4:11-cr-00260 (S.D.Tex. April 6, 2011).
25. *Supra* note 2.
26. U.S. Sentencing Guidelines Manual § 8C2.5(g).
27. FCPA Professor, 'Milestone Erased: Judge Matz Dismisses Lindsey Convictions, Says That "Dr. Lindsey and Mr. Lee Were Put through a Severe Ordeal" and That Lindsey Manufacturing, a "Small, Once Highly Respected Enterprise … Placed in Jeopardy"' (Dec. 1, 2011).
28. See DOJ, U.S. Attorney's Manual § 9-47.110.
29. William Jacobson, 'No Legislation Necessary: A Five-Part Test to Negate Corporate Criminal Liability in FCPA Cases,' Bloomberg BNA Criminal Law Reporter (April 11, 2012).
30. FCPA Professor, 'Friday Roundup' (May 31, 2013).
31. Report of Investigation Pursuant to Section 21(a) of the Securities Exchange Act of 1934 and Commission Statement on the Relationship of Cooperation to Agency Enforcement Decisions, Exchange Act Release No. 44969 (Oct. 23, 2001).
32. Press Release, SEC, SEC Announces Initiative to Encourage Individuals and Companies to Cooperate and Assist in Investigations (Jan. 13, 2010).
33. Affidavit of Joseph A. Grundfest at SEC v. Bank of America Corp (S.D.N.Y. 2009).
34. Memorandum of Plaintiff Securities and Exchange Commission in Support of Entry of the Proposed Consent, SEC v. Bank of America Corp. (S.D.N.Y. 2010).
35. Press Release, U.S. Dep't of Justice, 'InVision Technologies, Inc. Enters into Agreement with the United States' (Dec. 6, 2004).
36. FCPA Professor, 'DOJ Prosecution of Individuals – are Other Factors at Play?' (Jan. 29, 2013).
37. FCPA Professor, 'Year in Review Roundups' (Jan. 11, 2013) citing Gibson Dunn's annual 'Year End Update on Corporate Deferred Prosecution Agreements (DPAs) and Non-Prosecution Agreements (NPAs).'
38. Numerous examples of FCPA NPAs and DPAs can be found at http://www.justice.gov/criminal/fraud/fcpa/cases/a.html.
39. U.S. Government Accountability Office, 'Corporate Crime: DOJ Has Taken Steps to Better Track Its Use of Deferred and Non-Prosecution Agreements, but Should Evaluate Effectiveness' (2009).
40. Peter Spivak and Sujit Raman, 'Regulating the "New Regulators": Current Trends in Deferred Prosecution Agreement,' 45 American Criminal Law Review 159 (2008).
41. FCPA Professor, 'Add Alberto Gonzalez to the List of Former High-Ranking DOJ Officials Who Support an FCPA Compliance Defense' (Sept. 11, 2012).
42. Interview with David Pitofsky, 19 Corporate Crime Reporter (Nov. 28, 2005).
43. Candace Zierdt and Ellen S. Podgor, 'Corporate Deferred Prosecutions through the Looking Glass of Contract Policing,' 96 Kentucky Law Journal 1 (2007).
44. Press Release, U.S. Dep't of Justice, 'Assistant Attorney General Lanny A. Breuer Speaks at the New York City Bar Association' (Sept. 13, 2012).
45. *Supra* note 2.
46. FCPA Professor, 'Former Attorney General Alberto Gonzales Criticizes Various Aspects Of DOJ FCPA Enforcement' (April 4, 2013).
47. James Copland, 'The Shadow Regulatory State: The Rise of Deferred Prosecution Agreements' (May 2012).
48. Harvey Silverglate, 'Gibson Is Off the Feds' Hook. Who's Next?' (Aug. 19, 2012).

49. FCPA Professor, 'The "Muzzle" Clause' (March 26, 2013).
50. Numerous examples of SEC FCPA civil complaints resolved via 'neither admit nor deny' settlements can be found at http://www.sec.gov/spotlight/fcpa/fcpa-cases.shtml
51. Consent Decrees in Judicial or Administrative Proceedings, Securities Act Rel. No. 33-5337 (Nov. 28, 1972).
52. See e.g., FCPA Professor, 'Friday Roundup' (June 21, 2013).
53. SEC v. Citigroup, SEC'S Memorandum of Law in Response to Questions Posed by the Court Regarding Proposed Settlement, Case 1:11-cv-07387-JSR (S.D.N.Y. Nov. 7, 2011).
54. SEC v. Vitesse Semiconductor Corp., Case 1:10-cv-09239-JSR (S.D.N.Y. March 21, 2011).
55. SEC v. Citigroup, Case 1:11-cv-07387-JSR (S.D.N.Y. Nov. 28, 2011).
56. The text of the FCPA (in 50 different languages) can be found at http://www.justice.gov/criminal/fraud/fcpa/statutes/regulations.html
57. U.S. v. Kozeny, 493 F.Supp.2d 693, 697 (S.D.N.Y. 2007).
58. OECD, 'Phase 3 Report on Implementing the OECD Anti-Bribery Convention in the United States' (Oct. 2010).
59. U.S. Government Accountability Office, 'Corporate Crime: DOJ Has Taken Steps to Better Track Its Use of Deferred and Non-Prosecution Agreements, but Should Evaluate Effectiveness' (2009).
60. FCPA Professor, 'Prosecutorial Common Law' (Mar. 16, 2011).
61. FCPA Professor, 'Friday Roundup' (Mar. 1, 2013).
62. U.S. v. Bodmer, 342 F.Supp.2d 176 (S.D.N.Y. 2004); U.S. v. Giffen, 326 F.Supp.2d 497 (S.D.N.Y. 2004).
63. FCPA Professor, 'The Guidance Press Conference' (Nov. 15, 2012).
64. 'A Resource Guide to the U.S. Foreign Corrupt Practices Act' (Nov. 2012).
65. Joe Palazzolo and Christopher Matthews, Wall Street Journal, 'U.S. Attempts to Clarify Antibribery Law' (Nov. 14, 2012).
66. See 28 C.F.R. § 80.1.
67. *Supra* note 58.
68. Philip Urofsky and Danforth Newcomb, Recent Trends and Patterns in FCPA Enforcement, Shearman & Sterling LLP (Oct. 1, 2009).

3. The FCPA's anti-bribery provisions

This chapter provides a comprehensive analysis of the FCPA's anti-bribery provisions and its general elements: offering or paying money or anything of value, to a foreign official, to obtain or retain business, with a corrupt intent. For each element, legal sources of authority as well as non-legal sources of information will be discussed.

To state the obvious, providing a suitcase full of cash to a foreign government official to obtain a foreign government contract satisfies the elements of the anti-bribery provisions. However, you will learn that FCPA enforcement actions seldom involve such scenarios and the proper scope of the anti-bribery provisions is subject to much dispute in this new era as legal development of these elements is still in its infancy.

You will also learn that the FCPA's anti-bribery provisions prohibit not only direct payments to 'foreign officials' to 'obtain or retain business,' but also payments to 'any person' 'while knowing' that the payments will be provided to a 'foreign official.' Given the prevalence of foreign third parties, the FCPA's third-party payment provisions often present the greatest source of FCPA risk for companies competing in the global marketplace. In addition to the substantive elements of the anti-bribery provisions, jurisdictional issues will also be discussed including extra-territorial jurisdiction as to U.S. actors as well as the expansive jurisdictional theories advanced by the enforcement agencies in bringing FCPA enforcement actions against foreign actors.

Even if all of the substantive elements of the anti-bribery provisions have been met and there is jurisdiction over the actor, the final step in analyzing the anti-bribery provisions is determining whether the FCPA facilitating payment exception or the FCPA's affirmative defenses apply. After highlighting legal authority and non-legal sources of information relevant to the exception and affirmative defenses, the question is posed whether the FCPA's facilitating payment exception has any real meaning in the new era or whether the enforcement agencies have essentially repealed this exception through its enforcement theories.

Chapter 3 will conclude by highlighting other legal issues also relevant to FCPA enforcement in this new era including statute of limitations issues and how the FCPA is a supply-side statute targeting only one actor in a bribery scheme.

A. ANYTHING OF VALUE

The FCPA's anti-bribery provisions refer to the offer, payment, promise to pay, or authorization of the payment of any money, or offer, gift, promise to give, or authorization of the giving of 'anything of value.' The term 'anything of value' is obviously broad due to fact that 'foreign officials' can be influenced in many different ways other than cash payments. Indeed, in *U.S. v. Liebo* an appellate court concluded that there was sufficient evidence for the jury to convict the defendant based on payment of honeymoon airline tickets for a Niger official who was in a position of influence concerning the contract at issue.[1]

The FCPA Guidance states as follows concerning 'anything of value.'

> An improper benefit can take many forms. While cases often involve payments of cash [...] others have involved travel expenses and expensive gifts. Like the domestic bribery statute, the FCPA does not contain a minimum threshold amount for corrupt gifts or payments. Indeed, what might be considered a modest payment in the United States could be a larger and much more significant amount in a foreign country.

Although a few FCPA enforcement actions still involve actual suitcases full of cash, in most enforcement actions the things of value given to a 'foreign official' are less direct. For instance, in an enforcement action against Ashland Oil the thing of value was the purchase of a largely worthless mine owned by a 'foreign official' for a substantial price.[2] Likewise, in an enforcement action against individuals employed by Ports Engineering Consultants Corporation the thing of value included a 'foreign official's' receipt of dividend and bearer shares in a corporation.[3]

The most expansive interpretation of 'anything of value' was in enforcement actions against pharmaceutical companies Schering-Plough and Eli Lilly.[4] In both actions, the SEC alleged that the companies violated the FCPA when subsidiary companies recorded a bona fide charitable donation to a Polish foundation where the founder/president of the foundation was also the director of a government health fund (the 'Director' – an individual deemed by the SEC to be a 'foreign official') that provided money to hospitals throughout Poland for the purchase of pharmaceutical products. Although the companies ultimately resolved the matter via SEC neither admit nor deny settlements charging only FCPA books and records and internal controls violations, the enforcement actions are relevant to the 'anything of value' element. The SEC's tacit interpretation of the 'anything of value' element in these enforcement actions was significant because there was no allegation or indication that any tangible monetary benefit accrued to the Director. Rather, the SEC apparently concluded that the bona fide charitable donations constituted a 'thing of value' to the 'foreign official' because the donations were subjectively valued by the official and provided him with an intangible benefit of enhanced self-worth or prestige. In other words, the perception of the recipient and the subjective valuation of the thing conveyed may be a key factor in an enforcement agency analysis of whether 'anything of value' has been given to a 'foreign official.'

Various gifts and non-business travel and entertainment expenses to tourist destinations such as Disney World and Hawaii have also been frequent things of value alleged in FCPA enforcement actions. For instance, an enforcement against software company Paradigm involved the following things of value: travel and entertainment expenses including gifts, cash per diems, sightseeing and cash payments for shopping and a trip to Napa Valley that involved visits to wineries and dinners for an alleged Mexican foreign official and that coincided with his birthday.[5] Other things of value alleged in FCPA enforcement actions have included: handbags, watches, cameras, kitchen appliances and business suits, television sets, laptops and appliances, and tea sets and office furniture.

The take-away point from the first element of the FCPA's anti-bribery provisions is that 'anything of value' can include a variety of direct and indirect ways of influencing a 'foreign official' and there is no *de minimis* value associated with this element.

While the 'anything of value' element is relatively straightforward and intuitive, the enforcement agencies' interpretation of the 'foreign official' element of the FCPA's anti-bribery provisions is not and is subject to much dispute.

B. FOREIGN OFFICIAL

'Foreign official' is often viewed as the most important element of the FCPA's anti-bribery provisions. Simply put, even if something of value is corruptly provided to a person to obtain or retain business, the anti-bribery provisions apply only if that person is a 'foreign official.'

This section highlights legal sources of authority as well as non-legal sources of information relevant to 'foreign official' including: what types of persons may qualify as 'foreign officials,' whether the specific identity of a 'foreign official' must be proven by the enforcement agencies, and whether the defendant must have knowledge that a person is indeed a 'foreign official.'

As suggested by these issues, the 'foreign official' element of the FCPA's anti-bribery provisions is subject to much dispute and the legal development of this important element is still in its infancy.

Law

What is not subject to dispute is what the FCPA statutory text states. The FCPA defines 'foreign official,' as:

> any officer or employee of a foreign government or any department, agency, or instrumentality thereof, or of a public international organization, or any person acting in an official capacity for or on behalf of any such government or department, agency, or instrumentality, or for or on behalf of any such public international organization.

The FCPA does not define 'department,' 'agency,' or 'instrumentality.'

Legislative History

Chapter 1 concerning the FCPA's legislative history highlighted that in passing the FCPA, Congress was primarily concerned with the foreign policy implications of foreign government leaders being accountable to U.S. corporations because of improper payments. The scandals that motivated Congress to enact the FCPA included payments to the Japanese Prime Minister, the President of the Republic of Korea, the President of Gabon, a Saudi Arabian General, and Italian political parties.

Chapter 1 also highlighted how Congress learned of a wide variety of corporate payments to a wide variety of foreign recipients for a wide variety of reasons. As relevant to the disputed 'foreign official' element and judicial decisions discussed below, Congress was aware of the existence of state-owned or state-controlled enterprises ('SOEs') and that certain of the questionable payments uncovered or discovered may have involved such entities.[6]

Generally speaking, SOEs are profit-seeking enterprises that have many attributes of private business, such as publicly traded stock or other private investors, and SOEs may do business outside a foreign country's borders and employ nationals and non-nationals alike. Nevertheless, and not often transparent, a foreign government may hold an ownership interest in an SOE or exert some level of control (such as through appointment of directors or officers) over the business enterprise. Many of the world's largest companies (often in the oil and gas industry) are considered SOEs, and SOEs are found in most foreign countries and are most prevalent in certain Asian countries and the Middle East.

There is no express statement or information in the FCPA's extensive legislative history to support the enforcement agencies' legal interpretation that alleged SOEs are 'instrumentalities' (or 'departments' or 'agencies') of a foreign government and that employees of SOEs (regardless of rank, title, or position) are therefore 'foreign officials' under the FCPA and occupy a position equal to that of a Prime Minister or President.[7]

However, there are several statements, events, and information in the FCPA's legislative history that demonstrate that Congress did not intend the 'foreign official' definition to include SOE employees. Among other things, in certain of the competing bills introduced in Congress to address the foreign corporate payments discovered, the definition of 'foreign government' expressly included SOEs and Congress was provided an even more precise definition of 'foreign government' to include SOEs.[8] However, despite being aware of SOEs, despite exhibiting a capability for drafting a definition that expressly included SOEs in other bills, and despite being provided a more precise way to describe SOEs, Congress chose not to include such definitions or concepts in the bill that ultimately became the FCPA.

For most of the FCPA's history the 'foreign official' element presented little controversy as FCPA enforcement largely focused on payments to bona fide 'foreign officials' such as Presidents, other heads of state, political leaders, and other foreign government regulatory officials such as tax and customs officials.

To be sure, certain FCPA enforcement actions in this new era still focus on payments to such bona fide 'foreign officials' – mostly various regulatory officials – however, in this new era the 'foreign official' element has led to much dispute and controversy as many FCPA enforcement actions have nothing to do with the above recipient categories as highlighted in the below chart summarizing certain enforcement agency 'foreign official' allegations in corporate FCPA enforcement actions.

As indicated in Table 3.1, in many FCPA enforcement actions in this new era the alleged 'foreign officials' are employees of alleged SOEs. For instance, in 2012 approximately 40 percent of corporate FCPA enforcement actions involved, in whole or in part, SOE employees; in 2011 approximately 80 percent of corporate FCPA enforcement actions involved, in whole or in part, SOE employees; in 2010, approximately 60 percent of corporate FCPA enforcement actions involved, in whole or in

Table 3.1 Alleged 'foreign officials'

Health care providers who worked at publicly-owned hospitals in Argentina, Brazil, China, Greece, Poland, Romania, Bulgaria, Croatia, Kazakhstan, Czech Republic, Italy, Serbia, Indonesia, Pakistan and Russia.
Employees at a state-owned nuclear power plant in Lithuania.
Employees of Chinese state-owned and controlled entities, including airlines created, controlled, and exclusively owned by the Chinese government.
Employees of state-owned entities in Indonesia.
Employees of Chinese Design Institutes 'which were typically state-owned enterprises that provided design engineering and technical integration services' to end-user state-owned customers.
Employees of Haiti's state-owned national telecommunications company.
Employees of Costa Rica's state-owned insurance company.
Employees of government-controlled telecommunications companies in China and Vietnam.
Employees of Comision Federal de Electricidad, an electric utility company owned by the Mexican government.

part, SOE employees.[9] Given the 'carrots' and 'sticks' relevant to resolving corporate FCPA enforcement actions, this enforcement theory was not challenged in any of these corporate enforcement actions.

As the enforcement agencies began to bring more individual FCPA enforcement actions based on the enforcement theory that SOE employees are 'foreign officials' under the FCPA, individuals began to challenge this key enforcement agency interpretation resulting in non-binding trial court judicial decisions concerning: what types of persons may qualify as 'foreign officials;' whether the specific identity of a 'foreign official' must be proven by the enforcement agencies; and whether the defendant must have knowledge that the person is indeed a 'foreign official.'

Judicial Decisions

Judicial decisions regarding the FCPA's 'foreign official' element are discussed below, beginning with the issue of what types of persons may qualify as 'foreign officials.'

SOE employees as 'foreign officials'

In *U.S. v. Carson*, various former employees of valve manufacturer Control Components Inc. were criminally charged with FCPA anti-bribery violations in connection with alleged payments to employees of alleged SOEs in China, Malaysia, and the United Arab Emirates.[10]

In a pre-trial motion to dismiss, certain defendants argued that employees of SOEs 'can never be "foreign officials" under the FCPA and thus the indictment should be dismissed.' The defendants argued 'that the question of whether employees of state-owned companies are "foreign officials" under the FCPA is a legal issue that does not depend on the evidence.' Among other things, the DOJ argued that the motion to dismiss was 'premature because the Government intended to prove at trial that the state-owned companies charged in the indictment are "agencies" or "instrumentalities" under the FCPA.' Thus, the DOJ argued the motion was a 'challenge to the sufficiency of the evidence – an inappropriate challenge on a motion to dismiss.'

The court stated:

> The question of whether state-owned companies qualify as instrumentalities under the FCPA is a question of fact. [...] Simply assuming that a company is wholly-owned by the state is insufficient for the Court to determine as a matter of law whether the company constitutes a government 'instrumentality.' Several factors bear on the question of whether a business entity constitutes a government instrumentality, including:
>
> - The foreign state's characterization of the entity and its employees;
> - The foreign state's degree of control over the entity;
> - The purpose of the entity's activities;
> - The entity's obligations and privileges under the foreign state's law, including whether the entity exercises exclusive or controlling power to administer its designated functions;
> - The circumstances surrounding the entity's creation; and
> - The foreign state's extent of ownership of the entity, including the level of financial support by the state (e.g., subsidies, special tax treatment, and loans).

Such factors are not exclusive, and no single factor is dispositive. [...] Their chief utility is simply to point out that several types of evidence are relevant when determining whether a state-owned company constitutes an 'instrumentality' under the FCPA – with state ownership being only one of several considerations.

The court further stated:

> Admittedly, a mere monetary investment in a business entity by the government may not be sufficient to transform that entity into a governmental

> instrumentality. But when a monetary investment is combined with additional factors that objectively indicate the entity is being used as an instrument to carry out governmental objectives, that business entity would qualify as a governmental instrumentality. [...] The use of the term 'instrumentality' in the FCPA produces no such crisp exclusion of a state-owned entity. To the contrary, a state-owned entity – just like an agency or department – is a modality through which a government may conduct its business.

As to the FCPA's legislative history, the court stated: 'The statutory language of the FCPA is clear, that the statutory scheme is coherent and consistent, and that resort to the legislative history of the FCPA is unnecessary.'

In conclusion, the court stated: 'Some business entities may be considered an "instrumentality," but this is a fact-specific question that depends on the nature and characteristics of the business entity.'

The disputed legal issue of what types of persons may qualify as 'foreign officials' is still in its infancy and trial court decisions are not binding precedent. At present, there is no case law of precedent on the 'foreign official' element under the FCPA although an appeal is pending in the Joel Esquenazi and Carlos Rodriguez case, discussed in more detail in Chapter 5, concerning payments to alleged 'foreign officials' employed at Haiti Teleco, an alleged SOE. This appeal will be the first time in FCPA history that the 'foreign official' element of the anti-bribery provisions will be squarely before an appellate court.

As described in more detail in Chapter 8, the meaning of 'foreign official' matters because, based on the enforcement agencies' interpretation, companies spend significant time and money investigating the ownership structure of foreign customers and potential customers for any trace of foreign government ownership or control. Such a costly investigation is not motivated by the company's desire to make improper payments to the foreign customer or potential customer to obtain or retain business should the investigation reveal no foreign government ownership or control. Rather, the costly investigation is often motivated for the simple reason that the company wants to treat these foreign customers the same way it treats its other customers.

Identity of foreign official

In addition to the disputed legal issue of what types of persons may qualify as 'foreign officials' are the related issues of whether the specific identity of a 'foreign official' must be proven by the enforcement agencies and whether the defendant must have knowledge that the recipient of the alleged payment is indeed a 'foreign official.'

In *U.S. v. O'Shea*, the DOJ alleged that the defendant violated the FCPA by making payments to officials at a Mexican utility allegedly owned or controlled by the Mexican government. You will learn in Chapter 5 that the judge granted a motion for acquittal after the DOJ's evidence. In doing so, and as relevant to the identity of a 'foreign official' issue discussed here, the judge stated: 'You can't convict a man promising to pay unless you have a particular promise to a particular person for a particular benefit. If you call up [somebody] and say, look, I'm going to send you 50 grand, bribe somebody, that does not meet the statute.'[11]

However, the notion that the specific identity of a 'foreign official' must be proven by the enforcement agencies has been rejected by two other trial courts in individual FCPA enforcement actions. In *SEC v. Jackson*, an enforcement action discussed in more detail below concerning facilitating payments and statute of limitations issues, the court concluded, in ruling on a pre-trial motion to dismiss, that the 'government does not have to connect the payment to a particular official.'[12]

The court stated:

> The language of the statute does not appear to require that the identity of the foreign official involved be pled with specificity. [...] Nothing in the legislative history of the FCPA suggests that Congress intended to limit the application of [the FCPA] to those cases where the government could show that a defendant knew, either by name or job description, precisely which foreign officials would be receiving the illicit payments he had authorized. [...] It would be perverse to read into the statute a requirement that a defendant know precisely which government official, or which level of government official, would be targeted by his agent; a defendant could simply avoid liability by ensuring that his agent never told him which official was being targeted and what precise action the official took in exchange for the bribe.

Likewise in *SEC v. Straub*, an enforcement action discussed below in more detail concerning jurisdiction issues as to foreign actors, the court agreed with the above *Jackson* analysis in ruling on a pre-trial motion to dismiss and stated that 'the language of the [FCPA] does not appear to require that the identity of the foreign official involved be pled with specificity.'[13]

The court stated:

> Such a requirement would be at odds with the statutory scheme, which targets actions (such as making an 'offer' or 'promise') without requiring that the 'foreign official' accept the offer or reveal his specific identity to the payer. Indeed, the fact that the FCPA prohibits using 'any person' or an intermediary

to facilitate the bribe to any 'foreign official' or 'any foreign political party' suggests that the statute contemplates situations in which the payer knows that a 'foreign official' will ultimately receive a bribe but only the intermediary knows the foreign official's specific identity.

Knowledge of foreign official

Regarding the issue of whether a defendant must have knowledge that the person is indeed a 'foreign official,' in the *Carson* enforcement action discussed above, after the judge denied the defendants' motion to dismiss, the disputed 'foreign official' issue moved to the jury instructions and the judge issued a jury instruction titled 'knowledge of status of foreign official' which stated, in pertinent part, as follows:

> (4) The defendant offered, paid, promised to pay, or authorized the payment of money, or offered, gave, promised to give, or authorized the giving of anything of value to a foreign official;
>
> (5) The payment or gift at issue in element 4 was to (a) a person the defendant knew or believed was a foreign official or (b) any person and the defendant knew that all or a portion of such money or thing of value would be offered, given, or promised (directly or indirectly) to a person the defendant knew or believed to be a foreign official. Belief that an individual was a foreign official does not satisfy this element if the individual was not in fact a foreign official.[14]

As highlighted in Chapter 5 in more detail, soon after the judge in the *Carson* case issued this pro-defendant jury instruction, the DOJ offered the individual defendants lenient plea agreements to resolve the case without being put to its burden of proof on 'foreign official' issues.

In short, the enforcement agencies' 'foreign official' theories – most notably whether SOE employees may be 'foreign officials' under the FCPA – are subject to much dispute, and the legal development of 'foreign official' issues is still in its infancy.

Guidance

The FCPA Guidance states, in pertinent part, as follows.

> The FCPA broadly applies to corrupt payments to 'any' officer or employee of a foreign government and to those acting on the foreign government's behalf. The FCPA thus covers corrupt payments to low-ranking employees and high-level officials alike.
>
> […]

> Foreign officials under the FCPA include officers or employees of a department, agency, or instrumentality of a foreign government. When a foreign government is organized in a fashion similar to the U.S. system, what constitutes a government department or agency is typically clear (e.g., a ministry of energy, national security agency, or transportation authority). However, governments can be organized in very different ways. Many operate through state-owned and state-controlled entities, particularly in such areas as aerospace and defense manufacturing, banking and finance, healthcare and life sciences, energy and extractive industries, telecommunications, and transportation. By including officers or employees of agencies and instrumentalities within the definition of 'foreign official,' the FCPA accounts for this variability.
>
> The term 'instrumentality' is broad and can include state-owned or state-controlled entities. Whether a particular entity constitutes an 'instrumentality' under the FCPA requires a fact-specific analysis of an entity's ownership, control, status, and function.
>
> [...]
>
> While no one factor is dispositive or necessarily more important than another, as a practical matter, an entity is unlikely to qualify as an instrumentality if a government does not own or control a majority of its shares. However, there are circumstances in which an entity would qualify as an instrumentality absent 50% or greater foreign government ownership, which is reflected in the limited number of DOJ or SEC enforcement actions brought in such situations.

Notably, the above Guidance position on instrumentality conflicts with a previously issued rule promulgated by the SEC in connection with Section 1504 of the Dodd-Frank Wall Street Reform and Consumer Protection Act of 2010 concerning disclosure of payments to foreign governments by resource extraction issuers. Section 1504 defines 'foreign government' to mean a 'department, agency or instrumentality of a foreign government, or a company owned by a foreign government, as determined by the Commission' and in its final rules the SEC stated: 'The final rules clarify that a company owned by a foreign government is a company that is at least majority-owned by a foreign government.'[15]

In addition, the Guidance references only selective 'foreign official' information. For instance, while the Guidance discusses certain 'foreign official' jury instructions, missing from the discussion is reference to the above *Carson* jury instructions concerning 'knowledge of status of foreign official.'

Regardless of the dispute and controversy regarding the FCPA's key 'foreign official' element, the take-away point from this section is that given the enforcement agencies' interpretations, FCPA scrutiny can arise from business interactions with a variety of individuals and not just bona fide foreign government officials.

C. OBTAIN OR RETAIN BUSINESS

In addition to the 'foreign official' element, the FCPA's anti-bribery provisions are further qualified by the business purpose test in that the money or 'anything of value' to a 'foreign official' must be to influence or induce the recipient to assist in 'obtaining or retaining' business.

This section highlights legal sources of authority as well as non-legal sources of information relevant to the 'obtain or retain business' element of the FCPA. In this section you will learn that courts have found this element to be ambiguous and that the enforcement agencies have an overall losing record when put to its burden of proof in enforcement actions alleging that payments outside the context of foreign government procurement violate the FCPA's anti-bribery provisions. Nevertheless, the 'obtain or retain business' element is subject to much controversy as a significant number of corporate FCPA enforcement actions in this new era concern payments outside the context of foreign government procurement such as in connection with customs and tax issues or securing various foreign government licenses or permits.

Law

The FCPA's anti-bribery provisions apply to payments or things of value to 'foreign officials' for purposes of:

A. (i) influencing any act or decision of such foreign official in his official capacity, (ii) inducing such foreign official to do or omit to do any act in violation of the lawful duty of such official, or (iii) securing any improper advantage; or
B. inducing such foreign official to use his influence with a foreign government or instrumentality thereof to affect or influence any act or decision of such government or instrumentality in order to assist … in obtaining or retaining business for or with, or directing business to, any person.

Legislative History

The legislative history discussed in Chapter 1 evidences that despite learning of a wide range of foreign corporate payments, Congress limited the FCPA's payment provisions to a narrow range of payments involving foreign government procurement or influencing foreign government legislation or regulations. It is not necessary to restate this extensive legislative history here, but it bears repeating in this section the following language from the Conference Report immediately prior to the passage of the FCPA:

> The scope of the prohibition [in the Senate bill] was limited by the requirement that the offer, promise, authorization, payment, or gift must have as a purpose inducing the recipient to use his influence with the foreign government or instrumentality, influencing the enactment or promulgation of legislation or regulations of that government or instrumentality or refraining from performing any official responsibilities, so as to direct business to any person, maintain an established business opportunity with any person or divert a business opportunity from any person.
>
> The House amendment was similar to the Senate bill; however, the scope of the House amendment was not limited by the 'business purpose' test [...] The conferees clarified the scope of the prohibition by requiring that the purpose of the payment must be to influence any act or decision of a foreign official (including a decision not to act) or to induce such official to use his influence to affect a government act or decision so as to assist an issuer in obtaining, retaining or directing business to any person.[16]

For most of the FCPA's history the 'obtain or retain business' element presented little controversy as FCPA enforcement largely focused on payments in connection with foreign government procurement. However, in this new era of FCPA enforcement the 'obtain or retain' business element has led to much dispute and controversy as many FCPA enforcement actions have nothing to do with foreign government procurement. As the enforcement agencies brought more individual FCPA enforcement actions in connection with customs and tax issues or foreign licenses and permits, individuals began to challenge this interpretation theory.

Judicial Decisions

The enforcement agency theory that payments outside the context of foreign government procurement violate the FCPA's anti-bribery provisions has been subjected to judiciary scrutiny four times.

As previously highlighted in Chapter 1, in *U.S. v. Duran* a judge granted a defense motion of acquittal after the DOJ's evidence at trial in an enforcement action concerning payments to officials of the Dominican

Republic in order to obtain the release of two aircraft seized by the government.

In *U.S. v. Kay*, the DOJ charged David Kay and Douglas Murphy (the president and vice president of American Rice Inc. (ARI)), with FCPA anti-bribery violations based on allegations that the defendants made improper payments to Haitian foreign officials for the purpose of reducing customs duties and sales taxes owed by ARI to the Haitian government. The indictment, while specific as to other items, merely tracked the FCPA's 'obtain or retain business' language and did not specifically allege how the alleged payments assisted ARI in obtaining or retaining business in Haiti or what business was obtained or retained.

The trial court found the FCPA's 'obtain or retain business' element ambiguous and thus consulted the legislative history.[17] As to the legislative history, the court stated:

> A review of the legislative history confirms that in 1977, Congress chose to limit the scope of the prohibited activities under the FCPA and did not intend to cover payments made to influence any and all governmental decisions. This legislative history weighs against the Government's argument that the FCPA should be construed so broadly so as to encompass payments made to reduce customs duties or tax obligations. The Court thus determines that Congress has considered and rejected statutory language that would broaden the scope of the FCPA to cover the conduct in question here.

Accordingly, the court granted the defendants' motion to dismiss the indictment and held, as a matter of law, that the alleged payments were not payments made to 'obtain or retain business' and thus did not fall within the scope of the FCPA's anti-bribery provisions.

Shortly after the trial court decision in *Kay* in the Southern District of Texas, the court again considered whether payments made outside the context of foreign government procurement fell under the FCPA's anti-bribery provisions in *SEC v. Mattson*, a civil enforcement action against Baker Hughes Inc. employees Eric Mattson and James Harris in which the SEC alleged that the FCPA captured goodwill payments to an Indonesian tax official for a reduction in a tax assessment.[18]

The issue before the court in a pre-trial motion to dismiss was whether the FCPA prohibited goodwill payments for the purpose of reducing a tax assessment. The court noted that the *Kay* court already found that the FCPA did not prohibit goodwill payments to foreign government officials to reduce a tax obligation. However, the SEC attempted to distinguish the *Kay* ruling by arguing that in the civil enforcement context the FCPA's language should be construed more liberally than in criminal cases. The court rejected the SEC's argument, followed the trial court's analysis in

Kay, and held that the payments at issue to the Indonesian tax official did not violate the FCPA because it did not help Mattson's and Harris's employer 'obtain or retain business.'

The DOJ appealed the trial court dismissal of the criminal indictment in *Kay* and one issue on appeal was whether payments to foreign officials to obtain favorable tax and customs treatment can come within the scope of the FCPA's anti-bribery provisions.[19]

Like the trial court, the appellate court also found the FCPA's 'obtain or retain business' ambiguous and stated:

> Perhaps our most significant statutory construction problem results from the failure of the language of the FCPA to give a clear indication of the exact scope of the business nexus element; that is, the proximity of the required nexus between, on the one hand, the anticipated results of the foreign official's bargained-for action or inaction, and, on the other hand, the assistance provided by or expected from those results in helping the briber to obtain or retain business. Stated differently, how attenuated can the linkage be between the effects of that which is sought from the foreign official in consideration of a bribe (here, tax minimization) and the briber's goal of finding assistance or obtaining or retaining foreign business with or for some person, and still satisfy the business nexus element of the FCPA?

Like the trial court, the appellate court consulted the legislative history but came to a different conclusion than the trial court. The appellate court stated:

> We surmise that, in using the word 'business' … Congress intended for the statute to apply to bribes beyond the narrow band of payments sufficient only to 'obtain or retain government contracts.' […] In short, the 1977 legislative history … convinces us that Congress meant to prohibit a range of payments wider than only those that directly influence the acquisition or retention of government contracts or similar commercial or industrial arrangements. […] We cannot hold as a matter of law that Congress meant to limit the FCPA's applicability to cover only bribes that lead directly to the award or renewal of contracts. Instead, we hold that Congress intended for the FCPA to apply broadly to payments intended to assist the payer, either directly or indirectly, in obtaining or retaining business for some person, and that bribes paid to foreign tax officials to secure illegally reduced customs and tax liability constitute a type of payment that can fall within this broad coverage.
>
> […]
>
> Thus, in diametric opposition to the district court, we conclude that bribes paid to foreign officials in consideration for unlawful evasion of customs duties and sales taxes could fall within the purview of the FCPA's proscription. We hasten to add, however, that this conduct does not automatically constitute a violation of the FCPA: It still must be shown that the bribery was

> intended to produce an effect – here, through tax savings – that would 'assist in obtaining or retaining business.'

Indeed, the appellate court emphatically stated that not all such payments to a foreign official outside the context of foreign government procurement violate the FCPA; it merely held that such payments 'could' violate the FCPA. According to the court, the key question of whether the defendants' alleged payments constituted an FCPA violation depended on whether the payments were intended to lower ARI's costs of doing business in Haiti enough to assist ARI in obtaining or retaining business in Haiti.

The court then listed several hypothetical examples of how a reduction in custom and tax liabilities could assist a company in obtaining or retaining business in a foreign country. On the other hand, the court also recognized:

> There are bound to be circumstances in which such a cost reduction does nothing other than increase the profitability of an already-profitable venture or ensure profitability of some start-up venture. Indeed, if the government is correct that anytime operating costs are reduced the beneficiary of such advantage is assisted in getting or keeping business, the FCPA's language that expresses the necessary element of assisting in obtaining or retaining business would be unnecessary, and thus surplusage – a conclusion that we are forbidden to reach.

After the appellate court remanded the *Kay* case back down to the trial court, and after the defendants were convicted at trial, the defendants renewed their legal challenge by arguing that the FCPA failed to give fair notice of its prohibitions and was thus unconstitutionally vague.[20] The appellate court stated that even though the FCPA's 'obtain or retain business' language was ambiguous, the 'imprecise general language [in one of the elements] for a bribery conviction under the FCPA does not draw a line so vague that Defendants were not reasonably aware of their potential for engaging in illegal activity under the FCPA when they made payments to Haitian officials to reduce tax and duty burdens.' In the words of the appellate court: 'A man of common intelligence would have understood that ARI, in bribing foreign officials, was treading close to a reasonably-defined line of illegality.'

In short, the enforcement theory that payments to a foreign official outside the context of foreign government procurement fall under the FCPA's anti-bribery provisions has been subjected to judicial scrutiny four times. The enforcement agencies lost three of those cases and the fourth case – the appellate court decision in *Kay* – is equivocal. The decision merely holds that payments to a foreign official outside the context of foreign government procurement can, under appropriate circumstances, fall within the statute.

Given the facts and circumstances the *Kay* court found relevant, it is a highly fact-dependent question whether a payment to a foreign official outside the context of foreign government procurement is subject to the FCPA. The key portion from the *Kay* ruling would seem to be the following: 'there are bound to be circumstances' in which payments outside the context of foreign government procurement 'does nothing other than increase the profitability of an already-profitable venture or ensure profitability of some start-up venture' and thus presumably does not assist the payer in obtaining or retaining business.

Guidance

The FCPA Guidance states:

> The FCPA applies only to payments intended to induce or influence a foreign official to use his or her position 'in order to assist … in obtaining or retaining business for or with, or directing business to, any person.' This requirement is known as the 'business purpose test' and is broadly interpreted. […] The FCPA also prohibits bribes in the conduct of business or to gain a business advantage. For example, bribe payments made to secure favorable tax treatment, to reduce or eliminate customs duties, to obtain government action to prevent competitors from entering a market, or to circumvent a licensing or permit requirement, all satisfy the business purpose test. […] In short, while the FCPA does not cover every type of bribe paid around the world for every purpose, it does apply broadly to bribes paid to help obtain or retain business, which can include payments made to secure a wide variety of unfair business advantages.

Elsewhere, the Guidance asserts that 'in 1998, the FCPA was amended to conform to the requirements of the [OECD] Anti-Bribery Convention' and 'these amendments expanded the FCPA's scope to: include payments made to secure "any improper advantage."'

The notion however that the FCPA's 1998 amendments expanded the FCPA's scope to include payments made to secure 'any improper advantage' is false. Indeed, the DOJ's position on this specific issue was rejected by both the trial court and appellate court in *U.S. v. Kay*. The trial court decision stated:

> The OECD Convention had asked Congress to criminalize payments made to foreign officials 'in order to obtain or retain business or other improper advantage in the conduct of international business. […] Congress again

> declined to amend the "obtain or retain business" language in the FCPA' [...] Congress did not insert the 'improper advantage' language into the 'obtain or retain business' provision of the FCPA.

Although as highlighted above, the appellate court overruled the trial court's decision to grant defendants' motion to dismiss, the appellate court likewise stated as follows concerning the FCPA's 1998 amendments:

> When Congress amended the language of the FCPA, however, rather than inserting 'any improper advantage' immediately following 'obtaining or retaining business' within the business nexus requirement (as does the Convention), it chose to add the 'improper advantage' provision to the original list of abuses of discretion in consideration for bribes that the statute proscribes.

The Guidance rightly discusses *Kay*, the only case law of precedent on the FCPA's 'obtain or retain business element,' and accurately states its holding that payments outside the context of foreign government procurement 'could' fall within the meaning of the FCPA. However the Guidance discussion of *Kay* is selective at best. For instance, the Guidance fails to mention that the appellate court specifically rejected the DOJ's broad interpretation of the 'obtain or retain business' element when it stated:

> If the government is correct that anytime operating costs are reduced the beneficiary of such advantage is assisted in getting or keeping business, the FCPA's language that expresses the necessary element of assisting in obtaining business would be unnecessary, and thus surplusage – a conclusion that we are forbidden to reach.

Likewise, but not mentioned in the Guidance, the appellate court in *Kay* further stated 'that there are bound to be circumstances' in which payments outside the context of foreign government procurement merely increase the profitability of an existing profitable company and thus, presumably, do not assist the payer in obtaining or retaining business.

Further missing from the Guidance is any mention of the *Duran* or *Mattson* enforcement actions, discussed above, which represent the two other instances in FCPA history in which the enforcement agencies were put to its burden of proof that payments outside the context of foreign government procurement violate the FCPA.

In short, even though the Guidance boldly states that 'payments made to secure favorable tax treatment, to reduce or eliminate customs duties, to obtain government action to prevent competitors from entering a market, or to circumvent a licensing or permit requirement, all satisfy the business purpose test,' the legal authority discussed in this section demonstrates something much different when the enforcement agencies are put to its burdens of proof in FCPA enforcement actions concerning such payments. Rather than faithfully summarizing *Kay* or referencing other relevant judicial decisions, the Guidance discussion on the 'obtain or retain business' element cites resolved FCPA enforcement actions that were not subjected to any meaningful judicial scrutiny.

Notwithstanding the legal authority discussed above and despite *Kay's* equivocal holding, there has been a significant increase in corporate FCPA enforcement actions in this new era regarding alleged payments involving customs duties and taxes or payments alleged to have assisted the payer in securing foreign government licenses, permits, and certifications. In addition to other FCPA enforcement actions discussed throughout this book fitting this description (most notably the Customs Gate cases discussed in more detail below in connection with facilitating payments), Table 3.2 highlights certain representative corporate FCPA enforcement actions.

Table 3.2 Alleged Business 'obtained or retained'

Payments to Mexican veterinarians to influence their decisions in certifying product for export.
Payments to Brazilian customs agents to import certain unregistered products into Brazil.
Payments to various officials and representatives of the Argentine and Venezuelan customs services in connection with the importation and exportation of goods and equipment related to business operations in those countries.
Payments to Philippine customs officials to allow the firm to store shipments longer than otherwise permitted; to settle disputes with the Philippine Bureau of Customs; as well as payments to employees of state-owned airlines to induce the officials to improperly reserve space on airplanes.
Payments to officials in the Chinese State Intellectual Property Office in order to cause that office to approve the company's patent applications.
Payments to Nigerian tax officials to influence them to improperly reduce the amount of expatriate employment tax.
Payments to officials of the Turkish Ministry of Agricultural and Rural Affairs to obtain government reports and certifications necessary to operate in Turkey.

All of the above FCPA enforcement actions were resolved via a resolution vehicle not subjected to any meaningful judiciary scrutiny. Moreover, every enforcement action involved, as relevant to *Kay*'s holding, existing profitable companies.

Regardless of the dispute and controversy regarding application of the FCPA to payments outside the context of foreign government procurement, the take-away point from this section is that given the enforcement agencies' interpretation of the 'obtain or retain business' element, FCPA scrutiny can arise in many situations outside the context of foreign government procurement. It is this interpretation, coupled with the enforcement agencies seeming unwillingness to recognize the FCPA's facilitating payment exception discussed below, that has generated a large number of FCPA enforcement actions in this new era and why seemingly mundane corporate tasks such as securing foreign licenses and permits or interacting with customs and immigrations officials often presents FCPA risk.

D. INTENT

This section highlights legal authority and non-legal sources of information regarding the FCPA's often murky intent element.

Law

For there to be a violation of the FCPA's anti-bribery provisions, the thing of value offered, paid or promised to the 'foreign official' to 'obtain or retain business' must be made with a corrupt intent. This requirement applies to both business organizations as well as individuals charged with FCPA anti-bribery offenses. In addition, for an individual to be criminally liable under the anti-bribery provisions, proof of willfulness is required. The FCPA does not specifically define the terms 'corrupt' or 'willfully.'

As with any white-collar criminal law, the FCPA's *mens rea* requirements are often the most difficult to prove and assess given that, without incriminating documentary evidence, it is hard to get inside the minds of alleged criminal defendants.

Legislative History

A House Report stated as follows concerning corrupt intent:

> The word 'corruptly' is used in order to make clear that the offer, payment, promise, or gift, must be intended to induce the recipient to misuse his official position; for example, wrongfully to direct business to the payer or his client, to obtain preferential legislation or regulations, or to induce a foreign official to fail to perform an official function. The word 'corruptly' connotes an evil motive or purpose such as that required under 18 U.S.C. 201(b) which prohibits domestic bribery. As in 18 USC 201(b), the word 'corruptly' indicates an intent or desire wrongfully to influence the recipient. It does not require that the act [be] fully consummated or succeed in producing the desired outcome.[21]

A Senate Report further stated:

> [The anti-bribery provisions] cover payments and gifts intended to influence the recipient, regardless of who first suggested the payment or gift. The defense that the payment was demanded on the part of a government official as a price for gaining entry into a market or to obtain a contract would not suffice since at some point the U.S. company would make a conscious decision whether or not to pay a bribe. That the payment may have been first proposed by the recipient rather than the U.S. company does not alter the corrupt purpose on the part of the person paying the bribe. On the other hand extortion situations would not be covered by this provision since a payment to an official to keep an oil rig from being dynamited should not be held to be made with the requisite corrupt purpose.[22]

In terms of 'willfully,' a House Report stated:

> The bill [states that a person] must be found to have violated the law 'knowingly and willfully.' Consistent with the often-reiterated holdings of the courts that have interpreted a similar standard in the few places it is included in the federal securities laws, the knowledge required is merely that a defendant be aware that he is committing the act which constitutes the violation – not that he knows his conduct is illegal or has any specific intent to violate the law. [...] Indeed, even in the criminal context, neither knowledge of the law violated nor the intention to act in violation of the law is generally necessary for conviction, and the Committee does not intend that either be required here in either civil or criminal proceedings.[23]

Judicial Decisions

Given that the murky concepts of corrupt intent and willfulness are fact specific, it is not surprising that in the few litigated FCPA cases there are, *mens rea* issues have been contested giving rise to rare FCPA appellate decisions.

For instance, in *Stichting v. Schreiber* (a case occurring in the context of a civil malpractice action alleging erroneous legal advice by counsel regarding payments to a Panamanian official that caused the entity to violate the FCPA), an appellate court analyzed whether a company, in pleading guilty to FCPA anti-bribery violations, acknowledged acting with intent thus undermining its claims that the erroneous legal advice was the basis for its legal exposure.[24] The court stated:

> Knowledge by a defendant that it is violating the FCPA – that it is committing all the elements of an FCPA violation – is not itself an element of the FCPA crime. Federal statutes in which the defendant's knowledge that he or she is violating the statute is an element of the violation are rare; the FCPA is plainly not such a statute.

The court also stated as follows concerning 'corruptly' in the FCPA:

> It signifies, in addition to the element of 'general intent' present in most criminal statutes, a bad or wrongful purpose and an intent to influence a foreign official to misuse his official position. But there is nothing in that word or anything else in the FCPA that indicates that the government must establish that the defendant in fact knew that his conduct violated the FCPA to be guilty of such a violation.

FCPA *mens rea* issues were also the focus of an appellate decision in *U.S. v. Kay*, an enforcement action discussed earlier in this chapter in regards to the 'obtain or retain business' element.[25] After a jury convicted the defendants of FCPA anti-bribery violations, an appeal followed in which the defendants argued, among other things, that the trial court failed to adequately instruct the jury on *mens rea* issues.

As stated by the appellate court:

> The [district] court's instructions to the jury indicated that 'corruptly' was an element of the offense and defined a corrupt act as one that is 'done voluntarily and intentionally, and with a bad purpose or evil motive of accomplishing either an unlawful end or result, or a lawful end or result by some unlawful method or means.' The [district] court also instructed the jury on the definition of an act done 'knowingly' (thus incorporating the willfulness element into its instructions) and defined a knowing act as one 'done voluntarily and intentionally, not because of accident or mistake.'

The appellate court concluded:

> The FCPA does not define 'willfully,' and we therefore look to the common law interpretation of this term to determine the sufficiency of the jury instructions pertaining to the *mens rea* element. The definition of 'willful' in the criminal context remains unclear despite numerous opinions addressing this issue. Three levels of interpretation have arisen that help to clear the haze.

Under all three, a defendant must have acted intentionally – not by accident or mistake. The first and most basic interpretation of criminal willfulness is that committing an act, and having knowledge of that act, is criminal willfulness – provided that the actions fell within the category of actions defined as illegal under the applicable statute. In these cases, the defendant need not have known of the specific terms of the statute or even the existence of the statute. The defendant's knowledge that he committed the act is sufficient.

The second and 'intermediate' level of criminal willfulness requires the defendant to have known that his actions were in some way unlawful. Again, he need not have known of the specific statute, but rather he must have acted with the knowledge that he was doing a 'bad' act under the general rules of law. Under this intermediate level of criminal common law willfulness, 'the Government must prove that the defendant acted with knowledge that his conduct was unlawful.'

The strictest level of interpretation of criminal willfulness requires that the defendant knew the terms of the statute and that he was violating the statute. The courts have reserved this category to limited types of statutory violations involving 'complex' statutes – namely those governing federal tax law and antistructuring transactions. Although [this court] has not addressed the FCPA under this category, [the *Schreiber* case discussed above] has determined that the FCPA does not fall within this narrow category of complex statutes, and we agree.

The district court's jury instructions captured both the first and second levels of criminal willfulness [...] We find the instructions sufficient, since the strictest interpretation of criminal willfulness is reserved for complex statutes. Under the first and broadest definition of criminal willfulness, the term 'knowingly' in the context of willful criminal action 'merely requires proof of knowledge of the facts that constitute the offense.' [...]

The district court, by instructing the jury that a guilty verdict required a finding that defendant acted 'voluntarily and intentionally, and with a bad purpose or evil motive of accomplishing either an unlawful end or result,' and by including a separate 'knowing' instruction, correctly indicated that the jury must identify evidence amounting to 'knowledge of facts that constitute the offense' required by the traditional criminal definition of willfulness (which we have described as the first category of willfulness). The court's instructions also substantially covered the requested instruction that Defendants acted 'corruptly,' meaning they acted 'knowingly and dishonestly, with the specific intent to achieve an unlawful result by influencing a foreign public official's action in one's own favor.' The instructions suggested that illegal conduct under the FCPA defined the 'unlawful end or result' to which the court referred, since the jury had to have some standard by which to gauge lawfulness. Additionally, the instructions correctly indicated that to be guilty under the Act, Defendants must have knowingly (i.e., voluntarily and intentionally) acted with awareness of these unlawful ends.

[...]

> We find that the district court's jury instructions also capture our second, or intermediate, definition of criminal willfulness – a definition that we commonly follow – that a defendant knew that he was doing something generally 'unlawful' at the time of his action. This level of interpretation is stricter than the first because it does not only require that the defendant knew that he was committing an act (an act which, incidentally, falls within the definition of the relevant statute); the defendant must have known that the act was in some way wrong. The district court's jury instructions captured this level of intent well with their requirement that the jury find that Defendants acted 'with a bad purpose or evil motive.'
>
> [...]
>
> The instructions' requirements that Defendants acted corruptly, with an 'unlawful end or result,' and committed 'intentional' and 'knowing' acts with a bad motive sufficiently captured the definition of criminal willfulness that we follow. They also allowed Defendants to effectively put forth adequate defenses: Defendants could have argued lack of intent and that they were not acting with knowledge of unlawful means or ends. The district court's jury instructions adequately conveyed the 'willfulness' required for a conviction under the FCPA.

Guidance

The FCPA Guidance states as follows regarding *mens rea* issues:

> As long as the offer, promise, authorization, or payment is made corruptly, the actor need not know the identity of the recipient; the attempt is sufficient. Thus, an executive who authorizes others to pay 'whoever you need to' in a foreign government to obtain a contract has violated the FCPA – even if no bribe is ultimately offered or paid.
>
> The term 'willfully' is not defined in the FCPA, but it has generally been construed by courts to connote an act committed voluntarily and purposefully, and with a bad purpose, i.e. with 'knowledge that a defendant was doing a 'bad' act under the general rules of law. [...] 'As a general matter, when used in the criminal context, a "willful" act is one undertaken with a "bad purpose."' In other words, to establish a 'willful' violation of a statute, 'the Government must prove that the defendant acted with knowledge that his conduct was unlawful.'

While FCPA's *mens rea* requirements are murky and fact specific, the following take-away points are clear: (i) corrupt intent equates to an evil or wrongful motive and it does not matter if a payment is first proposed by a foreign official; (ii) to establish the willful requirement necessary for an individual FCPA criminal conviction, it is not necessary that the individual knew of the FCPA or its specific elements.

E. THIRD-PARTY PAYMENT PROVISIONS

As previously highlighted in Chapter 2, one reality of the global marketplace is the utilization of various third parties such as agents, distributors, and joint venture partners. According to survey data, approximately 80 percent of U.S. companies partner with a third party when doing business abroad and survey respondents (senior compliance executives from a variety of industry sectors) reported:

- 37 percent said they work with between 100 and 1,000 different third parties;
- 27 percent said they work with between 1,000 and 10,000 different third parties;
- 17 percent said they work with between 10,000 and 100,000 different third parties; and a small number said they worked with more than 100,000 different third parties.[26]

Utilizing a foreign third party is frequently an effective non-establishment form of doing business in a foreign country as the third party has an understanding and appreciation for the local business environment and has relationships with key business actors, both essential ingredients to a company's success in a foreign country.

Often times engaging a foreign third party or having a local sponsor is a requirement of doing business in a foreign country. In certain countries, a company may be required to enter into a joint venture with a local entity as a condition of doing business in the country. In certain industries, it is virtually guaranteed that a company will be required to have a foreign partner as a condition of doing business.

While beneficial in many respects, foreign third parties (whether engaged by choice or required pursuant to foreign local law) also present the greatest source of FCPA risk for companies in the global marketplace. In short, the upside of foreign third parties (i.e. they know how to get things done and expand business) is also the downside as companies subject to the FCPA can face legal liability for payments made by foreign third parties under the FCPA's third-party payment provisions if certain conditions are met.

This section highlights legal authority and non-legal sources of information relevant to the FCPA's third-party payment provisions.

Law

In passing the FCPA, Congress recognized that a direct prohibition alone on payments to 'foreign officials' to 'obtain or retain' business would be ineffective as payments could be funneled to 'foreign officials' through various third parties. Thus, the FCPA's anti-bribery provisions apply not only to direct payments or things of value to 'foreign officials' for the prohibited purposes, but also to payments or things of value to: 'any person, while knowing that all or a portion of such money or thing of value will be offered, given, or promised, directly or indirectly, to any foreign official …'

The FCPA defines 'knowing' as follows:

> (A) A person's state of mind is 'knowing' with respect to conduct, a circumstance, or a result if: (i) such person is aware that such person is engaging in such conduct, that such circumstance exists, or that such result is substantially certain to occur; or (ii) such person has a firm belief that such circumstance exists or that such result is substantially certain to occur.
>
> (B) When knowledge of the existence of a particular circumstance is required for an offense, such knowledge is established if a person is aware of a high probability of the existence of such circumstance, unless the person actually believes that such circumstance does not exist.

Legislative History

Chapter 1 detailed the FCPA's original 'while knowing or having reason to know' standard applicable to liability for the conduct of third parties and how even the enforcement agencies criticized this standard as being ambiguous. As previously noted, the 1988 amendments amended the third-party payment provisions to the standard highlighted above.

A Senate Report stated:

> [The provisions] are meant to prevent management from adopting 'head-in-the-sand' approach to bribery in order to avoid liability by ignoring facts and circumstances underlying the subject transaction which would indicate the payment of a bribe. […] On the other hand, the mere fact of doing business in a country where corrupt payments are common, or the employment of an agent with personal relationships with government officials in the country where the company seeks to do business, would not establish such a course of conduct. Similarly, the payment of a commission that is higher than customary would not by itself violate [the provisions] without other evidence that the increased amount of commission is to permit a corrupt payment to be made.[27]

A House Report likewise stated:

> The definition of 'knowing' is intended to make it clear that a 'head in the sand' approach to the payment of bribes through third parties will not be tolerated. Knowing is therefore defined to include conscious disregard of a high probability that a payment to a third payment will be transmitted by that party to a foreign official … .[28]

The House Report further stated:

> The statutory change makes it clear that mere negligence will not give rise to a civil prosecution under the FCPA. There must be a showing of reckless disregard or knowledge. […] The statutory change also makes it clear that neither mere negligence nor reckless disregard will give rise to a criminal prosecution under the FCPA. In order to bring a criminal prosecution for violation of the third party payments provisions, a showing of knowledge as defined in the [FCPA] would be required.

Judicial Decisions

The only judicial decision construing the FCPA's third-party payments provisions is *U.S. v. Bourke*.

The factual background of the case was unique in that it did not involve traditional uses of foreign third parties, but rather Bourke participated in an investment consortium and the DOJ alleged that he and others conspired to purchase assets in the privatization of the Azerbaijan state-owned oil company by bribing various Azeri officials. After being convicted of FCPA and related offenses at trial, Bourke appealed and one issue on appeal was whether the trial court properly instructed the jury on conscious avoidance.[29]

The appellate court concluded that there was 'ample evidence' to support a conviction at trial on a conscious avoidance theory under the FCPA's third-party payment provisions. The court stated:

> The testimony at trial demonstrated that Bourke was aware of how pervasive corruption was in Azerbaijan generally. Bourke knew of [a co-defendant's] reputation […] Bourke created the American advisory companies to shield himself and other American investors from potential liability from payments made in violation of FCPA, and joined the boards of the American companies instead of joining [a board of another company involved in the investment]. In so doing, Bourke enabled himself to participate in the investment without acquiring actual knowledge of [the other company's] undertakings. The strongest evidence demonstrating that Bourke willfully avoided learning whether corrupt payments were made came from tape recordings of a … phone conference with Bourke, [a] fellow investor, … and their attorneys, during which Bourke voiced concerns about whether [a co-defendant] and company were paying bribes. […] Finally, Bourke's attorney testified that he

> advised Bourke that if Bourke thought there might be bribes paid, Bourke could not just look the other way. Taken together, a rational juror could conclude that Bourke deliberately avoided confirming his suspicions that [co-defendant] and his cohorts may be paying bribes.

The Court further stated:

> It is not uncommon for a finding of conscious avoidance to be supported primarily by circumstantial evidence. Indeed, the very nature of conscious avoidance makes it unlikely that the record will contain directly incriminating statements. Just as it is rare to find direct record evidence of an employer stating, 'I am not going to give you a raise because you are a woman,' it is highly unlikely a defendant will provide direct record evidence of conscious avoidance by saying, 'Stop! I think you are about to discuss a crime and I want to be able to deny I know anything about it!' Here, the evidence adduced by the government at trial suffices to support the giving of a conscience avoidance charge.

In so holding, the Court specifically rejected Bourke's argument that the conscious avoidance charge improperly allowed the jury to convict him based on negligence rather than based on evidence that he avoided learning the truth. The Court stated: 'The record contains ample evidence that Bourke had serious concerns about the legality of [co-defendant's] business practices and worked to avoid learning exactly what [co-defendant] was doing.'

Guidance

The FCPA Guidance states:

> The FCPA expressly prohibits corrupt payments made through third parties or intermediaries. […] The fact that a bribe is paid by a third party does not eliminate the potential for criminal or civil FCPA liability. […] Because Congress anticipated the use of third-party agents in bribery schemes – for example to avoid actual knowledge of a bribe – it defined 'knowing' in a way that prevents individuals and businesses from avoiding liability by putting 'any person' between themselves and the foreign officials. […] A person has the requisite knowledge when he is aware of a high probability of the existence of such circumstance, unless the person actually believes that such circumstance does not exist. As Congress made clear, it meant to impose liability not only on those with actual knowledge of wrongdoing, but also on those who purposefully avoid actual knowledge.

A significant majority of corporate FCPA enforcements are based, in whole or in part, on allegations of improper payments made to 'foreign officials' via third parties.

For instance, an FCPA enforcement action against pharmaceutical company Eli Lilly was based, in part, on the conduct of third-party distributors in Brazil and the following allegations: Lilly sold drugs to the distributors at a discount; the distributors then resold the drugs to end users at a higher price and took the discount as their compensation; Lilly-Brazil approved 'unusually large discounts' to certain distributors; the distributors used a portion of the purchase price to 'bribe government officials from a Brazilian state so that the state would purchase Lilly product;' and the Lilly-Brazil sales and marketing manager who requested the discounts knew about the arrangement.[30]

Likewise, an FCPA enforcement action against infrastructure company Data Systems & Solutions was based on allegations that the company funneled payments to employees of alleged state-owned nuclear power plants in Eastern Europe through subcontractors who billed the company above market rates for services performed in connection with the projects.[31]

The take-away point from this section is that the FCPA's third-party payment provisions often present the greatest source of FCPA risk for companies competing in the global marketplace given the prevalent and extensive use of various third parties by business organizations subject to the FCPA. For this reason, one component of FCPA best practices discussed in Chapter 8 is specific policies and procedures concerning pre-engagement, engagement, and post-engagement of foreign third parties.

F. JURISDICTION

In addition to the substantive elements of the FCPA anti-bribery provisions discussed above, the jurisdictional elements of the FCPA must also be met in order for a business organization or individual to violate the FCPA's anti-bribery provisions. Due to FCPA amendments in 1998 that provided for extraterritorial jurisdiction as to U.S. actors, there are few disputed or controversial jurisdictional issues in FCPA enforcement actions against U.S. companies or citizens. However, as highlighted below there are several disputed and controversial jurisdictional issues in FCPA enforcement against foreign companies and citizens, and in this section you will learn of the expansive jurisdictional theories advanced by the enforcement agencies in bringing FCPA enforcement actions against foreign actors.

This section highlights legal authority and non-legal sources of information relevant to FCPA jurisdictional issues.

Law

The FCPA's anti-bribery provisions apply to 'issuers,' 'domestic concerns,' and 'persons' other than 'issuers' or 'domestic concerns.'

As previously highlighted, an issuer is a company (U.S. or foreign) that has a class of securities traded on a U.S. market or an entity that is otherwise required to file reports with the SEC. A 'domestic concern' is generally any business form (e.g., private corporations, limited liability companies, partnerships, sole proprietorships) with a principal place of business in the U.S. or organized under U.S. law. A 'domestic concern' also includes 'any individual who is a citizen, national, or resident of the U.S.' A 'person' other than an 'issuer' or 'domestic' concern includes foreign non-issuer business organizations as well as foreign nationals.

Jurisdiction under the FCPA's anti-bribery provisions depends on the type of business organization or person subject to the FCPA.

- As to *U.S.* 'issuers' and 'domestic concerns,' the FCPA contains both territorial jurisdiction and nationality jurisdiction. Territorial jurisdiction refers to 'use of the mails or any means or instrumentality of interstate commerce' in furtherance of an improper payment. Nationality jurisdiction means that an improper payment scheme is prohibited by the FCPA's anti-bribery provisions 'irrespective of whether [the U.S. person] makes use of the mails or any means or instrumentality of interstate commerce in furtherance' of an improper payment. Thus, as to *U.S.* 'issuers' and 'domestic concerns,' the FCPA's anti-bribery provisions have extraterritorial jurisdiction, meaning that the FCPA can be violated even if an improper payment scheme is devised and executed entirely outside of the U.S.
- As to foreign 'issuers,' the FCPA's anti-bribery provisions apply only to the extent there is territorial jurisdiction, in other words, 'use of the mails or any means of instrumentality of interstate commerce' in furtherance of an improper payment scheme.
- As to 'persons' other than an 'issuer' or 'domestic concerns,' the FCPA's anti-bribery provisions apply to the extent that, 'while in the territory of the U.S.,' the person 'makes use of the mails or any

means or instrumentality of interstate commerce' or engages in 'any other act in furtherance' of an improper payment scheme.

The first take-away point from the above jurisdictional analysis is that contrary to statements that the FCPA applies only to U.S. companies and citizens, the FCPA can also apply to foreign companies or foreign nationals.

Legislative History

The alternative nationality jurisdictional prong of the FCPA's anti-bribery provisions applicable to *U.S.* 'issuers' and 'domestic concerns' became part of the FCPA as a result of the 1998 amendments.

A relevant Senate Report stated:

> The OECD Convention calls on parties to assert nationality jurisdiction when consistent with national legal and constitutional principles. Accordingly, the Act amends the FCPA to provide for jurisdiction over the acts of U.S. businesses and nationals in furtherance of unlawful payments that take place wholly outside the United States. This exercise of jurisdiction over U.S. businesses and nationals for unlawful conduct abroad is consistent with U.S. legal and constitutional principles and is essential to protect U.S. interests abroad.[32]

Likewise, a relevant House Report stated:

> [The nationality jurisdictional prong] implements the OECD Convention by creating an additional basis for jurisdiction over foreign bribery by U.S. issuers [and domestic concerns] and U.S. persons that are officers, directors, employees, or agents, or stockholders of such issuers [or domestic concerns]. This section extends coverage for acts outside the United States to U.S. issuers [or domestic concerns] … and U.S. persons acting on such issuers' [or domestic concerns'] behalf.[33]

The 1998 amendments also added a new section to the FCPA's anti-bribery provisions applicable to 'persons' other than an 'issuer' or 'domestic concern.'

Relevant Senate and House Reports stated:

> [The amendment] creates a new section in the FCPA, providing for criminal and civil penalties over persons not covered under the existing FCPA provisions regarding issuers and domestic concerns. This section closes the gap left in the original FCPA and implements the OECD Convention's requirement that Parties criminalize bribery by 'any person.' The prohibited

acts are the same as those covered by [the existing provisions in the FCPA] with two qualifications.

First, the offense created under this section requires that an act in furtherance of the bribe be taken within the territory of the United States. The OECD Convention requires each Party to 'take such measures as may be necessary to establish its jurisdiction over the bribery of a foreign public official when the offense is committed in whole or in part in its territory.' The new offense complies with this section by providing for criminal jurisdiction in this country over bribery by foreign nationals of foreign officials when the foreign national takes some act in furtherance of the bribery within the territory of the United States. [...] As envisioned in the OECD the territorial basis for jurisdiction should be interpreted broadly so that an extensive physical connection to the bribery act is not required. [...] The second difference from the existing FCPA provisions is that this section expands the commerce nexus to include not only the use of the mails or any means or instrumentality of interstate commerce but 'any other act' within the United States.[34]

Judicial Decisions

As indicated above there are few disputed or controversial jurisdiction issues in FCPA enforcement actions against U.S. companies or citizens due to the FCPA's 1998 amendments that provided for expanded extra-territorial jurisdiction over U.S. actors.

However there are several disputed and controversial jurisdictional issues in FCPA enforcement against foreign companies and citizens. For instance, Chapter 2 highlighted how JGC Corporation of Japan was admonished by the DOJ for 'declining to cooperate' with its FCPA investigation 'based on jurisdictional arguments.' Perhaps mindful of the adverse consequences of its perceived failure to cooperate, JGC agreed to resolve its alleged FCPA scrutiny – based on the jurisdictional theory that certain alleged bribe payments to Nigerian officials flowed through U.S. bank accounts and that co-conspirators faxed or e-mailed information into the U.S. in furtherance of the bribery scheme – via a DPA not subjected to any meaningful judicial scrutiny.[35]

Expansive jurisdictional theories in individual FCPA enforcement actions against foreign actors have been subjected to judicial scrutiny three times and as highlighted below, the enforcement agencies have an overall losing record when put to its burden of proof.

In the manufactured Africa Sting action described in more detail in Chapter 5, one of the defendants, U.K. citizen Pankesh Patel, moved after the DOJ's evidence at trial for a judgment of acquittal of an FCPA charge based on his sending a DHL package – containing a purchase agreement in furtherance of the alleged bribery scheme – from the U.K. to the U.S.

The judge granted the acquittal and the hearing transcript indicates the following exchange between the judge and the DOJ prosecutor concerning the DOJ's jurisdictional theory that an act by a foreign national need not be in the territory of the U.S. for the FCPA to apply.

> *Judge*: 'Has the Supreme Court said that?'
>
> *DOJ*: 'Judge, no.'
>
> *Judge*: 'Has the D.C. Circuit said that?'
>
> *DOJ*: 'No.'
>
> *Judge*: 'How about the 2nd Circuit, where you used to prosecute?'
>
> *DOJ*: 'Judge, there's not a lot of case law on the FCPA, as Your Honor I think is well aware.'
>
> *Judge*: 'So is this a novel interpretation you want me to take?'
>
> *DOJ*: 'I don't know if it's a novel interpretation. I think it's an interpretation that's grounded in the law that's out there.'
>
> *Judge*: 'Is it grounded in the legislative record?'
>
> *DOJ*: 'We can go back and we can get Your Honor more particulars about the legislative history if Your Honor wants that.'
>
> *Judge*: 'I would think the more cautious, conservative interpretation would be that each act has to be while in the territory of the United States, wouldn't it?'[36]

The 2011 ruling in the Africa Sting case was significant in that it was the first instance of a foreign national defendant putting the DOJ to its burden of proof at trial on a jurisdictional issue.

In 2013 the SEC was put to its burden of proof in two individual FCPA enforcement actions involving foreign national defendants and the pre-trial results were mixed.

SEC v. Straub involved allegations that Hungarian nationals employed by issuer Magyar Telecom violated the FCPA's anti-bribery provisions in connection with a bribery scheme involving Macedonian 'foreign officials.'[37] The judge, ruling on a pre-trial motion to dismiss and an issue of first impression, concluded that the FCPA's territorial jurisdiction element (use of the mails or any means of instrumentality of interstate commerce) could be met based on allegations that e-mails in connection with the alleged bribery scheme were routed through and/or stored on network servers located within the U.S. even if the defendants did not personally know where the e-mails would be routed and/or stored. In so holding, the judge found the FCPA's territorial jurisdiction element ambiguous and thus turned to the legislative history. As stated by the judge: 'The legislative history reveals that, although Congress intended to make an "intent" or *mens rea* requirement for the underlying bribery, it expressed no corresponding intent to make such a requirement for the "make use of … any means or instrumentality of interstate commerce" element.'

SEC v. Steffen involved allegations that a German national formerly employed by issuer Siemens violated the FCPA's anti-bribery provisions in connection with a bribery scheme involving Argentine 'foreign officials.'[38] The judge granted the defendant's pre-trial motion to dismiss concluding that personal jurisdiction over the defendant exceeded the limits of due process. This non-FCPA specific issue is an initial threshold question in all U.S. actions involving foreign defendants and because the judge found general jurisdiction lacking, the judge did not address the FCPA's specific jurisdictional provisions like in the above *Straub* action.

Regarding the disputed issue of whether the SEC's complaint alleged sufficient facts to establish the two components of due process – minimum contacts and reasonableness – the judge stated as to minimum contacts:

> The SEC's allegations are premised on Steffen's role in encouraging [a co-defendant] to authorize bribes to Argentine officials that ultimately resulted in falsified [SEC] filings. While Steffen's actions may have been a proximate cause of the false filings – and that is a matter of some doubt – Steffen's actions are far too attenuated from the resulting harm to establish minimum contacts. Steffen was brought into the alleged scheme based solely on his connections with Argentine officials. In furtherance of his negotiations with those officials, Steffen 'urged' and 'pressured' [a co-defendant] to make certain bribes. However, [a co-defendant] did not agree to make the bribes until he communicated with several 'higher ups' whose responses he perceived to be instructions to make the bribes. Once [a co-defendant] agreed to make the bribes – following receipt of instructions from Siemens' management rather than Steffen – Steffen's alleged role was tangential at best. Steffen did not actually authorize the bribes. The SEC does not allege that he directed, ordered or even had awareness of the cover ups that occurred … much less that he had any involvement in the falsification of SEC filings in furtherance of those cover ups.

The judge further stated:

> Neither [a co-defendant's] call to Steffen from the United States nor the fact that a portion of the bribery payments were deposited in a New York bank provide sufficient evidence of conduct directed towards the United States to establish minimum contacts. First, Steffen did not place the calls to [a co-defendant]. Further, Steffen did not direct that the funds be routed through a New York bank. […] His conduct was focused solely on ensuring the

> continuation of the Siemens contract in Argentina. [...] If this Court were to hold that Steffen's support for the bribery scheme satisfied the minimum contacts analysis, even though he neither authorized the bribe, nor directed the cover up, much less played any role in the falsified filings, minimum contacts would be boundless. Illegal corporate action almost always requires cover ups, which to be successful must be reflected in financial statements. Thus, under the SEC's theory, every participant in illegal action taken by a foreign company subject to U.S. securities laws would be subject to the jurisdiction of U.S. courts no matter how attenuated their connection with the falsified financial statements. This would be akin to a tort-like foreseeability requirement, which has long been held to be insufficient. The allegations against Steffen fall far short of the requirement that he 'follow a course of conduct directed ... to the jurisdiction of a given sovereign, so that the sovereign has the power to subject the defendant to judgment concerning that conduct. Absent any alleged role in the cover ups themselves, let alone any role in preparing false financial statements the exercise of jurisdiction here exceeds the limits of due process ... '

As to reasonableness, the judge stated:

> The decision not to exercise jurisdiction in this case is bolstered by my conclusion that requiring Steffen to defend this case in the United States would be unreasonable. [...] When a defendant is not located in the United States, great care and reserve should be exercised when extending our notions of personal jurisdiction into the international context. Steffen's lack of geographic ties to the United States, his age, his poor proficiency in English, and the forum's diminished interest in adjudicating the matter, all weight against personal jurisdiction.

Guidance

The FCPA Guidance states, under the heading 'what jurisdictional conduct triggers the anti-bribery provisions' as follows:

> Placing a telephone call or sending an e-mail, text message, or fax from, to, or through the United States involves interstate commerce – as does sending a wire transfer from or to a U.S. bank or otherwise using the U.S. banking system, or traveling across state borders or internationally to or from the United States. [...] Those who are not issuers or domestic concerns may be prosecuted under the FCPA if they directly, or through an agent, engage in any act in furtherance of a corrupt payment while in the territory of the United States, regardless of whether they utilize the U.S. mails or a means or instrumentality of interstate commerce. Thus, for example, a foreign national who attends a meeting in the United States that furthers a foreign bribery scheme may be subject to prosecution, as may any co-conspirators, even if they did not themselves attend the meeting. A foreign national or company may also be liable under the FCPA if it aids and abets, conspires with, or acts

> as an agent of an issuer or domestic concern, regardless of whether the foreign national or company itself takes any action in the United States.

Missing from the Guidance is any discussion of the DOJ's unsuccessful prosecution of Patel described above. Instead of citing a relevant judicial decision, Guidance discussion of jurisdictional issues relevant to foreign actors cites resolved FCPA enforcement actions that were not subjected to any meaningful judicial scrutiny.

To be sure, there have been several such actions and, as highlighted in Chapter 5, nine of the top ten corporate FCPA settlements have been against foreign companies. A 2006 FCPA enforcement action against Norway-based oil and gas company Statoil was the first criminal FCPA enforcement action against a foreign company. In the action, based on allegations the company made improper payments to Iranian officials, the DOJ stated: 'Although Statoil is a foreign issuer, the [FCPA] applies to foreign and domestic public companies alike, where the company's stock trades on American exchanges. This prosecution demonstrates the Justice Department's commitment vigorously to enforce the FCPA against all international businesses whose conduct falls within its scope.'[39]

In addition to other FCPA enforcement actions discussed throughout this book against foreign companies, Table 3.3 highlights certain representative FCPA enforcement actions against foreign companies and the jurisdictional allegations asserted by the enforcement agencies.

On one level, it seems odd that the FCPA can apply to, for example, business interactions between a Hungarian company and a Macedonian foreign official or a Luxembourg company and an Uzbekistan foreign official. Yet the FCPA does allow for such jurisdiction over foreign actors in certain instances even though the legal contours of those instances have gone unexplored in corporate FCPA enforcement actions.

Jurisdiction is power to declare the law. In this regard the enforcement agencies' expansive theories of FCPA jurisdiction raise various policy issues. Why does the U.S. advance expansive jurisdictional theories in FCPA enforcement actions against foreign actors?

- Is it a moral obligation to hold bad actors accountable and help establish global norms as to corporate behavior and business ethics? If so, why, as discussed in Chapter 5, do certain companies in certain industries appear to be immune from FCPA anti-bribery charges and why does the general fight against bribery and corruption suffer from several double standards?

Table 3.3 Jurisdictional allegations

Company	Jurisdictional Allegations
Magyar Telecom (Hungary)	In connection with bribery scheme, company executive sent two e-mails to a Macedonian foreign official from his U.S. based e-mail address that passed through, were stored on, and transmitted from servers located in the U.S.
	Certain electronic communications made in furtherance of the scheme and the concealment of payments, including drafts of certain agreements and copies of certain contracts with intermediaries, were transmitted by company employees and others through U.S. interstate commerce or stored on computer servers located in the U.S.[a]
Bridgestone (Japan)	Company employees sent and received e-mail and fax communications to/from U.S. in connection with the bribery scheme involving Latin American 'foreign officials.'[b]
Tenaris (Luxembourg)	Payment to an agent via wire transfer through an intermediary bank located in New York in connection with a bribery scheme involving Uzbekistan foreign officials.[c]

Notes:

[a] Deferred Prosecution Agreement, U.S. v. Magyar Telecom plc, Case No. 11-cr-597, (E.D. Va., Dec. 29, 2011).
[b] Information, U.S. v. Bridgestone Corp., Case 4:11-cr-00651 (S.D. Tex., Sept. 15, 2011).
[c] Letter from Dennis McInerney, Chief, Fraud Section, U.S. Dep't of Justice (Criminal Div.), to Robert Giuffra, Attorney for Tenaris (Mar. 14, 2011).

- Is it to score political points and make the U.S. government look good in the eyes of civil society organizations?
- Is it to make money for the U.S. treasury and for FCPA Inc., an issue explored in more detail in Chapter 6?

Regardless of the answer, the take-away point from this section is that the FCPA's anti-bribery provisions do not just apply to U.S. actors. But perhaps restraint by the enforcement agencies is warranted. Indeed, during the 2010 Senate FCPA hearing, Senator Coons stated: 'Today we are the only nation that is extending extraterritorial reach and going after the citizens of other countries, we may someday find ourselves on the receiving end of such transnational actions.'[40]

As a matter of law, the FCPA does not provide extraterritorial jurisdiction against foreign actors, however as a matter of practice, this section has highlighted the expansive jurisdictional theories advanced by the enforcement agencies in bringing FCPA enforcement actions against foreign actors.

G. EXCEPTION AND AFFIRMATIVE DEFENSES

Even if all of the substantive elements of the FCPA anti-bribery provisions have been met and there is jurisdiction over the actor, the final step in analyzing the FCPA's anti-bribery provisions is determining whether the FCPA's facilitating payment exception or the FCPA's affirmative defenses apply. This section highlights legal authority and non-legal sources of information relevant to the exception and affirmative defenses.

Facilitating Payments Exception

While some view facilitating or 'grease' payments to be corrupt payments under a different name, the fact remains that the FCPA contains an express facilitating payments exception and it is this statute that the enforcement agencies are obligated to enforce.

After highlighting legal authority and non-legal sources of information relevant to this exception, the question is posed whether the FCPA's facilitating payment exception has any real meaning in this new era or whether the enforcement agencies have essentially repealed this exception through its enforcement theories.

Law

The FCPA states that the anti-bribery provisions 'shall not apply to any facilitating or expediting payment to a foreign official … the purpose of which is to expedite or to secure the performance of a routine government action by a foreign official … '.

The FCPA defines 'routine government action' as follows:

> The term 'routine governmental action' means only an action which is ordinarily and commonly performed by a foreign official in

> (i) obtaining permits, licenses, or other official documents to qualify a person to do business in a foreign country; (ii) processing governmental papers, such as visas and work orders; (iii) providing police protection, mail pick-up and delivery, or scheduling inspections associated with contract performance or inspections related to transit of goods across country; (iv) providing phone service, power and water supply, loading and unloading cargo, or protecting perishable products or commodities from deterioration; or (v) actions of a similar nature.

> The term 'routine governmental action' does not include any decision by a foreign official whether, or on what terms, to award new business to or to continue business with a particular party, or any action taken by a foreign official involved in the decision-making process to encourage a decision to award new business to or continue business with a particular party.

Legislative history

The legislative history discussed in Chapter 1 makes clear that in passing the FCPA Congress intended to capture only a narrow category of payments and chose not to capture so-called facilitating payments given the difficult and complex business conditions encountered in many foreign countries. It is not necessary to restate this extensive legislative history here, but it bears repeating in this section the following language from the relevant Senate and House Reports.

The Senate Report stated:

> In drafting the bill … the Committee deliberately cast the language narrowly, in order to differentiate between such payments [to a foreign official corruptly intended to induce the recipient to use his influence to secure business, influence legislation or regulations] and low-level facilitating payments sometimes called 'grease payments.' Thus, [the bill] would not reach a small gratuity paid to expedite shipment through Customs or the placement of a trans-Atlantic telephone call, to secure required permits, or to ensure that a corporation's warehouses were not put to the torch. In other words, payments made to expedite the proper performance of duties may be reprehensible, but it does not appear feasible for the United States to attempt unilaterally to eradicate all such payments. […] The Committee fully recognizes that the proposed law will not reach all corrupt payments overseas.[41]

The House Report likewise stated:

> The bill's coverage does not extend to so-called grease or facilitating payments. … The language of the bill is deliberately cast in terms which differentiate between such payments and facilitating payments, sometimes called 'grease payments'. In using the word 'corruptly', the committee intends to distinguish between payments which cause an official to exercise other than his free will in acting or deciding or influencing an act or decision and those

> payments which merely move a particular matter toward an eventual act or decision or which do not involve any discretionary action. [...] For example, a gratuity paid to a customs official to speed the processing of a customs document would not be reached by the bill. Nor would it reach payments made to secure permits, licenses, or the expeditious performance of similar duties of an essentially ministerial or clerical nature which must of necessity by performed in any event. While payments made to assure or to speed the proper performance of a foreign official's duties may be reprehensible in the United States, the committee recognizes that they are not necessarily so viewed elsewhere in the world and that it is not feasible for the United States to attempt unilaterally to eradicate all such payments. As a result, the committee has not attempted to reach such payments. [...] The committee fully recognizes that the proposed law will not reach all corrupt payments overseas.[42]

As previously noted in Chapter 1, the FCPA originally contained an indirect facilitating payment exception embedded in the 'foreign official' element by excluding from the definition of 'foreign official' 'any employee of a foreign government or any department, agency, or instrumentality thereof whose duties are essentially ministerial or clerical.'

In 1988, this indirect exception was removed from the definition of 'foreign official' in favor of an express stand-alone exception. The House Report indicates that Congress did not seek to disturb Congress's original intent and stated:

> The policy adopted by Congress in 1977 remains valid, in terms of both U.S. law enforcement and foreign relations considerations. Any prohibition under U.S. law against this type of petty corruption would be exceedingly difficult to enforce, not only by U.S. prosecutors but by company officials themselves. Thus while such payments should not be condoned, they may appropriately be excluded from the reach of the FCPA. U.S. enforcement resources should be devoted to activities that have much greater impact on foreign policy.[43]

Judicial decisions

There is little case law construing the FCPA's facilitation payments exception. However, a 2012 SEC enforcement action against Mark Jackson and James Ruehlen addressed an issue of first impression concerning facilitating payment pleading requirements.[44] At its core, the enforcement action concerned SEC allegations that the defendants (current and former employees of oil and gas services company Noble Corp.) violated 'the FCPA by participating in a bribery scheme to obtain illicit permits [Temporary Import Permits – 'TIPs'] for oil rigs in Nigeria in order to retain business under lucrative drilling contracts.' As relevant to facilitating payments, the defendants argued that the SEC had the burden of pleading the inapplicability of the facilitating payments exception whereas the SEC argued that the defendants had the burden of pleading the inapplicability of the exception. The court held that the SEC 'must bear the burden of negating the facilitating payments exception' and that the 'exception is best understood as a threshold requirement to pleading that a defendant acted "corruptly."'

Guidance

The FCPA Guidance terms the facilitation payments exception 'narrow' and states:

> Whether a payment falls within the exception is not dependent on the size of the payment, though size can be telling, as a large payment is more suggestive of corrupt intent to influence a non-routine governmental action. But, like the FCPA's anti-bribery provisions more generally, the facilitating payments exception focuses on the purpose of the payment rather than its value. [...] Labeling a bribe as a 'facilitating payment' in a company's books and records does not make it one. [...] As with any expenditure, facilitating payments may still violate the FCPA if they are not properly recorded in an issuer's books and records.

Notwithstanding the above legal authority, many corporate FCPA enforcement actions in this new era concern payments made in connection with securing foreign permits, licenses or other official documents needed to do business in a foreign country.

One of the most notable examples concerned 'Customs Gate' – related DOJ and SEC enforcement actions in 2010 against freight forwarder Panalpina and six oil and gas companies that utilized Panalpina's services in interacting with the notoriously corrupt Nigerian Customs Services ('NCS'). The core conduct at issue was the same as in the above SEC enforcement action against Jackson and Ruehlen and centered on payments allegedly made to NCS employees in connection with securing or renewing TIPS so that oil rigs could remain in Nigerian waters. Other allegations included that payments were made to NCS officials 'to expedite the delivery of goods and equipment into Nigeria.' Perhaps in a sign of how obvious the facilitating payments exception was to the conduct at issue, the DOJ twice stated in resolution documents that 'the payments [at issue] ... would not constitute facilitation payments for routine governmental actions within the meaning of the FCPA.'[45]

All of the Customs Gate enforcement actions were resolved via NPAs or DPAs in which the companies collectively agreed to pay approximately $236 million in combined settlement amounts.[46] The only individuals charged in connection with Customs Gate were Jackson and Ruehlen, and as described above, the defendants put the SEC to its burden of proof as to whether the payments violated the FCPA. In an ironic twist, two years after the enforcement agencies collected approximately $236 million in the corporate Customs Gate enforcement actions, the court ruled that the enforcement agency has the burden of proof to negate the facilitating payments exception.

The above enforcement actions, as well as many others in this new era that involve foreign licenses, permits, and the like raise the question of whether the facilitating payments exception has any real meaning or whether the enforcement agencies have essentially repealed this exception through its enforcement theories.

Indeed, the SEC's former Assistant Director of Enforcement has called the FCPA's facilitating payment exception 'illusory' and stated:

> The drafters of the FCPA recognized that such demands for 'grease payments' are a reality in many countries, and accordingly made clear that certain payments made to expedite the approval of permits or licenses, or to prompt the expeditious performance of similar low-level ministerial duties, fell outside the ambit of the statute's anti-bribery provisions. Yet that exception for 'facilitating payments' [...] is becoming harder and harder to rely on. [...] The DOJ and SEC have pressed a narrow view of the exception in recent years ... [...] Of course, the fact that the FCPA's twin enforcement agencies have treated certain payments as prohibited despite their possible categorization as facilitating payments does not mean a federal court would agree. But because the vast majority of enforcement actions are resolved through DPAs and NPAs, and other settlement devices, these cases never make it to trial. As a result, the DOJ and the SEC's narrow interpretation of the facilitating payments exception is making that exception ever more illusory, regardless of whether the federal courts – or Congress – would agree.[47]

As relevant to the *de facto* repealing of this statutory exception, a current Senior Investigations Counsel with the SEC's FCPA Unit stated, in his personal capacity: 'While the FCPA contains several core provisions that will always withstand the test of time, the facilitation payments exception is out of date in this modern-day era of commerce and sensibility.'[48]

Affirmative Defenses

In addition to the facilitating payments exception, the FCPA also contains two affirmative defenses. The first is for payments lawful under the written laws and regulations of a foreign country. The second is for payments of reasonable and bona fide expenditures directly related to products, services or the execution of a contract. As affirmative defenses, a business organization or individual under FCPA scrutiny has the burden of proving the elements of the defenses to be excused from liability for a payment that otherwise meets the requirements of the FCPA anti-bribery provisions.

Local law defense
Highlighted below is legal authority and non-legal sources of information relevant to the FCPA's local law affirmative defense.

Law
The FCPA provides that it shall be an affirmative defense to an anti-bribery violation if: 'the payment, gift, offer, or promise of anything of value that was made, was lawful under the written laws and regulations of the foreign official's … country.'

The key words from the statutory text are 'written' laws and regulations. In other words, just because a payment otherwise in violation of the FCPA's anti-bribery provisions may be common and accepted in a foreign country (and thus not prosecuted under foreign law), does not mean that the payment is 'lawful under the written laws and regulations' of the foreign country as required for the affirmative defense to apply.

Legislative history
The local law affirmative defense became part of the FCPA as a result of the 1988 amendments. A Senate Report stated: 'Under the affirmative defense provisions, a company must be able to defend its actions by documenting that they were in fact "lawful" in the host country.'[49] The House Conference report stated: 'The Conferees wish to make clear that the absence of written laws in a foreign official's country would not by itself be sufficient to satisfy this defense.'[50]

Judicial decisions
There has been one judicial decision regarding the FCPA's local law affirmative defense. In *U.S. v. Bourke*, an enforcement action previously discussed concerning an alleged bribery scheme in connection with the privatization of Azerbaijan's state-owned oil company, Bourke argued that the alleged payments were legal under Azeri law and thus under the FCPA given its local law affirmative defense.[51] Bourke's expert opined that under Azeri law a 'person who has given a bribe shall be free from criminal responsibility if, [among other things] the person after giving the

bribe voluntarily made a report of the occurrence.' The judge framed the disputed issue as follows: 'As a threshold matter, I must determine the meaning of "relieved (or free) from criminal responsibility." Bourkc contends that if an individual is relieved of criminal responsibility, his action was "lawful" and he may thus avail himself of the FCPA's affirmative defense.'

The judge disagreed and concluded:

> For purposes of the FCPA's affirmative defense, the focus is on the payment, not the payer. A person cannot be guilty of violating the FCPA if the payment was lawful under foreign law. But there is no immunity from prosecution under the FCPA if a person could not have been prosecuted in the foreign country due to a technicality (e.g., time-barred) or because a provision in the foreign law 'relieves' a person of criminal responsibility. An individual may be prosecuted under the FCPA for a payment that violates foreign law even if the individual is relieved of criminal responsibility for his actions by a provision of the foreign law.

As to the Azeri law at issue, the judge stated:

> The structure of the reporting exception to liability in [Azeri law] illustrates that the initial payment of a bribe was certainly not lawful. [Azeri law] relieves the payer of a bribe from criminal liability if the bribe is properly reported not because such an action retroactively erases the stain of criminality, but because the state has a strong interest in prosecuting the government official who received the bribe. By waiving liability for reporting payers, the state increases the likelihood that it will learn of the bribery. But at the moment that an individual pays a bribe, the individual has violated [Azeri law]. At that time, the payment was clearly not 'lawful under the written laws' of Azerbaijan. If the individual later reports the bribe, she can no longer be prosecuted for that payment. But it is inaccurate to suggest that the payment itself suddenly became 'lawful' – on the contrary, the payment was unlawful, though the payer is relieved of responsibility for it.

Guidance

The FCPA Guidance states as follows concerning the local law affirmative defense: 'The fact that bribes may not be prosecuted under local law is insufficient to establish the defense. In practice, the local law defense arises infrequently, as the written laws and regulations of countries, rarely, if ever, permit corrupt payments.'

When Congress enacted the FCPA in 1977 and amended the FCPA in 1988 to include the local law affirmative defense it recognized that no foreign country permitted bribery of its officials in its written laws. In this regard, the FCPA's affirmative defense for payments lawful 'under the written laws and regulations of the foreign official's … country' has always been curious. In short, the FCPA's local law affirmative defense is largely meaningless and it is difficult to imagine a circumstance in which it could be successfully invoked by a business organization or individual subject to FCPA scrutiny.

Reasonable and bona fide expenditures defense
Highlighted below is legal authority and non-legal sources of information relevant to the FCPA's reasonable and bona fide expenditures affirmative defense.

Law
The FCPA provides that it shall be an affirmative defense to an anti-bribery violation if:

> the payment, gift, offer, or promise of anything of value that was made, was a reasonable and bona fide expenditure, such as travel and lodging expenses, incurred by or on behalf of a foreign official … and was directly related to: (a) the promotion, demonstration, or explanation of products or services; or (b) the execution or performance of a contract with a foreign government or agency thereof.

All companies doing business in the global marketplace promote product and execute contracts. In connection with these common business practices, gifts, travel, hospitality and entertainment, and other 'good-will' expenses are often made. Most of these expenses are perfectly acceptable and legal, yet as demonstrated by FCPA enforcement actions below such expenses often morph into conduct giving rise to FCPA scrutiny.

It is for this reason why gifts, travel, and hospitality and entertainment are often the most worrying for companies, particularly in Asian countries where gift-gifting is a prominent feature of a business relationship. For instance, FCPA practitioners have noted:

> In China, building relationships, or guanxi, drives successful business development. These necessary relationships grow out of the exchange of favors and gifts, including meals and entertainment. Although not necessarily impermissible, these sorts of benefits, common in Chinese business, pose a serious corruption risk and serve to exacerbate what is already a very challenging anti-corruption compliance environment for foreign businesses in China.[52]

Likewise, an FCPA practitioner observed: 'Gifts, meals, entertainment and travel remain the part of the statute that companies still find the most vexing in terms of day-to-day compliance. Rarely a day goes by that I don't receive a call or email from a client with a question in this area.'[53]

Legislative history

The reasonable and bona fide expenditures affirmative defense became part of the FCPA as a result of the 1988 amendments. A Senate Rcport stated:

> The exceptions for reasonable and bona fide expenditures associated with selling or purchasing goods, or the performance of a contract with a foreign government or agency thereof must encompass only legitimate expenses made to or for the foreign official in payment for or reimbursement of that foreign official's expenses. These terms should, of course, be interpreted in a common sense manner.[54]

The House Conference report stated: 'If a payment or gift is corruptly made, in return for an official act or omission, then it cannot be a bona fide, good-faith payment, and this defense would not be available.'[55]

Judicial decisions

The FCPA's affirmative defense for reasonable and bona fide expenditures has never been directly addressed by a court. However, in *U.S. v. Liebo* discussed earlier in this chapter in regards to 'anything of value,' the defendant argued that there was insufficient evidence to show that he acted 'corruptly' by providing honeymoon airline tickets to a Niger official who was in a position of influence concerning a contract at issue. The court disagreed and was satisfied that sufficient evidence existed from which a reasonable jury could find that the airline tickets were given 'corruptly.' The court noted that the airline tickets were given to the foreign official shortly before a contract was approved and that the defendant classified the airline ticket for accounting purposes as a 'commission payment' which could allow a reasonable jury to infer that the defendant gave the tickets intending to influence the approval of the contract.[56]

Guidance

As to the FCPA's reasonable and bona fide expenditures affirmative defense, the FCPA Guidance generically references several DOJ Opinion Procedure Releases and states:

> DOJ and SEC have consistently recognized that businesses, both foreign and domestic, are permitted to pay for reasonable expenses associated with the promotion of their products and services or the execution of existing contracts. In addition, DOJ has frequently provided guidance about legitimate promotional and contract-related expenses – addressing travel and lodging expenses in particular – through several opinion procedure releases. Under the

circumstances presented in those releases, DOJ opined that the following types of expenditures on behalf of foreign officials did not warrant FCPA enforcement action:

- Travel and expenses to visit company facilities or operations;
- Travel and expenses for training; and
- Product demonstration or promotional activities, including travel and expenses for meetings.

Whether any particular payment is a bona fide expenditure necessarily reflects a fact-specific analysis. [...] Trips that are primarily for personal entertainment purposes, however, are not bona fide business expenses and may violate the FCPA's anti-bribery provisions. Moreover, when expenditures, bona fide or not, are mischaracterized in a company's books and records, or where unauthorized or improper expenditures occur due to a failure to implement adequate internal controls, they may also violate the FCPA's accounting provisions. Purposeful mischaracterization of expenditures may also, of course, indicate a corrupt intent.

The line between reasonable and bona fide expenditures and corrupt payments seeking influence disguised in other ways is often difficult to draw. However two corporate FCPA enforcement actions based primarily on excessive travel and entertainment expenses sheds light on how the enforcement agencies draw the line.

An FCPA enforcement action against telecommunications company UTStarcom ('UTSI') was based on allegations that the company provided travel and other things of value to employees of state-owned telecommunications firms in China. The NPA used to resolve the company's FCPA scrutiny stated: 'UTSI spent nearly $7 million on approximately 225 trips for customer employees pursuant to training provisions in systems contracts entered into between UTS-China and government-controlled municipal or provincial telecommunications companies.'[57]

According to the DOJ, the trips were to places such as Hawaii, Las Vegas and New York, and company senior management believed that these trips were 'necessary in order to obtain and retain the systems contracts.' The resolution documents do not specify the dollar value associated with these contracts but do state that China historically had been 'UTSI's most important market.' The SEC enforcement action contained additional allegations that 'UTSI provided other gifts and benefits to foreign government customers, including paying for them to attend executive training programs at U.S. universities.'[58] The SEC also alleged that 'UTSI's general manager in Thailand spent nearly $10,000 on French wine as a gift to agents of the government customer, including rare bottles that cost more than $600 each' and that the manager 'also spent $13,000 for entertainment expenses for the same customer in an attempt to secure the contract.'

Likewise an FCPA enforcement action against telecommunications company Lucent Technologies was based on similar allegations. The NPA used to resolve the company's FCPA scrutiny stated:

> Lucent provided approximately 315 trips for Chinese government officials that included primarily sightseeing, entertainment and leisure. These trips were requested and approved with the consent and knowledge of the highest Lucent China officials and with the assistance of Lucent employees in the United States, including at corporate headquarters. Lucent improperly recorded expenses for these trips in its books and records and failed to provide adequate internal controls to monitor the provision of travel and other things of value to Chinese government officials.[59]

According to the DOJ, although certain pre-sale trips included 'brief stops' at certain Lucent facilities, the majority of the trips consisted of visiting Boston, Las Vegas, the Grand Canyon and Hawaii 'for strictly entertainment, travel and leisure purposes.' Other trips included hosting an alleged Chinese foreign official in California for 'two and a half days of sightseeing, entertainment and leisure,' approved by the company 'after learning of the past and future revenues associated with this customer and [the] official's decision-making role.' Another trip included paying for an alleged Chinese 'foreign official' and his wife and daughter to travel 'to Thailand and Hong Kong for a seven-day vacation' and the planning for this trip indicated that the 'vacation was aimed at influencing the [foreign official] and "strengthening the customer relationship" to expand the business relationship with the customer.' Other trips included post-sale visits termed 'factory tours' which 'consisted primarily or entirely of sightseeing to locations such as Disneyland, Los Angeles, San Francisco, Universal Studios, the Grand Canyon, Las Vegas, tours of Washington D.C., tours of New York City, and stop-overs in Hawaii.'

The enforcement action also involved allegations that Lucent:

- 'paid or offered to pay for educational opportunities for relatives or associates of Chinese government officials, some of whom were in a position to influence China's use of Lucent-compatible technologies';
- 'approved payments totaling over $71,000 to cover the tuition and living expenses of an employee of a Chinese government ministry, who was obtaining a master's degree in international management' when that employee was 'an assistant to a committee chairman at the ministry' and the 'committee was at least partially responsible

  for choosing which mobile telecommunications platform China would adopt';
- paid, upon the request of a 'foreign official,' approximately $22,000 so that the individual could obtain an MBA; and
- 'provided a paid internship to the daughter of a Chinese government official working at the Chinese embassy in the United States' because 'it [was] very important for Lucent to continue building a good relationship with the Chinese embassy, which has close ties to leaders in China when it comes to wireless standards and vendor selections.'[60]

Several corporate FCPA enforcement actions have also included allegations concerning items such as wine, specialty foods, jewelry and handbags, karaoke bars, and spa treatments. The irony of course is that providing such items to certain customers would likely be deemed effective sales and marketing. However, the take-away point from this section is that providing such items to other customers (i.e. 'foreign officials') is deemed to be bribery by the enforcement agencies.

H. OTHER RELEVANT LEGAL ISSUES

In addition to the specific elements of an FCPA anti-bribery violation as well as the statutory exception and affirmative defenses discussed above, there are certain other legal issues also relevant to FCPA enforcement in this new era, including statute of limitation issues. In this section, you will also learn how the FCPA is a supply-side statute targeting only one actor in a bribery scheme.

Statute of Limitations

Statute of limitations are a fundamental legal principle which establish a set period of time for an action to be brought after the conduct at issue occurred. In 2013, in *Gabelli v. SEC* (an SEC enforcement action outside the FCPA context) the Supreme Court stated:

> Statute of limitations are intended to 'promote justice by preventing surprises through the revival of claims that have been allowed to slumber until evidence has been lost, memories have faded, and witnesses have disappeared.' They provide 'security and stability to human affairs.' [They] are 'vital to the welfare of society' [and] 'even wrongdoers are entitled to assume that their sins may be forgotten.' [...] It would be utterly repugnant to the genius of our laws if actions for penalties could 'be brought at any distance of time.'[61]

The Supreme Court further stated that statute of limitations are even more important in a government enforcement action compared to a case brought by a private plaintiff.

> There are good reasons why the fraud discovery rule has not been extended to Government enforcement actions for civil penalties. [...] The SEC, for example, is not like an individual victim who relies on apparent injury to learn of a wrong. Rather, a central 'mission' of the Commission is to 'investigate potential violations of the federal securities laws.' Unlike the private party who has no reason to suspect fraud, the SEC's very purpose is to root it out, and it has many legal tools at hand to aid in that pursuit. [...] Charged with this mission and armed with these weapons, the SEC as enforcer is a far cry from the defrauded victim the discovery rule evolved to protect. In a civil penalty action, the Government is not only a different kind of plaintiff, it seeks a different kind of relief. The discovery rule helps to ensure that the injured receive recompense. But this case involves penalties, which go beyond compensation, and are intended to punish, and label defendants wrongdoers.

The FCPA does not have a specific statute of limitations. Rather the five-year 'catch-all' provisions in 18 USC § 3282 (for criminal actions) and 28 USC § 2462 (for civil actions) apply to FCPA enforcement actions.

Despite this general five-year limitations period, if you dig into the details of most corporate FCPA enforcement actions you quickly discover that the alleged conduct at issued occurred 5–7 years, 7–10 years, and in some instances, 10–15 years prior to the enforcement action.

For instance, in a 2012 enforcement action against pharmaceutical company Biomet the conduct at issue went back to 2000; in a 2012 enforcement action against pharmaceutical company Pfizer the conduct at issue went back to 1997; and in a 2012 enforcement action against trading and investment firm Marubeni the conduct at issue went back to 1995.[62] Likewise, in a 2013 enforcement action against oil and gas company Total, the conduct at issue went back to 1995.[63] So old was the conduct giving rise to the Total enforcement action that the DOJ made the unusual statement in the DPA that 'evidentiary challenges' were present for both parties given that 'most of the underlying conduct occurred in the 1990s and early 2000s.'

Why, despite the importance of statute of limitations to our legal system and Supreme Court recognition that it 'would be utterly repugnant to the genius of our laws if actions for penalties could be brought at any distance of time,' do most corporate FCPA enforcement actions concern conduct well beyond the statute of limitations?

Simply put, because in corporate FCPA enforcement actions the fundamental black-letter legal principle of statute of limitations seems not to matter. Granted, counsel for a company under FCPA scrutiny based on conduct beyond the limitations period can argue about statute of limitation defenses around conference room tables behind closed doors in Washington, D.C. However, like with other FCPA issues, to truly challenge the enforcement agencies first requires that the company be criminally or civilly charged, something few corporate leaders are willing to let happen.

In short, and as detailed in Chapter 2, cooperation is the name of the game in corporate FCPA inquiries and to raise bona fide legal arguments such as statute of limitations is not cooperating in an investigation. Given the 'carrots' and 'sticks' relevant to resolving corporate FCPA enforcement actions, one of the first steps a company the subject of FCPA scrutiny often does to demonstrate its cooperation is agree to toll the statute of limitations or waive any statute of limitations defenses.

A former DOJ enforcement attorney noted:

> As a practical matter, companies, especially publicly held companies [...], typically make a strategic decision to fully cooperate with a DOJ investigation. Despite the potential success of a statute of limitations defense, a company will often make the judgment that the negative press of a protracted investigation and the uncertainty of the outcome at trial make cooperation the more prudent business judgment. The company's hope is that it will be given credit for the cooperation and it will achieve a better outcome than if it went to trial (i.e., avoid charges, a DPA, or a reduced fine).[64]

Given this dynamic, the enforcement agencies face little or no time pressure in bringing corporate FCPA enforcement actions. The end result is that the gray cloud of FCPA scrutiny often hangs over a company far too long. For instance, Pfizer's FCPA scrutiny began in 2004 but was not resolved until a 2012 enforcement action. Likewise, Total's FCPA scrutiny began in 2003 but was not resolved until a 2013 enforcement action.

In addition to the enforcement agencies not facing any meaningful time pressure in bringing corporate FCPA enforcement actions, other reasons for the typical long periods of FCPA scrutiny can include: the 'where else' question discussed in greater detail in Chapter 5; DOJ and SEC enforcement actions tend to be announced on the same day and it is common for one agency to wait for the other agency to conclude its investigation and deliberation; and attrition at the enforcement agencies tends to be high and it is not uncommon for simple employee turnover to prolong enforcement agency FCPA investigations.

Regarding the typical long periods of corporate FCPA scrutiny, an FCPA commentator stated:

> [Companies under FCPA scrutiny are] routinely asked to waive the statute of limitations. They could refuse but none do; refusal might trigger an instant enforcement action against the company or its people. So the waiver gives the feds limitless time to investigate, deliberate, or procrastinate. And no one can force the DOJ or SEC to move on, either with an enforcement action or a declination. The result? Companies [under FCPA scrutiny] get stuck in FCPA limbo. [...] But the DOJ and SEC should always keep one eye on the calendar. The threat of FCPA enforcement [...] casts a long shadow. It darkens the future for management, shareholders, lenders, customers, and suppliers. Exactly the problem the statute of limitations was supposed to fix.[65]

Regardless of the above, there are certain legitimate ways in which statute of limitations may be extended in the FCPA context.

The FCPA Guidance states as follows concerning criminal enforcement actions:

> In cases involving FCPA conspiracies, the government may be able to reach conduct occurring before the five-year limitations period applicable to conspiracies under 18 U.S.C. § 371. For conspiracy offenses, the government generally need prove only that one act in furtherance of the conspiracy occurred during the limitations period, thus enabling the government to prosecute bribes paid or accounting violations occurring more than five years prior to the filing of formal charges.
>
> Under 18 U.S.C. § 3292, the government may seek a court order suspending the statute of limitations posed in a criminal case for up to three years in order to obtain evidence from foreign countries. Generally, the suspension period begins when the official request is made by the U.S. government to the foreign authority and ends on the date on which the foreign authority takes final action on the request.

As to civil enforcement actions, the FCPA Guidance states:

> The five-year limitations period applies to SEC actions seeking civil penalties, but it does not prevent the SEC from seeking equitable remedies, such as an injunction or the disgorgement of ill-gotten gains, for conduct pre-dating the five-year period. In cases against individuals who are not residents of the United States, the statute is tolled for any period when the defendants are not 'found within the United States in order that proper service may be made thereon.'

As with most legal issues regarding FCPA enforcement, none of these enforcement agency positions regarding statute of limitations have been tested in a corporate FCPA enforcement action.

In individual FCPA enforcement actions, the enforcement agencies have a mixed record when put to its burden of proof on statute of limitation issues. For instance, in the *U.S. v. Bourke* enforcement action previously discussed the court dismissed certain criminal charges against various individuals.[66] The DOJ argued that the statute of limitations should be extended under 18 U.S.C. § 3292 based on the government's requests for foreign evidence from the Netherlands and Switzerland. However, the court rejected this argument and noted that the government did not move to 'suspend the running' of the statute of limitations until after it had expired and it was thus not entitled to any tolling. In so holding, the court noted that 'this problem can easily be avoided – and easily could have been avoided in this case,' but that 'the government waited almost nine full months after making the official request to the Netherlands before applying for a section 3292 suspension.' According to the court, 'the mere fact that the government could have easily avoided this dismissal does not change the result here' and the court noted that 'statutes of limitations must be enforced, even where it deprives society of its ability to prosecute otherwise viable criminal offenses; "that is the price we pay for repose."'

Likewise in the *SEC v. Jackson* enforcement action previously discussed, the court dismissed without prejudice SEC civil FCPA charges seeking monetary damages filed against individuals in connection with an alleged bribery scheme in Nigeria. Among the reasons cited by the court was the SEC's failure to plead any facts to support an inference that it acted diligently in bringing the action.[67]

However, in *SEC v. Straub* the SEC's statute of limitations theory survived a pre-trial motion to dismiss in an FCPA enforcement action against various foreign national defendants. The action raised an issue of first impression under 28 USC § 2462 which states:

> Except as otherwise provided by Act of Congress, an action, suit or proceeding for the enforcement of any civil fine, penalty, or forfeiture, pecuniary or otherwise, shall not be entertained unless commenced from the date when the claim first accrued if, within the same period, the offender or the property is found within the United States in order that proper service be made thereon.

The court noted that it was 'undisputed that more than five years have elapsed since the SEC's claims first accrued.'[68] However, the parties disagreed as to the plain meaning of section 2642 given that the Hungarian national defendants were not physically located within the United States during the limitations period. The court stated:

> The SEC argues that the statute of limitations has not run because the statute applies only 'if within the same period, the offender … is found within the United States.' Thus, according to the SEC, because Defendants were not 'found' in this country at any point during the limitations period in question, the Court's inquiry should end. The Court agrees. […] Here, the operative language in § 2462 requires, by its plain terms, that an offender must be physically present in the United States for the statute of limitations to run. In arguing otherwise, Defendants essentially seek to amend the statute to run against a defendant if he is either 'found within the United States' or subject to service of process elsewhere by some alternative means. Such a reading would be a dramatic restatement of the statutory language and would render the clause 'if … found within the United States' mere surplusage. […] Additionally, reading the statute to require a defendant's physical presence in the United States is not inconsistent with § 2462's statement of purpose, as was originally understood.

Regarding the defendants' argument that the Hague Service Convention has facilitated the serving of foreign defendants not found in the U.S., the court seemed to understand the logic of the position, yet exhibited restraint in concluding:

> [This] does not change the fact that Congress has maintained the statutory carve out for defendants not found within the United States. Indeed, although the purpose underlying the carve-out may no longer be as compelling as it might have once been in light of the possibilities opened by worldwide service of process, it is not for this Court to second-guess Congress and amend the statute on its own. Accordingly, the Court finds that the statute of limitations within § 2462 has not run on the SEC's claims.

The take-away point from this section is that while statute of limitations is a fundamental legal principle, in many corporate FCPA enforcement actions this black-letter legal principle seems not to matter as many actions are based on conduct beyond any conceivable limitations period.

Supply-Side Statute

Just as with the tango, it takes two in a bribery scheme – the payer and the recipient. As detailed in Chapter 2, few FCPA enforcement actions result from companies doing business in foreign markets intent on engaging in bribery as a business strategy. Rather, most FCPA enforcement actions and instances of FCPA scrutiny result from difficult and challenging business conditions in foreign markets in which, in the words of the DOJ's former FCPA Unit chief 'companies who seek to do the right thing can't help but confront corrupt officials – as customers, regulators and adjudicators – and confront them often.'[69]

Debating which actor in a payment scheme is more morally culpable and most deserving of prosecution is a moot point however, as courts have held that the FCPA is a supply-side statute targeting only the payer, not the recipient, of the improper payment.

For instance, in *U.S. v. Castle*, the DOJ conceded and the court recognized that the FCPA did not criminalize the receipt of a bribe by a foreign official. However, the court addressed the issue of whether the DOJ could prosecute two Canadian 'foreign officials' for conspiring to violate the FCPA. Based on the language and legislative history of the FCPA, the court found a 'legislative policy to leave unpunished a well-defined group of persons [i.e., 'foreign officials'] who were necessary parties to the acts constituting a violation of the substantive law.' Accordingly, the court held that the 'foreign officials' could not be prosecuted for conspiring to violate the FCPA and dismissed the criminal indictment against them.[70]

Nevertheless, in this new era the DOJ has used other criminal laws to charge certain 'foreign official' bribe recipients in connection with an FCPA enforcement action. For instance the DOJ charged, in the context of an FCPA enforcement action, alleged Haitian 'foreign officials' with money laundering conspiracy and substantive money laundering charges based on allegations that U.S. bank accounts owned by the 'foreign officials' were used in connection with the bribery scheme.[71] Likewise the DOJ charged, in the context of an FCPA enforcement action, alleged Thai 'foreign officials' with similar charges based on allegations that the individual FCPA defendants arranged for cash payments to be made to the 'foreign officials' during trips to the U.S.[72] The above charges followed an Attorney General speech to a global forum during which he announced a 'redoubled commitment on behalf of the DOJ to recover' funds obtained by foreign officials through bribery.[73] Pursuant to this commitment, the DOJ has established a Kleptocracy Asset Recovery Initiative under which prosecutors in the DOJ Asset Forfeiture and Money Laundering Section work in partnership with federal law enforcement agencies to forfeit the proceeds of foreign official corruption.

NOTES

1. 923 F.2d 1308 (8th Cir. 1991).
2. SEC v. Ashland Oil, Inc., Case 86-1904 (D.D.C. July 8, 1986).
3. Indictment, U.S. v. Warwick, Case 3:09-cr-00449-HEH (E.D. Va., Dec. 15, 2009).
4. Complaint, SEC v. Schering-Plough Corp., Case 1: O4-cv-0945 (D.D.C. June 9, 2004); Complaint, SEC v. Eli Lilly and Company Case 1:12-cv-02045 (D.D.C. Dec. 20, 2012).

5. Letter from Steven A. Tyrell, Chief, Fraud Section, U.S. Dep't of Justice (Criminal Div.), to Saul Pilchen, Attorney for Paradigm B.V. (Sept. 21, 2007).
6. The Activities of American Multinational Corporations Abroad: Hearings before the Subcomm. on Int'l Econ. Policy of the H. Comm. on Int'l Relations, 94th Cong. (1975); Foreign and Corporate Bribes: Hearings before the S. Comm. on Banking, Housing, and Urban Affairs, 94th Cong. (1976).
7. See Declaration of Professor Michael J. Koehler in Support of Defendants' Motion to Dismiss Counts One Through Ten of the Indictment, U.S. v. Carson, No. SACR 09-0007-JVS (C.D. Cal. Feb. 21, 2011).
8. Id.
9. Id.
10. 2011 WL 5101701 (C.D. Cal. 2011).
11. Trial Tr. 227:19–23, U.S. v. O'Shea, No. 09-629 (S.D. Tex. Jan. 16, 2012).
12. 908 F.Supp.2d 834 (S.D. Tex. 2012).
13. 2013 WL 466600 (S.D.N.Y. 2013).
14. Order Re: Select Jury Instructions, U.S. v. Carson, No. SACR 09-0007-JVS (C.D. Cal. Feb. 16, 2012).
15. SEC, 17 CFR Parts 240 and 249, Release No. 34-67717; File No. S7-42-10.
16. H.R. Rep. No. 95-831 (1977).
17. 200 F.Supp.2d 681 (S.D.Tex. 2002).
18. Memorandum and Order, SEC v. Eric Mattson et al., Case 4:01-cv-03106 (S.D.Tex. Sept. 9, 2002).
19. 359 F.3d 738 (5th Cir. 2004).
20. 513 F.3d 432 (5th Cir. 2007).
21. H.R. Rep. No. 95-640 (1977).
22. S. Rep. No. 95-114 (1977).
23. H.R. Rep. No. 95-640 (1977).
24. 327 F.3d 173 (2d Cir. 2003).
25. 513 F.3d 432 (5th Cir. 2007).
26. Kroll/Compliance Week, Anti-Bribery and Corruption Benchmarking Report (2013).
27. S. Rep. No. 100-85 (1987).
28. H.R. Rep. No. 100-40 (1987).
29. 667 F.3d 122 (2d Cir. 2011).
30. Complaint, SEC v. Eli Lilly and Co., No. 1:12-cv-02045 (D.D.C., Dec. 20, 2012).
31. Deferred Prosecution Agreement, U.S. v. Data Systems & Solutions LLC, Case 1:12-cr-00262-LO, (E.D.Va., June 18, 12).
32. S. Rep. No. 105-277 (1998).
33. H.R. Rep. No. 105-802 (1998).
34. S. Rep. No. 105-277 (1998); H.R. Rep. No. 105-802 (1998).
35. Deferred Prosecution Agreement, U.S. v. JGC Corp., Case 4:11-cr-00260 (S.D.Tex. April 6, 2011).
36. FCPA Professor, 'Significant dd-3 Development in Africa Sting Case,' (June 9, 2011).
37. 2013 WL 466600 (S.D.N.Y. 2013).
38. 2013 WL 603135 (S.D.N.Y. 2013).
39. Press Release, U.S. Dep't of Justice, 'U.S. Resolves Probe Against Oil Company That Bribed Iranian Official,' (Oct. 13, 2006).
40. 'Examining Enforcement of the Foreign Corrupt Practices Act, Hearing before the Subcommittee on Crime and Drugs of the Committee on the Judiciary,' Senate (Nov. 30, 2010).
41. S. Rep. No. 94-1031 (1976).
42. H.R. Rep. No. 95-640 (1977).
43. H.R. Rep. No. 100-40 (1987).
44. 908 F.Supp.2d 834 (S.D. Tex. 2012).

45. Letter from Dennis McInerney, Chief, Fraud Section, U.S. Dep't of Justice (Criminal Div.), to Mary Spearing, Attorney for Noble Corp. (Nov. 4, 2010).
46. Press Release, U.S. Dep't of Justice, 'Oil Services Companies and a Freight Forwarding Company Agree to Resolve Foreign Bribery Investigations and to Pay More Than $156 Million in Criminal Penalties,' (Nov. 4, 2010).
47. Richard Grime and Sara Zdeb, 'The Illusory Facilitating Payments Exception: Risks Posed By Ongoing FCPA Enforcement Actions and the U.K. Bribery Act,' (2011).
48. Jon Jordan, 'The OECD'S Call for an End to "Corrosive" Facilitation Payments and the International Focus on the Facilitation Payments Exception under the Foreign Corrupt Practices Act,' 13 Univ. of Pennsylvania Journal of Business Law 881 (2011).
49. S. Rep. No. 100-85 (1987).
50. H.R. Rep. No. 100-40 (1987).
51. 582 F.Supp.2d 535 (S.D.N.Y. 2008).
52. Joseph Warin, Michael Diamant, and Jill Pfenning, 'FCPA Compliance in China and the Gifts and Hospitality Challenge,' 5 Virginia Law and Business Review 33 (2010).
53. FCPA Professor, 'Can We Make the Expenditure in the First Place? Practical Advice for Navigating Gift, Travel and Entertainment Issues' (May 22, 2013).
54. S. Rep. No. 100-85 (1987).
55. H.R. Rep. No. 100-40 (1987).
56. 923 F.2d 1308 (8th Cir. 1991).
57. Letter from Steven Tyrrell, Chief, Fraud Section, U.S. Dep't of Justice (Criminal Div.), to Leo Cunningham, Attorney for UTStarcom, Inc. (Dec. 31, 2009).
58. Complaint, SEC v. UTStarcom, Inc., Case No. 09-cv-6094 (N.D. Cal., Dec. 31, 2009).
59. Letter from Steven Tyrrell, Chief, Fraud Section, U.S. Dep't of Justice (Criminal Div.), to Martin Weinstein, Attorney for Lucent Technologies Inc. (Nov. 14, 2007).
60. Complaint, SEC v. Lucent Technologies, Inc., Case No. 1:07-cv-02301 (D.D.C., Dec. 21, 2007).
61. 133 S.Ct. 1216 (2013),
62. FCPA Professor, 'Next Up – Biomet' (Mar. 27, 2012); FCPA Professor, 'Next Up – Pfizer' (Aug. 8, 2012); FCPA Professor, 'U.S. Bonny Island Bribery Bounty Grows,' (Jan. 19, 2012), containing links to original source documents.
63. FCPA Professor, '"Total"ly Milking the FCPA Cash Cow?' (June 3, 2013), containing links to original source documents.
64. Breon Peace, Ryan Becker and Elizabeth Hanley, Bloomberg Law, 'The FCPA Statute of Limitations – A Way Out for Wal-Mart?' (2012).
65. Richard Cassin, FCPA Blog, 'The FCPA's Long Shadow' (Aug. 6, 2012).
66. See 493 F.Supp.2d 693 (S.D.N.Y. 2007), affirmed 541 F.3d 166 (2d Cir. 2008).
67. 908 F.Supp.2d 834 (S.D. Tex. 2012).
68. 2013 WL 466600 (S.D.N.Y. 2013).
69. FCPA Professor, 'Former DOJ FCPA Chief Supports FCPA Compliance Defense' (Oct. 4, 2011).
70. 925 F.2d 831 (5th Cir. 1991).
71. FCPA Professor, 'Indicting a "Foreign Official"' (Dec. 8, 2009), containing links to original source documents.
72. FCPA Professor, 'Indicting a "Foreign Official" – Part II' (Jan. 21, 2010).
73. Press Release, U.S. Dep't of Justice, 'Attorney General Eric Holder at the Opening Plenary of the VI Ministerial Global Forum on Fighting Corruption and Safeguarding Integrity' (Nov. 7, 2009).

4. The FCPA's books and records and internal controls provisions

The FCPA has always been a law much broader than its name suggests. The anti-bribery provisions that were the focus of Chapter 3 are just one prong of the FCPA. Indeed, most FCPA enforcement actions do not involve *foreign* bribery.

A DOJ enforcement action against FalconStor Software is an example.[1] In the enforcement action, the DOJ alleged that the company conspired to pay bribes to U.S. bank executives to obtain lucrative electronic storage licensing contracts. FalconStor was also charged with conspiring to falsify its corporate books and records to cover up the bribery scheme. According to the DOJ, the bribes, including the grants of the stock options and restricted shares, were recognized in FalconStor's books and records, but were falsely recorded as 'compensation to an advisor' or as 'employment bonuses.' An SEC enforcement action against Gold Standard Mining is another example of an FCPA enforcement action not involving foreign *bribery*.[2] In the enforcement action, the SEC alleged that the company filed numerous reports about its purported Russian gold mining operations that were materially false and misleading. Among other things, the SEC alleged that the company: failed to devise and maintain a system of internal accounting controls; did not have a means to verify the amount of gold produced; did not have a means to determine the costs of producing the gold that was sold; and did not maintain records of inventory.

The above actions are 'non-FCPA FCPA enforcement actions' in that FCPA books and records and internal controls violations were among the statutory provisions charged even though the conduct at issue did not involve foreign bribery. Since the FCPA's enactment in 1977, there have been approximately 1,200 'non-FCPA FCPA enforcement actions.'[3] Thus, the first take-away point from this chapter is that the FCPA's books and records and internal controls provisions are among the most generic substantive legal provisions applicable to issuers.

The provisions generally provide that issuers shall: (i) maintain books and records which, in reasonable detail, accurately and fairly reflect issuer transactions and disposition of assets (the books and records provisions); and (ii) devise and maintain a system of internal accounting controls sufficient to provide reasonable assurances that transactions are properly authorized, recorded, and accounted for by the issuer (the internal controls provisions). The book and records and internal controls provisions are typically enforced civilly by the SEC. However, the FCPA also provides for criminal liability for 'knowingly' circumventing or failing to implement a system of internal controls as well as 'knowingly' falsifying any book, record, or account.

The books and records and internal controls provisions are further supplemented by SEC rules which generally provide that: (i) no person shall falsify or cause to be falsified, any book, record or account subject to the books and records provisions; and (ii) no director or officer of an issuer shall make or cause to be made a materially false or misleading statement to an accountant in connection with any audit, review or examination of the issuer's financial statements or the preparation or filing of any document or report required to be filed with the SEC.

Although allegations of foreign bribery are not necessary for the FCPA's books and records and internal controls provisions to be charged, the provisions are nearly always charged in issuer FCPA anti-bribery violations. The enforcement theory giving rise to book and records and internal controls charges in nearly every instance of issuer anti-bribery charges is that the alleged improper payments were misrecorded on company books and records. As to the internal controls provisions, the enforcement theory is that insufficient internal controls allowed the improper payments to occur.

While a dull read, the FCPA's books and records and internal controls provisions are potent particularly because they operate independently of the FCPA's anti-bribery provisions and can be charged even if all the elements of an FCPA anti-bribery violation are not met.

In this chapter you will learn that Congress intended for the FCPA's more glamorous anti-bribery provisions to operate in tandem with these generic provisions to reduce instances of corporate bribery. The chapter begins with a brief discussion of relevant legislative history which instructs that the books and records and internal controls provisions were intended to have a broad scope. However, the legislative history also instructs that Congress specifically qualified the provisions through concepts of reasonableness and good faith.

Against the backdrop of generic statutory language, this chapter next details legal authority and enforcement agency guidance concerning the books and records and internal controls provisions. From there, enforcement agency theories are introduced through actual FCPA enforcement actions and the question is posed whether certain theories are in fact consistent with relevant legal authority or even enforcement agency guidance.

A. LEGAL AUTHORITY

This section highlights the following legal authority concerning the books and records and internal controls provisions: legislative history, statutory text, and a judicial decision.

Legislative History and Statutory Text

During Congress's investigation and consideration of the foreign corporate payments problem discussed in Chapter 1, Congressional leaders were surprised to learn that existing corporate record-keeping and internal controls requirements were deficient in preventing the discovered payments. The following exchange between Senator Proxmire and SEC officials is instructive.

> *Senator Proxmire*: 'You stress the fact that in all nine of the SEC cases the corporate abuses were accompanied by false or inadequate corporate books and records and that most of the cases involved illegal or improper domestic and foreign payments. Does such falsification of corporate books and records constitute a violation of SEC's laws or regulations and do they constitute criminal violations?'
>
> *SEC Officials*: 'I can't say in all cases. There is no provision that prohibits just what you stated. There is no provision that provides, with respect to the kinds of companies we are talking about, that that could be a violation of law.'
>
> *Senator Proxmire*: 'Well, then, it would seem to me that maybe we ought to consider … making it a violation of the law.'[4]

Although the SEC wanted no part in enforcing what would become the FCPA's anti-bribery provisions, the SEC insisted that whatever legislation Congress deemed best to prevent future payments be supplemented by books and records and internal controls provisions.

The 1976 SEC Report stated:

> We believe that any legislation in this area should embody a prohibition against the falsification of corporate accounting records. The most devastating disclosure that we have uncovered in our recent experience with illegal or questionable payments has been the fact that, and the extent to which, some companies have falsified entries in their own books and records. […] We

> believe that any legislation in this area should also contain a prohibition against the making of false and misleading statements by corporate officials or agents to those persons conducting audits of the company's books and records and financial operations. Finally, we believe that any legislation should require management to establish and maintain its own system of internal accounting controls designed to provide reasonable assurances that corporate transactions are executed in accordance with management's general or specific authorization; and that such transactions as are authorized are properly reflected on the corporation's books and records in such a manner as to permit the preparation of financial statements in conformity with generally accepted accounting principles or any other criteria applicable to such statements.[5]

The SEC Report proposed legislation which embodied the following goals:

> (1) require issuers to make and keep accurate books and records; (2) require issuers to devise and maintain a system of internal accounting controls [...]; (3) prohibit the falsification of corporate accounting records; and (4) prohibit the making of false, misleading, or incomplete statements to an accountant in connection with an examination or audit.[6]

The goal of the books and records and internal controls provisions were thus to make explicit what was merely implicit in the existing securities laws prior to the FCPA's enactment. For instance, a Senate Report stated:

> While the Committee believes that the requirement that issuers maintain books, records, and accounts that accurately and fairly reflect the transactions and dispositions of the assets of the issuer is implicit in the existing securities laws, the Committee believes that such a basic requirement should be explicit.
>
> The committee recognizes that the SEC has broad authority to promulgate accounting standards for companies subject to jurisdiction under its existing authority. Nevertheless, the committee believes the Commission's current program for accurate accounting should be supplemented by an explicit statement of statutory policy. The accounting standards [...] are intended to operate in tandem with the criminalization provisions of the bill to deter corporate bribery [and express] a public policy which encompasses a unified approach to the matter of corporate bribery. This legislation imposes affirmative requirements on issuers to maintain books and records which accurately and fairly reflect the transactions of the corporation and to design an adequate system of internal controls to assure, among other things, that the assets of the issuer are used for proper corporate purposes. The committee believes that the imposition of these affirmative duties under our securities laws coupled with attendant civil liability and criminal penalties for failure to comply with the statutory standard will go a long way to prevent the use of corporate assets for corrupt purposes. Public confidence in the securities markets will be enhanced by assurance that corporate recordkeeping is honest.[7]

Similarly, the SEC Chairman stated during Senate testimony:

> I admit that it [the books and records and internal controls provisions] makes for dull reading, but these proposals will provide the teeth to assure that problems of this nature are brought to appropriate levels of corporate management and recorded in a manner that makes it far easier for us to discover them.[8]

Indeed, Senator Proxmire viewed such books and records and internal controls provisions as 'strengthening the SEC's ability to combat payment of bribes by American corporations overseas.'[9] A 1976 Senate Report likewise stated:

> The Committee expects that the requirement to maintain accurate books, records and management controls and the prohibition against falsifying such records or deceiving an auditor, will go a long way towards eliminating improper payments, which – almost by definition – require concealment. Taken in combination with the criminal prohibition against bribery, the accounting provisions should be adequate to the task of deterring corrupt payments even where transgressors take steps to evade the intent of the law.[10]

While the FCPA's books and records and internal controls provisions do indeed make for dull reading, the provisions are much broader in scope than the FCPA's anti-bribery provisions. Even with the enforcement agencies' aggressive and broad anti-bribery theories discussed in Chapter 3, the anti-bribery provisions are nevertheless narrowed by elements such as corrupt intent, 'foreign official' and 'obtain or retain business.' The FCPA's books and records and internal controls provisions have no such similar limitations and do not explicitly contain an intent requirement or materiality threshold.

Even so, Congress intended for the books and records and internal controls provisions to be qualified by concepts of reasonableness and good faith. This intent is best evidenced by a 1977 Senate Report which stated:

> The establishment and maintenance of a system of internal controls and accurate books and records are fundamental responsibilities of management. The expected benefits to be derived from the conscientious discharge of these responsibilities are of basic importance to investors and the maintenance of the integrity of our capital market system. The committee recognizes, however, that management must exercise judgment in determining the steps to be taken, and the cost incurred, in giving assurance that the objectives expressed will be achieved. Here, standards of reasonableness must apply. In this regard, the term 'accurately' does not mean exact precision as measured by some abstract principle. Rather it means that an issuer's records should

> reflect transactions in conformity with generally accepted accounting principles or other applicable criteria. While management should observe every reasonable prudence in satisfying the objections called for [in the books and records and internal controls provisions] the committee recognizes that management must necessarily estimate and evaluate the cost/benefit relationships to the steps to be taken in fulfillment of its responsibilities ... The size of the business, diversity of operations, degree of centralization of financial and operating management, amount of contact by top management with day-to-day operations, and numerous other circumstances are factors which management must consider in establishing and maintaining an internal accounting controls system.[11]

A 1977 House Conference Report likewise stated concerning the 'in reasonable detail' requirement of the books and records provisions: 'The conference committee adopted the "in reasonable detail" qualification to the accurate and fair requirement in light of the concern that such a standard, if unqualified, might connote a degree of exactitude and precision which is unrealistic.'[12]

In 1988, the FCPA's books and records and internal controls provisions were amended specifically as to an issuer's responsibility for the books and records and internal controls of minority subsidiaries, an important issue in this new era given that issuers often operate in foreign markets through subsidiaries or other indirect relationships.

The relevant provision added to the FCPA generally states, as to issuers which hold 50% or less of the voting power with respect to a firm, that the books and records and internal controls provisions:

> require only that the issuer proceed in good faith to use its influence, to the extent reasonable under the issuer's circumstances, to cause such [firm] to devise and maintain a system of internal accounting controls consistent [with the books and records and internal controls provisions]. Such circumstances include the relative degree of the issuer's ownership of the [firm] and the laws and practices governing the business operations of the country in which such firm is located. An issuer which demonstrates good faith efforts to use such influence shall be conclusively presumed to have complied with the requirements [of the books and records and internal controls provisions].'

As to the above provision, a 1988 House Conference Report stated:

> [The provision] recognizes that it is unrealistic to expect a minority owner to exert a disproportionate degree of influence over the accounting practices of a subsidiary. The amount of influence which an issuer may exercise necessarily varies from case to case. While the relative degree of ownership is obviously one factor, other factors may also be important in determining whether an issuer has demonstrated good-faith efforts to use its influence.[13]

The FCPA's books and records and internal controls provisions were further amended in 1988 by defining the terms 'reasonable assurance' and 'reasonable detail' to mean such level of detail and degree of assurance as would satisfy prudent officials in the conduct of their own affairs. Legislative history states as follows: 'The prudent man qualification [was adopted] in order to clarify that the current standard does not connote an unrealistic degree of exactitude or precision. The concept of reasonableness of necessity contemplates the weighing of a number of relevant factors, including the costs of compliance.'[14]

In short, while Congress intended for the FCPA's books and records and internal controls provisions to have broad scope and to operate in tandem with the anti-bribery provisions to reduce instances of corporate bribery, it is important to understand that the provisions are specifically qualified, as a matter of law and consistent with congressional intent, through concepts of reasonableness and good faith. These qualifications are best demonstrated through Figure 4.1, a word cloud (a graphical representation of word frequency in a source text) of FCPA's books and records and internal controls provisions.

Figure 4.1 Word frequency of FCPA's books and records and internal controls provisions

Source: author

Judicial Authority

In addition to statutory text and legislative history, judicial decisions are also another form of legal authority concerning the FCPA's books and records and internal controls provisions.

Notwithstanding the broad scope of the FCPA's books and records and internal controls provisions, there is only one judicial decision directly addressing the substance of these provisions. In many respects, this lack of case law is a function of the dynamics of resolving an FCPA enforcement action discussed in Chapter 2.

The one judicial decision that directly addresses the substance of the FCPA's books and records and internal controls provisions is *SEC v. World-Wide Coin Investments.*[15] Because it is the only directly on-point judicial decision concerning these provisions, it is highlighted below in detail.

Factually, *World-Wide Coin* was an egregious case and the FCPA issues addressed were not difficult for the judge in ruling on the SEC's request for a permanent injunction prohibiting future FCPA books and records and internal controls violations. Like many enforcement actions involving these provisions, *World-Wide Coin* was a 'non-FCPA FCPA enforcement action' in that the case had nothing to do with foreign bribery. Instead, the case involved a wide-ranging securities fraud involving World-Wide Coin, a business engaged primarily in the wholesale and retail sale of rare coins.

As the judge stated:

> The deterioration of World-Wide's internal controls and accounting procedures constituted the primary thrust of the SEC's complaint. The SEC contended that the combination of late filings, lack of internal controls, transactions unsupported by adequate documentation, and a total disregard for proper accounting procedures resulted in the precarious position of the company. [...] The company's accounting books were virtually ignored. General ledgers and general journals were not kept, and the checks written on World-Wide's five checking accounts were not reconciled.

The judge described the bookkeeper hired by the company as follows. '[She] was not a high school graduate; her only experience for this position consisted of five months of vocational school training and seven years of bookkeeping for a privately-held lumber company.' The judge's findings of fact further highlighted how the accounting firm retained by the company as an independent auditor wrote a letter to the company 'expressing grave concern over certain accounting procedures and lack of internal controls that [it] considered to be detrimental to the company.'

The judge stated:

> This letter [notified] World-Wide of its deficiencies in its internal accounting controls ... Yet, even with this official notice that improvements were needed, Hale [the company's Chairman of the Board, CEO, and President] and Seibert [a board member of the company and one-man audit committee] did nothing to remedy the situation, and the criticisms of [it] were virtually ignored. [...] The company's problems increased [...] mostly resulting from its chaotic bookkeeping practices and total disregard for an adequate internal control system.

The opinion goes into great detail concerning the 'problems that occurred at the company with respect to internal controls and accounting procedures' such as: '(1) inventory problems; (2) problems with separation of duties and the lack of documentation of transactions; and (3) problems with the books, records, and accounting procedures of the company.'

Turning to application of the law to the facts, the judge called the FCPA's books and records and internal controls provisions 'short and deceptively straight-forward' and stated in detail as follows:

> The only express congressional requirement for accuracy is the phrase 'in reasonable detail.' Although [the books and records provisions] expect management to see that the corporation's recordkeeping system is adequate and effectively implemented, how the issuer goes about this task is up to management; the FCPA provides no guidance, and this court cannot issue any kind of advisory opinion. Just as the degree of error is not relevant to an issuer's responsibility for any inaccuracies, the motivations of those who erred are not relevant. There are no words in [the books and records provisions] indicating that Congress intended to impose a scienter requirement … .
>
> Like the recordkeeping provisions of the Act, the internal controls provision is not limited to material transactions or to those above a specific dollar amount. While this requirement is supportive of accuracy and reliability in the auditor's review and financial disclosure process, this provision should not be analyzed solely from that point of view. The internal controls requirement is primarily designed to give statutory content to an aspect of management stewardship responsibility, that of providing shareholders with reasonable assurances that the business is adequately controlled.
>
> Internal accounting control is, generally speaking, only one aspect of a company's total control system; in order to maintain accountability for the disposition of its assets, a business must attempt to make it difficult for its assets to be misappropriated. The internal accounting controls element of a company's control system is that which is specifically designed to provide reasonable, cost-effective safeguards against the unauthorized use or disposition of company assets and reasonable assurances that financial records and accounts are sufficiently reliable for purposes of external reporting. […] Internal accounting controls must be distinguished from the accounting system typically found in a company. Accounting systems process transactions and recognize, calculate, classify, post, summarize, and report transactions. Internal controls safeguard assets and assure the reliability of financial records, one of their main jobs being to prevent and detect errors and irregularities that arise in the accounting systems of the company. Internal accounting controls are basic indicators of the reliability of the financial statements and the accounting system and records from which financial statements are prepared.
>
> Among the factors that determine the internal accounting control environment of a company are its organizational structure, including the competence of personnel, the degree and manner of delegation and responsibility, the

quality of internal budgets and financial reports, and the checks and balances that separate incompatible activities. The efficiency of the internal control system of a company cannot be evaluated without considering the company's organizational structure, the caliber of its employees, the strength of its audit committee, the effectiveness of its internal audit operation, and a host of other factors which, while not part of the internal control system itself, have an impact on the function of the system.

Although not specifically delineated in the Act itself, the following directives can be inferred from the internal controls provisions: (1) Every company should have reliable personnel … and all should be supervised. (2) Account functions should be segregated and procedures designed to prevent errors or irregularities. The major functions of recordkeeping, custodianship, authorization, and operation should be performed by different people to avoid the temptation for abuse of these incompatible functions. (3) Reasonable assurances should be maintained that transactions are executed as authorized. (4) Transactions should be properly recorded in the firm's accounting records to facilitate control, which would also require standardized procedures for making accounting entries. Exceptional entries should be investigated regularly. (5) Access to assets of the company should be limited to authorized personnel. (6) At reasonable intervals, there should be a comparison of the accounting records with the actual inventory of assets, which would usually involve the physical taking of inventory, the counting of cash, and the reconciliation of accounting records with the actual physical assets. Frequency of these comparisons will usually depend on the cost of the process and upon the materiality of the assets involved.

The main problem with the internal accounting controls provision of the FCPA is that there are no specific standards by which to evaluate the sufficiency of controls; any evaluation is inevitably a highly subjective process in which knowledgeable individuals can arrive at totally different conclusions. Any ruling by a court with respect to the applicability of both the accounting provisions and the internal accounting control provisions should be strictly limited to the facts of each case.

The judge then summarized the defendants' arguments as follows.

The defendants in the instant case contend that the SEC has misconstrued the provisions of the FCPA relating to a knowledge requirement, contending that the SEC must show scienter. The defendants further state that the SEC does not allege a knowing attempt to circumvent for an improper purpose an internal control system required by law and that the complaint ignores all considerations of the costs and benefits of internal accounting controls and seeks to require World-Wide to maintain a system of controls that would destroy the company.

The judge then stated:

> The definition of accounting controls does comprehend reasonable, but not absolute, assurances that the objectives expressed in it will be accomplished by the system. The concept of 'reasonable assurances' contained in [the internal controls provisions] recognizes that the costs of internal controls should not exceed the benefits expected to be derived. It does not appear that either the SEC or Congress, which adopted the SEC's recommendations, intended that the statute should require that each affected issuer install a fail-safe accounting control system at all costs. It appears that Congress was fully cognizant of the cost-effective considerations which confront companies as they consider the institution of accounting controls and of the subjective elements which may lead reasonable individuals to arrive at different conclusions. Congress has demanded only that judgment be exercised in applying the standard of reasonableness. The size of the business, diversity of operations, degree of centralization of financial and operating management, amount of contact by top management with day-to-day operations, and numerous other circumstances are factors which management must consider in establishing and maintaining an internal accounting controls system. However, an issuer would probably not be successful in arguing a cost-benefit defense in circumstances where the management, despite warnings by its auditors or significant weaknesses of its accounting control system, had decided, after a cost benefit analysis, not to strengthen them, and then the internal accounting controls proved to be so inadequate that the company was virtually destroyed. It is also true that the internal accounting controls provisions contemplate the financial principle of proportionality – what is material to a small company is not necessarily material to a large company.

The judge concluded his decision as follows.

> This court has already declined to adopt the defense offered by the defendants that the accounting controls provisions of the FCPA require a scienter requirement. The remainder of World-Wide's defense appears to be that such a small operation should not be required to maintain an elaborate and sophisticated internal control system, since the costs of implementing and maintaining it would financially destroy the company. It is true that a cost/benefit analysis is particularly relevant here, but it remains undisputed that it was the lack of any control over the inventory and inadequate accounting procedures that primarily contributed to World-Wide's demise. No organization, no matter how small, should ignore the provisions of the FCPA completely, as World-Wide did.
>
> […]
>
> Individually, the acts of the defendants do not appear so egregious as to warrant the full panoply of relief requested by the SEC nor to impose complete liability under the FCPA. However, the court cannot ignore the all-pervasive effect of the combined failure to act, failure to keep accurate records, failure to maintain any type of inventory control, material omissions and misrepresentations, and other activities which caused World-Wide to

> decrease from a company of 40 employees and assets over $2,000,000 to a company of only three employees and assets of less than $500,000. It is evident that World-Wide, Hale, and Seibert violated all provisions contained [in the books and records and internal controls provisions] and the SEC's rules promulgated thereunder.

As evident from the *World-Wide Coin* decision, the conduct at issue was egregious and factually it was not difficult for the judge to find violations of the FCPA's books and records and internal control provisions.

Nevertheless, the key language from *World-Wide Coin*, the only judicial decision that directly addresses the substance of the FCPA's books and records and internal control provisions, is fully consistent with congressional intent in enacting the provisions in that the decision states:

> The definition of accounting controls does comprehend reasonable, but not absolute, assurances that the objectives expressed in it will be accomplished by the system. The concept of 'reasonable assurances' contained in [the internal control provisions] recognizes that the costs of internal controls should not exceed the benefits expected to be derived. It does not appear that either the SEC or Congress, which adopted the SEC's recommendations, intended that the statute should require that each affected issuer install a fail-safe accounting control system at all costs. It appears that Congress was fully cognizant of the cost-effective considerations which confront companies as they consider the institution of accounting controls and of the subjective elements which may lead reasonable individuals to arrive at different conclusions. Congress has demanded only that judgment be exercised in applying the standard of reasonableness. [...] It is also true that the internal accounting controls provisions contemplate the financial principle of proportionality – what is material to a small company is not necessarily material to a large company.

Consistent with the *World-Wide Coin* holding, various courts have held (in the context of civil derivative actions in which shareholders seek to hold company directors liable for breach of fiduciary duties due to the company's alleged FCPA violations), that just because improper conduct allegedly occurred does not mean that internal controls must have been deficient.[16]

As you read certain of the FCPA enforcement actions discussed below, you can analyze whether the allegations giving rise to books and records and internal controls charges were consistent with the above legal authority.

B. NON-LEGAL SOURCES OF INFORMATION

The above sections highlighted legal authority regarding the FCPA's books and records and internal controls provisions. In addition to this legal authority, the SEC and DOJ have also issued formal guidance concerning these provisions. As explained in Chapter 2, while enforcement agency guidance lacks legal effect and is thus non-binding, such guidance remains relevant to those subject to the FCPA for the simple reason that the enforcement agencies enforce the law. In Chapter 2 reference was made to the 2012 FCPA Guidance issued by the DOJ and SEC. While the FCPA Guidance as to the books and records and internal controls provisions is discussed below, this section proceeds in chronological order beginning with SEC guidance soon after the FCPA was enacted.

1979 SEC Guidance

Soon after the FCPA was enacted in 1977, the SEC adopted rules in 1979 to supplement the FCPA's books and records and internal control provisions. In promulgating the rules, the SEC received numerous comments that 'false entries of insignificant or nominal amounts would give rise to a violation' and that 'in view of the large number of books, records and accounts kept by some corporations, particularly large corporations, application of the [provisions] to any falsification of such books, records and accounts would make compliance impossible.'[17]

The SEC responded to these concerns by referencing congressional intent, specifically that the provisions were 'qualified' by Congress to make clear that issuers are required to 'make and keep books, records and accounts, which *in reasonable detail*, accurately and fairly reflect the transactions and dispositions of the assets of the issuer.'[18] The SEC concluded that the 'presence of the words "in reasonable detail" in [the books and records provisions] should alleviate much of the concern expressed in comments …'. In addition, the SEC concluded that concerns expressed 'with respect to inadvertent and inconsequential errors is unwarranted' because the FCPA 'does not require perfection but only that books, records and accounts "*in reasonable detail*" accurately and fairly reflect the transactions and dispositions of the assets of the issuer.' The SEC further stated that 'the legislative history reflects that "standards of reasonableness" are to be used in applying the provisions.'

1981 SEC Guidance

In 1981, the SEC issued additional formal guidance concerning the FCPA's books and records and internal controls provisions. The guidance was in the form of a speech given by the SEC Chairman that was thereafter adopted as a formal statement of SEC policy.[19] Because this guidance is more extensive than the 2012 FCPA Guidance, it is highlighted below in detail.

The SEC Chairman began his remarks as follows:

> When viewed from an abstract perspective, the Act's accounting provisions seem merely to codify a basic and uncontroversial management principle: no enterprise of any size can operate successfully without maintaining effective controls over its transactions and the disposition of its assets. Perhaps in part because these provisions were considered truisms, the Act was passed without Congressional dissent. However, practical experience with new legislation – even a law thought to be noncontroversial – often will reveal unanticipated problems. Newly enacted standards, for example, may be subject to differing constructions or raise compliance difficulties and ambiguities unforeseen by their draftsmen. And, until these problems are resolved by an agency, the courts or the Congress, those who are subject to these laws are often faced, unfortunately, with some disquieting circumstances. The anxieties created by the FCPA – among men and women of utmost good faith – have been, in my experience without equal.

The Chairman noted that 'such uncertainty can have a debilitating effect on the activities of those who seek to comply with the law' and stated:

> My sense is that, as a consequence, many businesses have been very cautious – sometimes overly so – in assuring at least technical compliance with the Act. And, therefore, business resources may have been diverted from more productive uses to overly-burdensome compliance systems which extend beyond the requirements of sound management or the policies embodied in the Act. The public, of course, is not well served by such reactions.

As to the FCPA's books and records provisions, the Chairman stated:

> This provision is intimately related to the requirement for a system of internal accounting controls, and we believe that records which are not relevant to accomplishing the objectives specified in the statute for the system of internal controls are not within the purview of the recordkeeping provision. […] Nor could a company be enjoined for a falsification of which its management, broadly defined, was not aware and reasonably should not have known.

As to the FCPA's internal controls provisions, the Chairman stated:

> The Act does not mandate any particular kind of internal controls system. The test is whether a system, taken as a whole, reasonably meets the statute's specified objectives. 'Reasonableness,' a familiar legal concept, depends on an evaluation of all the facts and circumstances.
>
> [...]
>
> Private sector decisions implementing these statutory objectives are business decisions. And, reasonable business decisions should be afforded deference. This means that the issuer need not always select the best or the most effective control measure. However, the one selected must be reasonable under all the circumstances.
>
> [...]
>
> The accounting provisions principal objective is to reaching knowing or reckless conduct.

As to the 'purposes of the Act,' Williams provided a brief review of the 'events which led to the [FCPA]' and stated:

> Clearly, Congress went further than determining whether the payments which gave the new law its name were ethically and commercially justifiable. It also chose to consider the corporate accounting and control deficiencies which had been breeding grounds for these practices. And, by doing so, it addressed the far more serious issues raised by these disclosures. [...] These payments and falsifications were not only previously unknown to public investors and independent auditors, but many were also unknown to the payer's board and, in numerous examples, even to its senior management. In some of these instances, internal controls existed, but they were shown to be ineffective or easily subverted. Unauthorized payments and related falsifications of corporate records seemed to evidence – indeed, were fostered by – a lack of adequate accounting records and controls. Consequently, in the legislation which ultimately emerged from Congress, prohibiting questionable payments and mandating control and recordkeeping were inexorably interconnected.
>
> [...]
>
> The primary thrust of the Act's accounting provisions, in short, was to require those public companies which lacked effective internal controls or tolerated unreliable recordkeeping to comply with the standards of their better managed peers. That is the context in which these provisions should be construed.

The Chairman then addressed 'four of the most important' interpretative questions concerning the FCPA: 'first, the degree of exactitude in recordkeeping mandated by the Act; second, the deference it affords business decisions concerning internal controls; third, whether a particular state of mind is necessary for a violation to exist; and finally, liability for compliance by subsidiaries.'

As to the 'degree of exactitude,' the Chairman stated:

> I turn first to the question of whether the Act's text or purpose mandates that business records and controls conform to a standard of absolute exactitude or that a company's control system meet some absolute ideal. The answer is 'no.' Both of the Act's accounting provisions, it should be noted, are modified by the key term 'reasonable.' [...] In essence, therefore, the Act does provide a de minimus exemption, though not in absolute quantitative terms.

The Chairman noted that Congress specifically declined to adopt a materiality test and stated that 'internal accounting controls are not only concerned with misconduct that is material to investors, but also with a great deal of misconduct which is not.' He noted that while materiality is 'appropriate as a threshold standard to determine the necessity for disclosure to investors, [it] is totally inadequate as a standard for an internal control system.'

The Chairman stated that 'procedures designed only to uncover deficiencies in amounts material for financial statement purposes would be useless for internal control purposes' and noted that 'systems which tolerated omissions or errors of many thousands or even millions of dollars would not represent, by any accepted standard, adequate records and controls.' Indeed, he noted that many of the 'questionable payments that alarmed the public and caused Congress to act [...] were in most instances of far lesser magnitude than that which would constitute financial statement materiality.'

'Reasonableness, rather than materiality, is the appropriate test' and the Chairman stated:

> Reasonableness, as a standard, allows flexibility in responding to particular facts and circumstances. Inherent in this concept is a toleration of deviations from the absolute. One measure of the reasonableness of a system relates to whether the expected benefits from improving it would be significantly greater than the anticipated costs of doing so. Thousands of dollars ordinarily should not be spent conserving hundreds. Further, not every procedure which may be individually cost-justifiable need be implemented; the Act allows a range of reasonable judgments.

As to the 'specific recordkeeping requirement' in the FCPA, the Chairman stated:

> This provision is not an independent unrestrained mandate to the Commission to establish novel or unprecedented corporate recordkeeping standards; it is, rather, an integral part of Congress' efforts to assure that the business community records transactions and assets in such a way as to maintain

> adequate control over them. And this leads to two important conclusions: First, the Act does not establish any absolute standard of exactitude for corporate records. And, second, records which are not related to internal or external audits or to the four internal control objectives set forth in the Act are not within the purview of the Act's accounting provisions.

As to 'deference' with respect to 'issuer liability for recordkeeping violations,' the Chairman stated that the SEC 'will look to the adequacy of the internal control system of the issuer, the involvement of top management in the violation, and the corrective actions taken once the violation was uncovered.'

He then stated as follows, 'If a violation was committed by a low level employee, without the knowledge of top management, with an adequate system of internal control, and with appropriate corrective action taken by the issuer, we do not believe that any action against the company would be called for.'

The Chairman next turned to the 'state of mind needed to violate the Act's accounting provisions' and reiterated that the 'Act's principal purpose is to reach knowing or reckless misconduct.'

He stated:

> Depending on the circumstances, intentional circumventions of a company's system of records and of accounting controls by a low-level employee would not always be considered violations of the Act by the issuer. No system of adequate records and controls – no matter how effectively devised or conscientiously applied – could be expected to prevent all mistaken and improper transactions and disposition of assets. Given human nature, regardless of the adequacy of the system, a bookkeeper may still erroneously post entries, an overzealous agent may make unauthorized payments, or an unscrupulous employee may falsify records for his own purposes. The Act recognizes each of these limitations. Neither its text and legislative history nor its purposes suggest that occasional, inadvertent errors were the kind of problem that Congress sought to remedy in passing the Act. No rational federal interest in punishing insignificant mistakes has been articulated. And, the Act's accounting provisions do not require a company or its senior officials to be the guarantors of all conduct of company employees.

In concluding this portion of the speech, the Chairman stated:

> The test of a company's internal control system is not whether occasional failings can occur. Those will happen in the most ideally managed company. But, an adequate system of internal controls means that, when such breaches do arise, they will be isolated rather than systemic, and they will be subject to a reasonable likelihood of being uncovered in a timely manner and then remedied promptly. Barring, of course, the participation or complicity of

> senior company officials in the deed, when discovery and correction expeditiously follow, no failing in the company's internal accounting system would have existed. To the contrary, routine discovery and correction would evidence its effectiveness.

As to the SEC's enforcement policy, the Chairman concluded his remarks as follows.

> The genius – and challenge – of [the FCPA's books and records and internal controls provisions], it should be remembered, is their reliance on private sector decisionmaking – rather than specific federal edicts – to address an area of public concern. The Act's eventual success or failure will, therefore, depend primarily upon business's response. The Commission's obligation, in turn, is to provide a regulatory environment in which the private sector can address these issues meaningfully and creatively. In this regard, we must encourage public companies to develop innovative records and control systems, to modify and improve them as circumstances change, and to correct recordkeeping errors when they occur without a chilling fear of penalty or inference that a violation of the Act is involved.

In addition to the above 1981 formal statement of SEC policy, at various times the SEC has also affirmed statements of congressional intent relevant to the FCPA's books and records and internal controls provisions. For instance, in a 1999 SEC Staff Accounting Bulletin, the SEC cited with approval the following from the FCPA's legislative history:

> [Congress] adopted the prudent man qualification [in the FCPA's books and records and internal controls provisions] in order to clarify that the current standard does not connote an unrealistic degree of exactitude or precision. The concept of reasonableness of necessity contemplates the weighing of a number of relevant factors, including the costs of compliance.[20]

In the same Bulletin, the SEC also cited with approval various aspects of its 1981 formal statement of policy as reflected in the above speech. The Bulletin stated:

> The books and records provisions of the [FCPA] do not require registrants to make major expenditures to correct small misstatements. [...] As [the SEC] Chairman noted with respect to the internal control provisions of the FCPA, 'thousands of dollars ordinarily should not be spent conserving hundreds. [...] Because the judgment of ['reasonableness' under the accounting provisions] is not mechanical, the [SEC] staff will be inclined to defer to judgments that 'allow a business, acting in good faith, to comply with the Act's accounting provisions in an innovative and cost-effective way.'[21]

Enforcement agency guidance on the FCPA's books and records and internal controls provisions prior to this new era of FCPA enforcement is instructive on many levels. First, the guidance demonstrates that these provisions have always presented compliance difficulties for issuers. Second, the guidance demonstrates enforcement agency recognition of Congress's intent in enacting the provisions. Among other things, and in the words of the SEC: the 'principal objective [of the provisions] is to reach knowing or reckless conduct;' not all issuer books and records are 'within the purview' of the provisions; the provisions are not 'an independent unrestrained mandate to the Commission to establish novel or unprecedented corporate recordkeeping standards'; and 'thousands of dollars ordinarily should not be spent conserving hundreds' in attempting to comply with the provisions.

2012 FCPA Guidance

As referenced in Chapter 2, in 2012 the DOJ and SEC jointly issued FCPA Guidance setting forth its 'FCPA enforcement approach and priorities' and the FCPA Guidance contained a specific chapter regarding the FCPA's books and records and internal controls provisions. Like the previous enforcement agency guidance discussed above, the FCPA Guidance demonstrates enforcement agency recognition of Congress's intent in enacting the books and records and internal control provisions. Indeed, the FCPA Guidance cites legislative history or the FCPA itself for the following statements:

> *Books and Records Provision*
>
> The 'in reasonable detail' qualification was adopted by Congress 'in light of the concern that such a standard, if unqualified, might connote a degree of exactitude and precision which is unrealistic.'
>
> The term 'reasonable detail' is defined in the statute as the level of detail that would 'satisfy prudent officials in the conduct of their own affairs.' Thus, as Congress noted when it adopted this definition, 'the concept of reasonableness of necessity contemplates the weighing of a number of relevant factors, including the costs of compliance.'
>
> *Internal Controls Provision*
>
> Like the 'reasonable detail' requirement in the books and records provision, the Act defines 'reasonable assurances' as 'such level of detail and degree of assurance as would satisfy prudent officials in the conduct of their own affairs.'
>
> The Act does not specify a particular set of controls that companies are required to implement. Rather, the internal controls provision gives companies the flexibility to develop and maintain a system of controls that is appropriate to their particular needs and circumstances.

> Companies may not be able to exercise the same level of control over a minority-owned subsidiary or affiliate as they do over a majority or wholly-owned entity. Therefore, if a parent company owns 50% or less of a subsidiary or affiliate, the parent is only required to use good faith efforts to cause the minority-owned subsidiary or affiliate to devise and maintain a system of internal accounting controls consistent with the issuer's own obligations under the FCPA. In evaluating an issuer's good faith efforts, all the circumstances – including 'the relative degree of the issuer's ownership of the domestic or foreign firm and the laws and practices governing the business operations of the country in which such firm is located' – are taken into account.

These recent statements of enforcement agency policy serve as useful measuring sticks for analyzing enforcement agency theories. As with the legal authority discussed above concerning the FCPA's books and records and internal controls provisions, you can also analyze as you read certain of the FCPA enforcement actions discussed below whether the allegations giving rise to books and records and internal controls charges were consistent with even the guidance and policy positions of the enforcement agencies.

C. DISCUSSION AND ANALYSIS OF SELECTIVE ENFORCEMENT ACTIONS

As noted at the beginning of this chapter, although allegations of foreign bribery are not necessary for the books and records and internal controls provisions to be charged, the provisions are nearly always charged in issuer FCPA anti-bribery violations. In many such instances, the books and records and internal controls violations seem clear based on the enforcement agencies' allegations and thus the charging of these provisions is not controversial. Yet in many FCPA enforcement actions, the charging of these provisions is controversial and it is difficult to reconcile existing legal authority, as well as even enforcement agency guidance and policy, with the theories of enforcement advanced. This section discusses and analyzes enforcement actions that fit both categories.

Siemens

Siemens AG, a German company with shares listed on a U.S. exchange and thus subject to the FCPA, resolved parallel DOJ and SEC enforcement actions by agreeing to pay an FCPA record $800 million in combined fines and penalties.[22]

According to the DOJ, Siemens made payments totaling approximately $1.4 billion through various mechanisms. Of this amount, approximately $555 million was paid for unknown purposes, including approximately $341 million in direct payments to business consultants for unknown purposes. The remaining $805 million was intended, in whole or in part, as payments to foreign officials through various payment mechanisms including cash desks and slush funds. The DOJ stated that 'for much of its operations across the globe, bribery was nothing less than standard operating procedure for Siemens.' The SEC likewise stated that the 'pattern of bribery by Siemens was unprecedented in scale and geographic reach.'[23] At the press conference announcing the charges, government officials stated that: 'Siemens engaged in a systematic and widespread effort to make and hide hundreds of millions of dollars in bribe payments across the globe'; Siemens employees 'sometimes carried … cash in suitcases across international borders to pay bribes'; and that Siemens had a 'corporate culture in which bribery was tolerated and even rewarded at the highest levels of the company.'[24]

According to the DOJ, Siemens' 'compliance, legal, internal audit, and corporate finance departments' were areas of the company that played a significant role in the conduct at issue.

The DOJ information specifically alleged:

> From the mid-1990s to 2007, Siemens engaged in systematic efforts to falsify its corporate books and records and circumvent existing internal controls. These systematic efforts included, but were not limited to: (a) using off-book accounts for corrupt payments even after compliance risks associated with such accounts were raised at the highest levels of management; (b) entering into purported business consulting agreements with no basis, sometimes after Siemens had won the relevant project; (c) engaging former Siemens employees as purported business consultants to act as conduits for corrupt payments to government officials; (d) justifying payments to purported business consultants based on false invoices; (e) mischaracterizing corrupt payments in the corporate books and records as consulting fees and other seemingly legitimate expenses; (f) limiting the quantity and scope of audits of payments to purported business consultants; (g) accumulating profit reserves as liabilities in internal balance sheet accounts and then using them to make corrupt payments through business consultants as needed; (h) using removable Post-It notes to affix signatures on approval forms authorizing payments to conceal the identity of the signers and obscure the audit trail; (i) allowing third party payments to be made based on a single signature in contravention of Siemens' [policy]; (j) drafting and backdating sham business consulting agreements to justify third party payments; and (k) changing the name of purported business consulting agreements to agency agreements or similar titles to avoid detection and conceal noncompliance … .[25]

The SEC complaint likewise alleged that 'the success of Siemens' bribery system was maintained by lax internal controls over corruption-related activities and an acceptance of such activities by members of senior management and the compliance, internal audit, legal and finance departments.'[26]

The FCPA books and records and internal controls violations in the Siemens enforcement action seem clear and fully consistent with legal authority as well as enforcement agency guidance and policy.

Daimler

Daimler AG, also a German company with shares listed on a U.S. exchange and thus subject to the FCPA, resolved parallel DOJ and SEC enforcement actions by agreeing to pay approximately $185 million in combined fines and penalties.[27] According to the DOJ, the company and certain of its subsidiaries 'brazenly offered bribes in exchange for business around the world' and the company 'saw foreign bribery as a way of doing business.' The SEC likewise stated:

> It is no exaggeration to describe corruption and bribe-paying at Daimler as standard business practice. [...] The bribery was so pervasive in Daimler's decentralized corporate structure that it extended outside of the sales organization to internal audit, legal, and finance departments. These departments should have caught and stopped the illegal sales practices, but instead they permitted or were directly involved in the company's bribery practices.[28]

The DOJ criminal information alleged:

> Daimler's longstanding violations of the FCPA resulted from a variety of factors, including: (1) an inadequate compliance structure; (2) a highly decentralized system of selling vehicles through a myriad of foreign sales forces, subsidiaries, and affiliates, with no central oversight; (3) a corporate culture that tolerated and/or encouraged bribery; and (4) the involvement of certain key executives, such as the then head of its overseas sales division, the then head of internal audit, and the then CEO's of several subsidiaries and affiliates.[29]

The information also alleged specific improper conduct at the highest levels of the company. For instance, during a Daimler Board of Management meeting, Daimler's then head of internal audit proposed that the company adopt an integrity code that included anti-bribery provisions. However, the information alleged that 'participants in the meeting discussed that adopting such policies (and stopping the practice of making "useful payments") would result in Daimler losing business in certain countries.' Even though the company did adopt 'an integrity code with anti-bribery provisions' at the meeting, the information alleged that Daimler, among other things, 'failed to make sufficient efforts to cnforce the code, train employees on compliance with the FCPA or other applicable anti-bribery statutes' or 'otherwise attempt to ensure that the company was not continuing to make improper payments in order to obtain or retain government business overseas.'

Elsewhere, the information alleged that 'Daimler's internal audit department was aware that Daimler employees had made and could make bribe payments' and that the department drafted a document identifying fourteen separate improper payment mechanisms. According to the information, the same document noted that 'payment of "useful expenditures" through these methods was subject to criminal prosecution in countries such as the United States.' However, the document also noted the 'level of difficulty' law enforcement authorities would have in 'proving corruption carried out through the various methods.'

Similar to the DOJ's allegations, the SEC alleged that Daimler's 'improper payments were made possible in part as a result of the falsification of corporate records' and specifically alleged that Daimler: internally referred to various of the improper payments as 'N.A.' payments (a German abbreviation for 'useful expenditures' or 'useful payments'); used bogus pricing mechanisms such as 'price surcharges,' 'price inclusions,' or excessive commissions, 'discounts' or 'rebates'; and otherwise improperly booked corrupt payments in several expense accounts designated as 'key accounts,' 'costs of goods sold,' 'gifts line,' 'petty cash' and 'broker commissions.'[30]

Like in the Siemens enforcement action, the FCPA books and records and internal controls violations in the Daimler enforcement action seem clear and fully consistent with legal authority as well as enforcement agency guidance and policy.

Iraq Oil-for-Food Program Actions

As referenced earlier in this chapter, the FCPA's books and records and internal controls provisions operate independently of the FCPA's anti-bribery provisions and can be charged even if all the elements of an FCPA anti-bribery violation are not met. Numerous Iraq Oil-for-Food Program enforcement actions are an instructive example of this dynamic. Between 2007 and 2011, approximately 20 percent of FCPA enforcement actions concerned business conduct in connection with this program.[31]

The Oil-for-Food Program ('OFFP') was set up in 1995 by the United Nations and provided certain limited exceptions to the Iraq sanctions regime that allowed Iraq to sell its oil on the condition that the proceeds from the oil sales be used by the Iraqi government to purchase various humanitarian supplies for the Iraqi people.[32] Under the OFFP program, a supplier of humanitarian goods contracted with an Iraqi government ministry or other department of the Iraqi government to sell goods to the government. According to the allegations in the OFFP enforcement actions, beginning in 2000 the 'Iraqi government demanded that the suppliers of humanitarian goods pay a kickback, usually valued at 10% of the contract price, to the Iraqi government in order to be awarded a contract by the government.' The actions further alleged that these kickbacks were often termed 'after sales service fees' ('ASSFs'), but did not represent any actual service being performed by the supplier. According to the allegations, 'some suppliers labeled the ASSFs as such, thereby leading the U.N. to believe that actual after-sales services were being provided by the supplier' whereas 'other suppliers disguised the ASSFs by inserting fictitious line items into the contracts for goods or services that were not being provided' whereas 'other suppliers simply inflated their contract prices by 10% to account for the payments they would make, or cause to be made, to the Iraqi government.'

Because the OFFP actions involved payments to the Iraqi government or government ministries, but not specific 'foreign officials' as required for there to be an FCPA anti-bribery violation, the above conduct under the OFFP program did not result in anti-bribery violations. However, numerous companies (such as Chevron, Azko Nobel, El Paso, Novo Nordisk, AGCO, ABB, Innospec, Ingersoll-Rand, Textron, York, AB Volvo, Flowserve, General Electric and Fiat) resolved enforcement actions charging FCPA books and records and internal controls violations.

The enforcement action against agriculture company AGCO is an instructive example of the books and records and internal controls issues present in many of the OFFP enforcement actions.[33] At its core, the enforcement action involved payments through a Jordanian agent of approximately $6 million in kickback payments to Iraq in the form of ASSFs to secure contracts worth approximately $14 million. According to the SEC, the payments were disguised or improperly recorded in subsidiary books and records and 'AGCO knew or was reckless in not knowing that kickbacks were paid in connection with its subsidiaries' transactions.'

Specifically, the SEC alleged a number of books and records and internal control deficiencies including the following:

- the 'accrual account [where the kickback payments were recorded] was created by AGCO Ltd.'s marketing staff with virtually no oversight from AGCO Ltd.'s finance department';

- 'no one questioned the existence of the dual accounts';
- 'no one questioned why the [accrual account] contained approximately ten percent of the contract value despite the fact that there was no contract in place requiring that such ten percent be paid to the ministry or anyone else';
- 'when the finance department authorized payments from the [accrual account], it did not ask for or receive any proof of service to warrant the payments';
- an employee cautioned the business manager for Iraq and his supervisor that 'we don't want the auditors raising any questions on Iraq Business!';
- 'sales and marketing personnel were able to enter into contracts without review from the legal or finance departments';
- 'an accounting employee described the Finance Department employees as "blind loaders" who input information into AGCO's books without any adequate oversight role';
- 'marketing personnel were able to create accrual accounts […] without any oversight and caused accounts to be created and payments to be made without proper documentation';
- 'AGCO Ltd.'s structure at the time allocated inappropriate accounting and finance responsibilities to the marketing department';
- 'turnover in the marketing department […] was high and employees were forced to shoulder a great deal of the accounting burden';
- 'AGCO did not conduct any due diligence on the [Jordanian] agent or require that the agent undergo FCPA training'; and
- 'agent contracts with AGCO did not accurately explain the agent's services and payments, and lacked any FCPA language.'[34]

The Siemens, Daimler, and Iraq Oil for Food FCPA books and records and internal controls enforcement actions demonstrate that the FCPA's less glamorous provisions can be potent whether coupled with FCPA anti-bribery charges or charged independently because an element of an FCPA anti-bribery violation is not met.

Yet issuer internal control breakdowns of the sort evidenced by the above enforcement actions are rarely the reason why books and records and internal controls violations are charged by the enforcement agencies.

In many FCPA enforcement actions, charging of these provisions is controversial and it is difficult to reconcile existing legal authority, as well as even enforcement agency guidance and policy, with the theories of enforcement advanced. Such representative actions are discussed and analyzed below. Before turning to such enforcement actions, it is useful to review the following.

Based on the legal sources of authority discussed earlier in this chapter, you know that the FCPA's books and records and internal controls provisions do not require an unrealistic degree of exactitude and precision. Rather, the provisions are qualified by concepts such as reasonableness and good faith and the concept of reasonableness contemplates the weighing of a number of factors including the cost of compliance. As stated in *World-Wide Coin*, the provisions contemplate 'reasonable, but not absolute assurances' and the 'costs of internal controls should not exceed the benefits expected to be derived.' The decision further noted that neither 'the SEC or Congress … intended that the statute should require that each affected issuer install a fail-safe accounting control system at all costs.'

You further know from legal authority that as to issuers which hold 50% or less of the voting power with respect to a firm, the FCPA's books and records and internal controls provisions 'require only that the issuer proceed in good faith […] to cause such [firm] to devise and maintain a system of internal accounting controls' and that an 'issuer which demonstrates good faith efforts to use such influence shall be conclusively presumed to have complied with the requirements' of the provisions.

Beyond relevant legal authority, you further know that enforcement agency guidance concerning the books and records and internal controls provisions stands for the following propositions: not all books and records are within the purview of the provisions; issuers should not face liability when its management was not aware and reasonably should not have known of the conduct at issue; the principal objective of the provisions is to reach knowing or reckless conduct; thousands of dollars ordinarily should not be spent conserving hundreds; the provisions are not an independent unrestrained mandate to establish novel or unprecedented corporate recordkeeping standards; if conduct was engaged in by a low-level employee, without the knowledge of top management, and with appropriate corrective action taken, an enforcement action against the issuer is not warranted; and the provisions do not require a company or its senior officials to be guarantors of all conduct of company employees.

It is difficult to reconcile this legal authority, as well as even enforcement agency guidance and policy, with the theories of enforcement advanced in many FCPA enforcement actions, including those discussed below which appear to advance issuer strict liability.

Dow Chemical

The SEC charged Dow Chemical Company with violating the FCPA's books and records and internal controls provisions based on alleged conduct by Dow's 'fifth-tier subsidiary' in India.[35] The SEC alleged that the entity, through third parties, made payments to 'Indian government officials to register several agro-chemical products slated for marketing in time for India's growing season.'

Without making a single allegation that Dow participated in or had knowledge of the conduct at issue (indeed, the SEC's complaint specifically stated that 'the payments were made without knowledge or approval of any Dow employee'), and without alleging the absence of good faith concerning Dow's oversight of indirect subsidiaries, the SEC nevertheless charged Dow with FCPA books and records and internal controls violations.

Avery Dennison

Similar to the Dow enforcement action, the SEC charged Avery Dennison ('Avery,' a manufacturer of self-adhesive materials and products) with FCPA books and records and internal controls violations.[36] To connect Avery, the issuer, to the conduct at issue requires the following narrative. Avery operated in China through an 'indirect subsidiary,' Avery (China) Co. Ltd. ('Avery China'). Avery China was incorporated under the laws of China and wholly-owned by Avery Dennison Hong Kong BV, which in turn was wholly-owned by Avery Dennison Group Danmark ApS, which in turn was wholly-owned by Avery. The conduct at issue focused on alleged 'kickbacks, sightseeing trips, and gifts' of approximately $30,000 to alleged Chinese foreign officials as well as conduct by employees of a company Avery acquired and allegations that the employees continued their pre-acquisition practice of making petty cash payments to customs and other officials in several countries.

Without making a single allegation that Avery participated in or had knowledge of the conduct at issue, and without alleging the absence of good faith concerning Avery's oversight of its indirect subsidiaries, the SEC nevertheless charged Avery with FCPA books and records and internal controls violations. In conclusory fashion, the SEC merely stated: 'Avery failed to accurately record [the payments] at issue and gifts in the company's books and records, and failed to implement or maintain a system of internal accounting controls sufficient to detect and prevent such illegal payments or promises of illegal payments.'

Veraz Networks

Given its neither admit nor deny settlement policy, the SEC likely realizes that it will never be put to its burden of proof in corporate FCPA enforcement actions. Thus, the end result is often resolution documents full of uninformative, bare-bones statement of facts with legal conclusions. An instructive example is the SEC enforcement action against Veraz Networks charging FCPA books and records and internal controls violations.[37]

The SEC alleged that 'Veraz resellers, consultants, and employees made and offered payments to employees of government-controlled telecommunications companies in China and Vietnam with the purpose and effect of improperly influencing these foreign officials to award or continue to do business with Veraz.'

In China, the SEC alleged approximately $4,500 worth of gifts were made by a consultant as well as a consultant's attempt to offer an approximate $35,000 payment in connection with a transaction. As to the latter offer, the complaint specifically alleged that 'Veraz discovered this improper offer of payment prior to receiving any money from the transaction and cancelled the sale.'

In Vietnam, the complaint alleged, with little detail, that a 'Veraz employee, through a Singapore reseller' made or offered payments to a customer and that 'Veraz also approved or reimbursed its employees for questionable expenses … including gifts and entertainment for [the customer's] employees and flowers for the wife of the CEO [of the customers].'

As to both the China and Vietnam allegations, the SEC merely stated in conclusory fashion as follows.

> Veraz failed to accurately record these improper payments on the Company's books and records, and failed to implement or maintain a system of effective internal accounting controls to prevent them in violation of the FCPA which requires public companies to keep books and records that accurately reflect their operations, and to put in place internal controls that are reasonably designed to ensure that their books and records are accurate.

So bare-bones was the Veraz complaint that a former SEC FCPA enforcement attorney stated that 'the complaint disclosed little information about the specifics of the alleged misconduct' and was 'remarkably ambiguous about the substance of the alleged violations.'[38]

NATCO Group

The SEC charged oil field services provider NATCO Group with violating the FCPA books and records and internal control provisions based on the conduct of its subsidiary, TEST Automation & Controls, Inc., which maintained a branch office in Kazakhstan ('TEST Kazakhstan').[39]

The SEC acknowledged in the complaint that TEST-Kazakhstan expatriate workers were the victims of extortionate demands by Kazakhstan officials, specifically that Kazakh immigration prosecutors 'threatened to fine, jail or deport the workers if TEST Kazakhstan did not pay cash fines.' 'Believing the prosecutor's threats to be genuine,' the SEC complaint alleged that TEST Kazakhstan employees 'used personal funds to pay the prosecutors' and 'then obtained reimbursement' from the company. According to the SEC, NATCO Group violated the FCPA's books and records and internal controls provisions because its subsidiary described the reimbursements as 'an advance against bonus' or 'payroll advance' in its wire instructions to the bank.

Oracle

The SEC charged Oracle with FCPA books and records and internal controls violations based on the alleged conduct of its Indian subsidiary. The SEC complaint alleged, in summary fashion, as follows.

> This matter involves violations of the books and records and internal controls provisions of the FCPA by Oracle Corporation. From 2005 to 2007, certain employees of Oracle's Indian subsidiary ['Oracle India'] secretly 'parked' a portion of the proceeds from certain sales to the Indian government and put the money to unauthorized use, creating the potential for bribery or embezzlement. These Oracle India employees structured more than a dozen transactions so that a total of around $2.2 million was held by the Company's distributors and kept off Oracle India's corporate books. The Oracle India employees would then direct its distributor to disburse payments out of the unauthorized side funds to purported local 'vendors.' Several of the 'vendors' were merely storefronts that did not provide any services. Oracle failed to accurately record these side funds on the Company's books and records, and failed to implement or maintain a system of effective internal accounting controls to prevent improper side funds in violation of the FCPA, which requires public companies to keep books and records that accurately reflect their operations.[40]

Specifically, the SEC complaint alleged:

> On approximately 14 occasions related to 8 different government contracts between 2005 and 2007, certain Oracle India employees created extra margins between the end user and distributor price and directed the distributors to hold the extra margin in side funds. Oracle India's employees made these margins large enough to ensure a side fund existed to pay third parties. At the direction of the Oracle India employees, the distributor then made payments out of the side funds to third parties, purportedly for marketing and development expenses. Some of the recipients of these payments were not on Oracle's approved local vendor list; indeed, some of the third parties did not exist and were merely storefronts. Because the Oracle India employees concealed the existence of the side fund, Oracle did not properly account for these side funds. These funds constituted prepaid marketing expenses incurred by Oracle India and should have been recorded as an asset and rolled up to Oracle's corporate books and records. These marketing expenses should then have been reflected in the income statement once they were used. Instead, the parked funds were not reflected on Oracle India's books and were not properly recorded as prepaid marketing expenses. This incorrect accounting in turn affected Oracle's books and records.

The SEC further alleged:

> Oracle lacked the proper controls to prevent its employees at Oracle India from creating and misusing the parked funds. For example, Oracle knew distributor discounts created a margin of cash from which distributors received payments for their services. Before 2009, however, the company failed to audit and compare the distributor's margin against the end user price to ensure excess margins were not being built into the pricing structure. In addition, although Oracle maintained corporate policies requiring approvals for payment of marketing expenses, Oracle failed to seek transparency in or audit third party payments made by distributors on Oracle India's behalf. This control would have enabled Oracle to check that payments were made to appropriate recipients.

In a release, the SEC stated:

> Through its subsidiary's use of secret cash cushions, Oracle exposed itself to the risk that these hidden funds would be put to illegal use. It is important for U.S. companies to proactively establish policies and procedures to minimize the potential for payments to foreign officials or other unauthorized uses of company funds.[41]

The FCPA enforcement action against Oracle diluted FCPA enforcement to a new level. The only allegations against Oracle itself is that it failed to audit distributor margins against end user prices and that it failed to audit third party payments made by distributors.

It is common for large multinational companies like Oracle to engage thousands of third parties across the globe to assist in business development. Because of this, audits Oracle was held liable for not conducting are not practical or cost-effective *absent* red flags suggesting improper conduct. The SEC did not allege any such red flag issues. In fact, the SEC alleged that Oracle's Indian subsidiary 'concealed' and kept 'secret' the conduct from Oracle.

You were asked at the beginning of this section to reconcile existing legal authority, as well as even enforcement agency guidance, with the theories of enforcement advanced in many FCPA enforcement actions. Regardless of your answer to the question of whether many FCPA enforcement actions charging books and records and internal controls violations are warranted, all can agree that the provisions, as currently enforced by the enforcement agencies, are potent supplements to the FCPA's more glamorous anti-bribery provisions.

Based on the enforcement theories, it would seem that nearly all issuers doing business in the global marketplace could, upon a thorough investigation of their entire business operations, discover conduct implicating the books and records and internal controls provisions. For instance, the SEC alleged in an FCPA enforcement action against pharmaceutical company Eli Lilly that the company violated the books and records and internal controls provisions because sales representatives at the company's China subsidiary submitted false expense reports for items such as wine, specialty foods, a jade bracelet, visits to bath houses, card games, karaoke bars, door prizes, spa treatments and cigarettes.[42] If the SEC's position is that an issuer violates the FCPA's books and records and internal controls provisions because some employees, anywhere within its world-wide organization, submit false expense reports for such nominal and inconsequential items, then every issuer has violated and will continue to violate the FCPA.

Indeed, such nominal and inconsequential matters often occur in an issuer's domestic business. For instance, think of how often a company's suite at a sports stadium is used for questionable business purposes, or how often gifts are provided or meals expensed for questionable business purposes. Because the FCPA's books and records and internal controls provisions can apply even if the conduct does not involve allegations of foreign bribery, one would think that such domestic books and records and internal controls charges would be numerous. However, few FCPA books and records and internal controls actions are based on domestic conduct of the type and degree highlighted in many FCPA enforcement actions involving alleged foreign bribery.

What is it about business conduct in the global marketplace that attracts greater FCPA scrutiny and how did the enforcement agencies learn of the alleged improper conduct in all of the questionable enforcement actions detailed above? One answer is that all of the questionable enforcement actions discussed above originated from corporate voluntary disclosures. As highlighted in the next chapter, voluntary disclosures are the single largest originating source of FCPA enforcement actions, and as explored in Chapter 6, one of the reasons for the general increase in FCPA enforcement in this new era may be that voluntary disclosures are often the fuel that feeds a vibrant and lucrative industry known as FCPA Inc.

NOTES

1. Press Release, U.S. Dep't of Justice, 'Long Island-Based FalconStor Software, Inc. Charged with Conspiring to Bribe J.P. Morgan Chase Executives and Related Securities Law Violations' (June 27, 2012).
2. Press Release, SEC, 'SEC Charges Gold Standard Mining Corp. and Others for False and Misleading Statements Concerning Russian Gold Mining Operations' (July 3, 2012).
3. Searle Civil Justice Center, 'The Foreign Corrupt Practices Act: An Empirical Examination of Enforcement Trends' (Sept. 2012).
4. Abuses of Corporate Power: Hearings before the Subcomm. on Priorities and Econ. in Gov't of the Joint Econ. Comm., 94th Cong. (1976).
5. SEC, 'Report of the Securities and Exchange Commission on Questionable and Illegal Corporate Payments and Practices' (1976), reprinted in Special Supplement, Sec. Reg. & L. Rep. (BNA) No. 353 (May 19, 1976).
6. Id.
7. S. Rep. No. 114 (1977).
8. Prohibiting Bribes to Foreign Officials: Hearing before the S. Comm. on Banking, Housing, and Urban Affairs, 94th Cong. (1976).
9. Cong. Record – Senate at S 6977 (May 12, 1976).
10. S. Rep. No. 94-1031 (1976).
11. S. Rep. No. 95-114 (1977).
12. H. Conf. Rep. No. 94-831 (1977).
13. H. Conf. Rep. No. 100-576 (1988).
14. Id.
15. 567 F.Supp. 724 (N.D. Ga. 1983).
16. 2009 WL 6799492 (S.D. Tex. 2009); 803 F.Supp.2d 630 (S.D. Tex. 2011).
17. 44 Fed. Reg. 10, 968 (Feb. 23, 1979).
18. Id.
19. SEC Release No. 17500 (Jan. 29, 1981).
20. SEC Staff Accounting Bulletin: No. 99 – Materiality, 17 CFR Part 211 [Release No. SAB 99], Staff Accounting Bulletin No. 99 (Aug. 12, 1999).
21. Id.
22. Press Release, U.S. Dep't of Justice, 'Siemens AG and Three Subsidiaries Plead Guilty to Foreign Corrupt Practices Act Violations and Agree to Pay $450 Million in Combined Criminal Fines' (Dec. 15, 2008).

23. Press Release, SEC, 'SEC Charges Siemens AG for Engaging in Worldwide Bribery' (Dec. 15, 2008).
24. Press Release, U.S. Dep't of Justice, 'Transcript of Press Conference Announcing Siemens AG and Three Subsidiaries Plead Guilty to Foreign Corrupt Practices Act Violations' (Dec. 15, 2008).
25. Information, U.S. v. Siemens, No. 08-cr-367-RJL (D.D.C., Dec. 12, 2008).
26. Complaint, SEC v. Siemens, No. 1:08-cv-02167 (D.D.C., Dec. 12, 2008).
27. Press Release, U.S. Dep't of Justice, 'Daimler AG and Three Subsidiaries Resolve Foreign Corrupt Practices Act Investigation and Agree to Pay $93.6 Million in Criminal Penalties' (Apr. 1, 2010).
28. Press Release, SEC, 'SEC Charges Daimler AG with Global Bribery' (Apr. 1, 2010).
29. Information, U.S. v. Daimler, No. 1:10-cr-00063-RJL (D.D.C., Mar. 22, 2010).
30. Complaint, SEC v. Daimler, No. 1:10-cv-00473 (D.D.C., Mar. 22, 2010).
31. FCPA Professor, 'Keeping FCPA Enforcement Statistics in Perspective' (Jan. 23, 2013).
32. See e.g., Information, U.S. v. AGCO Limited, No. 1:09-cr-00249-RJL (D.D.C., Sept. 30, 2009).
33. Id., Complaint, SEC v. AGCO Limited, No. 1:09-cv-01865 (D.D.C., Sept. 30, 2009).
34. Id.
35. Complaint, SEC v. Dow Chemical (D.D.C. Feb. 13, 2007).
36. Complaint, SEC v. Avery Dennison Corp., No. CV09-5493 (C.D. Cal., July 28, 2009).
37. Complaint, SEC v. Veraz Networks Inc., No. CV10-2849 (N.D. Cal., June 29, 2010).
38. Richard Grime et al., O'Melveny & Myers LLP, 'SEC Levies $300,000 FCPA Penalty for Misrecording Gifts and Entertainment' (July 13, 2010).
39. Complaint, SEC v. Natco Group, No. 4:10-cv-00098 (S.D. Tex., Jan. 11, 2010).
40. Complaint, SEC v. Oracle Corp., No. CV1204310 (N.D. Cal., Aug. 16, 2012).
41. Press Release, SEC, 'SEC Charges Oracle Corporation with FCPA Violations Related to Secret Side Funds in India' (Aug. 16, 2012).
42. Complaint, SEC v. Eli Lilly and Co., No. 1:12-cv-02045 (D.D.C., Dec. 20, 2012).

5. FCPA enforcement

The previous two chapters provided a comprehensive analysis of the FCPA's anti-bribery and books and records and internal controls provisions. Yet just because these provisions may be violated does not mean that an FCPA enforcement action will result. To state the obvious, the enforcement agencies must first learn of the improper conduct. This chapter begins by highlighting the typical origins of FCPA enforcement actions including the prominent role voluntary disclosures play in serving as the basis for most corporate FCPA enforcement actions.

Next, this chapter introduces you to the 'three buckets' of FCPA financial exposure. The first bucket is pre-enforcement action professional fees and expenses and you will learn the importance of the 'where else' question. The second bucket is fine, penalty and disgorgement amounts in an actual FCPA enforcement action and you will learn how such amounts are calculated as well as certain controversial aspects regarding these amounts. The third bucket is post-enforcement action professional fees and expenses and you will learn that a company's financial exposure rarely ends on enforcement action day. Of these 'three buckets,' while settlement amounts in an actual FCPA enforcement action tend to get the most attention, pre-enforcement action professional fees and expenses are often the most expensive aspect of FCPA scrutiny and enforcement.

This chapter then analyzes and compares corporate FCPA enforcement and individual FCPA enforcement. After highlighting various facts and figures regarding corporate FCPA enforcement, certain uncomfortable truths regarding corporate FCPA enforcement will be exposed including how certain companies in certain industries appear to be immune from FCPA anti-bribery charges and how the general fight against bribery and corruption suffers from several double standards.

After highlighting various facts and figures regarding individual FCPA enforcement, this chapter demonstrates that despite enforcement agency rhetoric to the contrary, FCPA enforcement in this new era is largely corporate enforcement only. However, on occasion individuals are also charged with FCPA offenses and various dynamics will be discussed relevant to resolving FCPA individual enforcement actions. Unlike business organizations subject to FCPA scrutiny, individuals are often more motivated to put the enforcement agencies to its burden of proof at trial and this chapter also highlights how the enforcement agencies have generally struggled when put to its burden of proof in individual enforcement actions.

This chapter concludes with a discussion of sentencing issues in individual FCPA enforcement actions and how sentencing judges often see shades of gray in FCPA enforcement actions that the DOJ often portrays to be black and white.

A. ENFORCEMENT ACTION ORIGINS

This section discusses the typical origins of FCPA enforcement actions. Corporate voluntary disclosures are the single largest source of FCPA enforcement actions and this section also highlights other origins of FCPA enforcement including foreign law enforcement investigations, industry sweeps, and others.

Voluntary Disclosures

Business organizations often learn of conduct that might implicate the FCPA through internal audits or other internal reporting mechanisms. After an internal investigation, the company's lawyers might disclose the conduct that could implicate the FCPA to the DOJ and SEC as well if the company is an issuer. This disclosure is made even though, in most instances, the enforcement agencies likely would not otherwise learn of the conduct.

Goodyear Tire and Rubber Company's FCPA voluntary disclosure is a representative example. In an SEC filing, the company stated:

> … An anonymous source reported, through our confidential ethics hotline, that our majority-owned joint venture in Kenya may have made certain improper payments. […] An employee of our subsidiary in Angola reported that similar improper payments may have been made in Angola. Outside counsel and forensic accountants were retained to investigate the alleged improper payments in Kenya and Angola, including our compliance in those countries with the FCPA. […] Following our internal investigation, we have implemented, and are continuing to implement, appropriate remedial measures and have voluntarily disclosed the results of our investigation to the DOJ and the SEC, and are cooperating with those agencies in their review of these matters.[1]

Nothing in the FCPA required Goodyear to make the disclosure. While issuers are required by the securities laws to disclose all material information to investors, conduct implicating the FCPA seldom rises to the level of materiality for most companies. Nevertheless, the SEC has stated that materiality includes a qualitative component and that all conduct in violation of the FCPA can be considered qualitatively material because it may automatically trigger a books and records violation.[2] Based on this theory, even if dubious for the reasons discussed in Chapter 4 regarding the FCPA's books and records and internal controls provisions, SEC officials have stated that it is 'prudent' for any issuer to approach the SEC with any 'suspicion' of conduct in violation of the FCPA 'as soon as' the company learns of the improper conduct.[3]

The main motivation of business organizations subject to the FCPA to make voluntary disclosures would seem not to be legal, but based on the 'carrots' and 'sticks' previously discussed in Chapter 2. As previously noted, under the DOJ's Principles of Prosecution, a company's 'timely and voluntary disclosure of wrongdoing' is one factor the DOJ will consider in determining whether to bring criminal charges against a business organization or negotiate an agreement (such as an NPA or DPA) to resolve potential criminal charges. Likewise, the Sentencing Guidelines allow for a lower criminal fine if a company 'reported the offense to appropriate government authorities.' Furthermore, one factor the SEC will consider in determining how to resolve an enforcement action is whether the 'company promptly, completely and effectively disclosed the existence of the misconduct to the public, to regulators and to self-regulators.'

Enforcement agency officials have been vocal about voluntary disclosure in the FCPA context. For instance, the DOJ Assistant Attorney General has 'strongly urged any corporation that discovers an FCPA violation to seriously consider making a voluntary disclosure and always to cooperate with the Department' and assured the business community of the DOJ's 'commitment to meaningfully reward voluntary disclosures.'[4] Recognizing that the 'question of whether to self-report is a difficult one,' the Assistant Attorney General nevertheless stated:

> If you do not voluntarily disclose your organization's conduct, and we discover it on our own, or through a competitor or a customer of yours, the result will not be the same. [...] There is no doubt that a company that comes forward on its own will see a more favorable resolution than one that doesn't.[5]

It is easy to understand why the enforcement agencies favor and encourage voluntary disclosure. Simply put, it makes their job easier and it is cost-effective from a budget and resource standpoint.

Nevertheless, despite frequent enforcement agency statements about the tangible benefits of voluntary disclosure, whether voluntary disclosure in the FCPA context is indeed rewarded is the subject of much dispute and debate. For instance, one study analyzed approximately 40 FCPA enforcement actions and compared the ratio between bribes and fines for companies that do and do not voluntary disclose and found that there did not appear to be any benefit to voluntary disclosure.[6] The authors of another study concluded: 'We cannot rule out the possibility that voluntary disclosure does result in some form of leniency [...] but the fact that we could not find any evidence of the benefits of voluntary disclosure suggests that current enforcement practices are not creating clear incentives.'[7]

Although the lack of transparency regarding FCPA fine and penalty amounts discussed later in this chapter may have impacted the soundness of the above studies, the fact remains that many are skeptical whether the enforcement agencies sufficiently reward voluntary disclosure in the FCPA context.

Given the controversies surrounding voluntary disclosure, corporate counsel and others making business decisions on behalf of an organization need to understand that thoroughly investigating an issue, promptly implementing remedial measures, and effectively revising and enhancing compliance policies and procedures – all internally and without disclosing to the enforcement agencies – is a perfectly acceptable, legitimate, and legal response to FCPA issues in but all the rarest of circumstances.

As noted by a former SEC enforcement attorney and a former DOJ enforcement attorney:

> Not all potential [FCPA] problems, however, are appropriate for disclosure. After investigation, allegations of misconduct may not result in a determination that illicit activity has occurred. [...] Prematurely attracting the government's attention may, as a practical matter, shift the burden to the company to prove the absence of a corruption problem. Enforcement officials may feel the need as a matter of basic human nature to seek some type of resolution to a case where they have invested significant time and effort. Companies need to weigh the potential benefits of cooperation against the significant costs of initiating a potentially unwarranted government investigation.[8]

Similarly, the former Chief of the DOJ's Fraud section has stated:

> It often will not be in a company's best interest to disclose if, for example, the allegations prove not to be credible or if it is unclear whether the conduct even amounts to a violation of law. Under those circumstances, a disclosure could unnecessarily embroil the company in a lengthy and costly government investigation and result in other repercussions such as triggering civil litigation and harm to a company's reputation that could otherwise be avoided. It's a challenging calculus. [...] However, the fact that a company doesn't disclose a problem that ultimately comes to DOJ's attention is not necessarily going to damage the company's credibility with DOJ. Regulators recognize that not every allegation should be of interest to them – and, frankly, having counsel that knows when they'll be interested and when they won't is really important.[9]

Nevertheless, because of the 'carrots' and 'sticks' relevant to FCPA enforcement, as well as perhaps nudging by FCPA counsel (an issue discussed in Chapter 6), many risk-averse business organizations choose to disclose conduct that could implicate the FCPA to the enforcement agencies. The take-away point is that voluntary disclosures are the single largest source of corporate FCPA enforcement actions. For instance, in 2012, 50 percent of all corporate FCPA enforcement actions were the result of voluntary disclosures.[10]

Foreign Law Enforcement Investigations

In addition to voluntary disclosures, the origins of several FCPA enforcement actions, including some of the largest in FCPA history in terms of settlement amounts, have been foreign, not U.S., law enforcement investigations and actions.

For instance, the record-setting Siemens enforcement action originated, in the words of the DOJ, when 'the Munich Public Prosecutor's Office conducted raids on multiple Siemens offices and the homes of Siemens employees in and around Munich, Germany, as part of an investigation of possible bribery of foreign public officials and falsification of corporate books and records.'[11] Shortly after these raids, Siemens disclosed to the DOJ and SEC 'potential violations of the FCPA in multiple countries and initiated a sweeping global internal investigation.' Likewise, several FCPA enforcement actions concerning business conduct at Bonny Island, Nigeria in connection with a liquefied natural gas plant began in 2003 in France when a former executive at French oil and gas company Technip was charged with embezzlement in an unrelated matter and informed a French magistrate of the Bonny Island conduct.[12]

In 2010, the former chief of the DOJ's FCPA unit stated that a priority of his while at the DOJ was 'forging relationships with foreign prosecutors and regulators who were tackling foreign bribery cases and collaborating with them' in building a 'network of prosecutors.'[13] Likewise, in 2013, the Acting DOJ Assistant Attorney General discussed the importance of foreign law enforcement cooperation and stated:

> Another important shift in the anti-corruption realm [is] the development of stronger anti-bribery enforcement programs in foreign countries, the continuing and encouraging rise in cross-border cooperation, and the increasing efforts of our foreign law enforcement partners to hold individual perpetrators accountable. [...] It is safe to say that we are cooperating with foreign law enforcement on foreign bribery cases more closely today than at any time in history.[14]

Industry Sweeps

During this new era of FCPA enforcement, the term 'industry sweep' has been added to the FCPA vocabulary as such sweeps have served as an additional basis for several FCPA enforcement actions.

An industry sweep generally refers to 'investigations that grow out of perceived FCPA violations by one company that enforcement agencies believe may reflect an industry-wide pattern of wrongdoing.' An FCPA practitioner has observed:

> Industry sweeps are often led by the SEC which has broad subpoena power as a regulatory agency, arguably broader oversight authority than prosecutors. They are different from internal investigations or traditional government investigations, and present different challenges to companies. Because the catalyst may be wrongdoing in a single company, agencies may have no evidence or suspicion of specific violations in the companies subject to an industry sweep. A sweep may thus begin with *possible cause*, not probable cause. In sweeps, agencies broadly solicit information from companies about their past FCPA issues or present practices. And they may explicitly encourage companies to volunteer incriminating information about competitors. This practice not only fuels the 'salesman's defense' (that 'everybody does it'), but can also generate anecdotal or speculative information that simply leads to additional rounds of inquiries. Inevitably, industry sweeps become organic and evolve, with government investigators using information from one company as the basis for additional requests to others. Pooling information about unreliable third parties, suspect government instrumentalities, and information about employees who have worked for multiple companies can prolong an investigation or cause its scope to expand or turn in new directions.[15]

For instance several FCPA enforcement actions originated from an investigation of Swiss freight-forwarder Panalpina and its interactions with Nigerian customs officials on behalf of several oil and gas service companies.[16] Likewise, several FCPA enforcement actions and instances of FCPA scrutiny of healthcare companies likely resulted from a voluntary disclosure and resulting FCPA enforcement action against Johnson & Johnson. Indeed, in the DPA used to resolve the action, the DOJ stated: 'J&J has cooperated and agreed to continue to cooperate with the [DOJ] in the [DOJ's] investigations of other companies and individuals in connection with business practices overseas in various markets.'[17]

Industry sweeps are certainly a central feature of this new era of FCPA enforcement and FCPA scrutiny of one industry participant can also attract FCPA scrutiny of other industry participants or an entire industry. In addition to the above examples, the following industries are also reportedly in the middle of industry sweeps: financial services, Hollywood film studies, and retailers doing business in emerging markets concerning various license and permit issues.

On one level, FCPA industry sweeps represent effective law enforcement. Yet on another level, industry sweeps have the potential to turn into boundless enforcement agency fishing expeditions, the costs of which are borne by the companies subject to the sweep. When the origins of the sweep are based on aggressive enforcement theories that are not subjected to any meaningful judicial scrutiny – as is often the case given the frequent use of NPAs and DPA in the FCPA context – the effects of such boundless sweeps raise a host of policy issues, including that such sweeps seem to represent an indirect tax on an entire industry.

Others

Although voluntary disclosures, foreign law enforcement investigations, and industry sweeps are the origins for most FCPA enforcement actions in this new era, there are several other origins that deserve mention including: sting operations and undercover investigations; unrelated government investigations; civil litigation; and whistleblowers.

In 2009, perhaps sensing the valid perception that the DOJ was reactionary when it came to FCPA enforcement, the Assistant Attorney General stated that the DOJ does not 'simply react to self-disclosures and rely on internal corporate investigations' in bringing FCPA enforcement actions.[18] Rather, the Assistant Attorney General stated that the DOJ would be 'proactive and aggressive' and he predicted that the 'number of FCPA prosecutions – of corporations and individuals alike – will continue to rise.'

In retrospect it would seem that the Assistant Attorney General's 2009 remarks were foreshadowing the 2010 arrest of 22 individuals in the military and law enforcement products industry in a manufactured sting operation. As discussed in more detail later in this chapter concerning individual FCPA enforcement actions, the so-called Africa Sting case involved FBI agents, with the assistance of an individual who had already pleaded guilty to real, unrelated FCPA offenses, posing as representatives of the Gabon Minister of Defense. In connection with the case, the Assistant Attorney General stated 'from now on, would-be FCPA violators should stop and ponder whether the person they are trying to bribe might really be a federal agent.'[19]

While the Africa Sting case was not the first use of proactive, undercover investigative techniques in an FCPA enforcement action, it was certainly the largest and most dramatic use of such techniques in the FCPA's history and the full force of the government's surveillance capabilities were used against individuals from mostly small private companies located across America. Even though you will learn that the Africa Sting case proved disastrous for the DOJ when put to its burden of proof, the FBI has stated that it will continue to use undercover investigative tactics in FCPA inquiries, and in the words of an FBI official 'we will do it again – see you out there.'[20]

Unrelated government investigations have also served as the origins for FCPA enforcement actions. For instance, in 2013 the DOJ announced FCPA enforcement actions against several individuals associated with broker-dealer Direct Access Partners (DAP).[21] As a broker-dealer, DAP was subject to periodic SEC examination and during an examination it was discovered that individuals employed by the company directed kickback payments to an employee of an alleged Venezuelan state-owned bank in exchange for executing bond trades with the company. Likewise, a 2011 enforcement action against Bridgestone Corporation, a Japanese company that manufacturers tires and rubber products, involved both FCPA charges and antitrust charges and originated in a U.S. government investigation regarding the company's involvement in international cartel activities relating to the sale of marine hose.[22]

FCPA enforcement actions have also originated from civil litigation. For instance, the FCPA enforcement action against David Kay and Douglas Murphy, an enforcement action that resulted in several notable judicial decisions as highlighted in Chapter 3, began as follows:

> In 1999 [American Rice, Inc. ('ARI') – Kay and Murphy's employer] retained a prominent Houston law firm to represent it in a civil suit. Preparing for this suit, the lawyers asked Kay for background information on ARI's rice

> business in Haiti. Kay volunteered that he had taken the actions [i.e., made or authorized payments to Haitian customs officials], explaining that doing so was part of doing business in Haiti. Those lawyers informed ARI's directors. The directors self-reported these activities to government regulators. The SEC launched an investigation into ARI, Murphy, and Kay. Murphy and Kay were eventually indicted.[23]

FCPA scrutiny and enforcement actions have also originated from whistleblower complaints. For instance, the 2010 Daimler FCPA enforcement action – which involved 'a decade-long scheme involving tens of millions of dollars' and 'bribes in exchange for business around the world' – originated, per the DOJ's sentencing memorandum, as follows:

> In 2004, a former Daimler employee filed a whistleblower complaint with the U.S. Department of Labor's Occupational Safety & Health Administration [...] In the complaint, the former employee alleged that he was terminated for voicing concerns about Daimler's practice of maintaining secret accounts, including accounts in its books and records, for the purpose of bribing foreign government officials. [...] The SEC granted its staff a formal order to investigate whether Daimler violated the FCPA. Thereafter, the DOJ opened its own investigation as to whether any such violations were criminal in nature.[24]

The number of FCPA enforcement actions originating from whistleblower complaints may increase as a result of the Dodd-Frank Wall Street Reform and Consumer Protection Act of 2010. The financial reform law contained whistleblower provisions applicable to all securities laws violations and you will recall that the FCPA is part of the Securities and Exchange Act. Under the provisions, any whistleblower who voluntarily provides original information to the SEC that leads to an enforcement action resulting in monetary sanctions exceeding $1 million shall be entitled to an award between 10 to 30 percent of the monetary sanctions in an enforcement action.[25]

As highlighted in this section, FCPA enforcement actions have many origins, from voluntary disclosures, to foreign law enforcement investigations, to industry sweeps to several others. Regardless of the origins, FCPA enforcement actions can expose a business organization to significant monetary consequences and the next section introduces you to the 'three buckets' of FCPA financial exposure.

B. THE 'THREE BUCKETS' OF FCPA FINANCIAL EXPOSURE

The 'three buckets' of FCPA financial exposure are: (i) pre-enforcement action professional fees and expenses; (ii) fine, penalty and disgorgement amounts in an actual FCPA enforcement action; and (iii) post-enforcement action professional fees and expenses. Of these 'three buckets,' while settlement amounts in an actual FCPA enforcement action tend to get the most attention, pre-enforcement action professional fees and expenses are often the most expensive aspect of FCPA scrutiny and enforcement because of the 'where else' question. In this section, you will also learn how settlement amounts in FCPA enforcement actions are calculated as well as certain controversial aspects associated with these amounts, and how a company's financial exposure rarely ends on enforcement action day.

Pre-Enforcement Action Professional Fees and Expenses

Every instance of FCPA scrutiny has a point of entry – in other words a set of facts which give rise to the scrutiny in the first place. This point of entry is often the beginning of a long and expensive journey for the company under scrutiny and the first bucket of FCPA financial exposure is pre-enforcement action professional fees and expenses.

For instance, in 2008 beauty products company Avon disclosed that it was conducting an FCPA internal investigation regarding compliance in China. The investigation soon spread to other countries and five years later, the internal investigation is still active and the company has disclosed approximately $350 million in pre-enforcement action professional fees and expenses.[26] Even though Avon's internal investigation expenses have tapered off, the company is still spending, five years later, approximately $110,000 per working day to address its FCPA scrutiny.[27]

Wal-Mart's FCPA scrutiny has resulted in even higher pre-enforcement action professional fees and expenses. As highlighted in more detail in Chapter 9, in late 2011 Wal-Mart disclosed that it was conducting an FCPA internal investigation concerning certain permitting, licensing and inspection issues. Wal-Mart has since disclosed that more than 300 legal and accounting professionals are assisting the company in its FCPA internal investigation and compliance review and that its 2012 FCPA-related professional fees and expenses were approximately $73 million. This represents approximately $1.16 million per working day in pre-enforcement action professional fees and expenses.[28]

It is not just large multinational companies the subject of high-profile FCPA scrutiny that are spending millions of dollars in pre-enforcement action professional and expenses. Rather, such amounts have become the norm even in routine FCPA enforcement actions. For instance, in the NATCO enforcement action discussed in Chapter 4, the company agreed to pay a $65,000 civil penalty to resolve an SEC enforcement action. The company's pre-enforcement action professional fees and expenses were reported to be $11 million and caused the company cash-flow problems.[29] Likewise, in the Veraz Networks enforcement action also previously discussed, the company agreed to pay a $300,000 civil penalty to resolve an SEC enforcement action. The company's pre-enforcement action professional fees and expenses were approximately $3 million.[30]

The above examples highlight how pre-enforcement action professional fees and expenses are typically the most expensive aspect of FCPA scrutiny and enforcement. The examples also foreshadow an issue discussed in more detail in Chapter 6 – how FCPA Inc. participants have a potential conflict of interest in advising business organizations on voluntary disclosures because attracting enforcement agency scrutiny and an actual FCPA enforcement can lead to substantial work. In this regard, it is notable that both the NATCO Group and Veraz Networks enforcement actions, like so many others in this new era, originated from corporate voluntary disclosures. In short, voluntary disclosures are like a rainbow, and waiting on the other side for FCPA Inc. is often a pot of gold in the form of pre-enforcement action and post-enforcement action professional fees.

That pre-enforcement action professional fees and expenses are typically the most expensive aspect of FCPA scrutiny is a fact. The question is why are pre-enforcement action professional fees and expenses so expensive?

Resolution documents from the 2010 FCPA enforcement action against telecommunication company Alcatel-Lucent provide insight into the expansive nature of FCPA scrutiny. The DOJ noted:

> At the request of the government, [Alcatel-Lucent] undertook a 'Global Review' to evaluate its relationship with agents, interactions with government officials, and gifts, travel and entertainment provided in countries around the world. [...] In particular, Alcatel-Lucent and its outside counsel conducted investigations of 34 countries around the world to uncover potential misconduct. The internal investigation examined Alcatel-Lucent's agent and consultant approval, review, and termination processes, the activities of a number of terminated agents, and the knowledge and involvement of senior management in any potential wrongdoing. This effort was closely coordinated with the government. [...] [As part of its agent and consultant approval

> process review], Alcatel-Lucent retained an independent investigative firm to review all of Alcatel-Lucent's 300 then-existing agents and consultants. [...] Additionally, [...] Alcatel-Lucent commenced a review of its Board of Directors' and other senior management's knowledge of, and involvement in, any of the wrongdoing. As part of this review, interviews were conducted of 26 individuals who were either current high-ranking members of Alcatel-Lucent's management, former high-ranking members of Alcatel's management, or were in a position to provide information relevant to the review. Alcatel-Lucent and its counsel also reviewed documents collected from these individuals. [...] Overall, Alcatel-Lucent's outside counsel interviewed over 330 witnesses as part of these investigations, collected data from 201 individuals, and reviewed over 2 million documents, of which over 200,000 documents were produced to the government.[31]

As hinted at above, a main reason pre-enforcement action professional fees and expenses are typically the most expensive aspect of FCPA scrutiny and enforcement is because of the 'where else' question.

The 'where else' question generally works as follows. A company voluntary discloses to the enforcement agencies specific conduct that occurred in country X that could implicate the FCPA. Before the enforcement agencies will agree to resolve any enforcement action concerning the conduct in country X, the enforcement agencies will often ask 'where else.' In other words, if the conduct giving rise to FCPA scrutiny occurred in country X, how do the enforcement agencies know that similar conduct did not also occur in countries A, B, C, D, etc. In short, the 'where else' question asked in instances of FCPA scrutiny often results in a company conducting a world-wide compliance review of its entire operations.

Because cooperation with the government's investigation is an important factor the enforcement agencies weigh in deciding whether to bring an enforcement action, business organizations invariably, yet reluctantly, accept FCPA's counsel's recommendation to broaden the internal investigation to demonstrate cooperation to the enforcement agencies. The next thing the company knows, it is paying for a team of lawyers (accompanied by forensic accountants and other specialists) to travel around the world to answer the 'where else' question even though the voluntary disclosure that got the whole process started involved only specific conduct in a specific country.

Where an instance of FCPA scrutiny is prompted by board of director or senior executive conduct that raises the possibility of a culture of corruption within a company, the 'where else' question would seem like a legitimate law enforcement question. However, the 'where else' question is asked in nearly every instance of FCPA scrutiny as evidenced by FCPA resolution documents. For example, the Magyar Telekom FCPA enforcement action focused on business conduct in Macedonia and Montenegro, but in resolving its FCPA scrutiny the company, in the words of the DOJ, conducted a 'thorough global internal investigation concerning bribery and related misconduct.'[32] Likewise, the Tenaris FCPA enforcement action focused on business conduct in Uzbekistan, but in resolving the action the DOJ cited the company's 'voluntary investigation of the Company's business operations throughout the world.'[33]

The 'where else' question is even asked in instances of FCPA scrutiny focused on conduct in foreign subsidiaries that comprise a meaningless percentage of the company's overall operations. For instance, the Tyson Foods FCPA enforcement action focused on conduct in Mexico involving a subsidiary company that 'comprised less than one percent of Tyson's global net sales.' Even though approximately 85 to 90 percent of Tyson's sales were domestic, in resolving the enforcement action, Tyson 'subjected to rigorous FCPA reviews' all of its wholly-owned production facilities including those located outside of Mexico.[34]

An FCPA practitioner, formerly an SEC FCPA enforcement attorney, stated as follows regarding the 'where else' question:

> *Q*: 'What percentage of FCPA enforcement actions that you have been involved in have resulted in the 'where else' question being asked?'
>
> *A*: 'In my time as a regulator at the Securities and Exchange Commission's Division of Enforcement and in private practice, the 'where else' question has been asked in virtually every single FCPA matter in which I have been involved. I have asked it and it has been asked of me.'
>
> *Q*: 'Do you believe the 'where else' question was appropriate in these instances?'
>
> *A*: 'In some instances it was entirely appropriate for the SEC, the DOJ, and other regulators to ask the 'where else' question. In others, however, the allegations did not support a 'where else' question and it appeared to be more of a fishing expedition and boiler plate question than a well-reasoned question under the facts. 'Where else' is a reasonable and appropriate question when the alleged misconduct appears to be systemic and/or the company under investigation appears to lack the controls necessary to prevent the payment of bribes to foreign government officials. It is not, however, an appropriate question where it is intended to force companies to conduct multi-country internal investigations with little more than the uninformed hunch of a government official who has little or no experience in how businesses work around the world.'[35]

That the 'where else' question is asked in the absence of any meaningful check or judicial oversight raises a host of problematic issues. For instance, FCPA attorneys to whom the 'where else' question is posed have little incentive to pushback as the question often leads to multi-year, multi-country billing bonanzas. Further, the enforcement agency attorneys who frequently ask the 'where else' question increase the demand for FCPA Inc. services and, as you will learn in Chapter 6, often leave government service for FCPA Inc.

Regardless of the merits of the 'where else' question in most instances, and regardless of the necessity of many pre-enforcement action professional fees and expenses, the take-away point is that such fees and expenses are often the most expensive aspect of FCPA scrutiny and enforcement in this new era.

Enforcement Action Day – Fines, Penalties, Disgorgement

Fine, penalty and disgorgement amounts in an actual FCPA enforcement action represent the 'second bucket' of FCPA financial exposure. In this section you will learn how such amounts are calculated by the enforcement agencies as well as certain controversial aspects regarding such amounts.

As explained below, even though the FCPA provides specific criminal fine and civil penalty amounts, the statutory amounts are often of little importance in arriving at actual fine and penalty amounts in a corporate FCPA enforcement action because of the Alternative Fines Act.

Criminal fines

Under the Alternative Fines Act, fines in a criminal enforcement action can be based on up to twice the benefit sought or obtained through the improper conduct.[36] Moreover, the advisory Sentencing Guidelines provide the following general formula used to calculate an advisory fine range in an FCPA enforcement action.

- The starting point under the Guidelines is the base offense level relevant to an FCPA anti-bribery violation – that is offering, giving or soliciting or receiving a bribe.
- This base offense level can be increased based on the value of the benefit received from the improper payment. This results in a total offense level and a base fine amount under the Guidelines.
- From there, a business organization's culpability score is calculated based on a number of factors including: the number of employees in the organization; whether high-level personnel were involved in or condoned the improper conduct; prior criminal history; whether

the organization had a pre-existing compliance and ethics program; voluntary disclosure; cooperation; and acceptance of responsibility.

- A business organization's culpability score then yields a multiplier ratio (such as 1.4 to 2.8), that is then applied to the base fine amount, which then yields an advisory fine range. The DOJ then selects a number based on that fine range (and often times below the fine range) that the business organization then agrees to pay to resolve its alleged FCPA scrutiny.[37]

The above general framework best demonstrates the 'carrots' embedded in the Guidelines that were previously discussed in Chapter 2. In short, a company subject to FCPA scrutiny will receive a lower culpability score based on voluntary disclosure, cooperation and acceptance of responsibility, which then yields a lower multiplier, which then yields a lower fine range. In addition, in cases of voluntary disclosures and cooperating corporate defendants, the DOJ typically selects a fine amount approximately 25 percent below the minimum amount suggested by the Guidelines range.[38]

The DOJ's Guidelines calculations are generally publicly available at least when a DPA or plea agreement is used to resolve a corporate FCPA enforcement action. When an NPA is used to resolve an FCPA enforcement action, the ultimate fine amount and how it as calculated is not transparent.

Even with corporate DPAs and plea agreements, there remains little transparency regarding FCPA criminal fine amounts, particularly as to the value of the benefit allegedly received through the improper payment. The DOJ simply cites a number. The irony in many corporate FCPA enforcement actions is that the company is otherwise viewed as selling the best product or service for the best price. With such companies, can it truly be said that the alleged improper payments were the sole reason the company secured the contract or other benefit received? Does a but-for analysis have a place in arriving at FCPA fine and penalty amounts? In other words, should it be relevant that the company would likely have secured the contract or other benefit at issue anyway, regardless of the improper payment?

A paper titled 'Economic Analysis of Damages under the FCPA' rightly noted that 'to date there has been little consideration of the true benefit of the bribe,' but 'with fines in the hundreds of millions of dollars and increasing enforcement, it is necessary to clearly understand what effect a bribe had on profits and to carefully establish what the but-for profits would have been without the bribe.'[39] The paper noted that 'while a bribe may have led to very high gains, the but-for profits could have been high (and the gain from the bribe low) if the bribe would have little effect on the probability of winning the work or if alternative projects were similarly profitable.'

Civil penalties and disgorgement

Because most FCPA enforcement actions against issuers include both a DOJ and SEC component, it is also important to understand how civil penalties and disgorgement are calculated. Although the FCPA also provides civil penalty amounts, in an SEC FCPA enforcement action the predominate monetary sanction is a non-statutory disgorgement amount of alleged ill-gotten gains. The equitable remedy of disgorgement was first used in an SEC FCPA enforcement action in 2004, and has since been used in the majority of cases and comprises the most significant amount of the SEC's recovery. For instance, in 2012 approximately 85 percent of SEC FCPA settlement amounts consisted of disgorgement and prejudgment interest and in 2011 and 2010 approximately 95 percent of settlement amounts consisted of disgorgement and prejudgment interest.[40]

The shift away from statutory penalty amounts towards disgorgement in most SEC FCPA enforcement action 'raises significant concerns' and it has been noted: 'The history surrounding the passage of the FCPA indicates that it is unclear whether Congress intended that the SEC pursue disgorgement in FCPA enforcement. This fact alone should at least give pause to question the normative function of disgorgement.'[41]

Even with a less than enlightening legislative history, disgorgement of ill-gotten gains would seem to have an intuitive appeal, subject to the but-for issues raised above, in an SEC FCPA enforcement action charging violations of the anti-bribery provisions, given that the company allegedly obtained or retained business because of the improper payment.

However, the SEC's use of the disgorgement remedy has not been limited to cases involving anti-bribery charges. Rather, the SEC also routinely seeks a disgorgement remedy when only charging violations of the FCPA's books and records and internal controls provisions, a practice referred to as no-charged bribery disgorgement.[42] Even more troubling is that in the 2013 SEC enforcement action against Ralph Lauren resolved via an NPA, the SEC obtained a disgorgement remedy even though the company was not charged with anything.[43]

One of the most vocal critics of the SEC's no-charged bribery disgorgement practice is a former SEC Associate Director of Enforcement who has noted:

> Settlements invoking disgorgement but charging no primary anti-bribery violations push the law's boundaries, as disgorgement is predicated on the common-sense notion that an actual, jurisdictionally-cognizable bribe was paid to procure the revenue identified by the SEC in its complaint. [...] No-charged bribery disgorgement settlements appear designed to inflict punishment rather than achieve the goals of equity. [...] Given the bedrock principle that a court's equitable power to order such disgorgement goes only as far as the scope of the violation, it is difficult to determine how a court could lawfully allow disgorgement of profits for uncharged violations without the remedy crossing the line into 'punishment' for the violations actually charged. Although settling companies that willingly accept disgorgement as a remedy in such cases may have important strategic interests at stake – e.g., avoiding primary anti-bribery charges – even these companies (as well as the SEC) must consider that the federal courts may at some point step in and forbid such settlements as beyond 'the bounds of fairness, reasonableness, and adequacy.' [...] At some point [...] Congress may well determine that the practice of seeking 'disgorgements' in cases in which there is no jurisdictionally-cognizable bribery charged by the SEC is an inappropriate use of the agency's authority. In light of these serious legal issues, the Commission itself may wish to re-examine its settlement practices in this arena.[44]

Non-FCPA disgorgement case law clearly holds that because 'disgorgement primarily serves to prevent unjust enrichment,' a 'court may exercise its equitable power only over property causally related to the wrongdoing.'[45] This case law makes clear that while the remedy of disgorgement 'may well be a key to the SEC's efforts to deter others from violating the securities laws ... disgorgement may not be used punitively.'

It is thus difficult to see how a disgorgement remedy premised solely on FCPA books and records and internal controls charges (or no actual charges at all) is not punitive. As FCPA practitioners have noted, 'whether or not a false entry in a company's books and records (or a failure to implement adequate internal controls) truly results in increased profits is open to question.'

No-charged bribery disgorgement is not the only controversial aspect of SEC FCPA enforcement. In most FCPA enforcement actions involving a DOJ and SEC component in which the SEC seeks disgorgement, the DOJ and SEC seek recovery of money for the same conduct in what can only be called double-dipping.

This aspect of SEC FCPA enforcement has caught the attention of Congress. In a 2011 letter from Senator Mike Crapo to the SEC Chairman, Senator Crapo asked, among other FCPA questions, 'under what circumstances, if any, is it appropriate for both the SEC and the

DOJ to seek the recovery of penalties from the same entity for the same conduct.' The SEC Chairman stated:

> The Commission and DOJ do not obtain duplicative penalties in FCPA cases. Typically, the Commission will obtain monetary sanctions in the form of disgorgement (ill-gotten gains) while the DOJ obtains monetary sanctions in the form of penalties. In those rare cases where both the Commission and the DOJ obtain penalties, the total penalty assessed against the company is no greater than it would be if either the Commission or DOJ alone obtained the penalty.[46]

Despite the SEC Chairman's answer, the fact remains as discussed above, that DOJ criminal fines are calculated pursuant to the Sentencing Guidelines in which a key factor determining the ultimate penalty amount is the value of the benefit received by the company from the conduct at issue.

For instance, the 2013 Total enforcement action involved parallel DOJ and SEC enforcement actions and the company agreed to pay approximately $398 million (the third-largest FCPA settlement in history) to resolve its FCPA scrutiny.[47] The DOJ component included a $245 million fine and the SEC component included approximately $153 in disgorgement and prejudgment interest.

It is clear from the enforcement agency documents that approximately $150 million represented a double-dip. The DOJ DPA set forth the Sentencing Guidelines calculation and noted that the base fine was $147 million 'which corresponds to the value of the benefit received in return for the unlawful payments.'[48] The SEC's order stated that the company's improper payments 'netted Total approximately $150 million in profits.' Based on this figure, the SEC ordered Total to pay $153 million in disgorgement and prejudgment interest.[49] In other words, Total repaid the approximate $150 million benefit it received from the alleged improper payments twice – first to the DOJ and then to the SEC. This can only be called double-dipping and it is not unique to the Total enforcement action.

FCPA reform is a topic discussed in more detail in Chapter 9, but one FCPA reform proposal relevant to the issue at hand is to 'eliminate overlapping [FCPA] enforcement jurisdiction' meaning that the 'SEC should get out of the anti-bribery business.' The former DOJ Assistant Chief of the Fraud Section has stated:

> The SEC's enforcement of the anti-bribery provisions raises a fundamental matter of fairness. Take two companies, one public and one private, and assume that both violate the FCPA and realize the same illicit gain from the

> violation. The private company will be subject only to DOJ's jurisdiction and will therefore be exposed to a criminal fine of up to twice its gain. The public company, on the other hand, will be subject both to that criminal fine and to a civil fine and disgorgement of the illicit proceeds, thus potentially paying a third more in fines than the private company for the same conduct.[50]

Others have also argued that the SEC should stop enforcing the FCPA's anti-bribery provisions because 'fighting global corruption is not part of the SEC's mission.'[51] Should the SEC be removed from enforcing the FCPA's anti-bribery provisions, and many FCPA reform bills in the mid-1980s contained such provisions, it could be called 'granting the wish' as the FCPA legislative history makes clear that the SEC never wanted any part in enforcing the FCPA anti-bribery provisions.[52]

Regardless of the controversy and lack of transparency surrounding various aspects of corporate FCPA fine, penalty and disgorgement amounts, FCPA enforcement actions in this new era have resulted in several large settlements. Table 5.1 contains the largest FCPA corporate settlement amounts in history as of August 2013.

What is interesting to note about the above figures is that in 2007 the largest FCPA corporate settlement in history was a 'mere' $44 million.[53] Simply put, FCPA settlement amounts have come a long way in a short amount of time. Even though FCPA enforcement actions in this new era have resulted in several large settlement amounts, it would be inaccurate to conclude from the above chart that every FCPA enforcement action in this new era yields settlement amounts in the hundreds or tens of million. Indeed, many FCPA enforcement actions in this new era have been resolved for under $5 million in combined fine, penalty and disgorgement amounts.[54]

Post-Enforcement Action Professional Fees and Expenses

The financial exposure of FCPA scrutiny and enforcement continues even after enforcement action day. In this section you will learn about the 'third bucket' of FCPA financial exposure – post-enforcement action professional fees and expenses.

As previously noted in Chapter 2, nearly all corporate FCPA enforcement actions in this new era are resolved via NPAs or DPAs. A common clause in such agreements is a requirement that the company report to the enforcement agencies during the usual two- to three-year term of the agreement regarding, among other things, its implementation of an FCPA compliance program and its ongoing compliance efforts.[55] While such a requirement may seem simple and straightforward, it often involves

Table 5.1 Largest FCPA corporate settlements

Company	Amount	Year
Siemens	$800 million (DOJ – $450 million) (SEC – $350 million)	2008
KBR/Halliburton	$579 million (DOJ – $402 million) (SEC – $177 million)	2009
Total	$398 million (DOJ – $245 million) (SEC – $153 million)	2013
Snamprogetti/ENI	$365 million (DOJ – $240 million) (SEC – $125 million)	2010
Technnip	$338 million (DOJ – $240 million) (SEC – $ 98 million)	2010
JGC	$219 million (DOJ – $219 million)	2011
Daimler	$185 million (DOJ – $94 million) (SEC – $91 million)	2010
Alcatel-Lucent	$137 million (DOJ – $92 million) (SEC – $45 million)	2010
Magyar Telekom/Deutsche Telekom	$95 million (DOJ – $64 million) (SEC – $31 million)	2011
Panalpina	$82 million (DOJ – $71 million) (SEC – $11 million)	2010

internal reviews, follow-up reviews, and written reports that occupy FCPA Inc. participants for hundreds of hours and often cost the company millions of dollars in professional fees and expenses.

In addition to the above standard post-enforcement action compliance obligation in a typical FCPA NPA or DPA, the enforcement agencies are also often imposing 'enhanced compliance obligations' on companies as a condition of settlement.

For instance, healthcare company Johnson & Johnson (J&J) resolved an FCPA enforcement action focused on subsidiary conduct in Greece, Poland, and Romania. The enforcement action was resolved via a DPA, and the DOJ specifically noted: 'J&J had a pre-existing compliance and ethics program that was effective and the majority of problematic operations globally resulted from insufficient implementation of the J&J compliance and ethics program in acquired companies.'[56] The DPA contained the standard compliance obligations found in typical FCPA DPAs, but also included 'enhanced compliance obligations' that J&J is required to abide by during the three-year term of the DPA.

Even though the DPA stated that J&J, as part of the voluntary disclosure process, 'conducted an extensive, global review of all of its operations to determine if there were problems elsewhere,' the 'enhanced compliance obligations' nevertheless require J&J to 'conduct risk assessments of markets where [the company] has government customers and/or other anticorruption compliance risks on a staggered, periodic basis.'

In what seems like an FCPA Inc. full employment act, the DPA also requires J&J to 'identify no less than five operating companies that are high risk for corruption because of their sector and location and [...] conduct FCPA audits of those operating companies at least once every three years.' As stated in the DPA, 'FCPA audits of other operating companies that pose corruption risk shall occur no less than once every five years.'

Pursuant to the DPA, 'each FCPA audit shall include' the following:

> (i) on-site visits by an audit team comprised of qualified auditors who have received FCPA and anticorruption training; (ii) where appropriate, participation in the on-site visits by personnel from the compliance and legal functions; (iii) review of a statistically representative sample appropriately adjusted for the risks of the market, of contracts with and payments to individual health care providers; (iv) creation of action plans resulting from issues identified during audits; and (v) where appropriate, feasible, and permissible under local law, review of the books and records of distributors which, in the view of the audit team, may present corruption risk.

Such 'enhanced compliance obligations' would seem wholly inappropriate given the DOJ's conclusion that J&J already had generally 'effective' compliance policies and procedures and given that the company, prior to resolving the enforcement action, already 'conducted an extensive, global review of all of its operations to determine if there were problems elsewhere …'.

Likewise the FCPA enforcement action against pharmaceutical company Pfizer also required the company to adhere to 'enhanced compliance obligations' notwithstanding the following pertinent facts alleged by the enforcement agencies:

> (i) the substantial bulk of the enforcement action concerned conduct by entities Pfizer acquired in 2003 and 2009; (ii) in the 18 months following its 2009 acquisition of an entity giving rise to its scrutiny, Pfizer conducted a due diligence and investigative review of the entity's business operations and integrated Pfizer's internal controls system into the business entities; (iii) there was no allegation or suggestion that anyone at corporate headquarters knew of or approved the conduct at issue; (iv) as soon as the problematic conduct came to the attention of Pfizer's corporate headquarters, it made a timely voluntary disclosure to the enforcement agencies; and (v) Pfizer's self-investigation was thorough and wide-ranging.[57]

As to this later point, the DOJ stated: 'From 2004 to the present, Pfizer, using external counsel and forensic accountants, internal Legal, Compliance, and Corporate Audit personnel, conducted an extensive, global review of its operations regarding allegations of improper payments to Government officials and government doctors …'. Likewise, the SEC stated: '[Since 2004, Pfizer] diligently and thoroughly undertook a global internal investigation of its operations in no less than 19 countries …'.

According to the enforcement agencies, Pfizer also undertook early and extensive remedial efforts and made substantial and continuing improvements to its global anti-corruption compliance policies and procedures. Specifically, the DOJ stated:

> [S]tarting immediately in 2004, Pfizer launched extensive remedial actions including: undertaken a comprehensive review of its compliance program, implementing enhanced anti-corruption compliance policies and procedures on a worldwide basis, developing global systems to support employee compliance with the enhanced procedures, adding FCPA-specific reviews to its internal audits, performing proactive anti-corruption compliance reviews in approximately ten markets annually, and conducting comprehensive anti-corruption training throughout the organization.

Thus, since learning of potential FCPA issues and for approximately eight years therafter, Pfizer did the right thing and when the enforcement agencies use words like thorough, wide-ranging, extensive, global, worldwide, diligent, comprehensive, proactive, significant, innovative and sophisticated, there can be no reasonable doubt about this. Yet, just as in the J&J enforcement action, the Pfizer DPA required the company to adhere to similar 'enhanced compliance obligations.'

Given the enforcement agencies' allegations and findings as to J&J and Pfizer, were the 'enhanced compliance obligations' truly necessary? Or were these 'enhanced compliance obligations' examples of companies being required by the government (under risk of prosecution for failure to do so) to engage in fishing expeditions when the company has already gone fishing just for the sake of going fishing again? If so, the 'enhanced compliance obligations' represent a boundless and unconstrained government-required transfer of shareholder wealth to FCPA Inc. Such fishing expeditions are of course lucrative for FCPA Inc., hence one reason not many in the industry have raised concerns about the emerging trend of 'enhanced compliance obligations.'

In addition to standard post-enforcement action compliance obligations or 'enhanced compliance obligations' as a condition of resolving a corporate FCPA enforcement action, certain companies have also been required to engage an independent compliance monitor as a condition of settlement. For instance, in 2012 approximately 35 percent of corporate DOJ FCPA enforcement actions required the engagement of a compliance monitor.[58]

As noted in the FCPA Guidance, 'a monitor is an independent third party who assesses and monitors a company's adherence to the compliance requirements of an agreement that was designed to reduce the risk of recurrence of the company's misconduct.' The term monitor is a bit misleading as it suggests a single person. The reality is that a monitor, while a single person, is more like the conductor of a large orchestra and a monitorship can become an expensive and distracting requirement of resolving an FCPA enforcement action.

FCPA practitioners have observed:

> Few penalties imposed on a corporate criminal offender cause as much consternation as do compliance monitors. After the late-night crisis management meetings, after the invasive and expensive internal investigation, after the shakeup of senior managers, and after the protracted negotiations with federal authorities, companies just want to get back to business. They want to sell their goods and services, be profitable, invest, and grow. In short, they want to move on. Fundamentally, the corporate compliance monitor stands in the way of forgetting the past and going back to 'business as usual' – at least when it comes to obeying the law. The monitor's purpose is to see that the company follows applicable laws and regulations going forward and institutes the proper policies and procedures to help ensure compliance. Corporations will never welcome this 'tail' to their criminal prosecutions. Monitorships inevitably involve significant expenditures of funds and time.[59]

According to the FCPA Guidance, the enforcement agencies consider the following factors when determining whether a compliance monitor is an appropriate requirement of a corporate FCPA enforcement action: seriousness of the offense; duration of the misconduct; pervasiveness of the misconduct, including whether the conduct cuts across geographic and/or product lines; nature and size of the company; quality of the company's compliance program at the time of the misconduct; and subsequent remediation efforts.

Based on these factors, it was not surprising that Siemens was required to engage a compliance monitor when resolving its FCPA enforcement action in 2008. As previously highlighted, in resolving the largest FCPA enforcement action of all-time, the enforcement agencies stated that 'for much of its operations across the globe, bribery was nothing less than standard operating procedure for Siemens' and that Siemens had a 'corporate culture in which bribery was tolerated and even rewarded at the highest levels of the company.'

In 2012, the term of Siemens' monitor ended and the DOJ determined that Siemens satisfied its settlement obligations with respect to the monitor. The DOJ's filing provides an informative insight into the extent of the monitor's work and stated:

> In accordance with the plea agreement, the Monitor conducted an initial review and three subsequent reviews of Siemens's anti-corruption compliance program, and documented the Monitor's findings and recommendations in four annual reports [...]. Over the course of those four years, the Monitor conducted on-site or remote reviews of Siemens' activities in 20 countries; conducted limited or issue-specific reviews in or relating to an additional 19 countries; reviewed over 51,000 documents totaling more than 973,000 pages in 11 languages; conducted interviews of or meetings with over 2,300 Siemens employees; observed over 180 regularly scheduled company events; and spent the equivalent of over 3,000 auditor days conducting financial studies and testing.[60]

Siemens has not disclosed its post-enforcement action professional fees and expenses, including the monitor costs, but one can safely assume such fees and expenses were in the hundreds of millions of dollars and in addition to the approximate billion dollars the company spent in pre-enforcement action professional fees and expenses as well as the $800 million the company agreed to pay to resolve its FCPA scrutiny.

Monitor costs can also reach into the millions of dollars even in less high-profile FCPA enforcement actions. For instance, oil and gas services company Willbros Group agreed to pay approximately $32 million in combined fines and penalties to resolve parallel DOJ and SEC FCPA enforcement actions concerning conduct in Nigeria, Ecuador and Bolivia. Pursuant to the DPA, the company was required to engage a compliance monitor and the company disclosed total monitor expenses of approximately $10 million.[61] Likewise, Faro Technologies agreed to pay approximately $3 million in combined fines and penalties to resolve parallel DOJ and SEC FCPA enforcement concerning conduct in China.

Pursuant to the DPA, the company was required to engage a compliance monitor and the company disclosed monitor expenses of $1 million in just one quarter.[62]

Regardless of which of the 'three buckets' the money falls into, the take-away point from this section is that FCPA scrutiny and enforcement are expensive and the fines and penalties announced in an FCPA enforcement action are often just the tip of the iceberg in terms of a company's overall financial exposure.

Yet the question is asked: does FCPA scrutiny and enforcement need to be so expensive? Does Wal-Mart really need to be spending $1.1 million per day in pre-enforcement action professional fees and expenses to address its FCPA scrutiny? Did Siemens' monitor really need to have meetings with 2,300 employees? Did Willbros Group really need to spend $10 million on its FCPA compliance monitor?

Or has FCPA scrutiny and enforcement turned into a government-sanctioned boondoggle for many in FCPA Inc?

C. CORPORATE ENFORCEMENT ACTIONS

The last two sections of this chapter analyze and compare corporate FCPA enforcement and individual FCPA enforcement. Simply put, there are two different FCPA enforcement regimes with different dynamics and issues.

Facts and Figures

This section begins by highlighting certain facts and figures regarding corporate FCPA enforcement. Next, certain uncomfortable truths regarding corporate FCPA enforcement are exposed, including how certain companies in certain industries appear to be immune from FCPA anti-bribery charges and how the fight against bribery and corruption suffers from several double standards.

For most of the FCPA's history, FCPA risk was generally found in the oil and gas industry, other resource extraction companies, or those actually doing business with foreign governments. This of course was consistent with Congressional intent in enacting the FCPA, including that the anti-bribery provisions were intended to capture payments in the context of foreign government procurement and seeking to influence foreign laws and legislation. However, given the enforcement theories in this new era discussed in Chapters 3 and 4, particularly 'foreign official' and 'obtain or retain business,' no industry is immune from FCPA scrutiny.

While the oil and gas and resource extraction industries continue to comprise a meaningful percentage of FCPA enforcement actions, companies in the following industries have also recently resolved FCPA enforcement actions: apparel; liquor; electronics; various manufacturing sectors; telecommunications; pharmaceutical, healthcare and medical devices; insurance; airlines and airline service; technology; power; financial services; food and agriculture; and military and law enforcement products.

Conduct giving rise to an FCPA enforcement action can occur in any foreign country, and recent FCPA enforcement actions have involved business conduct in Mexico, Panama, Nigeria, Poland, Argentina, Indonesia, China, Brazil, Russia, Thailand and Saudi Arabia.[63]

During this new era, the enforcement agencies have received praise for their FCPA enforcement efforts. For instance, in the OECD's 2010 review of U.S. enforcement of the FCPA, the OECD 'commended the United States for its […] substantial enforcement, and commitment from the highest levels of the U.S. Government' and noted that 'the United States has investigated and prosecuted the most foreign bribery cases among the Parties to the Anti-Bribery Convention.'[64] In the immediate aftermath of the OECD report, the DOJ, SEC, State Department and Commerce Department jointly issued a press release titled 'OECD Commends United States for Its Efforts to Fight Transnational Bribery.'[65] In the release, the DOJ Assistant Attorney General stated: 'The United States has risen to the forefront of enhanced global efforts to combat foreign bribery, including through our vigorous enforcement of the FCPA.' Likewise, a Commerce Department official stated: 'This report shows that the United States is serious about fighting corruption in international business transactions, and sets a high standard for global cooperation in this fight.'

The enforcement agencies also frequently boast about the number of FCPA enforcement actions they are bringing. For instance in 2013, the Acting Assistant Attorney General stated 'our stellar FCPA Unit continues to go gangbusters, bringing case after case' and 'we are not going away … our efforts to fight foreign bribery are more robust than ever.'[66]

There is no question that during this new era of FCPA enforcement the enforcement agencies have been 'successful' in piggybacking off foreign law enforcement actions and processing corporate voluntary disclosures in bringing corporate FCPA enforcement actions. In large measure, the enforcement agencies do not actually enforce the FCPA against corporate actors. Rather, the enforcement agencies exercise leverage and the ability to bring actual charges against risk-averse corporate actors who are mindful of the 'carrots' and 'sticks' relevant to resolving an FCPA enforcement action. As previously highlighted, nearly all corporate FCPA enforcement actions in this new era are resolved via NPAs or DPAs, are often based on dubious legal theories, and are negotiated behind closed doors in the absence of meaningful judicial scrutiny. Are these dynamics something to praise or something to lament?

Moreover, in this new era 'success' seems to be measured by quantity of enforcement actions and settlement amounts. But is this an appropriate proxy for success? One of the ironies of the OECD's Report was this contradiction: while loudly praising the U.S. for its 'high level' of enforcement, the Report quietly criticized and questioned many of the policies and enforcement theories which yield the 'high level' of enforcement. For instance, the Report noted that the FCPA's language 'does not specifically convey' that cases concerning 'an operating license or permit to operate a business, or a reduction in tax or import duty' are in violation of the statute. Yet, many FCPA enforcement actions are based on this theory. Further, the Report noted that 'due to an absence of explicit language in the definition of foreign official' it is an open question whether employees of so-called state-owned or state-controlled enterprises are 'foreign officials' under the FCPA. Yet, numerous FCPA enforcement actions are based on this theory. The Report also noted that the increase in NPAs and DPAs is 'one of the reasons for the impressive FCPA enforcement record in the U.S.,' yet also noted that these agreements are subject to little or no judicial scrutiny.

Success in enforcing a law, whether in the corporate context or individual context discussed later in this chapter, is best measured by instances in which an enforcement agency is actually put to its burden of proof in an adversarial proceeding. Using this measure of success, the DOJ is 0–2 in corporate FCPA enforcement actions and it is believed that the SEC has never been put to its burden of proof in a corporate FCPA enforcement action.

Chapter 1 previously highlighted the 1990 enforcement action against Harris Corporation and certain of its executives that resulted in a judgment of acquittal based on insufficient evidence. A 2010 FCPA enforcement action against Lindsey Manufacturing Company and two of its executives (CEO Keith Lindsey and CFO Steve Lee) is the only other instance in FCPA history of a corporate defendant putting the DOJ to its burden of proof at trial. The DOJ charged the defendants with FCPA offenses for their alleged roles in a conspiracy to pay bribes to alleged Mexican 'foreign officials.'[67] The company and its executives were found guilty of various FCPA charges after a five-week jury trial and the DOJ issued a same-day press release calling the verdict an 'important milestone' in its FCPA enforcement efforts as Lindsey Manufacturing was the first company ever to be tried and convicted of FCPA offenses.[68]

However, the trial was flawed and the milestone was short-lived as the trial judge, after months of post-trial legal wrangling, vacated the convictions and dismissed the indictment after finding numerous instances of prosecutorial misconduct. In the words of the judge, the instances of misconduct were so varied and occurred over such a long period of time 'that they add up to an unusual and extreme picture of a prosecution gone badly awry.'[69] The judge specifically cited the following missteps:

> The Government team allowed a key FBI agent to testify untruthfully before the grand jury, inserted material falsehoods into affidavits submitted to magistrate judges in support of applications for search warrants and seizure warrants, improperly reviewed e-mail communications between one defendant and her lawyer, recklessly failed to comply with its discovery obligations, posed questions to certain witnesses in violation of the Court's order, engaged in questionable behavior during close arguments and even made misrepresentations to the court.[70]

In a striking close to his order dismissing the case, the judge stated:

> Dr. Lindsey and Mr. Lee were put through a severe ordeal. Charges were filed against them as a result of a sloppy, incomplete and notably over-zealous investigation, an investigation that was so flawed that the Government's lawyers tried to prevent inquiry into it. In some instances motives, statements and conduct were attributed to them that were wholly unfounded or were obtained unlawfully. [...] The financial costs of the investigation and trial were immense, but the emotional drubbing [Lindsey and Lee] absorbed was even worse. As for [Lindsey Manufacturing], the very survival of that small, once highly-respected enterprise has been placed in jeopardy.[71]

Uncomfortable Truths

In 2012, the DOJ Assistant Attorney General stated: 'We in the United States are in a unique position to spread the gospel of anti-corruption, because there is no country that enforces its anti-bribery laws more vigorously than we do. The DOJ's record of accomplishment in this area is a signature achievement of ours ...'.[72]

However, there are certain uncomfortable truths regarding corporate FCPA enforcement in this new era that are exposed in this section, including how certain companies in certain industries appear to be immune from FCPA anti-bribery charges and how the general fight against bribery and corruption suffers from several double standards.

Bribery, yet no bribery

Equal treatment and absence of discrimination are commonly accepted rule of law principles. These fundamental principles are also found in Article 5 of the OECD Convention which states, under the heading 'Enforcement,' that prosecution of bribery offenses 'shall not be influenced by considerations of national economic interest, the potential effect upon relations with another State or the identity of the natural or legal persons involved.'

However, several high-profile instances of corporate bribery seemingly violate these principles in that the companies were not charged with violating the FCPA's anti-bribery provisions in what can be called bribery, yet no bribery enforcement actions.

For instance, while Siemens resolved the largest FCPA enforcement action in history and agreed to pay a record $800 million in combined fines and penalties, the company was not charged with violating the FCPA's anti-bribery provisions despite clear allegations supporting such charges. Among other allegations, the DOJ alleged that certain Siemens subsidiary companies with offices in the U.S. participated in the bribery scheme. If ever a company deserved to be prosecuted for FCPA anti-bribery violations, it was Siemens. Yet, the DOJ criminal information charged Siemens only with violating the FCPA's books and records and internal controls provisions.[73] A key factor the DOJ considered in resolving the case against Siemens in the way it did was the 'collateral consequences' that could have resulted from criminal anti-bribery charges including the 'risk of debarment and exclusion from government contracts.'[74]

Another example of a bribery, yet no bribery enforcement action involved BAE Systems ('BAE'). For years, British defense contractor BAE Systems had been under intense scrutiny concerning allegations that it engaged in widespread bribery and corruption. In 2010, the DOJ filed a criminal information against BAE. Among other allegations, the information charged that BAE served as the 'prime contractor to the U.K. government following the conclusion of a Formal Understanding between the U.K. and the Kingdom of Saudi Arabia ('KSA')' in which BAE sold several Tornado and Hawk aircraft, 'along with other military hardware, training and services' to the U.K. government, which sold the material and services to the Saudi government.[75] The information refers to these frequent arrangements as the 'KSA Fighter Deals.'

In connection with these deals, the information alleged that 'BAE provided substantial benefits to one KSA public official, who was in a position of influence regarding the KSA Fighter Deals (the 'KSA Official'), and to the KSA Official's associates.' According to the information, BAE 'provided these benefits through various payment mechanisms both in the territorial jurisdiction of the U.S. and elsewhere.' The information contained additional allegations that clearly demonstrated that BAE's bribery scheme had a U.S. nexus. For instance, the information alleged that BAE 'provided support services to [the] KSA Official while in the territory of the U.S.' and that these benefits 'included the purchase of travel and accommodations, security services, real estate, automobiles and personal items.' The information alleged that during one year a single BAE employee submitted over $5 million in invoices for benefits provided to the KSA Official.

The information also alleged that BAE 'used intermediaries and shell entities to conceal payments to certain advisors who were assisting in the solicitation, promotion and otherwise endeavoring to secure the conclusion or maintenance of the KSA Fighter Deals.' Specifically, the information alleged that 'in connection with the KSA Fighter Deals, BAE agreed to transfer sums totaling more than £10,000,000 and more than $9,000,000 to a bank account in Switzerland controlled by an intermediary.' According to the information, 'BAE was aware that there was a high probability that the intermediary would transfer part of these payments to the KSA Official.' Though unnamed in the DOJ information, the Saudi intermediary was widely reported to be Saudi Prince Bandar bin Sultan – at the time the Saudi Ambassador to the U.S.

Despite the above allegations, the DOJ's criminal information merely charged BAE with one count of conspiracy for 'making certain false, inaccurate and incomplete statements to the U.S. government and failing to honor certain undertakings given to the U.S. government, thereby defrauding the United States' and 'causing to be filed export license applications with [various U.S. government entities] that omitted a material fact' concerning fee and commission payments.

In other words, BAE was not charged with FCPA anti-bribery violations even though among the false statements BAE was alleged to have made to the U.S. government was its commitment to not knowingly violating the FCPA. This was the only mention of the FCPA in the criminal information despite the above allegations concerning the KSA Fighter Deals – facts that clearly implicated the FCPA's anti-bribery provisions.

Like in the Siemens enforcement action, a key factor the DOJ considered in resolving the case against BAE in the way it did was the 'collateral consequences' that could have resulted from criminal anti-bribery charges including the risk of debarment and exclusion from government contracts.[76]

BAE did plead guilty to the criminal information and agreed to pay a $400 million fine.[77] Thus, like Siemens, BAE clearly did not escape liability for its egregious conduct, but the lack of FCPA anti-bribery violations against BAE is just as startling as in the Siemens matter.

Under the rule of law and consistent with OECD Article 5, facts are to be applied to the law, and the law is to be applied equally to all subject to the law. However, Siemens and BAE were no ordinary companies. Siemens is a major U.S. government contractor and its diverse business units have contracts with a wide range of U.S. government agencies, including Department of Defense, Department of the Air Force, Department of the Army, Department of Transportation, Department of Health and Human Services, Department of Energy, Department of Commerce, Department of Housing and Urban Development, and the General Services Administration. Likewise, BAE is a major U.S. government contractor and the criminal information specifically stated that the company is the largest defense contractor in Europe and the fifth largest in the U.S. as measured by sales.

The uncomfortable truth is that some of the most egregious FCPA violators, per the DOJ's own allegations, are some of the largest and most important U.S. government contractors or suppliers including of goods and services critical to national security.

The manner in which the Siemens and BAE enforcement actions were resolved significantly undermines numerous enforcement agency statements regarding its FCPA enforcement program. More broadly, maximum deterrence is not achieved when the FCPA is enforced in an inconsistent fashion and where the end result is that certain companies in certain industries are essentially immune from FCPA anti-bribery charges.

For these companies, as well as the U.S. government, notwithstanding egregious allegations of corporate bribery, business continues as usual. For instance, on the same day Siemens agreed to resolve the record-setting FCPA enforcement action, the company announced that the U.S. government issued a formal determination declaring Siemens a 'responsible contractor,' a designation that assisted the company in continuing to do business with the U.S. government even though an entity found in violation of the FCPA may be barred from doing business with the federal government.[78] Likewise, in the aftermath of the BAE enforcement actions, the FBI, the same agency that investigated BAE's conduct and issued a press release stating that 'corporations and individuals who conspire to defeat [competition] not only cause harm but ultimately shake the public's confidence in the entire system,' awarded the company a $40 million contract.[79]

Double standard

Another uncomfortable truth regarding FCPA enforcement in this new era is that the general fight against bribery and corruption suffers from several double standards. For instance, what if bribery occurs with the knowledge and support of the highest levels of the U.S. government? You learned in Chapter 1 that this was one of the most troubling aspects of the foreign corporate payments problem Congress became aware of during the FCPA legislative process.

A notable FCPA enforcement action regarding the oil and gas industry demonstrates that this troubling aspect has not disappeared. In 2003, James Giffen was criminally charged with 'making more than $78 million in unlawful payments to two senior officials of the Republic of Kazakhstan in connection with six separate oil transactions, in which the American oil companies Mobil Oil, Amoco, Texaco and Phillips Petroleum acquired valuable oil and gas rights in Kazakhstan.'[80]

However, Giffen's defense was that his actions were made with the knowledge and support of the CIA, the National Security Council, the Department of State and the White House.[81] The DOJ did not dispute that Giffen had frequent contacts with senior U.S. intelligence officials or that he used his ties within the Kazakh government to assist the United States. With the court's approval, Giffen sought discovery from the government to support his public authority defense, and much of the delay in the case was due to the government's resistance to such discovery and who was entitled to see such discovery. In 2010, the enforcement action took a sudden and mysterious turn when Giffen agreed to plead guilty to a one-paragraph superseding indictment charging a misdemeanor tax violation. The enforcement action ended with the presiding judge imposing no jail time on Giffen and stating that he was a Cold War hero and that the enforcement action should have never been brought in the first place.[82]

Giffen presumably prevailed over the DOJ not because of the facts or the law, but because he possessed significant leverage over the U.S. government in that he asserted his actions were taken with the knowledge and support of the highest levels of the government. A *Foreign Policy* columnist noted that Giffen's legal team 'understood correctly that he could set up a collision between the DOJ and the CIA in which the latter would probably prevail.'[83] Likewise, a *Harpers* columnist noted that the Giffen enforcement action had 'been the focus of political manipulation concern for years' and that the end of the case seemed to ratify that view and 'the notion of an independent, politically insulated criminal-justice administration in America [took] another severe hit.'[84]

It is troubling to think that the U.S. government condones bribery when done with the approval or the wink and nod of government officials while aggressively prosecuting business organizations competing in the global marketplace subject to many difficult and complex conditions.

Another aspect of the double standard relevant to the general fight against bribery and corruption concerns how corporate interactions with 'foreign officials' are subject to greater scrutiny and different standards of enforcement than corporate interactions with U.S. officials. After all, the U.S. domestic bribery statute (18 USC § 201) has elements very similar to the FCPA.

For instance, imagine a foreign country in which the president is actively seeking corporate money to fund inaugural festivities. You would be correct to spot many FCPA red flags associated with this activity. But wait, the above scenario describes not a foreign country, but the United States and President Obama's 2013 inauguration in which his fundraising advisers offered exclusive access to an array of inaugural festivities to corporations and other institutions that contribute $1 million.[85]

At the same time however, the enforcement agencies are bringing FCPA enforcement actions against business organizations for conduct that includes providing bottles of wine, watches, cameras, kitchen appliances, business suits, and executive education classes to foreign physicians or individuals employed by foreign companies that are allegedly state-owned or state-controlled.

Consider as well the following examples.[86]

A company learns of potential legislation that will negatively affect its business. A company representative reportedly begs a government official (who heads a key committee that will decide the fate of the legislation) to vote in a way that serves the company's interest and the company otherwise spends millions to seek to influence the legislative body. The government official reverses his prior position and votes in a way that serves the company's interest. One month later, the company's CEO and the government official appear at an event in which the company announces it is making a $30 million charitable donation, $11 million of which will benefit schools in the government official's district, the largest gift ever to the city's schools.

Businesses are prohibited from making campaign contributions to a government official. So businesses give money to a foundation set up by the government official's wife months after the official took office. Even though the charity is named and led by the official's wife, the government official is pictured alongside his wife on the corporate solicitation page of the charity's website and the official's chief fundraiser is listed as the charity's treasurer.

A government official sets up a foundation to aid local organizations. It is funded by business entities that often turn to the government official for help and usually succeed in getting such help. Over a six-week period, a company sends at least $45,000 in donations to four charitable programs founded by government officials just as the companies were seeking approval of favorable legislation. Another company supports a fundraiser for the scholarship fund of a government official. Another company sponsors a sports competition to help the favorite food bank of a government official. Another company subsidizes a spa outing in a popular tourist destination to aid the charity of a government official. Another company helps sponsor a golf tournament benefiting the foundation of a government official. Another company acknowledges that it participates in government officials' charitable events to get access to the officials to push the company's agenda.

A prudent FCPA professional would immediately see the red flags and counsel the companies at issue to conduct an internal investigation as to the conduct at issue and related conduct and – mindful of the enforcement agencies guidance and cognizant of the 'carrots' and 'sticks' they possess – likely suggest voluntarily disclosure of the investigative findings.

But wait. The government officials in all of the above actual scenarios were not 'foreign officials,' they were U.S. government officials!

Scrap those internal investigation plans, forget about voluntary disclosure, and slim chance there will be an enforcement action. Some will say nobody said the U.S. system was perfect, but that is just how the system works. But why should business interactions with 'foreign officials' be subject to different standards than business interactions with U.S. officials? Is the FCPA enforced too aggressively or is enforcement of the U.S. domestic bribery statute too lax? Ought not there be some consistency between these two laws?

At the very least, the enforcement actions and other actual scenarios discussed in this section should cause us to pause and reflect whether, in the words of the DOJ, 'we in the United States are in a unique position to spread the gospel of anti-corruption, because there is no country that enforces its anti-bribery laws more vigorously than we do.'

As previously highlighted, the FCPA's legislative history contained the following statement as to the basic issue of defining bribery:

> There will be countless situations in which a fair-minded investigator or judge will be hard-put to determine whether a particular payment or practice is a legitimate and permissible business activity or a means of improper influence. [...] Reasonable men and even angels will differ on the answers to these and similar questions. At the very least such distinctions should make us less sweeping in our judgments and less confident of our solutions.[87]

Thirty-five years later this statement still holds true given the uncomfortable truths concerning certain aspects of FCPA enforcement as well as the general fight against bribery and corruption.

D. INDIVIDUAL ENFORCEMENT ACTIONS

This section concerns individual FCPA enforcement actions. Key to achieving deterrence in the FCPA context is prosecuting individuals to the extent the individual's conduct legitimately satisfies the elements of an FCPA violation. For a corporate employee with job duties that provide an opportunity to violate the FCPA, it is easy to dismiss corporate money being used to pay corporate FCPA fines and penalties. On the other hand, it is not easy to dismiss hearing of an individual with a similar background and job duties being criminally indicted and sent to federal prison for violating the FCPA.

The enforcement agencies have long recognized that an FCPA enforcement program based solely on corporate fines is not effective and does not adequately deter future FCPA violations. For instance, in 1986 the DOJ Deputy Assistant Attorney General stated:

> If the risk of conduct in violation of the [FCPA] becomes merely monetary, the fine will simply become a cost of doing business, payable only upon being caught and in many instances, it will be only a fraction of the profit acquired from the corrupt activity. Absent the threat of incarceration, there may no longer be any compelling need to resist the urge to acquire business in any way possible.[88]

In 2010, the DOJ Deputy Chief of the Fraud Section likewise stated that a corporate fine-only FCPA enforcement program allows companies to calculate FCPA settlements as the cost of doing business.[89] In this new era, the DOJ has consistently stated that prosecution of individuals is a 'cornerstone' of its FCPA enforcement strategy, and in a 2012 speech the Assistant Attorney General stated: 'If you look at the FCPA over the past four years, you'll see we really have been vigorous about holding individuals accountable.'[90]

However, despite enforcement agency rhetoric, this section demonstrates that FCPA enforcement in this new era is largely corporate enforcement only. The vast majority of corporate FCPA enforcement actions lack related individual prosecutions and reasons for this apparent contradiction will be explored. Further, empirical data will be highlighted raising the issue of whether there are two tiers of justice in this new era of FCPA enforcement.

To be sure, on occasion individuals are prosecuted for FCPA violations. Like the 'carrots' and 'sticks' relevant to resolving corporate FCPA enforcement actions discussed in Chapter 2, this section also highlights various 'carrots' and 'sticks' relevant to resolving individual FCPA enforcement actions and how these 'carrots' and 'sticks' likewise often induce individuals subject to FCPA scrutiny to resolve enforcement actions for reasons of risk aversion and not necessarily because the enforcement agency has a superior legal position.

This section also documents how the enforcement agencies have generally struggled when put to its burden of proof in individual enforcement actions prompting the question – what percentage of enforcement agency losses in FCPA individual prosecutions is acceptable? Finally, this section concludes with a discussion of sentencing issues in individual FCPA enforcement actions and how sentencing judges often see shades of gray in FCPA enforcement that the DOJ portrays to be black and white.

Facts and Figures

From 2005 to 2012, the DOJ has charged 93 individuals with FCPA criminal offenses. The breakdown is as follows.

- 2005 – 3 individuals
- 2006 – 6 individuals
- 2007 – 7 individuals
- 2008 – 14 individuals
- 2009 – 18 individuals
- 2010 – 33 individuals
- 2011 – 10 individuals
- 2012 – 2 individuals[91]

An analysis of the numbers reveals some interesting points.

Most of the individuals, 77 (or 83 percent), were charged since 2008. Thus, on one level the DOJ is correct when it states that individual prosecutions are a 'cornerstone' of its FCPA enforcement strategy and that it has been 'vigorous about holding individuals accountable,' at least as measured against the historical average in that between 1978 and 2004, the DOJ charged 53 individuals with FCPA criminal offenses.

Yet on another level, a more meaningful level given that there was much less overall DOJ FCPA enforcement between 1978 and 2004, the DOJ's rhetoric that it is 'vigorous about holding individuals accountable' proves hollow as demonstrated by the below figures.

Of the 77 individuals criminally charged with FCPA offenses by the DOJ since 2008:

- 22 individuals were in the Africa Sting case;
- 9 individuals were in an enforcement action concerning Haiti Teleco;
- 8 individuals were in connection with the Control Components enforcement action;
- 8 individuals were in connection with the Siemens enforcement action;
- 4 individuals were in connection with the Lindsey Manufacturing enforcement action;
- 4 individuals were in connection with an enforcement action concerning Hondutel; and
- 4 individuals were in connection with the Nexus Technologies enforcement action.[92]

In other words, 61 percent of the individuals charged by the DOJ with FCPA criminal offenses since 2008 have been in just four cases and 77 percent of the individuals charged by the DOJ since 2008 have been in just seven cases. Considering that there has been 53 corporate DOJ FCPA enforcement actions since 2008, this is a rather remarkable statistic. Of the 53 corporate DOJ FCPA enforcement actions, 39 (or 74 percent), have not (at least yet) resulted in any DOJ charges against company employees. In short, contrary to DOJ rhetoric that prosecution of individuals is a 'cornerstone' of its FCPA enforcement program, the actual enforcement statistics paint a different picture.

An interesting and significant picture also emerges when analyzing DOJ individual FCPA prosecutions based on whether the business employing or otherwise involved with the individual criminally charged was a public or private entity. Of the 77 individuals charged by the DOJ with FCPA criminal offenses since 2008, 54 of the individuals (70 percent) were employees or otherwise affiliated with private business entities.[93] This is a striking statistic given that 42 of the 53 corporate DOJ FCPA enforcement actions since 2008 (79 percent) were against publicly traded corporations. In the 11 private entity DOJ FCPA enforcement actions since 2008, individuals were charged in connection with 6 of those cases (55 percent). In contrast, in the 42 public entity DOJ FCPA enforcement actions since 2008, individuals were charged in connection with 8 of those cases (19 percent).

In short, and based on actual enforcement statistics, a DOJ FCPA enforcement action against a private entity is approximately three times more likely to have a related DOJ FCPA criminal prosecution of an individual than a public entity DOJ FCPA enforcement action.

As noted throughout this book, the FCPA has dual enforcers and the SEC can also bring civil FCPA enforcement actions against individuals employed by or associated with issuers. Like the DOJ, the SEC frequently speaks in lofty rhetoric concerning holding individuals accountable under the FCPA and SEC FCPA officials have stated that the SEC 'will vigorously hold accountable' individuals for FCPA violations.[94]

From 2005 to 2012, the SEC has charged 49 individuals with FCPA civil offenses. The breakdown is as follows.

- 2005 – 1 individual
- 2006 – 8 individuals
- 2007 – 7 individuals
- 2008 – 5 individuals
- 2009 – 5 individuals
- 2010 – 7 individuals
- 2011 – 12 individuals
- 2012 – 4 individuals[95]

An analysis of the numbers also reveals some interesting points.

Similar to the above DOJ figures, most of the individuals charged, 33 (or 67 percent), were charged since 2008. Thus, on one level the SEC is also correct when it states that individual prosecutions are a focus of its FCPA enforcement program, at least as measured against the historical average in that between 1978 and 2004 the SEC charged 32 individuals with FCPA civil offenses.

Yet on another level, a more meaningful level given that there was much less overall SEC FCPA enforcement between 1978 and 2004, the SEC's rhetoric likewise proves hollow as demonstrated by the below figures.

Of the 33 individuals charged with civil FCPA offenses by the SEC since 2008:

- 7 individuals were in connection with the Siemens enforcement action;
- 4 individuals were in connection with the Willbros Group enforcement action;
- 4 individuals were in connection with the Alliance One enforcement action;
- 3 individuals were in connection with the Magyar Telekom enforcement action; and
- 3 individuals were in connection with the Noble Corp. case.[96]

In other words, 64 percent of the individuals charged by the SEC with FCPA civil offenses since 2008 have been in just five enforcement actions. Considering that there have been 57 corporate SEC FCPA enforcement actions since 2008, this is also a rather remarkable statistic. Of the 57 corporate SEC FCPA enforcement actions, 45 (or 79 percent), have not (at least yet) resulted in any SEC charges against company employees. It is notable that this figure is higher than the above DOJ figure even though the SEC, as a civil law enforcement agency, has a lower burden of proof in an FCPA enforcement action.

The above facts and figures regarding individual FCPA enforcement actions have rightfully caused alarm and concern. After all, business organizations can only act through employees and agents and if a business organization resolves an FCPA enforcement action it would seem to suggest that provable facts exist that an actual employee or agent acted in violation of the FCPA.

During a 2010 Senate FCPA hearing, Senator Arlen Specter pointedly asked the DOJ witness: 'You talk about collecting more in criminal fines than anyone else, prosecuted more cases than other countries who are parties to the convention, and you say you do not hesitate to go after individuals. But whom have you sent to jail?'[97]

Indeed, during the same hearing, written testimony noted that the lack of individual prosecutions in most FCPA enforcement actions 'causes one to legitimately wonder whether the conduct was engaged in by ghosts.'[98]

It was noted at the hearing however that there is an equally plausible reason why so few corporate enforcement actions result in related FCPA charges against individuals. The reason has to do with the quality and legitimacy of the corporate enforcement action in the first place. As highlighted in Chapter 2, the 'carrots' and 'sticks' relevant to resolving corporate FCPA enforcement actions often motivate business organizations subject to FCPA scrutiny to resolve enforcement actions for reasons of risk aversion and not necessarily because the enforcement agency has a superior legal position.

In analyzing whether NPAs or DPAs represent over-prosecution of the FCPA, a suitable proxy is comparing the number of individual prosecutions that follow corporate NPAs or DPAs compared to individual prosecutions that follow actual criminal charges against a company. The hypothesis is that the latter represents a higher-quality FCPA enforcement action whereas the former represents a lower-quality FCPA enforcement action. A compelling data point is that since NPAs and DPAs were first introduced to the FCPA context, only 6.5 percent of corporate enforcement actions resolved solely with an NPA or DPA have resulted in related criminal charges of company employees.[99] In stark contrast, 83 percent of corporate enforcement actions that were the result of a criminal indictment or resulted in a guilty plea by a corporate entity have resulted in related criminal charges of company employees.[100]

In other words, perhaps the more appropriate question regarding the general lack of individual FCPA charges in connection with most corporate DOJ FCPA enforcement actions is not 'why were no individuals charged' but rather do NPA and DPAs always represent provable FCPA violations?

Unlike business organizations, individuals can be put in jail, and have their liberty, as well as their personal assets and reputation, at stake in an FCPA enforcement action. Thus, individuals are more likely to contest DOJ FCPA charges and put it to its high burden of proof at trial and potentially expose the DOJ's dubious legal theories or its interpretation of facts giving rise to the related corporate enforcement action. Indeed, every judicial decision highlighted in Chapter 3 concerning the FCPA's anti-bribery provisions involved individual FCPA defendants.

Against this backdrop, it is understandable why few corporate FCPA enforcement actions result in related individual enforcement actions. Perhaps the enforcement agencies do not have sufficient evidence to establish provable FCPA violations against individuals even though the 'carrots' and 'sticks' relevant to resolving corporate FCPA enforcement actions yielded a corporate settlement. Perhaps the enforcement agencies are hesitant to expose certain enforcement theories to judicial scrutiny in an individual enforcement action and risk losing the theory to extract corporate FCPA settlements.

For instance, you learned in Chapter 1 that the main reason motivating Congress to enact the FCPA was the foreign policy implications of payments to foreign government officials such as the Prime Minister of Japan, the President of Korea, the President of Gabon, and Italian political parties. In this new era, FCPA enforcement actions seldom involve such a recipient category as highlighted in the 'foreign official' table (Table 3.1) in Chapter 3. Rather, the enforcement agencies have created other 'foreign official' theories, such as physicians, nurses, midwives and laboratory personnel of various foreign health care systems are 'foreign officials' under the FCPA and thus occupy the same status as Prime Ministers and Presidents.

First used in a corporate enforcement action in 2002, this dubious enforcement theory has since been used as the basis, in whole or in part, in approximately 15 corporate FCPA enforcement actions.[101] This enforcement theory is so prominent that 50 percent of corporate enforcement actions in 2012 (representing approximately 65 percent of the settlement amounts in 2012 corporate FCPA enforcement actions) were against pharmaceutical or other health care companies based, in whole or in part, on this theory.[102] All of these enforcement actions were resolved via an NPA or DPA and there was no meaningful judicial scrutiny of this enforcement theory.

A noteworthy data point in examining the legitimacy and validity of this enforcement theory is that despite extracting numerous corporate settlements based on the theory, the DOJ has never charged an individual based on this theory.[103]

As to the general lack of individual FCPA charges in connection with SEC corporate FCPA enforcement actions, the issue is not so much NPAs or DPAs, but rather the SEC's 'neither admit nor deny' settlement policy discussed in Chapter 2. As previously noted, SEC enforcement actions 'typically omit mention of valid defenses and of countervailing facts or mitigating circumstances that, if proven at trial, could cause the Commission to lose its case.' Even the SEC has acknowledged that a settled SEC enforcement action 'does not necessarily reflect the triumph of one party's position over the other.' Individuals in an SEC FCPA enforcement, even if only a civil action and even if allowed to settle on 'neither admit nor deny' terms, have their personal reputation at stake and are thus more likely than corporate entities to challenge the SEC and force it to satisfy its burden of proof at trial. In other words, and like in the DOJ context, perhaps the more appropriate question regarding the lack of individual FCPA prosecutions in most corporate SEC FCPA enforcement actions is not 'why were no individuals charged' but rather do SEC corporate FCPA settlements necessarily represent provable FCPA violations?

Resolution Dynamics

Notwithstanding the above statistics, on occasion individuals are also prosecuted for FCPA violations. Like the 'carrots' and 'sticks' relevant to resolving corporate FCPA enforcement actions discussed in Chapter 2, there are also 'carrots' and 'sticks' relevant to resolving individual FCPA enforcement actions.

Unlike the three options relevant to corporate FCPA enforcement (charge, do not charge, or resolve via an NPA or DPA), enforcement agencies have generally adhered to the traditional two option charge or do not charge approach in individual FCPA enforcement actions. An individual criminally charged in an FCPA enforcement action thus confronts a stark choice: plead guilty or exercise their constitutional right to a jury trial and put the DOJ to its high burden of trial. Like in the corporate context, the Sentencing Guidelines relevant to individual criminal prosecutions also provide a 'carrot' for cooperating in the DOJ's investigation and accepting responsibility through a plea agreement.

The significant adverse consequences of testing one's innocence are highlighted in the next section regarding FCPA sentences. At present, you should understand that it is extremely risky for individuals to test their innocence in an FCPA enforcement action because, by testing one's innocence at trial, the individual defendant faces a significantly longer jail sentence if they lose than if they pleaded guilty.

As to this risk, it has been noted:

> Our existing legal system places the risk of going to trial, and in some cases even being charged with a crime so high, that innocence and guilt no longer become the real considerations. [...] [Rather] maneuvering the system to receive the least onerous consequences may ensure the best result for the accused party, regardless of innocence. [...] Innocence becomes irrelevant as the real question becomes whether it is worth the risk of testing an innocence claim.[104]

Thus, given the prospect of missing out on a child's life or growing old in jail, many white collar individual defendants choose the lesser of two evils, accept a plea, and play a game in which 'innocence and guilt no longer become the real considerations.'[105]

As highlighted by an article titled 'Federal Guilty Pleas Soar as Bargains Trump Trial,' a 'growing number of federal defendants [plead guilty] often to avoid the lengthy prison sentences that can come with losing at trial.' The article noted:

> Federal sentencing guidelines not only toughened punishments but also formalized a system to reward defendants who plead guilty by reducing sentences if they accept responsibility or cooperate with prosecutors, among other things. As part of plea deals, federal prosecutors often drop additional charges that could add years, or decades, to a sentence. Going to trial bring none of those benefits for the accused.[106]

Indeed, an academic study has shown that approximately 55 percent of individuals who were innocent in a control group pleaded guilty and demonstrated 'a strong compulsion [by the individuals] to have the matter resolved even if it meant confessing to something that they really didn't do.'[107]

This is not merely an academic issue, but one with real-world consequences. For instance, Si Chan Wooh, an employee of SSI International (a wholly-owned subsidiary of Schnitzer Steel) was criminally charged and pleaded guilty to conspiring to violate the FCPA by allegedly making cash payments to officers and employees of foreign government-owned steel production companies in China to induce employees of those companies to do business with and provide preferential sales terms to Schnitzer Steel.[108] However, four years later 'the Justice Department informed Wooh's counsel that a FBI agent assigned to the investigation of Schnitzer and its employees had written a letter to a high-ranking prosecutor in Washington D.C. saying Wooh should not have been charged in connection with the case.'[109] The DOJ then moved to dismiss the case 'out of prosecutorial discretion in the interests of justice and the efficient use of government resources.'[110]

The reality of the dynamics relevant to individual FCPA enforcement actions are that when the DOJ senses it may have a difficult time meeting its high burden of proof at trial, it can offer individual defendants a lenient plea agreement to resolve the case in the absence of meaningful judicial scrutiny.

For example, one of the notable instances of individual FCPA charges in connection with a corporate FCPA enforcement action concerned Control Components Inc. ('CCI'). In 2009, six former CCI employees were criminally charged in a wide-ranging indictment for allegedly engaging in 'a conspiracy to secure contracts by paying bribes to officials of foreign state-owned companies as well as officers and employees of foreign and domestic private companies.'[111] Like most individual FCPA defendants, two of the defendants quickly pleaded guilty, perhaps mindful of the relevant 'carrots' and 'sticks.'[112] However, four defendants mounted a legal defense most notably on the 'foreign official' issue discussed in greater detail in Chapter 3. As noted in Chapter 3, even though the judge denied the motion to dismiss, before trial the judge issued a pro-defense jury instruction relevant to the 'foreign official' issue. Shortly thereafter, the DOJ offered the defendants a lenient plea agreement and all of the defendants, likely mindful of the high costs of testing their innocence, did what most rational, risk-averse actors in their position would do – they agreed to plead guilty to substantially reduced charges compared to the conduct originally charged in the indictment.[113]

As highlighted in the sentencing chart in the next section, two defendants (Stuart Carson and David Edmonds) were sentenced to four months in prison, whereas the other two defendants did not receive a prison sentence. In sentencing one of the defendants, the court stated:

> The Court also takes into account the strength of the Government's case had the matter gone to trial. While the Court found no legal impediment to the prosecution in the face of numerous challenges, the ultimate outcome of a number of issues on appeal was uncertain to a greater or lesser degree.[114]

After sentencing, counsel for one of the defendants issued the following provocative press release:

> [Counsel] and counsel for three other defendants … conducted a worldwide investigation and developed evidence suggesting the government's evidence was incomplete … Ultimately, most companies bought CCI valves because they were the best in the world (not because of bribes); most of the supposed 'public officials' denied receiving any bribes; and, in most cases, the alleged improper payments were never actually made …
>
> Further, through an aggressive litigation and motion strategy, counsel were able to obtain jury instructions that highlighted the government's heavy burden of proof at trial. For example, the trial court agreed with defense counsel that the government was obligated to prove defendants knew they were dealing with 'foreign officials,' something that would have been extremely difficult for the government to prove. The supposed bribery recipients worked for companies that appeared to operate like private companies in the United States, making it very unlikely that the defendants realized they were dealing with 'government officials.'
>
> [Counsel] and other defense counsel raised several other issues that brought the government's ability to obtain a conviction, or defend an appeal, into serious doubt.[115]

While the guilt or innocence of individual FCPA defendants will likely only be known by the defendants themselves, the following comments by FCPA defendant Garth Peterson speak to the pressures facing defendants in criminal enforcement actions. During a Q&A on CNBC, Peterson was asked as follows.

> *Q*: 'So, why did you plead guilty to anything?'
>
> *A*: 'You know, it's – I think, hopefully most people will never be in the position I had to be in. But when you're an individual against the weight of the U.S. Government – and the U.S. Government, the DOJ, the SEC, perhaps it's their way of doing things. They can have – a heavy stick, you know. That if you don't cooperate with us, you'll – you know, we're going to do all these

> other things. And so, I just cooperated. You know, everybody's different. Some people are fighters. I guess I'm not.'
>
> *Q*: 'But, I mean, you – you're giving away a lot. You're – potentially giving away your freedom for a number of years?'
>
> *A*: 'In some sense, they took that away a long time ago in reality. Because once I started to cooperate – when they wanted to speak to me, I had to go speak to them. They were – literally, the SEC was harassing my family for years. But – at the end of the day, like I said, I agreed to cooperate, and so, I took that path.'[116]

Like in Chapter 2 concerning the dynamics relevant to resolving corporate FCPA enforcement actions, discussion of the dynamics relevant to resolving individual FCPA enforcement actions is not meant to suggest, or even imply, that no individual has ever violated the FCPA. Rather, the goal of this section was to provide a proper background concerning the dynamics relevant to resolving individual FCPA enforcement actions and to demonstrate that just because an individual defendant pleads guilty in an FCPA enforcement action (as most individual defendants do) does not necessarily mean that the DOJ would have prevailed at trial.

Enforcement Agency Struggles when put to its Burden of Proof

As noted earlier in this chapter concerning corporate FCPA actions, success in enforcing a law is best measured by instances in which an enforcement agency is actually put to its burden of proof in the context of an adversarial proceeding.

To be sure, the DOJ has experienced some success in individual FCPA prosecutions when put to its burden of proof in this new era. In 2009, Gerald and Patricia Green were found guilty by a jury of FCPA and other charges concerning a bribery scheme involving an official at the Tourism Authority of Thailand ('TAT').[117] Also in 2009, Frederic Bourke was found guilty by a jury for conspiring to pay bribes to Azerbaijan officials and, as noted in Chapter 3, this conviction was affirmed on appeal. Although an appeal is pending, in 2011 Joel Esquenazi and Carlos Rodriguez were found guilty by a jury of FCPA and other charges concerning a bribery scheme involving officials at Haiti Teleco, an alleged state-owned telecommunications company.[118]

The above successes however are countered by many failures in this new era when the enforcement agencies have been put to their burdens of proof in individual FCPA enforcement actions.

Bringing criminal charges and marshaling the full resources of the government against an individual is an awesome power that the DOJ possesses. Because that power alters the lives of real people and their families, sidetracks real careers, empties real bank accounts in mounting a defense, and causes often irreversible damage to real reputations, it ought to be exercised with real discipline and prudence. While it is unrealistic, and probably not desirable from a policy perspective, to expect the DOJ to win 100% of its FCPA prosecutions against individuals when put to its burden of proof, given the above dynamics, it is realistic, and desirable from a policy perspective, to expect the DOJ to win a very high percentage of its FCPA prosecutions against individuals. In this new era of FCPA enforcement, the DOJ has fallen short of this desirable objective, raising the question: what percentage of DOJ FCPA losses is acceptable?

In addition to the previously discussed DOJ failures in the Lindsey Manufacturing case which also involved the prosecution of two individuals, as well as several enforcement agency failures highlighted in Chapter 3 as to various FCPA elements, the DOJ failed dramatically in the Africa Sting action as well as an enforcement action against John O'Shea.

Africa Sting action

The DOJ's most spectacular failure when put to its burden of proof occurred in the Africa Sting action. As highlighted earlier in this chapter, in January 2010, the DOJ filed criminal charges against 22 executives and employees of companies in the military and law enforcement products industry for engaging in a scheme to pay bribes to the minister of defense of an African country. However, there was no actual involvement from any minister of defense. Rather, FBI agents, with the assistance of an individual who had already pleaded guilty to real, unrelated FCPA offenses, posed as representatives of the Gabon Minister of Defense. While it was not the first use of proactive, undercover investigative techniques in an FCPA enforcement action, it was certainly the largest and most dramatic use of such techniques in the FCPA's history, and the full force of the government's surveillance capabilities were used against individuals from mostly small private companies located across America.

In announcing the criminal charges, the DOJ Assistant Attorney General called the manufactured case a 'turning point' in the DOJ's FCPA enforcement program, and otherwise trumpeted that the charges represented the 'largest single investigation and prosecution against individuals in the history of DOJ's enforcement of the FCPA.' All but one of the charged individuals was arrested at the industry's leading trade show in Las Vegas, and in a sophomoric statement, the Assistant Attorney

General said, 'this is one case where what happened in Vegas doesn't stay in Vegas.'[119] In a press release that foreshadowed the conduct of the FBI agents involved in the sting operation, the FBI stated that the undercover operation was like a 'ruse [that] played out with all the intrigue of a spy novel.'[120] A good spy novel often involves sex, drugs, and criminals, and the FBI's conduct in carrying out the manufactured case touched upon all such subjects. Indeed, the FBI agents openly wondered who would portray them when Hollywood made a movie about the case.

The presiding judge immediately expressed strong skepticism of the DOJ's enforcement theories and the difficulties of trying such a large group of defendants, and ultimately decided that the defendants would be tried in four separate groups. The first Africa Sting trial started in May 2011 and involved four defendants. At the close of the DOJ's case, the judge dismissed a substantive FCPA charge against one defendant, dismissed another substantive FCPA charge against another defendant, and dismissed the money laundering count against all defendants.[121] In July 2011, the judge declared a mistrial as to all remaining counts against all defendants.

At this point, prudence might have suggested a reevaluation of the DOJ's 'turning point' prosecution. However, the DOJ quickly announced that it would retry the remaining charges against the first group of defendants. In addition, the DOJ plowed ahead against the second group of six defendants, and the second trial in the manufactured case began in September 2011. At the close of the DOJ's case in December 2011, the judge dismissed the conspiracy charge against all defendants.[122] Because one defendant faced only that conspiracy charge, he was exonerated by the decision. The trial proceeded, the charges went to the jury, the jury deliberated, and in January 2012 the jury found two defendants not guilty.[123] The jury hung as to the remaining defendants, and once again the judge declared a mistrial as to all remaining counts against the remaining three defendants.[124]

It is rare for a jury foreman to go public after a stint of public service, but what happened next may have turned the direction in the DOJ's 'turning point' prosecutions. Soon after the judge declared a mistrial in the second Africa String trial, the jury foreman published a post on the website FCPA Professor. The jury foreman, a non-practicing attorney, described numerous facets of the trial and the jury's deliberations including its assessment of the government's witnesses. The foreman stated that 'the jury with near unanimity found nearly all of the prosecution witnesses to be evasive and combative' and further stated:

> The very low view of their credibility was also based on the concerns of many jurors related to the nature of the sting operation. Though, in the end, I am not sure the credibility concerns were an important aspect of this case because the jury had the most difficult time ascertaining the state of mind and intent of the defendants.[125]

The foreman also stated that 'a number of jurors were troubled by the nature of the FBI sting operation' and stated that the underlying view of the jury was that 'the defendants had acted in good faith and the FBI/DOJ in bad faith.'

The jury foreman concluded the FCPA Professor post as follows:

> The government has the option to try [the defendants on which the jury hung] again. As a taxpayer, I sincerely hope they will instead dismiss the charges. The evidence simply does not exist, even if they get their witnesses to behave better under cross, to convict. This is a case that makes one wish that a supermajority was sufficient to acquit. Prolonging this prosecution is a waste of government resources. At some point in the deliberations, I described this sting and prosecution as a quarterback sneak. Although I came to regret that analogy for the frequency with which it was recalled in the jury room, I think it apt. The FBI and DOJ designed a play to get the ball just across the goal line. Unfortunately, in the ensuing pileup, no camera angle shows the ball with clarity and it is anyone's guess as to whether they scored.

According to knowledgeable sources, the jury foreman's FCPA Professor post soon reached high levels in the DOJ. Two weeks later, the DOJ moved to dismiss with prejudice the criminal charges against all of the remaining Africa Sting defendants. The DOJ's filing stated that 'continued prosecution of this case is not warranted under the circumstances.'[126]

The next day, the judge granted the DOJ's motion to dismiss and stated:

> This appears to be the end of a long and sad chapter in the annals of white collar criminal enforcement. Unlike takedown day in Las Vegas, however, there will be no front page story in the New York Times or the Post for that matter tomorrow reflecting the government's decision today to move to dismiss the charges against the remaining defendants in this case. Funny, isn't it, what sells newspapers? The good news, however, is that for these defendants, agents, prosecutors, defense counsel and the court we can get on with our professional and personal lives without the constant strain and burden of three to four more eight-week trials hanging over our heads. I for one hope this very long, and I'm sure very expensive, ordeal will be a true learning experience for both the DOJ and the FBI as they regroup to investigate and prosecute FCPA cases against individuals in the future. Two years ago, at the very outset of this case, I expressed more than my fair share of concerns on the record regarding the way this case has been charged and

was being prosecuted. Later, during the two trials that I presided over, I specifically commented again on the record regarding the government's very, very aggressive conspiracy theory that was pushing its already generous elasticity to its outer limits. Of course, in the second trial that elastic snapped in the absence of the necessary evidence to sustain it. In addition, in that same trial, I expressed on a number of occasions my concerns regarding the way this case had been investigated and was conducted especially vis-a-vis the handling of [the undercover cooperator]. I even had an occasion, sadly, to chastise the government in a situation where the government's handling of the discovery process constituted sharp practices that have no place in a federal courtroom. Notwithstanding all of this water over the dam, and there has been a lot of water, I'm happy to see and I applaud the DOJ for having the wisdom and courage of its convictions to face up to the limitations of its case as revealed in the past 26 weeks of trial and the courage to do the right thing under the circumstances. Having served at the higher levels of the DOJ, I know that that was not an easy decision. They never are, when so much has been invested, and the agents and the prosecutors are so convinced of the righteousness of their position. I for one however am confident this will be in the end a positive, if not painful, lesson that results in better prosecutions of individuals in the future under the FCPA. As for the defendants, I hope the healing process is a swift one and that they get back to their normal lives in the very near future. [...] And so without further adieu I grant the government's motion to dismiss. The defendants are excused.[127]

The DOJ's 'turning point' FCPA prosecution, the 'largest single investigation and prosecution against individuals in the history of DOJ's enforcement of the FCPA,' failed spectacularly. The defendants' lives were damaged, as were their real reputations, their real careers were sidetracked, and their real bank accounts were emptied in mounting a defense.

The press release issued by defendant Lee Tolleson's attorneys after the dismissal best captured the human element of the Africa Sting action:

Lee Tolleson and his family are elated that this unnecessary and worthless nightmare is now over with the Government dismissing the multi-count indictment with prejudice. Lee was a victim of a scheme by the Government, which was the mother of all gigantic taxpayers' waste of dollars, to entrap him and others by faking an overseas business scam. The prosecutors were testing the FCPA by setting up a sting to raise a national awareness of the law, but the little guy suffers. The Government went to great expense to attempt to sucker many businesses into a fake business deal in Gabon, West Africa. The Government pinned its entire investigation on a despicable character, [the undercover cooperator], who manipulated Federal Agents throughout the investigation, in order to save his soul for his misdeeds. Ultimately, the Government finally did the right thing today and should think twice about going after honest business people in the future. Now, where does Lee go to

> get back his good name? He is from a small Arkansas town with a GED and has a home school education. His family has been devastated financially by this process. Two things have kept him grounded; his faith in God and his family.[128]

In the aftermath of its spectacular Africa Sting failure, a DOJ spokesperson merely stated that the DOJ's 'FCPA enforcement efforts are broader than one case.'[129] This statement, of course, is true, but it is also true that the Africa Sting case was not the only DOJ FCPA individual prosecution that failed in this new era.

O'Shea action

In 2009, the DOJ issued a press release when John Joseph O'Shea was arrested and charged with FCPA and related offenses. As stated in the DOJ release, 'the indictment alleges that while acting as the general manager of a Texas business unit of a U.S. subsidiary of [ABB Ltd.], O'Shea arranged and authorized payments to multiple officials at [Comision Federal de Electricida ('CFE') – a utility allegedly owned or controlled by the Mexican government] in exchange for lucrative contracts.'[130] O'Shea proceeded to trial, and in early 2012, following the DOJ's case, the judge dismissed the FCPA charges against O'Shea. In doing so, the judge stated: 'The problem here is that the principal witness against Mr. O'Shea … knows almost nothing.'[131]

As evident from the case record, this was not the only deficiency in the DOJ's case. The judge was also troubled by the DOJ's 'foreign official' position and its lack of preparation as to the unique attributes of CFE to support its position that employees of CFE were 'foreign officials' under the FCPA. During a hearing, the judge stated that the DOJ 'is supposed to know before it brings the indictment that it can prove that it is a governmental entity … in fact you should have to convince the grand jury of it.'[132] The judge further commented that 'it does trouble me […] that the Government did not present evidence on governmental status on which a reasonable grand jury could have relied.' The following exchange between the DOJ prosecutor and the judge then followed.

> *DOJ*: 'I believe, Your Honor, that we presented evidence that it was a state-owned company.'
>
> *Judge*: 'The statute is more subtle than that. I'm not saying you couldn't have done it or they wouldn't have indicted him.'
>
> *DOJ*: 'The statute says an instrumentality of a foreign government. I think in fairness, Your Honor, it is not a stretch to think that a company that is created by, owned by and operated by a foreign government, could be considered an

instrumentality. I think in the sharp relief of a trial in which we are going to be challenged on those issues, we needed to have been more prepared and we were not.'

Judge: 'I don't know what was presented to the Grand Jury, but as I observed several days ago, the Government should have been prepared before they brought the charges to the Grand Jury. It's something you have to prove. And you shouldn't indict people on stuff you can't prove.'[133]

O'Shea, a married grandfather with two children and 35 years of business experience, 'lost his job, savings and home while fighting to prove his innocence.' After the decision, O'Shea's counsel stated, 'Deflecting blame for bribery in corruption-ridden countries onto unknowing executives is both Cervantian and unfair.'[134]

The DOJ's numerous FCPA losses in this new era when put to its burden of proof would have been troubling even if, for instance, all of the losses were based on a single issue such as an aggressive interpretation of the same FCPA substantive element. However, such a common thread was not present in the recent string of DOJ losses. Rather, and more problematic, the DOJ's losses were for a variety of reasons: apparent jury resentment of a bad-faith sting operation, aggressive legal theories, insufficient evidence, and numerous instances of prosecutorial misconduct. Moreover, the losses were not merely adverse jury verdicts, but rather instances in which judges took the unusual step of refusing to allow the trial or specific charges to proceed after the DOJ's case; a judge issuing a rare post-verdict dismissal of a case because of prosecutorial misconduct; the DOJ dismissing a case after the defendant had pleaded guilty; and the DOJ dismissing several cases before the trials even occurred. If there is a common theme in the recent DOJ losses in FCPA enforcement actions, it is this: the DOJ's aggressive theories and tactics, when subjected to scrutiny, failed.

Against this backdrop, it would be prudent for the DOJ to take a step back and contemplate the future direction of its FCPA enforcement program. However, it appears that the DOJ's spectacular failures have not yielded such a result. Rather, the head of DOJ's FCPA unit stated,

> I know there is a lot of commentary out there about what this [DOJ's recent FCPA setbacks] portends for the FCPA program [and] certain law enforcement techniques. I would caution everybody not to draw too much from that. In terms of pursuing cases moving forward, I don't think a lot is going to change.[135]

The substance of the DOJ's statement is akin to the following. A company is found to be in violation of the FCPA and states that not 'a lot is going to change' about its future foreign business practices. The DOJ would not tolerate such a cavalier stance from a company and such a cavalier stance should not be tolerated from a law enforcement agency.

One would hardly know of these numerous DOJ FCPA losses if one's only source of information were enforcement agency speeches. For instance, in 2013 the DOJ Acting Assistant Attorney General stated that 'our recent string of successful prosecutions of corporate executives is worth highlighting' and that 'our stellar FCPA Unit continues to go gangbusters, bringing case after case.'[136]

The fact remains that the last three times the DOJ has been put to its burden of proof in FCPA cases the end results were either acquittals or dismissals, including for prosecutorial misconduct.

Sentencing Issues

This chapter concludes with a discussion of sentencing issues in individual FCPA enforcement actions. You will learn how FCPA sentences are calculated and a range of recent FCPA sentences will be highlighted. As discussed throughout this book, while FCPA enforcement is largely devoid of judicial scrutiny, sentencing of individual defendants remains a judicial function and provides an opportunity for someone other than the enforcement agencies to weigh in on issues relevant to FCPA enforcement. For this reason, FCPA sentencing transcripts and orders provide a wealth of information concerning this new era of FCPA enforcement. This section highlights how sentencing judges often see shades of gray in FCPA enforcement actions that the DOJ portrays to be black and white.

The FCPA provides for a maximum five years' imprisonment for each instance of violating the anti-bribery provisions. The sentencing of individual criminal defendants, in the FCPA context and otherwise, is based on the following general procedure.

- The U.S. Probation Office applies the advisory Sentencing Guidelines to calculate the defendant's total offense level. The offense level is based on among other things, the value of the improper payment, whether the defendant accepted responsibility, and the defendant's criminal history. The total offense level then yields an advisory sentencing range.
- In cases of cooperating defendants, the DOJ often moves for a downward departure based on the defendant's substantial assistance in the prosecution of others.
- Based on the advisory sentencing range and any downward departure, the DOJ makes a sentencing recommendation to the court.

- The defendant is then given an opportunity to respond to the DOJ's sentencing recommendation. In doing so, FCPA defendants often highlight certain unique factors such as age, health, education, family support, and low probability of recidivism in seeking a lighter sentence than recommended by the DOJ.
- The court then takes into consideration the DOJ's sentencing recommendation, the specific facts of the case, and other various factors such as the need to afford adequate deterrence of criminal conduct and orders a specific sentence.[137]

In the words of the Supreme Court, a sentencing judge 'considers every convicted person as an individual and every case as a unique study in the human failings that sometimes mitigate, sometimes magnify, the crime and the punishment to ensue.'[138] Because most FCPA individual defendants come from successful business careers and lack a criminal history prior to the FCPA enforcement action, most FCPA individual defendants are sentenced to substantially less than five years.

Set forth in Table 5.2 are selected recent federal prison sentences for individuals in FCPA enforcement actions. In many of the long sentences highlighted, the defendants were sentenced on multiple FCPA charges and/or related offenses such as making false statements or money laundering. Not included in this table are numerous recent instances of cooperating FCPA defendants receiving no prison sentence, but rather terms of probation, home detention and/or supervised release.

As evident from the chart, the sentences of Joel Esquenazi and Carlos Rodriguez are significant outliers and prompt the question: what did these defendants do that warranted such long sentences? Simply put, Esquenazi and Rodriguez – unlike most other individual defendants highlighted who pleaded guilty and cooperated with the DOJ – tested their innocence and exercised their constitutional right to a jury trial and were convicted.

It is useful to compare the conduct of Esquenazi and Rodriguez with the conduct of Albert Stanley and Jeffrey Tesler to demonstrate the high costs of testing innocence in an individual FCPA enforcement.[139] Stanley and Tesler were charged in connection with a massive, decades-long bribery scheme and were accused of paying over $100 million in bribes to Nigerian 'foreign officials' to obtain more than $6 billion in contracts at Bonny Island, Nigeria. Both individuals pleaded guilty, accepted responsibility, and cooperated. As indicated in the chart, Stanley was sentenced to 30 months in federal prison and Tesler was sentenced to 21 months. Esquenazi and Rodriguez were charged and convicted for

Table 5.2 Selected sentences of FCPA defendants (2010–2013)

Defendant	Prison sentence
Paul Novak	15 months
Stuart Carson	4 months
David Edmonds	4 months
Garth Peterson	9 months
Richard Bistrong	18 months
Albert Stanley	30 months
Jeffrey Tesler	21 months
Antonio Perez	24 months
Juan Diaz	57 months
Joel Esquenazi	180 months
Carlos Rodriguez	84 months
Manual Salvoch	10 months
Jorge Granados	46 months
Manual Caceres	23 months
Gerald and Patricia Green	6 months
Ousama Naaman	30 months
Charles Jumet	87 months
Leo Smith	6 months
Nam Nguyen	16 months
An Nguyen	9 months

paying $890,000 to shell companies to be used for bribes to Haiti ‘foreign officials’ to receive preferred telecommunication rates from the alleged state-owned telecommunications company. In short, Esquenazi and Rodriguez’s conduct paled in comparison to Stanley and Tesler’s conduct, but Esquenazi and Rodriguez received a significantly harsher sentence because they tested their innocence.

Is this justice or is this merely knowing how to play a game? Were Stanley and Tesler sentenced too lightly or were Esquenazi and Rodriguez sentenced too harshly? Given the vast disparity in these sentences, what message is sent to future FCPA individual defendants who might want to exercise their constitutional right and test their innocence?

In addition to federal prison sentences or terms of probation, home confinement and/or supervised release, FCPA individual defendants can also be ordered to pay criminal fines or forfeit money or property. For instance, Jeffrey Tesler, the U.K. consultant at the center of the massive Bonny Island bribery scheme, agreed to forfeit approximately $149 million as part of his plea agreement.[140] Likewise, Paul Novak was ordered to pay a $1 million criminal fine, among the largest individual criminal fines in FCPA history.[141]

While much of the focus in individual FCPA enforcement actions tends to be criminal actions and resulting prison sentences, the SEC also has authority to bring FCPA charges against individuals associated with issuers. As a civil law enforcement agency only, the SEC lacks the ability to sentence defendants, but it can obtain significant monetary sanctions in FCPA enforcement actions. For instance, in resolving an SEC FCPA enforcement action concerning conduct in Iraq, Ousama Naaman agreed to disgorge approximately $850,000 in commissions he received from chemical company Innospec for his role in funneling bribe payments to foreign officials.[142] Likewise, Innospec's former chief financial officer, Paul Jennings, agreed to disgorge approximately $120,000 and pay a $100,000 civil penalty in a related enforcement action.[143]

Sentencing of individual FCPA defendants is a judicial function and FCPA sentencing transcripts and orders provide a wealth of useful information. These documents provide a rare public glimpse of someone other than the enforcement agencies weighing in on issues relevant to FCPA enforcement.

One mitigating factor individual FCPA defendants often raise in seeking a lighter sentence is the cultural context in which the payments were made. Judges have viewed cultural context in different ways in sentencing FCPA defendants. For instance, one judge stated:

> The Court does not give credit to the fact that [the defendant] was educated in China, and has spent her career in a business environment that at a minimum raises potential conflicts with the FCPA. There is no cultural defense to the present crime or any other under black letter law.[144]

Other judges have appeared more sympathetic to cultural issues in FCPA enforcement actions. Although, as indicated in the above chart, Garth Peterson was sentenced to nine months in prison, his sentence was substantially less than the 51–60 months the DOJ recommended and the sentencing memoranda contain an interesting back-and-forth concerning cultural context, specifically the concept of Chinese guanxi.

Peterson's sentencing memo contained a specific section titled 'Cultural Context' and stated:

> Peterson committed an FCPA offense without stepping foot in the United States while working for a Chinese subsidiary of a United States company. Peterson's tenuous connection with the United States, despite being a U.S. citizen, makes this case very unusual and makes Chinese cultural considerations relevant. Peterson admitted at his plea hearing that he helped the

> Chinese Official to invest personally in a Morgan Stanley investment at a beneficial price and that by misleading Morgan Stanley about this fact with another person, he conspired to violate the FCPA. The Chinese Official was a close friend of Peterson's – in many ways a father figure to him – and Peterson helped him in order to repay the help that the Chinese Official had given him through his career. This type of favor is called 'guanxi' in China, a term that describes the exchange of gifts or favors in a professional setting. Guanxi is the traditional way that business relationships are developed in China. Peterson has spent much of his life living in Asia. He learned Asian cultural traditions, and they are as familiar, if not more familiar to him, than United States cultural traditions. […] As part of Peterson's Asian cultural understanding, he learned the Chinese business culture of gift giving, or 'guanxi.' […] We ask the Court to consider … the cultural context of Peterson's crime when sentencing him.[145]

The DOJ responded:

> Peterson's assertion that he gave [the Chinese Official] a $3 million-plus interest in [the investment at issue] as an expression of 'guanxi' is demonstrably false. Peterson says that 'guanxi' is 'a term that describes the exchange of gifts or favors in a professional setting.' The source upon which Peterson relies, […] describes the parameters of guanxi, which typically involves small tokens: the 'exchange of gifts, favors, and banquets.' Here, Peterson stole a $7 million piece of a building and gave a Chinese public official a piece worth more than $3 million. The grant of an ill-gotten, multimillion dollar interest in an apartment building is hardly the type of item one typically exchanges in Chinese culture. Any suggestion to the contrary borders on the offensive. […] Even if Peterson's […] 'guanxi' arguments were based upon a true factual recitation – which they are not – they are legally irrelevant. […] Corrupting a Chinese official in the course of stealing an interest in a building cannot be dismissed as a symptom of Peterson's affinity for China or its culture. If anything, his actions demonstrate quite the opposite.[146]

In reply, Peterson stated:

> The Government argues that Peterson's inclusion of the Chinese Official [in the investment] was not an expression of 'guanxi' because the value of the Chinese Official's interest was too great to fit within the technical definition of 'guanxi.' Whether the term 'guanxi' applies misses the point. Peterson seeks to provide the Court with the full context for his actions, including the cultural and relationship-based motivations for his offense. Peterson acknowledges that the Chinese culture and Peterson's own desire to build his relationship with the Chinese Official do not justify his offense. Cultural context and motives, however, can be relevant to a defendant's character for sentencing purposes, and Peterson asks the Court to consider those factors here.[147]

FCPA sentencing transcripts and orders not only capture advocacy moments seldom seen in FCPA enforcement but also often capture telling unscripted comments concerning this new era of FCPA enforcement. For instance, the enforcement agencies and others often portray bribery as a black-and-white issue. However, judges sentencing FCPA individual defendants often see shades of gray.

In the Ousama Naaman FCPA enforcement action concerning conduct in Iraq, the DOJ sought a 90-month federal prison sentence. However, the judge sentenced Naaman to 30 months and in doing so dismissed the DOJ's rhetoric and refused to make Naaman the 'poster child' the DOJ wanted. The DOJ wanted the judge to give Naaman a harsh sentence so that it could be used as a benchmark for future cases. During the hearing, the DOJ prosecutor stated as follows.

> What this Court does with respect to Mr. Naaman will set a benchmark of what other courts will do, and that has an impact. [...] We are bringing more of these enforcement efforts, other judges will look to what this court does with respect to Mr. Naaman and then sentence others below him if they believe their conduct is not as egregious.[148]

The DOJ then cited the usual statistics regarding corruption.

> The World Bank estimates that corruption is three percent of the world economy; a trillion dollars of bribes every single year. That is not something that the U.S. Government, even working with all of our foreign partners around the world, can scratch the surface in enforcing. The only way to try to change the corrupt conduct, to try to change the behavior is to change businesses, to change individuals from conducting, from choosing to commit these crimes of choice.[149]

The judge then stated:

> This analogy is not apt. And I don't mean to suggest it's like drugs, but, you know, the American companies want to do the business, and they engage in these practices to get the business and hire people to help them get the business. It's like the demand in this country for drugs. We are not willing to give up operating in these countries, to say the least; nor should we. But you know, you are looking at a way to solve the problem that is somewhat limited in your vision, it seems to me. I mean, I cannot take this position that I, in some way, am really solving a large, worldwide problem of corruption. If you go to any other part of the world, the American companies want to participate, and they engage in practices that we have outlawed for good reason. I understand that. But just – I am not going to take on my shoulders what you are trying to put. I just don't see it that way.[150]

The DOJ prosecutor then stated:

> Let me just state very clearly that we have gone from a nascent fight against corruption where the DOJ was doing it essentially by itself, where we have now broadened that where Russia has passed new laws. China has passed new laws. I would not say that our vision, the DOJ's vision, is short. It would say it's long-term. This is not a project which is going to be five years. It is not a project that's ten years. This is a project which is thirty years. And that Your Honor, I think, is the most important thing to remember, that your sentence with Mr. Naaman will last beyond any period of incarceration that Mr. Naaman faces … .[151]

The judge refused to bear the cross the DOJ wanted her to bear and stated:

> It is a mixed, sort of complicated situation. I, for one, have traveled a lot in this world, and it is very complicated to say that our morality is necessarily that of other peoples. And I don't suggest that we should not try. But to say that in the early 2000's, that I should ignore context, that because Iraq has contributed – or collaborated with us in order to clean it up – [Naaman] cannot be the poster child that [DOJ] would like.[152]

The sentencing of Gerald and Patricia Green provides another notable instance of a judge seeing shades of gray in an FCPA enforcement action. After the Greens were convicted by a jury, the sentencing judge rejected the DOJ's ten-year sentencing recommendation and sentenced the Greens to six months in prison.

The sentencing transcript indicates that the judge believed the Greens helped make the Thai Film Festival, the focus of the bribery scheme, a success and that they performed the services they were engaged to perform in a professional manner and thereby increased revenue for the country. The judge stated:

> Insofar as the nature of the crimes are concerned, the jury found that the defendants bribed the head official of the TAT in order to obtain contracts to operate the Bangkok International Film Festival between 2002 and 2006. The Court finds that by engaging in that scheme the defendants were not trying to get money from the Thai government without performing the services or even to engage in those services in a slipshod manner. Prior to the Greens' involvement, the Bangkok International Film Festival was not a particularly successful endeavor in any sense of the word. Through the Greens' management the Bangkok International Film Festival gained in stature, reputation and increased revenue for the country. The defendants are claiming that the nation of Thailand profited in the sum of 140 million. I find that that figure is somewhat excessive. Although, I do feel that the evidence does show that

> there was a profit when everything was said and done, including any payments that were made either to the Greens or to [the TAT official]. Therefore, the Court would find that the Greens' efforts and also actually their scheme did not actually cause any monetary loss for the country.[153]

The sentencing of Frederic Bourke and Bobby Elkin also provide other notable instances of judges seeing shades of gray in FCPA enforcement action. As previously noted, Bourke was convicted by a jury of conspiring to pay bribes to Azerbaijan officials. In rejecting the DOJ's ten-year sentencing recommendation, the judge sentenced Bourke to approximately 12 months in prison and stated 'after years of supervising this case, it's still not entirely clear to me whether Mr. Bourke is a victim or a crook or a little bit of both.'[154]

Elkin, a former Country Manager of a tobacco company operating in Kyrgyzstan, pleaded guilty to conspiracy to violate the FCPA for making payments to officials of alleged state-owned enterprises and other public officials in Kyrgyzstan to secure business. The DOJ sought a 38-month prison sentence, but the judge sentenced Elkin to three years probation and waived the usual travel restrictions associated with probation allowing Elkin to return to Kyrgyzstan to resume work with another tobacco company. In sentencing Elkin, the judge noted that the CIA routinely bribes Afghan warlords, but the CIA's conduct is not illegal and that this parallel 'sort of goes to the morality of the situation.'[155]

The above examples of judges significantly rejecting DOJ sentencing recommendations in individual FCPA enforcement actions are the norm, not the exception. Indeed, a 2011 study of FCPA sentences found:

> Over the past four years, approximately 58% of all federal sentences were within the Guidelines range and 40% were below the range, according to U.S. Sentencing Commission data. In FCPA cases, however, the opposite is true: a Guidelines sentence is the exception rather than the norm. Since 1998, a total of 36 individuals have been sentenced in FCPA cases. Only nine of the 36 defendants, or 25%, received sentences within the Guidelines range. The remaining 27 defendants – a remarkable 75% of the total – were sentenced below the range. [Since 2005], the percentage of below-Guidelines sentences is even higher: 81%.[156]

The study concluded: 'Many judges have failed to see the wisdom of imprisoning [individual FCPA defendants] for many years in order to "send a message" to the business community that violations of the FCPA will not be tolerated. Instead, courts seem to be sending a message of their own to the DOJ.'

Sentencing is one of the few areas of FCPA enforcement in which the judiciary plays an active role and in which an adversarial process is on display. Thus, while largely unnoticed and unexplored, FCPA sentencing transcripts and orders are some of the most important and revealing documents concerning this new era of FCPA enforcement. As highlighted above, judges sentencing FCPA individual defendants often see shades of gray on issues the DOJ often portrays as black and white. In many respects, sentencing judges in this new era of FCPA enforcement are confronting the same issues Congress confronted in passing the FCPA – bribery is not the simple, safe issue it seems to be at first blush.

NOTES

1. Goodyear Tire and Rubber Co., Form 10-K (filed Feb. 14, 2012).
2. FCPA Professor, 'World Bribery & Corruption Compliance Forum – Comments by U.S. Officials,' (Sept. 16, 2010).
3. Id.
4. Lanny Breuer, Assistant Attorney General, Criminal Division, Prepared Address to the 22nd Annual National Forum on the Foreign Corrupt Practices Act (Nov. 17, 2009).
5. Press Release, U.S. Dep't of Justice, 'Assistant Attorney General Lanny A. Breuer Speaks at the 24th National Conference on the Foreign Corrupt Practices Act,' (Nov. 16, 2010).
6. Bruce Hinchey, 'Punishing the Penitent: Disproportionate Fines in Recent FCPA Enforcements and Suggested Improvements,' 40 Public Contract Law Journal 393 (2011).
7. Steven Choi and Kevin Davis, 'Foreign Affairs and Enforcement of the Foreign Corrupt Practices Act,' (2012).
8. Timothy Peterson and Robertson Park, Inside Counsel, 'Regulatory: Investigating Potential Bribery Means Looking Beyond the FCPA,' (May 29, 2013).
9. Steven Tyrrell, The Metropolitan Corporate Counsel, 'FCPA: Compliance and Enforcement Insights,' (June 2012).
10. FCPA Professor, 'Year-In-Review Roundups' (Jan. 11, 2013).
11. Department's Sentencing Memorandum, U.S. v. Siemens, Case No. 1:08-cr-00367-RJL (D.D.C., Dec. 12, 2008).
12. Russell Gold and Charles Fleming, Wall Street Journal, 'In Halliburton Nigeria Probe, A Search for Bribes to a Dictator' (Sept. 29, 2004).
13. Mark Mendelsohn, The Metropolitan Corporate Counsel, 'Recent Top DOJ Official Shares Insights into FCPA Policies, Enforcement Strategies, Public-Private Cooperation and Role of the OECD' (August 2010).
14. Press Release, U.S. Dep't of Justice, 'Acting Assistant Attorney General Mythili Raman Delivers Keynote Address at the Global Anti-Corruption Congress' (June 17, 2013).
15. FCPA Professor, 'Industry Sweeps' (Jan. 25, 2012).
16. Press Release, U.S. Dep't of Justice, 'Oil Services Companies and a Freight Forwarding Company Agree to Resolve Foreign Bribery Investigations and to Pay More Than $156 Million in Criminal Penalties' (Nov. 4, 2010).

17. Deferred Prosecution Agreement, U.S. v. Johnson & Johnson, Case 1:11-cr-00099-JDB, (D.D.C., Apr. 8, 2011).
18. Lanny Breuer, Assistant Attorney General, Criminal Division, Prepared Remarks to the National Association of Criminal Defense Lawyers at the 5th Annual 'Defending the White Collar Case – in and out of Court' Seminar (Oct. 1, 2009).
19. Press Release, U.S. Dep't of Justice, 'Twenty-Two Executives and Employees of Military and Law Enforcement Products Companies Charged in Foreign Bribery Scheme' (Jan. 19, 2010).
20. FCPA Professor, 'Friday Roundup' (Apr. 5, 2013).
21. FCPA Professor, 'SEC Examination Leads to Criminal FCPA Charges against Bond Traders' (May 8, 2013).
22. Press Release, U.S. Dep't of Justice, 'Bridgestone Corporation Agrees to Plead Guilty to Participating in Conspiracies to Rig Bids and Bribe Foreign Government Officials' (Sept. 15, 2011).
23. 513 F.3d 432.
24. U.S.'s Sentencing Memorandum, U.S. v. Daimler, Case No. 1:10-cr-00063-RJL (D.D.C., Mar. 24, 2010).
25. See Section 922 of the Dodd-Frank Wall Street Reform and Consumer Protection Act.
26. See e.g., Peter Henning, New York Times DealBook, 'The Mounting Costs of Internal Investigations' (Mar. 5, 2012) (discussing pre-enforcement action professional fees and expenses as of March 2012).
27. FCPA Professor, 'Friday Roundup' (May 3, 2013).
28. FCPA Professor, 'Friday Roundup' (May 17, 2013).
29. Nathan Vardi, Forbes, 'The Bribery Racket' (June 7, 2010).
30. FCPA Professor, 'Disconnected … Another Telecommunications Company Settles an FCPA Enforcement Action' (June 30, 2010).
31. Memorandum in Support of the Proposed Plea Agreements and Deferred Prosecution Agreement, U.S. v. Alcatel-Lucent France S.A., et al., Case No. 10-cr-20906 (S.D. Fl. May 23, 2011).
32. FCPA Professor, 'A Q&A with Claudius Sokenu on "Where Else"' (Apr. 4, 2012), containing links to original source documents.
33. Id.
34. FCPA Professor, 'Tyson Foods Settles FCPA Enforcement Action Involving Mexican Veterinarians and Their No-Show Wives' (Feb. 11, 2011), containing links to original source documents.
35. FCPA Professor, 'A Q&A with Claudius Sokenu on "Where Else"' (Apr. 4, 2012).
36. 18 U.S.C. § 3571(d).
37. See for instance the Sentencing Guidelines calculation in Deferred Prosecution Agreement, U.S. v. Parker Drilling Co., Case 1:13-cr-00176 (E.D. Va., Apr. 16, 2013).
38. FCPA Professor, 'DOJ Enforcement of the FCPA – Year in Review' (Jan. 9, 2013).
39. Dr. Patrick Conroy and Dr. Graeme Hunter, Nera Economic Consulting, 'Economic Analysis of Damages under the FCPA' (May 5, 2011).
40. FCPA Professor, 'SEC Enforcement of the FCPA – Year in Review' (Jan. 8, 2013).
41. David Weiss, 'The Foreign Corrupt Practices Act, SEC Disgorgement of Profits, and the Evolving International Bribery Regime: Weighing Proportionality, Retribution, and Deterrence,' 30 Michigan Journal of Int'l Law 471 (2009).
42. Debevoise & Plimpton, FCPA Update, 'Do FCPA Remedies Follow FCPA Wrongs? "Disgorgement" in Internal Controls and Books and Records Cases' (Aug. 2011).
43. SEC News Release, 'SEC Announces Non-Prosecution Agreement with Ralph Lauren Corporation Involving FCPA Misconduct' (Apr. 22, 2013).
44. *Supra* note 42.

45. See e.g., SEC v. First City Fin. Corp. Ltd., 890 F.2d 1215 (D.D.C. 1989).
46. FCPA Professor, 'SEC Chairman Schapiro's FCPA Responses' (Oct. 7, 2011), containing links to original source documents.
47. FCPA Professor, 'Double-Dipping' (June 4, 2013), containing links to original source documents.
48. Id.
49. Id.
50. Philip Urofsky, et al., 'How Should We Measure the Effectiveness of the Foreign Corrupt Practices Act? Don't Break What Isn't Broken – the Fallacies of Reform,' 73 The Ohio Law Journal 1145 (2012).
51. Barbara Black, 'The SEC and the Foreign Corrupt Practices Act: Fighting Global Corruption is Not Part of the SEC's Mission,' 73 Ohio State Law Journal 1093 (2012).
52. Mike Koehler, 'The Story of the Foreign Corrupt Practices Act,' 73 Ohio State Law Journal 929 (2012).
53. Press Release, U.S. Dep't of Justice, 'Baker Hughes Subsidiary Pleads Guilty to Bribing Kazakh Official and Agrees to Pay $11 Million Criminal Fine as Part of Largest Combined Sanction Ever Imposed in FCPA Case' (Apr. 26, 2007).
54. FCPA Professor, 'Year in Review Roundups' (Jan. 11, 2013).
55. See for instance the Deferred Prosecution Agreement, U.S. v. Parker Drilling Co., Case 1:13-cr-00176 (E.D. Va., Apr. 16, 2013).
56. Deferred Prosecution Agreement, U.S. v. Johnson & Johnson, Case 1:11-cr-00099-JDB, (D.D.C., Apr. 8, 2011).
57. Deferred Prosecution Agreement, U.S. v. Pfizer H.C.P. Corp. (D.D.C. Aug. 7, 2012).
58. FCPA Professor, 'DOJ Enforcement of the FCPA – Year in Review' (Jan. 9, 2013).
59. Joseph Warin et al., 'Somebody's Watching Me: FCPA Monitorships and How They Can Work Better,' 13 U. of Pennsylvania Journal of Business Law 321 (2011).
60. FCPA Professor, 'The Work of a Monitor and Checking in on Siemens' (Jan. 22, 2013), containing links to original source documents.
61. FCPA Professor, 'Friday Roundup' (Apr. 13, 2012), containing links to original source documents.
62. FCPA Professor, 'Faro's Monitor – Late and Expensive' (Dec. 27, 2010).
63. The following website contains an interactive map allowing users to learn of FCPA violations in specific countries, as well as industry specific FCPA data – www.fcpamap.com.
64. OECD, 'Phase 3 Report on Implementing the OECD Anti-Bribery Convention in the United States' (Oct. 2010).
65. SEC Release, 'OECD Commends U.S. Regulators for Efforts to Fight Transnational Bribery' (Oct. 20, 2010).
66. FCPA Professor, 'Our Stellar FCPA Unit Continues to Go Gangbusters, Bringing Case after Case' (May 6, 2013); FCPA Professor, 'We Are Not Going Away … Our Efforts to Fight Foreign Bribery Are More Robust Than Ever' (June 9, 2013).
67. Press Release, U.S. Dep't of Justice, 'California Company and Two Executives Indicted for Their Alleged Participation in Scheme to Bribe Officials at State-owned Electrical Utility in Mexico' (Oct. 21, 2010).
68. Press Release, U.S. Dep't of Justice, 'California Company, Its Two Executives and Intermediary Convicted by Federal Jury in Los Angeles on All Counts for Their Involvement in Scheme to Bribe Officials at State-Owned Electrical Utility in Mexico' (May 10, 2011).
69. Order Granting Motion to Dismiss, U.S. v. Noriega, et al., Case 2:10-cr-01031-AHM (Dec. 1, 2011).
70. Id.
71. Id.

72. Press Release, U.S. Dep't of Justice, 'Assistant Attorney General Lanny A. Breuer Speaks at the American Conference Institute's 28th National Conference on the Foreign Corrupt Practices Act' (Nov. 16, 2012).
73. Information, U.S. v. Siemens, Case No. 08-CR-367-RJL (D.D.C., Dec. 12, 2008).
74. Government's Sentencing Memorandum, U.S. v. Siemens, Case No. 08-CR-367-RJL (D.D.C., Dec. 12, 2008).
75. Information, U.S. v. BAE Systems, Case No. 10-CR-035-JDB (D.D.C., Feb. 4, 2010).
76. Government's Sentencing Memorandum, U.S. v. BAE Systems, Case No. 10-CR-035-JDB (D.D.C., Feb. 4, 2010).
77. Press Release, U.S. Dep't of Justice, 'BAE Systems PLC Pleads Guilty and Ordered to Pay $400 Million Criminal Fine' (Mar. 1, 2010).
78. FCPA Professor, 'Siemens… the Year After' (Dec. 14, 2009).
79. FCPA Professor, 'FBI Awards BAE $40 Million Contract' (Sept. 28, 2010).
80. Complaint, U.S. v. James Giffen, Case No. 03-MAG-663 (S.D.N.Y., Mar. 28, 2003).
81. FCPA Professor, 'The Giffen Gaffe – the Final Chapter' (Nov. 22, 2010), containing links to original source documents.
82. Id.
83. Steve Levine, Foreign Policy, 'James Giffen's trial ends: A Slap on the Wrist, and the Triumph of American Putinism' (Aug. 10, 2010).
84. Scott Horton, Harpers, 'Kazakhgate Ends with a Whimper' (Aug. 9, 2010).
85. FCPA Professor, 'Friday Roundup' (Nov. 30, 2012).
86. See FCPA Professor, entries under the 'Double Standard' subject matter tab.
87. Foreign Payments Disclosure: Hearings before the Subcomm. on Consumer Prot. and Fin. of the H. Comm. on Interstate and Foreign Commerce, 94th Cong. 2 (1976).
88. Response to Written Questions of Senator D'Amato from John C. Keeney, Business Accounting and Foreign Trade Simplification Act, Joint Hearing before the Subcommittee on International Finance and Monetary Policy and the Subcommittee on Securities of the Committee on Banking, Housing, and Urban Affairs, United States Senate, 99th Congress, Second Session, on S. 430 (June 10, 1986).
89. Aruna Viswanatha, Main Justice, 'Targeting Executives in FCPA Cases Can Lead to Industry-Wide Probes' (June 23, 2010).
90. FCPA Professor, 'Empty Rhetoric' (Nov. 8, 2012).
91. FCPA Professor, 'A Focus on DOJ FCPA Individual Prosecutions' (Jan. 28, 2013).
92. Id.
93. Id.
94. SEC Release, 'SEC Charges Former CEO of Innospec for Role in Bribery Scheme' (Jan. 24, 2011).
95. FCPA Professor, 'A Focus on SEC FCPA Individual Actions' (Jan. 30, 2013).
96. Id.
97. 'Examining Enforcement of the Foreign Corrupt Practices Act, Hearing before the Subcommittee on Crime and Drugs of the Committee on the Judiciary, Senate' (Nov. 30, 2010).
98. Id.
99. FCPA Professor, 'DOJ Prosecution of Individuals – Are Other Factors at Play?' (Jan. 29, 2013).
100. Id.
101. FCPA Professor, 'The Origins and Prominence of a Theory' (Sept. 13, 2012).
102. FCPA Professor, 'Year in Review Roundups' (Jan. 11, 2013).
103. FCPA Professor, 'The Origins And Prominence of a Theory' (Sept. 13, 2012).
104. Ellen Podgor, 'White Collar Innocence: Irrelevant in the High Stakes Risk Game,' 85 Chicago Kent Law Review 77 (2010).

105. Id.
106. Gary Fields and John Emshwiller, Wall Street Journal, 'Federal Guilty Pleas Soar as Bargains Trump Trials' (Sept. 23, 2012).
107. Id.
108. Press Release, U.S. Dep't of Justice, 'Former Senior Officer of Schnitzer Steel Industries Inc. Subsidiary Pleads Guilty to Foreign Bribes' (June 29, 2007).
109. Joe Palazzolo, Wall Street Journal Corruption Currents, 'DOJ Drops Bribery Charges Against Whistleblower in Schnitzer Steel Case' (Oct. 18, 2011).
110. United States' Unopposed Motion to Dismiss the Information, U.S. v. Wooh, Case 3:07-cr-00244-KI (D. Ore., Oct. 14, 2011).
111. Press Release, U.S. Dep't of Justice, 'Six Former Executives of California Valve Company Charged in $46 Million Foreign Bribery Conspiracy' (Apr. 8, 2009).
112. Press Release, U.S. Dep't of Justice, 'Former Finance Director of California Valve Company Pleads Guilty to Bribing Foreign Government Officials' (Feb. 3, 2009).
113. See e.g., FCPA Professor, 'Edmonds Pleads Guilty as Trial Nears' (June 18, 2012).
114. FCPA Professor, 'Carson Sentencing Issues' (Nov. 12, 2012).
115. Press Release, 'BMK Obtains Non-Prison Resolution for Client in Criminal FCPA Case' (Jan. 17, 2013).
116. Transcript, CNBC Exclusive: CNBC Senior Correspondent Scott Cohn Speaks with Former Morgan Stanley Managing Director Garth Peterson (Aug. 17, 2012).
117. Press Release, U.S. Dep't of Justice, 'Film Executive and Spouse Found Guilty of Paying Bribes to a Senior Thai Tourism Official to Obtain Lucrative Contracts' (Sept. 14, 2009).
118. Press Release, U.S. Dep't of Justice, 'Two Telecommunications Executives Convicted by Miami Jury on All Counts for Their Involvement in Scheme to Bribe Officials at State-Owned Telecommunications Company in Haiti' (Aug. 5, 2011).
119. John Smith, Las Vegas Review, 'FBI Stung after Sting Involving Corrupt Foreign Practices' (Feb. 29, 2012).
120. FBI Release, 'Corporate Corruption – a Historic Takedown' (Jan. 26, 2010).
121. FCPA Professor, 'First Africa Sting Trial Results in Mistrial' (July 8, 2011).
122. FCPA Professor, 'Africa Sting Development – "Mr. Giordanella You Are Excused … You Are Free to Go"' (Dec. 22, 2011).
123. FCPA Professor, 'Africa Sting – Caldwell and Godsey Not Guilty – Jury Still out as to Other Defendants' (Jan. 30, 2012).
124. FCPA Professor, 'Judge Leon Declares Mistrial as to Remaining Africa Sting Defendants' (Jan. 31, 2012).
125. FCPA Professor, 'A Guest Post from the Africa Sting Jury Foreman' (Feb. 6, 2012).
126. Government's Motion to Dismiss, U.S. v. Amaro Goncalves, No. 09-CR-335-RJL (D.D.C. Feb. 21, 2012).
127. Transcript of Judge Leon's Remarks Dismissing the Indictments with Prejudice for Amaro Goncalves and 15 Co-Defendants, U.S. v. Amaro Goncalves, No. 09-CR-335-RJL (D.D.C. Feb. 21, 2012).
128. FCPA Professor, 'Africa Sting – a "Long and Sad Chapter in The Annals of White Collar Criminal Enforcement"' (Feb. 22, 2012).
129. Leslie Wayne, New York Times, 'Bribery Case Falls Apart, and Tactics Are Doubted' (Feb. 23, 2012).
130. Press Release, U.S. Dep't of Justice, 'Former General Manager of Texas Business Arrested for Role in Alleged Scheme to Bribe Officials at Mexican State-Owned Electrical Utility' (Nov. 23, 2009).
131. FCPA Professor, 'Did "Foreign Official" Impact the O'Shea Acquittal?' (July 11, 2012).
132. Id.

133. Id.
134. Dane Schiller, Houston Chronicle, 'After Losing Everything, Mexico Bribery Suspect Acquitted' (Jan. 17, 2012).
135. Kevin Gray, Thompson Reuters News & Insight, 'U.S. Prosecutor Says Tough Tactics to Remain in Bribery Fight' (Mar. 1, 2012).
136. *Supra* note 66.
137. Sentencing Memorandum, U.S. v. Carson, No. SACR 09-0007-JVS (C.D. Cal. Nov. 5, 2012).
138. Koon v. U.S., 518 U.S. 81 (1996).
139. FCPA Professor, 'Testing Innocence' (Feb. 27, 2012).
140. Press Release, U.S. Dep't of Justice, 'Former Chairman and CEO of Kellogg, Brown & Root Inc. Sentenced to 30 Months in Prison for Foreign Bribery and Kickback Schemes' (Feb. 23, 2012).
141. Press Release, U.S. Dep't of Justice, 'Former Consultant for Willbros International Sentenced in Connection with Foreign Bribery Scheme' (May 3, 2013).
142. SEC Release, 'SEC Files Settled Charges Against David P. Turner and Ousama M. Naaman for Engaging in Bribery' (Aug. 5, 2010).
143. SEC Release, 'SEC Charges Former CEO of Innospec for Role in Bribery Scheme' (Jan. 24, 2011).
144. FCPA Professor, 'Carson Sentencing Issues' (Nov. 12, 2012), containing links to original source documents.
145. FCPA Professor, 'A Focus On Chinese Guanxi' (Aug. 21, 2012), containing links to original source documents.
146. Id.
147. Id.
148. FCPA Professor, 'In Sentencing Naaman, Judge Huvelle Dismisses DOJ's Rhetoric and Refuses to Make Naaman the "Poster Child" the DOJ Would Like' (Jan. 23, 2012).
149. Id.
150. Id.
151. Id.
152. Id.
153. FCPA Professor, 'Shades of Gray' (Aug. 28, 2012).
154. FCPA Professor, '366 Days' (Nov. 11, 2009).
155. FCPA Professor, 'Judge (Again) Significantly Rejects DOJ's Recommendation in Sentencing Bobby Elkins' (Oct. 25, 2010).
156. Gary Stein, 'Sentencing of Individuals in FCPA Cases,' Business Crimes Bulletin (Jan. 2011).

6. Reasons for the increase in FCPA enforcement

That FCPA enforcement has increased in this new era begs the question why? This chapter offers several practical and provocative reasons for the increase in FCPA enforcement. Practical reasons highlighted include that there is more international business than ever before, the introduction of NPAs and DPAs to the FCPA context, and the impact another law – Sarbanes Oxley – has had on FCPA enforcement. A provocative reason highlighted is that many believe FCPA enforcement has increased because it is lucrative for the government. In addition, one of the effects of this new era of FCPA enforcement has been the emergence of a thriving and vibrant anti-bribery complex called FCPA Inc., and the issue will be explored whether FCPA Inc. itself is one of the reasons for the increase in FCPA enforcement and scrutiny.

Even though FCPA enforcement has trended upward during this new era, enforcement statistics need to be viewed in the proper context. This chapter concludes by placing FCPA enforcement statistics in the proper perspective and demonstrating that the FCPA is not nearly the boogeyman it is often portrayed to be.

A. PRACTICAL REASONS

There are several practical reasons for the increase in FCPA enforcement during this new era including: more companies are doing business than ever before in international markets, particularly in FCPA high risk jurisdictions; more companies and individuals than ever before are subject to the FCPA; NPAs and DPAs have provided enforcement agencies with more options in bringing enforcement actions; and Sarbanes-Oxley requires corporate management to assess internal controls including at foreign subsidiaries.

More International Business

The FCPA is a law most logically implicated when doing business in international markets. In this new era, business organizations (large and small and across a variety of industry sectors) are doing more business in international markets than ever before. According to a recent analysis, 'U.S. companies conduct almost as much business overseas as they do in the U.S.' and approximately 50 percent of production, sales and profits of U.S. companies in the S&P 500 are from overseas operations.[1] This compares to approximately 30 percent a decade ago.

Financial information of companies across a variety of industry sectors highlights the prominence of international business. Consumer products company Procter & Gamble derives approximately 60 percent of its sales from outside of North America, its products are sold in approximately 180 countries and it has facilities in approximately 40 countries. Dow Chemical derives approximately 65 percent of its sales from outside the U.S., it serves customers in approximately 160 countries, and it has facilities in approximately 35 countries. Nike derives approximately 60 percent of its revenue from outside the U.S. and it has approximately 400 stores outside the U.S. as well as 16 distribution centers.

For many companies, doing business in the global marketplace, including FCPA high-risk jurisdiction such as China, India and Brazil, is necessary to sustain growth and satisfy shareholder demand for profits. As the CEO of a large multi-national company rhetorically asked, 'Where do you think the growth in the world is going to come from? Would you bet on the U.S.? Would you bet on Western Europe? It's going to come from emerging markets.'[2]

Simply put, more business in international markets means more engagement of foreign third parties, more points of contact with 'foreign officials,' and more exposure to difficult and challenging foreign business conditions and trade barriers that often create the conditions in which bribery can flourish. Against this backdrop, it is not surprising that there has been more FCPA enforcement in this new era for the same reason that more cars on the road results in more accidents, traffic violations and speeding tickets.

More Companies and Individuals Subject to the FCPA

Another practical reason for the increase in FCPA enforcement is that more companies and individuals are subject to the FCPA than ever before. As detailed in Chapter 3 regarding the FCPA's jurisdiction, foreign companies with shares listed on U.S. exchanges are subject to the books and records and internal controls provisions, as well as the anti-bribery provisions to the extent a bribery scheme has a U.S. nexus. When the FCPA was passed in 1977, few foreign companies had shares listed on a U.S. exchange, but in this new era approximately 1,000 foreign companies have shares listed on U.S. exchanges. Indeed, most of the top FCPA enforcement actions in terms of settlement amounts detailed in Chapter 5 have been against foreign companies such as Siemens, Total, Eni/Snamprogetti, Technip, JGC Corp., Daimler, Alcatel-Lucent, and Magyar Telekom.

In addition, in 1998 the FCPA was amended resulting in certain other foreign companies and foreign nationals becoming subject to the FCPA's anti-bribery provisions to the extent a bribery scheme has a U.S. nexus. Enforcement agencies have invoked this newest prong of the FCPA in bringing enforcement actions against, among others, companies from Korea, Germany, Japan, Switzerland, Russia and China, as well as citizens of Japan, the United Kingdom, and Israel.

Non-Prosecution and Deferred Prosecution Agreements

As previously highlighted in Chapter 2, for most of the FCPA's history the DOJ had two choices when faced with conduct that might implicate the FCPA: prosecute or do not prosecute. In this new era, the third option of NPAs and DPAs dominate FCPA enforcement and use of these alternative resolution vehicles is one of the more obvious reasons for the general upward trend in FCPA enforcement. For instance, the former chief of the DOJ's FCPA unit stated that if the DOJ did not have the option of resolving FCPA enforcement actions with NPAs or DPAs the DOJ 'would certainly bring fewer cases.'[3] Likewise, the OECD Report stated that 'it seems quite clear that the use of these agreements is one of the reasons for the impressive FCPA enforcement record in the U.S.'[4]

Sarbanes Oxley

The passage of Sarbanes Oxley ('SOX') in 2002 is also one of the practical reasons for the increase in FCPA enforcement. Enacted in the aftermath of several corporate financial scandals approximately a decade ago, Section 404 of SOX ('Management of Assessment of Internal Controls') requires issuers to assess and report on the effectiveness of internal controls over financial reporting. Among other things, the SOX requirement caused issuers to more actively assess internal controls across its business operations, particularly in foreign subsidiaries because such books and records are consolidated with the issuers for purposes of financial reporting.

Such assessments have resulted in questionable payments or transactions being reported to corporate headquarters and SOX has been specifically cited by the DOJ as one of the reasons for the increase in FCPA enforcement. During a 2010 Senate FCPA hearing, a DOJ representative stated: 'We are getting a significant number of disclosures from corporations about their own criminal conduct. I think that, in part, relates to the passage of Sarbanes-Oxley legislation, which encourages corporations to review their own books and records.'[5]

Similarly, during a 2011 House FCPA hearing, the same DOJ representative stated:

> At least one likely cause for this increase in cases is disclosures by companies consistent with their obligations under the Sarbanes-Oxley Act, which requires senior corporate officers to certify the accuracy of their financial statements. This has led to more companies discovering FCPA violations and making the decision to disclose them to the SEC and DOJ.[6]

Other Reasons

Other factors that have contributed to a general increase in FCPA enforcement include changes in technology and increased monitoring and reporting of business conduct by non-governmental organizations, civil society, and the media.

In terms of technology, think about how the average person today communicates – via e-mail, text message, cell phone, and other electronic means. There are often permanent records of all these communications, unlike in prior eras when various forms of communication were often temporary and incapable of being retrieved at the touch of a button. Modes of current communication have provided law enforcement agencies with mounds of information and data that often provide key evidence in enforcement actions, including FCPA enforcement actions which often include direct references to e-mails or other electronic communications. Increased capabilities to monitor global financial transactions in the aftermath of the September 11th terrorist attacks have also provided law enforcement agencies with additional evidence-gathering tools. Moreover, the DOJ and its law enforcement partner, the FBI, have also made greater use of undercover investigative tactics in FCPA enforcement actions. For instance, the Africa Sting action made extensive use of such methods and the following information and materials were collected: 615 audio and video recordings of more than 150 meetings; 5,287 recorded telephone calls; nearly 3000 pages of text messages; and approximately 242,000 pages of documents, electronic media, including desktop computers, laptop computers, USB drives, zip discs, memory cards and DVDs, among other items, seized during thirteen search warrants.[7]

In addition to several practical reasons for the general increase in FCPA enforcement in this new era, there are also certain provocative reasons as well.

B. PROVOCATIVE REASONS

Many believe that FCPA enforcement has increased because it is lucrative for the government. In addition, one of the effects of this new era of FCPA enforcement is FCPA Inc. and the issue will be explored whether the industry itself is one of the reasons for the increase in FCPA enforcement and scrutiny.

FCPA Enforcement is Lucrative for the U.S. Government

The term cash cow refers to a business unit that generates unusually high profit margins, so high that the business unit is responsible for a large amount of the company's operating profit and thus a reliable source of money. There are many who believe that FCPA enforcement in this new era represents a cash cow for the government as settlement amounts in FCPA enforcement actions simply flow into the U.S. treasury.[8] The Chamber of Commerce has stated that 'FCPA prosecutions have turned into a cash cow for the Justice Department,' but that 'using the justice system as an ATM wasn't what the authors of the FCPA had in mind.' Others have noted that 'the profitability enforcement has garnered for the government' is one of the reasons for the increase in FCPA enforcement and that 'quite simply, [FCPA enforcement] is lucrative for the government.'

There is statistical evidence to support the notion that FCPA enforcement has become a cash cow for the government. For instance, in 2010, 50 percent of the total fine and penalty amounts secured by the DOJ criminal division (a law enforcement agency that enforces approximately 900 laws) were in FCPA (or related) enforcement actions.[9] Commenting on the rise in FCPA enforcement, a former DOJ prosecutor stated: 'You have to think of the SEC and the DOJ as businesses. They are looking for growth areas, too.'[10]

The notion that FCPA enforcement has increased because it is lucrative for the government is hard to dismiss, given that some of the most forceful comments on this issue have come from former DOJ and SEC enforcement attorneys, including those in the DOJ's FCPA unit. For instance, a former DOJ prosecutor stated: 'FCPA is a cash cow. Big companies, most of whom are quite vulnerable, will do anything to avoid a civil or criminal trial. FCPA becomes a cost of doing business. The money flows into the government.'[11] A former Assistant Director of the SEC's Enforcement Division likewise stated that one reason for the increase in FCPA enforcement is a 'very simple reason – it's lucrative.'[12] Most prominently, the former Assistant Chief of the DOJ's FCPA unit stated: 'The government sees a profitable program, and it's going to ride that horse until it can't ride it anymore.'[13]

The 2013 FCPA enforcement actions against oil and gas company Total would seem to advance the belief that FCPA enforcement represents a cash cow for the government. The salient points regarding the $398 million FCPA enforcement action (the third-largest in FCPA history) are as follows.

- The enforcement action was against a French oil and gas company for making improper payments to an Iranian foreign official through use of an employee of a Swiss private bank and a British Virgin Islands company.
- The vast majority of the alleged improper conduct took place between 1995 and 1997 (that is 16 to 18 years ago).
- The sole U.S. jurisdictional nexus (a required legal element for an anti-bribery violation since Total was a foreign issuer) was a 1995 wire transfer of $500,000 (representing less than 1 percent of the alleged bribe payments at issue) from a New York-based account.
- The same exact conduct at issue was the focus of a French law enforcement investigation (i.e. Total's 'home' country).
- So old was the conduct giving rise to the enforcement action that the DOJ made the unusual statement in the DPA that 'evidentiary challenges' were present for both parties given that 'most of the underlying conduct occurred in the 1990s and early 2000s.'[14]

As highlighted in Chapter 3, the Total enforcement is just one of many corporate FCPA enforcement actions based on conduct significantly beyond the statute of limitations period. Other than an inflow into the U.S. treasury (as well as a boon to FCPA Inc.), what is really being accomplished by bringing an enforcement action based on such old conduct? For instance, the SEC's mission is 'to protect investors, maintain fair, orderly, and efficient markets, and facilitate capital formation.' How is this mission accomplished by an enforcement action concerning conduct that took place 10 to 15 years ago?

Moreover, as detailed throughout this book, much of the largeness of FCPA enforcement in this new era has resulted from aggressive enforcement theories (whether 'foreign official,' 'obtain or retain business,' or jurisdictional theories) resolved through NPAs and DPAs that are seldom subject to any meaningful judicial scrutiny. Indeed, the former chief of the DOJ's FCPA unit was asked about the increase in FCPA enforcement and candidly stated that 'what's really changed is not so much the legislation, but the enforcement and approach to enforcement by U.S. authorities.'[15] In short, these new enforcement theories and approach to enforcement have made FCPA enforcement a lucrative cash cow for the government.

FCPA Inc. and the Business of Bribery

One of the effects of this new era of FCPA enforcement has been the emergence and rapid rise of a lucrative industry called FCPA Inc. Because most corporate FCPA enforcement actions result from voluntary disclosures, FCPA Inc. law firm participants often serve as gatekeepers, and their decisions often play an important role in determining whether a business organization embarks on a lengthy and costly FCPA investigation and ultimately whether an FCPA enforcement action will follow. Indeed, as the former chief of the DOJ Fraud section has stated, 'if you get two of these [FCPA investigations] a year as a partner, you're pretty much set.'[16]

This section highlights various aspects of FCPA Inc., including how the industry markets this new era of FCPA enforcement and explores the issue of whether FCPA Inc. itself is one of the reasons for the increase in FCPA enforcement and scrutiny. This section also examines the typical career path of a DOJ or SEC FCPA enforcement attorney and highlights how most of the architects of this new era of FCPA enforcement are now making millions of dollars providing private sector FCPA investigative and compliance services to business organizations subject to the new era of FCPA enforcement they helped create.

The rise of FCPA Inc.

The rise of FCPA Inc. has been well documented. A *Washington Post* article titled 'Cashing in on Corruption' observed: 'FCPA business is booming, a welcome growth area for Washington law offices. [...]

Sharing in the bonanza [are] accounting firms, forensic computer specialists and a growing army of compliance consultants.'[17]

A *Newsweek* article titled 'Going after Graft' noted:

> With prosecutions likely to continue – the FBI has doubled the number of agents tasked to FCPA cases – business is responding in kind. Law firms are competing for top FCPA talent, banks financing international deals are insisting on anti-bribery stipulations in contracts, and a new cottage industry of experts has emerged, offering country-by-country advice on gifts and local laws.[18]

A *Forbes* article titled 'The Bribery Racket' highlighted how this new era of FCPA enforcement is 'good business for law firms [...] good business for accounting firms, [... and] good business for consulting firms, [and] the media.'[19]

A *Wall Street Journal* article titled 'FCPA Inc.: The Business of Bribery' observed that the FCPA is 'one of the few sort of crown-jewel practices right now' and reported that the annual compensation for top lawyers specializing in the FCPA is approximately $2 million per year.[20]

Others have noted that 'newcomers [some of whom 'discover they can spell FCPA and it's suddenly on their résumé'] are all clamoring for FCPA business,'[21] and it has been observed as follows.

> It is getting pretty crowded these days out in the Anti-Corruption Compliance space. There are more and more companies, consultants, software providers and other entities offering to provide the right mix of information and data needed to support a due diligence review of a third-party, joint venture partner or acquisition target. These companies, consultants and investigators are at the infancy of this new and sophisticated industry. Just look on the Internet for information and you will be overwhelmed.[22]

The emergence and rapid rise of FCPA Inc. caused the *Wall Street Journal* to ask whether the FCPA is 'just a full-employment act for the private bar?'[23] Even the judiciary has noticed the rise of FCPA Inc. For instance, in sentencing an FCPA individual defendant the judge noted: 'I know it's a growth industry, isn't it, the FCPA? It's keeping a lot of white collar lawyers busy; is that fair?'[24]

There is of course nothing inherently wrong with the emergence and rapid rise of a niche industry. However, with any new industry it is proper to explore the market conditions which gave rise to the industry as well as examine which people contributed to the market conditions and what they are doing now. These issues will be explored in more detail below, but first it is important to recognize how FCPA Inc. participants often serve as gatekeepers in this new era of FCPA enforcement.

FCPA Inc. as gatekeepers

Because most corporate FCPA enforcement actions result from voluntary disclosures, FCPA Inc. law firm participants often serve as gatekeepers and their decisions often play an important role in determining whether a business organization embarks on a lengthy and costly FCPA investigation and ultimately whether an FCPA enforcement action will follow.

Forbes described the path of a typical FCPA investigation and enforcement action as follows. 'Companies can find themselves getting extorted in foreign lands, only to get extorted again by Washington. It works generally like this: A company that suspects bribery overseas hires a battery of lawyers, accountants and investigators who may then report any findings to DOJ in hopes of some undefined leniency.'[25]

Even the DOJ understands the key role FCPA Inc. plays in a typical FCPA enforcement action as the DOJ Assistant Attorney General stated that the DOJ 'absolutely need companies through their firms to provide us with their investigations.'[26]

That FCPA voluntary disclosures are often the fuel that ignites an FCPA enforcement action is obvious as highlighted by the statistics in Chapter 5 regarding the origins of FCPA enforcement actions. Less obvious is that voluntary disclosures are like a rainbow, and waiting on the other side for FCPA Inc. is often a pot of gold in the form of pre-enforcement action professional fees, which as highlighted in Chapter 5 are often the largest financial component of FCPA scrutiny. Post-enforcement action professional fees can also climb into the millions of dollars per year as most corporate FCPA enforcement actions impose compliance and reporting requirements on the company necessitating the need for FCPA Inc. services even after the enforcement action has been resolved.

While the decision to voluntarily disclose is of course the company's and that of its board of directors and/or audit committee, it must be recognized that FCPA counsel has an inherent conflict of interest in advising the company on voluntary disclosure issues.

Simply put, if the company does not voluntarily disclose, the matter for all practical purposes and in all likelihood is over and the need for FCPA Inc. services ends. However, if the company does voluntarily disclose to the enforcement agencies, the matter gains new steam – the 'where else' question will be asked by the enforcement agencies, to answer the 'where else' question a team of lawyers and other industry participants will travel the globe, and FCPA Inc. services will be needed for years to come.

Is there any other area of law where those subject to the law race to Washington D.C. to tell the government about potential violations? The 'carrots' and 'sticks' that may motivate FCPA voluntary disclosures are present in every enforcement agency investigation regardless of the substantive area of law at issue. The question is posed: why then is corporate voluntary disclosure such a prominent feature of FCPA enforcement, but less prominent in other areas of law? An answer may be that corporate voluntary disclosures are often the fuel that feeds FCPA Inc.

In short, voluntary disclosures represent a pot of gold for FCPA Inc. and the disclosure decision is often a multi-million dollar decision for a business organization. The proverbial 'elephant in the room' is that the decision is also often a multi-million dollar decision for FCPA counsel advising the company.

By highlighting the role of FCPA Inc. as gatekeepers, this section merely points out the potential conflict of interest that is present in a typical FCPA investigation and enforcement action. This potential conflict of interest however is seldom highlighted as few outside of FCPA Inc. realize how FCPA enforcement actually works. Another issue seldom discussed, but highlighted below, is that the same enforcement agency officials who encourage voluntary disclosure and speak of the credit that will be given to a company that makes such a disclosure are the same individuals who frequently move to FCPA Inc. after articulating this enforcement agency policy while at the government.

Marketing the new era of FCPA enforcement

The FCPA is a law that keeps corporate counsel up at night.[27] Some of this angst is a rational response to the FCPA risks business organizations face when doing business in the global marketplace as well as the FCPA's long tentacles discussed in Chapter 7. On the other hand, some of this angst is an irrational response to the flood of information disseminated by FCPA Inc. participants who frequently, and with presumed business interests in mind, highlight the increase in FCPA enforcement and other doomsday scenarios.

The *Washington Post* article referenced above stated: 'don't think law firms aren't playing off those fears by aggressively marketing their services as investigators, risk mitigators and compliance counselors.' An FCPA commentator observed, under the heading 'scare the crap out of them' as follows.

> Our dirty little secret, if this could rightly be called that, is that we practitioners vastly overstate the risk that the FCPA brings to companies. [...] The degree to which the industry that has popped up around the FCPA has an inherent interest in puffing up the underlying risk creates at the least an apparent bias. We all feed off it: risk equals fear equals action equals money

for consultants, lawyers, compliance people (in the form of jobs, resources, and budgets), training suppliers, and everyone down the line. It's not a flattering equation.[28]

Fear-based marketing is common among FCPA Inc. participants as demonstrated by the following industry ads.

- The life sciences 'industry sweep' is in full swing. Recent high-profile settlements by two large, multi-national pharmaceutical manufacturers for violations of the FCPA make one fact clear – this is only the beginning;
- We are in a new era of corruption mitigation. Heralded by the increased enforcement of the [FCPA] … the noose of regulators has tightened;
- The stakes are getting higher and failure to demonstrate a sound FCPA strategy could be disastrous to your organization;
- FCPA enforcement actions can be 'bet the company' events with the huge potential for civil and criminal penalties; and
- With FCPA enforcement on the rise, it's never been more important to train your staff. [The enforcement agencies] are aggressively pursuing cases and recently settled with Siemens AG for an unprecedented $800 million.[29]

The last example is indicative of a common marketing device of using the largest fine and penalty amount in FCPA history to portray a false reality. The actual reality is that the Siemens enforcement action was a significant outlier and most FCPA enforcement actions are resolved for significantly lower amounts.

Another common FCPA Inc. marketing device involves the number of FCPA enforcement actions. It would seem like a basic question: how many FCPA enforcement actions are there in a given year? However, how one answers this question may depend on one's objective and motivation such as marketing FCPA compliance products and services.

For instance, various FCPA Inc. participants inflate the number of FCPA enforcement actions. Consider the following graphical depiction of FCPA enforcement actions per year by an FCPA Inc. participant (Figure 6.1).

The reality is something much different and the number of FCPA enforcement actions are often inflated, as in the chart in Figure 6.1, by: (i) double counting related DOJ and SEC enforcement actions based on the same core set of conduct; and (ii) counting individual enforcement

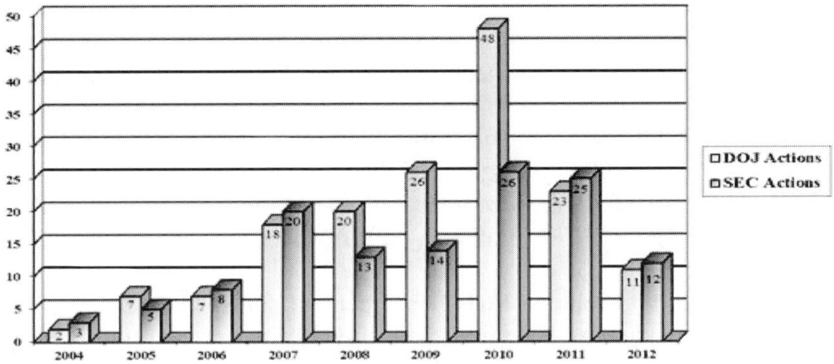

Source: Gibson, Dunn & Crutcher LLP

Figure 6.1 FCPA enforcement actions per year

actions separately from the corporate enforcement action based on the same core set of conduct. Nevertheless, these numbers are often carried forward by publications such as the *Wall Street Journal*, and all of a sudden the business community is led to believe that 'since 2009, the [DOJ] has brought 108 FCPA cases while the SEC has brought 77.'[30]

To demonstrate how FCPA enforcement actions are inflated consider just two examples: the Africa Sting action and the Siemens enforcement action.

As previously discussed in Chapter 5, the manufactured Africa Sting action involved 22 individuals allegedly engaged in the same core conduct. You can decide whether it is more accurate to count the Africa Sting action as one core enforcement action or 22 different enforcement actions. The chart in Figure 6.1 counted the Africa Sting action as 22 enforcement actions, thus the apparent spike in FCPA enforcement in 2010.

The record-setting Siemens enforcement action had the following components: (i) in 2008, the DOJ and SEC brought related corporate enforcement actions – the DOJ component included an action against Siemens AG and related enforcement actions against Siemens Argentina, Siemens Bangladesh, and Siemens Venezuela – the SEC component included an action against Siemens AG; and (ii) in 2011, the DOJ brought a related enforcement action against eight individuals and the SEC brought a related enforcement action against seven individuals.[31] All of the enforcement actions were based, in whole or in part, on the same core conduct. Again, you can decide whether it is more accurate to count the Siemens enforcement actions as one core enforcement action or 20 different enforcement actions. The chart in Figure 6.1 counted the Siemens individual enforcement actions in 2011 as 15 enforcement actions.

Inflating FCPA enforcement statistics in the way many FCPA Inc. participants do results in highly misleading statistics concerning the actual amount of FCPA enforcement. This is an important issue given the growing interest in FCPA statistical information and empirical FCPA-related research.

High-quality and reliable FCPA enforcement statistics reflecting what is actually occurring and without distorting reality are best achieved by using the core approach. The core approach focuses on the corporate conduct at issue regardless of whether the conduct at issue involved a DOJ or SEC enforcement action or both (as is frequently the case), regardless of whether the corporate enforcement action involved a parent company, a subsidiary or both (as is frequently the case), and regardless of whether the DOJ and/or SEC brought any related individual enforcement actions (as is occasionally the case).

Notably, the DOJ has endorsed the core approach to counting FCPA enforcement actions. The DOJ's FCPA Unit Chief stated:

> We don't count statistics the way I guess some of the people, whether it's the commentators or the media, or law firms and the like. [...] And so, you know, we count slightly differently by the way, than a lot of people in the public. If you have a parent and two subs plead guilty, and the parent gets a DPA, we don't count that as three actions. That's one matter from our perspective, and I think internally it just makes sense for us.[32]

Using the core approach, since 2009 there have been approximately 55 FCPA enforcement actions, not approximately 185 as suggested by the FCPA Inc. chart in Figure 6.1 and as carried forward by the others.

The FCPA's revolving door problem and the solution

The public policy concerns of government enforcement attorneys aggressively enforcing a law and then leaving government service to provide private sector defense and compliance services related to that law have been well documented. For instance a study concerning the so-called 'revolving door' found that lawyers who leave the SEC to join law firms that specialize in defending clients against the SEC are associated with stronger enforcement efforts.[33]

A *Forbes* columnist described the public policy concerns of DOJ enforcement attorneys leaving government service for the private sector as follows.

> From an outside perspective, [such moves seem] like a zero-consequence decision: corporations now have lawyers who understand the federal prosecutorial machinery and, importantly, maintain their relationships with former colleagues remaining in government service. And, of course, the federal government will easily enough be able to find replacements among the many eager law school graduates seeking these plum positions. Everybody wins, right? Everybody, that is, except for the justice system as a whole. Underlying the revolving door is a pernicious underbelly of overzealous and often unfair prosecutions, juked conviction stats, and a culture of plea-bargaining that is spiraling out of control, all in order to bring down some of the biggies in the business world. In short, the revolving door is facilitated by a federal criminal justice system geared more for making prosecutors' reputations on the scalps of private sector companies and executives, than for achieving true justice. [...] The revolving door between the DOJ and white shoe law firms is a phenomenon that deserves more attention by the press and other elements of civil society ... .[34]

The phenomenon deserves even more attention in the context of FCPA enforcement given the unique attributes of FCPA enforcement described in Chapter 2, including the DOJ's specific centralized enforcement policy that results in just a few individuals, from a supervisory and discretionary standpoint, controlling FCPA enforcement.

In this section, you will learn of the typical career path of a DOJ or SEC FCPA enforcement attorney and how the primary architects of this new era of FCPA enforcement are currently making millions of dollars in the private sector providing FCPA investigative and compliance services to business organizations subject to the new era of FCPA enforcement they helped create. Indeed, the law firms employing these former FCPA enforcement attorneys specifically market their prior government experience and inside knowledge in seeking clients.

As previously highlighted, in 2010 the DOJ Assistant Attorney General proclaimed, 'we are in a new era of [FCPA] enforcement; and we are here to stay.' During this individual's (the former AAG) tenure at the DOJ, he was responsible for enforcement of all criminal laws, not just the FCPA. However, the substantive law of most interest to the former AAG while at DOJ appeared to be the FCPA, and by his own admission he spoke about the FCPA and related issues 'perhaps more than on any other subject and all over the world.'[35] In 2013, a law firm announced that the former AAG would become Vice Chair of that firm, and the *New York*

Times reported his position was created especially for him, a 'Washington insider,' and that his first-year salary was going to be approximately $4 million.[36]

The law firm release stated that the former AAG 'established himself as a national leader on a range of federal law enforcement priorities' including the FCPA. Media reports stated that the former AAG hoped his white-collar practice will grow following his stint at the DOJ and that he expects to have clients in areas such as foreign bribery. The *Wall Street Journal* stated that the former AAG 'plans to leverage his government experience with money laundering and FCPA cases into more international work for the firm' and quoted the former AAG as follows: 'I think I have a pretty good sense of what the department and what the government looks for.'[37]

Indeed, the former AAG's law firm bio states that he 'specializes in helping clients navigate [among other things] anti-corruption matters' and that while at the DOJ he 'oversaw numerous prosecutions that set new benchmarks across a host of enforcement areas, including anti-corruption …'.[38]

Commenting on the former AAG's new position, the president of a public interest group stated:

> Nothing is more corrosive to the American people's trust in government than the revolving door where too many officials turn their so-called public service into multi-million dollar riches unimaginable to most Americans. […] [The former AAG] spinning through it is only the latest example: partner at big DC law firm representing corporate clients before the DOJ, then becomes a senior official at the DOJ making decisions whether or not to prosecute those same or similar corporate clients, then leaves to go back to private practice representing those same or similar corporate clients with legal issues before, bingo, the DOJ. Isn't much of his new multi-million dollar pay package due to the high level connections, high-profile and intimate knowledge of the DOJ he gained while doing his 'public service' at the DOJ?[39]

Prior to the former AAG leaving government service for the private sector, it was the Assistant Chief of the DOJ's FCPA Unit. In 2013, a law firm announced that the individual (the former Assistant Chief) would join the firm to provide FCPA investigative and compliance services. The law firm's release stated:

> In recent years, [the former Assistant Chief] was responsible for directly supervising up to half of the DOJ's investigations into transnational bribery. He also drafted portions of the FCPA Resource Guide … which details the contours of the FCPA legal regime, the policy positions underlying the enforcement strategy, and the relevance of past enforcement positions taken

> by the DOJ and the SEC. During [the former Assistant Chief's] tenure, the DOJ has investigated and resolved more cases against corporations and has charged, tried, and convicted more individuals under the FCPA than in any other similar period in history.[40]

In the release, the law firm touted the former Assistant Chief's 'connections to U.S. government agencies' and he stated to the media that 'FCPA investigations and enforcement has increased in recent years and that the practice would likely continue to be robust for attorneys.'[41]

Prior to the Assistant Chief leaving government service for the private sector, it was the DOJ Deputy Assistant Attorney General. In 2012, a law firm announced that the individual (the former Deputy AAG) would join the firm to provide FCPA investigative and compliance services. The law firm's release stated that the former Deputy AAG, while at the DOJ, 'was involved in policy and enforcement issues' relating to the FCPA, and on his law firm bio page the former Deputy AAG noted that while at the DOJ he 'managed' many of the DOJ's white-collar prosecutions, including the DOJ's FCPA program, and that he 'represented' the DOJ on FCPA issues before Congress.[42]

Prior to the former Deputy AAG leaving government service for the private sector, it was another Assistant Chief of the DOJ's FCPA Unit. In 2012, a law firm announced that the individual (the former Assistant Chief) would join the firm to provide FCPA investigative and compliance services. The law firm's release stated:

> [The former Assistant Chief] brings a wealth of experience and insight from his years in government. The unique perspective he has gained from prosecuting … FCPA cases on behalf of the federal government will add tremendously to our Corporate Criminal Investigations Practice. We're delighted he's chosen [the law firm] for his return to the private sector.[43]

Prior to another Assistant Chief leaving government service for the private sector, it was the chief of the DOJ's FCPA Unit.[44] While the FCPA Unit chief between 2005 and 2010, this individual (the former FCPA Unit chief), in the words of the *Wall Street Journal*, oversaw 'a hot field in prosecution' and that 'it has been up to the Justice Department – and specifically to [the FCPA Unit chief] – to interpret the law.'[45] Others noted that the individual 'transformed the FCPA from a legal backwater to a headline practice' and 'led a revival of FCPA enforcement when the law had lain largely dormant for more than 20 years.'[46] In 2010, a law firm announced that the former FCPA Unit chief would join the firm to provide FCPA investigative and compliance services. The law firm's release stated that he 'was responsible for overseeing all investigations and prosecutions under the FCPA' and that his 'background and experience will be an enormous asset to our clients, which are facing increased scrutiny' on FCPA issues.[47]

It was reported that the FCPA Unit chief would be making approximately $2.5 million per year and the *Wall Street Journal* noted that this was a significant sum 'particularly for a lawyer arriving at firm without a ready list of clients.'[48] The FCPA Unit chief's law firm bio page states:

> Prior to joining [the law firm, the FCPA Unit chief] served as the deputy chief of the Fraud Section of the Criminal Division of the DOJ and is internationally acknowledged and respected as the architect and key enforcement official of the DOJ's modern FCPA enforcement program. [...] The FCPA Unit chief was responsible for overseeing all DOJ investigations and prosecutions under the FCPA.[49]

It is not just high-ranking DOJ FCPA enforcement attorneys that typically leave government service for the private sector to provide FCPA investigative and compliance services to business organizations subject to the new era of FCPA enforcement they helped create. In 2011, the chief of the SEC's FCPA Unit also left for the private sector. The law firm's release stated as follows.

> As head of the SEC's FCPA practice, [the former SEC FCPA Unit chief] played a role in all of the SEC's recent major FCPA cases and acted as the SEC liaison with the DOJ and regulators around the world. [...] In recent years, the SEC and other regulatory bodies have increased their focus on identifying violations under the FCPA. [The former SEC FCPA Unit chief's] experience and insight ... will be extremely beneficial to our clients.[50]

The *Wall Street Journal* observed as follows regarding the move. 'In recent years amid an uptick in FCPA investigations as well as a huge increase in fines for offenses, [the former SEC FCPA Unit chief] has had a hand in every major FCPA investigation the agency carried out and has worked closely with the DOJ FCPA team.'[51]

Numerous other examples could also be cited, but the point is clear: the primary architects of this new era of FCPA enforcement are currently making millions of dollars in the private sector providing FCPA investigative and compliance services to business organizations subject to the new era of FCPA enforcement they helped create. As to this dynamic, an FCPA practitioner candidly stated: 'What I don't understand is this – FCPA prosecutors consider companies to be the dark empire. Why then are they so attracted to represent the dark empire just a few years later – other than the money?'[52]

Indeed, as *Forbes* highlighted, this new era of FCPA enforcement has been good for 'Justice Department lawyers who create the marketplace and then get [themselves] a job.' *Forbes* asked:

> What are these prosecutors accomplishing? Maybe they are fighting for truth and justice. Maybe, that is, it makes sense for the U.S. to hold its corporations to a higher standard of integrity than the French or Chinese outfits they compete against when trying to win business abroad. The prosecutors, though, are doing something else at the same time. They are creating a lucrative industry – FCPA defense work – in which they will someday be prime candidates for the cushy assignments. A former prosecutor, to be sure, does not work on the defense of the same case he had as a government lawyer. But there is nothing to stop prosecutors from ginning up cases that will feed the lawyers who used to have their jobs or from looking forward to a payday in the private sector that will be made possible by their busy successors at Justice.[53]

The public policy problems associated with the FCPA's revolving door are many, including that former FCPA enforcement attorneys can market and benefit from the reality they helped create and can backtrack on the FCPA policy positions they articulated while at the government.

For instance, a law firm publication titled 'Overview of the Foreign Corrupt Practices Act: A Practical Guide for Businesses' stated:

- Although Congress indicated its intent to exclude certain widespread practices from the scope of the Act, it is often difficult to determine where the lines are to be drawn.
- In addition to pushing the boundaries of jurisdiction for substantive FCPA charges, U.S. enforcement officials have employed other tools to target international bribery with some link to the United States.
- U.S. enforcement personnel have interpreted [the FCPA's 'obtain or retain business' element] broadly to encompass any business purpose, and thereby to apply to payments made to avoid or reduce customs, income or other taxes, to bypass customs, health, or other inspections, or otherwise to change the enforcement or application of laws or regulations.
- It is not necessarily easy to identify the dividing line between a permitted facilitating payment and a prohibited bribe … .
- In addition to the severe penalties that can apply to violations, there are very good reasons why issuers and U.S. companies have committed significant resources to FCPA compliance in recent years. The language of most of the relevant FCPA provisions is

> broadly phrased and broadly interpreted by the DOJ and SEC. […] Very few issues of interpretation have been litigated. By and large, business entities are extremely reluctant to litigatc FCPA enforcement cases, and virtually all DOJ and SEC enforcement cases against business entities are settled.[54]

The lead author of the law firm publication was the former FCPA Unit chief who proclaims on his law firm bio page that he 'is internationally acknowledged and respected as the architect and key enforcement official of the DOJ's modern FCPA enforcement program' and was responsible 'for overseeing all DOJ investigations and prosecutions under the FCPA.'

Another example concerns the above-mentioned former Deputy AAG who was the face and voice of the DOJ at both the 2010 Senate and 2011 House FCPA hearings. During his testimony, the individual encouraged companies to voluntarily disclose conduct that could implicate the FCPA. Now that he is in private practice, the former Deputy AAG appears to have a different position on voluntary disclosure. In an interview with *Corporate Crime Reporter,* he stated: 'not every issue that a company uncovers should necessarily be disclosed. Some of it depends on size and scale – hundreds, or thousands or tens of thousands of dollars – it may not rise to the level where you would need to bring it to the DOJ's attention.'[55]

Likewise, during his congressional testimony the former Deputy AAG stated that an FCPA compliance defense 'is a novel and somewhat risky approach, the time is not right to adopt such a compliance defense.' Now that he is in private practice, the individual appears to have softened his position. In the same interview he was asked:

> *Q*: 'You were with the government when the government was saying no compliance defense is necessary. Is that your view now?'
>
> *A*: 'I don't know that I would take a specific view on that. I'm certainly aware of what the government's arguments were in favor [of rejecting such a defense].'[56]

The *Corporate Crime Reporter* interview also demonstrated how former high-ranking FCPA enforcement attorneys can benefit from the priorities and policy they articulated while at the government. For instance, during his congressional testimony, the former Deputy AAG stated: 'The investigation and prosecution of transnational bribery is an important priority for the DOJ and we have been hard at work.' In the interview he was asked 'what part of your [current private] practice is FCPA' and the former Deputy AAG responded: 'At the moment a large part. That remains a large focus of the government's white collar program. Our practice reflects in part the priorities of the DOJ. And clearly the FCPA is one.'[57]

Of course, just because *Forbes* noted that 'there is nothing to stop prosecutors from ginning up cases that will feed the lawyers who used to have their jobs or from looking forward to a payday in the private sector that will be made possible by their busy successors at Justice,' does not mean that government FCPA enforcement attorneys are 'ginning up cases.'

However, the unique attributes of FCPA enforcement and the special government policies that impact enforcement and thus make it a highly niched area of law, warrant special solutions. As to DOJ and SEC FCPA enforcement attorneys who have supervisory and discretionary positions and articulate government FCPA policies, it is in the public interest that such individuals be prohibited, when leaving government service, from providing FCPA defense or compliance services in the private sector for a five-year period.

This reform proposal would not have a material impact on the future career prospects of affected individuals (after all such individuals presumably obtained their high-level positions given their broad-based legal skills and experience), nor would it affect many people given the highly centralized nature of FCPA enforcement.

However, the reform proposal would: (i) restore public confidence in the rule of law and transparency; (ii) lessen the conflicting incentives government enforcement attorneys, as rational actors, may encounter in resolving sensitive legal matters or enforcing a niche law in such a way as to create a market for their future services; (iii) dissipate the appearance that taxpayer-financed positions are often launching pads to lucrative post-government careers; and (iv) lessen the incentives private law firms have to hire former government attorneys for their connections.

Some will say that the revolving door is just how Washington D.C. works. That is hardly a persuasive response. Imagine a foreign country where enforcement of a specific law is vested solely in the hands of a few individuals; where the individuals have declared new eras of enforcement and set policy objectives relevant to the specific law; where the individuals enforce the specific law against business organizations largely behind closed doors in the absence of meaningful judicial scrutiny and little case law setting the parameters of the specific law; and where the individuals then leave government service for million-dollar jobs in the private sector to provide defense and compliance services to business organizations subject to the new era of enforcement they helped create. Do you have concerns with such a system?

Thus far this chapter has highlighted various reasons for the increase in FCPA enforcement. Whether you believe that the increase is the result of practical reasons, provocative reasons, or some combination of both, it is important to keep FCPA enforcement statistics in the proper perspective.

C. A PROPER PERSPECTIVE ON FCPA ENFORCEMENT STATISTICS

Even though FCPA enforcement has trended upward during this new era, the increase in enforcement needs to be viewed in the proper context. This chapter concludes by providing a proper perspective on FCPA enforcement statistics and demonstrating that the FCPA is not nearly the boogeyman it is often portrayed to be.

Table 6.1 uses the core approach described above and provides a summary of corporate FCPA enforcement data (DOJ and SEC combined) for the years 2007–2012, and also highlights notable circumstances that significantly skewed enforcement data statistics for a particular year.[58]

As indicated above, just a few unique historical events had a significant impact on FCPA enforcement statistics in this new era. The events were: (i) publication in 2005 of the so-called Volcker Report on the United Nations Iraq Oil for Food Program which served as a ready-made list of enforcement actions; (ii) in 2003, a former top official at French oil and gas company Technip shared information with French investigators concerning a $6 billion dollar project at Bonny Island, Nigeria; and (iii) several oil and gas companies utilized the services of Panalpina.

As indicated in Tables 6.2–6.4, these unique historical events had a significant impact on FCPA enforcement data between 2007 and 2011.

As demonstrated in Tables 6.2–6.4, the combined effect of just three unique historical events – Iraq Oil for Food, Bonny Island conduct, and use of Panalpina – had a significant impact on FCPA enforcement statistics in this new era. These events served as the foundation for 35 percent of all corporate enforcement actions and resulted in 55 percent of the settlement amounts between 2007 and 2011. Adding only the 2008 Siemens enforcement action to the settlement amount calculation results in just four unique historical events accounting for 77 percent of settlement amounts in corporate enforcement actions between 2007 and 2011.

Table 6.1 Corporate FCPA enforcement actions (2007–2012)

Year	Enforcement actions	Settlement amounts	Of note
2007	15	$149 million	Six enforcement actions involved Iraq Oil for Food conduct and these enforcement actions comprised 40% of all enforcement actions and approximately 50% of the $149 million amount.
2008	10	$885 million	The $800 million Siemens enforcement action comprised approximately 90% of the $885 million amount.
2009	11	$645 million	The $579 million KBR/Halliburton Bonny Island, Nigeria enforcement action comprised approximately 90% of the $645 million amount.
2010	21	$1.4 billion	Six enforcement actions, all resolved on the same day, centered on various oil and gas companies use of Panalpina in Nigeria. Panalpina also resolved an enforcement action on the same day. Two enforcement actions (Technip and Eni/Snamprogetti) involved Bonny Island conduct and comprised approximately 50% of the $1.4 billion amount.
2011	16	$503 million	The JGC Bonny Island enforcement action comprised approximately 44% of the $503 million amount.
2012	12	$260 million	
	Total 85	**Total** $3.9 billion	

Recognizing how just a few unique events have impacted FCPA enforcement in this new era should provide comfort to corporate counsel and business managers inundated with FCPA Inc. doomsday marketing material. While FCPA risk should indeed be an issue on a company's risk management radar screen, FCPA enforcement is not nearly the boogeyman it is often portrayed to be by FCPA Inc.

Table 6.2 Corporate FCPA enforcement actions based on Iraq Oil for Food Conduct (2007–2011)

Enforcement actions	Total enforcement Action percentage	Settlement amounts	Total settlement amount percentage
14	19%	$267 million	7%

Table 6.3 Corporate Bonny Island, Nigeria FCPA enforcement actions (2007–2011)

Enforcement actions	Total enforcement action percentage	Settlement amounts	Total settlement amount percentage
4	5%	$1.5 billion	41%

Table 6.4 Corporate Panalpina-related FCPA enforcement actions (2007–2011)

Enforcement actions	Total enforcement action percentage	Settlement amounts	Total settlement amount percentage
8	11%	$262 million	7%

For instance, in 2007, corporate FCPA enforcement actions were the result of 15 unique events; in 2008, the result of 10 unique events; in 2009, the result of 11 unique events; in 2010, the result of 14 unique events; in 2011, the result of 16 unique events; and in 2012, the result of 12 unique events.

Considering that all U.S. business organizations, all foreign companies with shares listed on a U.S. exchange, and certain other foreign business organizations are all subject to the FCPA, you can decide whether the above numbers represent boogeyman-like numbers.

Refreshing words were offered by an FCPA practitioner who stated:

> Over the past five years, the [FCPA] has solidified itself as an industry brimming with expert forums, company departments and substantial news

> coverage. Is this statute really the bear in the woods some say it is? [...] The existence of the FCPA industry (and professionals who are available to conduct internal investigations at a high price) does not mean that this reaction is what is always required. What is required first and foremost is reasonable judgment exercised by directors and professionals who seek both compliance and solutions – without assuming a bear is present at every turn.[59]

Nevertheless, the FCPA is often a law that keeps corporate counsel and business managers up at night. Perhaps one reason is that in this new era the FCPA has long tentacles, an issue explored in the next chapter.

NOTES

1. Rick Ferri, Forbes, 'Going Foreign with the S&P 500' (Aug. 14, 2011).
2. Jonathan Rockoff, Wall Street Journal, 'Abbott Looks to India for Shot in Arm' (Aug. 26, 2010).
3. 'Mark Mendelsohn on the Rise of FCPA Enforcement,' 24 Corporate Crime Reporter 35 (Sept. 10, 2010).
4. OECD, 'Phase 3 Report on Implementing the OECD Anti-Bribery Convention in the United States' (Oct. 2010).
5. 'Examining Enforcement of the Foreign Corrupt Practices Act, Hearing before the Subcommittee on Crime and Drugs of the Committee on the Judiciary, Senate (Nov. 30, 2010).
6. 'Foreign Corrupt Practices Act,' Hearing before the Subcommittee on Crime, Terrorism, and Homeland Security of the Committee on the Judiciary, House of Representatives (June 14, 2011).
7. FCPA Professor, 'Africa Sting – Will Economic Realities Result in Additional Pleas?' (May 11, 2010).
8. FCPA Professor, '"Total"ly Milking the FCPA Cash Cow?' (June 3, 2013) (highlighting numerous statements).
9. Press Release, U.S. Dep't of Justice, 'Department of Justice Secures More Than $2 Billion in Judgments and Settlements as a Result of Enforcement Actions Led by the Criminal Division' (Jan. 21, 2011).
10. FCPA Professor, '"Total"ly Milking the FCPA Cash Cow?' (June 3, 2013) (highlighting numerous statements).
11. Id.
12. Id.
13. Joseph Rosenbloom, The American Lawyer, 'Here Come the Payoff Police' (May 17, 2010).
14. Deferred Prosecution Agreement, U.S. v. Total S.A., No. 1:13-cr-239 (May 29, 2013).
15. This Week in the Boardroom, Webcast Interview with Mark Mendelsohn (Nov. 5, 2010).
16. Joe Palazzolo, Wall Street Journal, 'FCPA Inc.: The Business of Bribery' (Oct. 2, 2012).
17. Steven Pearlstein, Washington Post 'Cashing in on Corruption' (Apr. 25, 2008).
18. Andrew Bast, Newsweek, 'Going after Graft' (Oct. 23, 2010).
19. Nathan Vardi, Forbes, 'The Bribery Racket' (June 7, 2010).

20. Joe Palazzolo, Wall Street Journal, 'FCPA Inc.: The Business of Bribery' (Oct. 2, 2012).
21. Sue Reisinger, Corporate Counsel, 'TRACE Launches World's First Accreditation Program for FCPA Compliance' (Feb. 4, 2011).
22. Corruption Crime & Compliance, 'The First Step in Any Due Diligence Inquiry' (Dec. 13, 2011).
23. Ashby Jones, Wall Street Journal Law Blog, 'Is the FCPA Just a Full-Employment Act for the Private Bar?' (May 7, 2010).
24. Richard Cassin, FCPA Blog 'It's a Growth Industry, Isn't It?' (Jan. 12, 2012).
25. *Supra* note 19.
26. *Supra* note 20.
27. Ashby Jones, Wall Street Journal, 'Legal Maze's Murkiest Corners Worry Companies' (Dec. 23, 2012).
28. Open Air Blog, 'Scare the Crap out of Them' (Nov. 28, 2011).
29. FCPA Professor, 'FCPA Inc. and the Business of Bribery' (Feb. 21, 2012).
30. Christopher Matthews et al., Wall Street Journal, 'U.S. Probes Microsoft Bribery Allegations' (Mar. 19, 2013).
31. FCPA Professor, 'In Depth on the Siemens Argentina Enforcement Action' (Dec. 14, 2011), containing links to original source documents.
32. FCPA Professor, 'Friday Roundup' (Mar. 22, 2013).
33. Ed DeHaan et al., 'Does the Revolving Door Affect the SEC's Enforcement Outcomes?' (July 2012).
34. Harvey Silverglate, Forbes, 'The Revolving Door at the Department of Justice' (June 22, 2011).
35. Mike Koehler, Bloomberg BNA White Collar Crime Report, 'Lanny Breuer and Foreign Corrupt Practices Act Enforcement' (Mar. 22, 2013).
36. FCPA Professor, 'Former Assistant Attorney General Lanny Breuer Joins FCPA Inc.' (Mar. 29, 2013), containing links to original source documents.
37. Id.
38. Id.
39. Corporate Crime Reporter, 'Lanny Breuer Back to Covington' (March 28, 2013).
40. FCPA Professor, 'Friday Roundup' (Mar. 15, 2013), containing links to original source documents.
41. Id.
42. FCPA Professor, 'New Position, New Positions' (Dec. 17, 2012), containing links to original source documents.
43. FCPA Professor, 'Friday Roundup' (Jan. 6, 2012), containing links to original source documents.
44. See Mike Koehler and Ethan Burger, Academy of Criminal Justice Studies, ACJS Today, 'Recent High-Level Department of Justice Departure Raises Recurring Questions That Require Prompt Action' (Dec. 2010), citing original source documents.
45. Id.
46. Id.
47. Id.
48. Id.
49. Id.
50. FCPA Professor, 'Scarboro to Simpson Thatcher' (June 3, 2011), containing links to original source documents.
51. Id.
52. 'DLA Piper's Sharie Brown on the FCPA, UK Hype, and the Dark Empire,' 25 Corporate Crime Reporter 5 (Jan. 31, 2011).
53. *Supra* note 19.

54. Paul Weiss LLP, 'Overview of the Foreign Corrupt Practices Act: A Practical Guide for Businesses' (2012).
55. *Supra* note 42.
56. Id.
57. Id.
58. FCPA Professor, 'Keeping FCPA Enforcement Statistics In Perspective' (Jan. 3, 2013).
59. Pamela Marple, NACD Director Advisory, 'The FCPA: A New Bear in the Woods?' (July 19, 2012).

7. The FCPA's long tentacles

Throughout this book the FCPA has been examined as a law enforced by the DOJ and the SEC. This chapter explores the FCPA's long tentacles and demonstrates how actual FCPA enforcement actions brought by the enforcement agencies are often just one consequence of FCPA scrutiny in this new era.

Indeed, when the dust settles on a corporate FCPA enforcement action, the company may become the subject of a foreign law enforcement investigation or action based on the same core conduct alleged in the FCPA enforcement action. After all, the U.S. action was based on allegations that the company, or someone on its behalf, made payments to a foreign official to obtain or retain business. It is thus understandable why foreign law enforcement agencies may also investigate the conduct and seek monetary fines and penalties. This chapter begins with a discussion of foreign law enforcement investigations and actions that are increasingly following FCPA enforcement actions.

Next, this chapter focuses on the business effects of FCPA scrutiny and enforcement. You will learn from various case studies how FCPA scrutiny can impact a company's business operations and strategy in a variety of ways from market capitalization, to cost of capital, to merger and acquisition activity, to impeding or distracting a company from achieving other business objectives. For these reasons, FCPA scrutiny and exposure is not just a legal issue, but a business issue as well that needs to be on the radar screen of business leaders operating in the global marketplace.

FCPA scrutiny and enforcement can also expose corporate directors and executives to private FCPA-related civil suits. Although courts have held that the FCPA does not provide a private right of action, in this new era plaintiff's lawyers representing shareholders often target corporate leaders with civil suits alleging, among other things, breach of fiduciary duty or securities fraud. This section highlights the trend of FCPA-related shareholder litigation and explores whether such suits serve a purpose or are merely parasitic actions which feed off FCPA scrutiny and enforcement in this new era.

This chapter next discusses an emerging trend. Ordinarily, companies are in a defensive posture when it comes to the FCPA. However, in this new era the FCPA is increasingly being used 'offensively' to achieve a business objective or to further advance a litigating position.

In short, the FCPA has long tentacles and there are many reasons to comply with the FCPA in addition to the obvious reason that non-compliance can expose a company and culpable individuals to an enforcement agency action. At the same time, because of the FCPA's long tentacles and the feeding frenzy that often follows FCPA scrutiny or enforcement actions, it is important, as discussed throughout this book, that FCPA enforcement be subject to judicial scrutiny and that enforcement actions represent legitimate instances of provable FCPA violations, not merely settlements entered into for reasons of risk aversion.

A. RELATED FOREIGN LAW ENFORCEMENT INVESTIGATIONS AND ACTIONS

For most of the FCPA's history, companies with FCPA exposure could sleep well at night after resolving a U.S. enforcement agency action. However, the landscape has changed and in this new era U.S. enforcement agency actions are often just one consequence of FCPA scrutiny.

After resolving a corporate FCPA enforcement action the company may also become the subject of a foreign law enforcement investigation or action based on the same core conduct alleged in the FCPA enforcement action. After all, the U.S. action was based on allegations that the company, or someone on its behalf, made payments to a foreign official to obtain or retain business.

Given the ease in which information now flows and the growing interest in cracking down on bribery and corruption, FCPA enforcement actions are frequently read around the world by foreign media, foreign-based non-governmental organizations, and even foreign governments themselves. Thus, it is not surprising that when the dust settles on corporate FCPA enforcement actions many remain interested in the conduct at issue, including the foreign governments whose alleged 'foreign officials' were implicated in the conduct at issue.

For the foreign government involved, it is potentially embarrassing to have 'one of its own' implicated in a bribery and corruption scandal without doing something about it 'at home.' Thus, with increasing frequency FCPA enforcement actions are followed by 'tag-a-long' or 'carbon-copy' foreign law enforcement investigations and enforcement actions.[1]

For instance, Ralph Lauren Corporation resolved an FCPA enforcement action based on the conduct of its subsidiary in Argentina. The alleged improper payments were made to Argentine customs officials 'to assist in improperly obtaining paperwork necessary for goods to clear customs, to permit clearance of items without the necessary paperwork, to permit the clearance of prohibited items, and to avoid inspection.' A few days later, the head of Argentina's tax agency wrote to the U.S. Ambassador to Argentina stating that it was 'necessary for the Argentine government to have names and more detailed information about the alleged bribery to aid in a newly launched criminal investigation into the matter.'[2]

Likewise, tobacco companies Alliance One International Inc. and Universal Corporation resolved FCPA enforcement actions principally based on allegations of improper payments to Thai government officials to secure contracts with an alleged Thai government agency for the sale of tobacco leaf.[3] Soon thereafter, Thai law enforcement officials began an investigation of the conduct at issue.[4]

It is an open question, and the answer will often depend on the passage of time, whether such 'carbon copy' foreign law enforcement investigations are sincere and bona fide investigations or merely politically expedient investigations. However, certain related foreign law enforcement investigations have resulted in corporate payment of millions of dollars to foreign law enforcement officials for the same conduct at issue in the previously resolved FCPA enforcement.

A notable example involved Halliburton Company and its related entities concerning conduct at Bonny Island, Nigeria. In resolving related DOJ and SEC FCPA enforcement actions, Halliburton and its affiliated entities agreed to pay $579 million in fine, penalty, and disgorgement amounts, which as noted in Chapter 5 is the second-largest FCPA settlement in history.

Thereafter, Halliburton announced resolution of an investigation by the Nigerian government arising out of the same conduct.[5] Pursuant to the settlement agreement with Nigerian law enforcement authorities, all lawsuits and charges against Halliburton, its related entities, and associated persons were withdrawn, and Nigerian authorities agreed not to bring any further criminal or civil charges in exchange for Halliburton paying approximately $33 million to Nigerian authorities as well as approximately $2.5 million for attorneys' fees and other expenses of the Nigerian authorities.

Regarding such 'carbon-copy' prosecutions, it has been noted:

> The net effect of [DOJ and SEC FCPA settlement policies] is that when a company enters into a negotiated resolution with the DOJ – particularly in those cases with parallel SEC enforcement actions – it is essentially powerless

> to defend against, much less deny, the factual basis on which the resolution is based. This all but ensures that a company that settles with the DOJ – or both the DOJ and SEC in parallel proceedings – will have little or no choice but to settle with foreign authorities, should such authorities choose to exercise jurisdiction and enforce their corollary anticorruption laws.[6]

'Carbon copy' prosecutions are not only a concern for companies that resolve FCPA enforcement actions, but also for individuals associated with the company. For instance, in the Halliburton case among the individuals charged by Nigerian authorities was former Vice President Dick Cheney who previously served as CEO of Halliburton from 1995 to 2000. In filing the criminal charges against Cheney, a Nigerian law enforcement official stated: 'Dick Cheney was head of Halliburton. There's no way such amount of money would've been moved to bribe Nigeria officials without his approval and without his knowledge, this is what we're saying.'[7] The criminal charges against Cheney and other individuals associated with Halliburton were dropped pursuant to the Nigerian settlement agreement referenced above.

The above examples, and numerous others that could also be cited, demonstrate that the enforcement landscape has changed and that enforcement actions brought by U.S. enforcement agencies are often just one consequence of FCPA scrutiny. With increasing frequency, when the dust settles on corporate FCPA enforcement actions, related foreign law enforcement investigations and actions may follow.

On one level such 'tag-a-long' investigations and enforcement actions are hardly surprising or controversial. After all, in an FCPA enforcement action the U.S. government alleged that a company, or someone on its behalf, made payments to a foreign official to obtain or retain business. Against this backdrop, it seems entirely reasonable for a foreign law enforcement agency to exercise its sovereign authority to bring an action where the conduct actually took place and whose officials were allegedly bribed. Indeed, in most instances, the foreign government would seem to have a greater and more direct interest in the conduct at issue compared to the U.S. government.

Yet on another level, such 'tag-a-long' investigations and enforcement actions are akin to a piñata breaking at a party, with multiple hands eager to catch the resulting candy. Indeed, in seeming recognition of how aggressive enforcement of bribery and corruption laws can become a cash cow for the enforcing government, a 2010 report from Transparency International (a global civil society organization) stated that certain bribery and corruption settlements in Western countries 'should also make clear to laggard governments that investing in adequate enforcement can have substantial returns.'[8] Likewise, a former DOJ prosecutor stated, concerning the global trend of increased enforcement:

> I think a lot of it is looking at the numbers … I think a lot of the global anti-bribery movement is driven by regulators around the world saying, Okay, a German company just paid $300 million to the U.S. That's sort of funny to us. Where are we in this? I think there is some international pressure. There is the pressure of raising the bar, but there's also a very cynical pressure of raising money. We're in an economic climate today where I don't think there's a single government in the world that isn't struggling to find resources. This area has emerged, again, as a money making center, which is kind of bizarre.[9]

Another aspect related to foreign law enforcement investigations and actions in this new era, separate and distinct from the issue discussed above regarding 'home' country actions, is the increasing frequency of multiple sovereigns asserting jurisdiction over an alleged bribery scheme.

For instance, the Halliburton Bonny Island, Nigeria bribery scheme involved not only a 2009 U.S. FCPA enforcement action and a 2010 Nigeria enforcement action, but also a 2011 U.K. enforcement action against M.W. Kellogg Limited ('MKWL'). MKWL, a wholly-owned U.K. subsidiary of KBR to which Halliburton owed an indemnification obligation, was the entity that originally formed the investment consortium at the center of the Bonny Island bribery scheme. In the U.K. enforcement action, the Serious Fraud Office ('SFO') ordered MKWL to pay approximately $11.2 million.[10]

Another example of a joint U.S.–U.K. enforcement action was against chemical company Innospec. On the same day the DOJ and SEC announced resolution of a $40.2 million FCPA enforcement action, the SFO also announced a $12.7 million enforcement action against the company's U.K. subsidiary for conduct also at issue in the U.S. enforcement action.[11]

Given that many bribery schemes involve multinational companies with subsidiaries in various countries, and because improper payments are often conceived of or facilitated through use of e-mails or bank accounts that span the world, it is not surprising that multiple sovereigns might have jurisdiction over a bribery scheme.

Indeed, the OECD Convention provides: 'When more than one Party has jurisdiction over an alleged offence described in this Convention, the Parties involved shall, at the request of one of them, consult with a view to determining the most appropriate jurisdiction for prosecution.'[12]

Yet despite the aspirational pledge of cooperation in the OECD Convention, given the substantial returns that can result from bribery and corruption enforcement actions and the political points that can be scored for bringing such actions, the reality is that countries often find themselves in competition with each other to bring enforcement actions based on the same core conduct and/or divide the enforcement proceeds.

Public documents in the U.K. Innospec action highlight this tension. In his sentencing remarks, the U.K. judge noted:

> In September 2009, when it was anticipated that an acceptable settlement would be reached, discussions began between the SFO and the DOJ about the manner in which the authorities in the US and the SFO should proceed to implement any settlement and divide up the monetary amount to be paid. The discussions took place against the background that it had been agreed that the SFO would have primacy in respect to the Indonesian corruption and the DOJ in respect of the Iraq corruption.[13]

The sentencing remarks then note that 'the SFO began by suggesting a 50:50 split based upon the fact that the criminality had been orchestrated and arranged from the UK in respect of the corruption in both Iraq and Indonesia.' However, as noted in the remarks, the 'DOJ would not accept this,' but rather proposed a 'methodology that in the result produced a split which was approximately one third to the DOJ, one third to the SFO and one third to the SEC …'. As noted in the sentencing remarks, 'after much further discussion on the SFO agreed to a split that was approximately one third to the DOJ, one third to the SEC … and one third to the SFO.'

With cross-border investigations and global settlements increasingly becoming a new norm, the following comments by the U.K. judge in the Innospec matter regarding uniform financial penalties were noteworthy: 'There is every reason for states to adopt a uniform approach to financial penalties for corruption of foreign government officials so that the penalties in each country do not discriminate either favorably or unfavorably against a company in a particular state.'

The enforcement action against U.K. defense company BAE Systems, previously discussed in Chapter 5, also highlights the tension common in cross-border bribery investigations when multiple sovereigns operating under different legal principles claim jurisdiction over an alleged bribery scheme.

Both the U.S. and U.K. investigation of BAE involved, among other things, conduct in Central and Eastern Europe. The U.S. enforcement action against BAE alleged undisclosed payments associated with the lease of fighter jets in the Czech Republic and Hungary, and the U.K. criminally charged a former BAE agent with 'conspiracy to corrupt' and for 'conspiring with others to give or agree to give corrupt payments

[...] to officials and other agents of certain Eastern and Central European governments, including the Czech Republic, Hungary and Austria as inducements to secure, or as rewards for having secured, contracts from those governments for' fighter jets.[14]

However, the U.K. enforcement action against BAE, in which the company agreed to pay a £30 million penalty, related solely to the company's failure 'to keep reasonable and accurate accounting records in relation to its activities in Tanzania.' Public documents filed in connection with the U.K. BAE plea agreement shed light on the tension between the U.S. and U.K. enforcement authorities.[15] The documents detailed as follows.

- From the beginning of March 2009, the SFO had been involved in plea discussions with BAE. The position of the SFO was that it would be satisfied with pleas to charges in respect to some, but not necessarily all, the strands of its investigation.
- By September 30, 2009 ('the SFO imposed deadline') no agreement had been reached and 'discussions in England were discontinued.' 'By that time, it was known that plea discussions between the DOJ and BAE in the U.S. had also failed to produce any agreement.'
- In late January–early February 2010 there was a material change in circumstances. First on January 29, the DOJ contacted the SFO and indicated that a plea agreement with BAE was imminent. The agreement involved BAE entering pleas of guilty with respect of offenses in connection to the investigations concerning Eastern Europe and Saudi Arabia and a payment of $400 million.
- The SFO 'received advice from counsel that the Eastern Europe aspect of the proposed U.S. agreement was highly likely to have the effect of preventing prosecution for the offenses under consideration in respect of the Eastern European investigation in England, on the basis of the application of the principle of double jeopardy.'

Even though, as previously highlighted, the offense BAE pleaded guilty to in the U.S. was not an FCPA offense, the U.K. was limited in the charges it could bring against BAE under its double jeopardy principles because of the U.S. first-filed action. The SFO Director responded to a Q&A as follows:

> *Q*: 'Are you suggesting that simply because facts are alleged in a U.S. prosecution to support a non-corruption charge, that the U.K. is thereby prohibited from bringing a corruption charge as to those facts?'

> *A*: 'Yes. Our double jeopardy law looks at the facts in issue in the other jurisdiction and not the precise offence. Our law does not allow someone to be prosecuted here in relation to a set of facts if that person has been in jeopardy of a conviction in relation to those facts in another jurisdiction. As a result I could not continue to consider whether to prosecute BAE for an offence relating to Central and Eastern Europe once BAE had pleaded guilty in the US.'[16]

As highlighted by the BAE action, enforcement competition is real. At times enforcement of alleged corporate bribery seems like a new global arms race to see which country can bring the most enforcement actions and secure the most settlement dollars. With good reasons, return on investment is not a concept typically linked to justice and the rule of law. However, Transparency International's statement (i.e. that certain bribery and corruption settlements in various Western countries 'should also make clear to laggard governments that investing in adequate enforcement can have substantial returns') and those of other civil society organizations that champion a 'get tough on bribery' position seemingly oblivious to the broader public policy implications of such an approach help facilitate this new global arms race.

Whatever the motivations of related foreign law enforcement investigations and actions and regardless of the public policy implications which flow from them, the take-away point from this section is that just because an FCPA enforcement action may be over does not necessarily mean that all the dust has settled. Indeed, as explored in the next section, an FCPA enforcement action or the mere mention of FCPA scrutiny can also impact a company's business operations and strategy in a variety of ways.

B. THE BUSINESS EFFECTS OF FCPA SCRUTINY AND ENFORCEMENT

There are many reasons to comply with the FCPA in addition to the obvious reason that non-compliance can expose a company and culpable individuals to an enforcement agency action and, with increasing frequency, related foreign law enforcement investigations and actions.

This section highlights another reason to comply with the FCPA and documents the negative business effects often associated with FCPA scrutiny and enforcement. Such negative effects demonstrate that FCPA compliance is not just a legal issue, but a business issue as well that needs to be on the radar screen of business leaders operating in the global marketplace.

Before highlighting the variety of ways that FCPA scrutiny and enforcement can impact a company, it bears repeating that the negative business effects of FCPA scrutiny and enforcement, and other examples of the FCPA's long tentacles discussed in this chapter, are one of the most important reasons why FCPA enforcement be subjected to judicial scrutiny and that enforcement actions represent legitimate instances of provable FCPA violations, not merely settlements entered into for reasons of risk aversion.

Companies that pursue bribery as a business strategy or companies that lack a commitment to FCPA compliance are deserving of the wide-ranging negative business effects that can impact the company upon instances of FCPA scrutiny or an enforcement action.

However, companies that have pre-existing FCPA compliance policies and procedures and are making good faith efforts to comply with the FCPA in the challenging global marketplace are not deserving of the wide-ranging negative business effects that can impact the company upon instances of FCPA scrutiny or an enforcement action when a non-executive employee or agent acts contrary to those policies and procedures. Similarly, companies that agree to resolve instances of FCPA scrutiny via NPAs or DPAs, or via SEC 'neither admit nor deny' settlements for reasons of risk aversion and not necessarily because the conduct at issue violates the FCPA, are not deserving of the wide-ranging negative business effects that can impact the company.

Yet the reality in this new era is that such negative business effects often do not distinguish between different types of FCPA scrutiny or different types of FCPA enforcement actions. Several case studies highlighted below demonstrate how FCPA scrutiny can impact a company's market capitalization, its cost of capital, its merger and acquisition activity, and have other negative business effects as well. These business effects are in addition to the significant financial impact FCPA scrutiny and enforcement actions can have on a company, as discussed previously in Chapter 5 in terms of the 'three buckets' of FCPA financial exposure.

Market Capitalization

Market capitalization refers to the total market value of a public company's outstanding shares and is calculated by multiplying a company's shares by the current market price of one share. Market capitalization is an important data point for investors and an important metric by which business manager performance is judged. Because FCPA scrutiny or FCPA enforcement actions can impact a company's share price, a company's market capitalization can likewise be impacted by FCPA scrutiny.

Two examples of FCPA scrutiny – one involving a large well-known company the other involving a small lesser-known company – highlight this issue.

Wal-Mart's FCPA scrutiny, discussed in more detail in Chapter 9, was front-page news in 2012 when the *New York Times* published an article concerning alleged conduct in Mexico. Even though Wal-Mart disclosed its FCPA scrutiny in a 2011 SEC filing, the market reacted swiftly to the *Times* article. On the last trading day before the *Times* article, Wal-Mart's stock closed at $62.45. The first trading day after the *Times* article, the stock dropped 4.7 percent and continued a downward trend for several days eclipsing approximately $20 billion in shareholder value. Investors were likely spooked by the intense media coverage and also likely grew paranoid by predictions that Wal-Mart could face approximately $13 billion in ultimate fines and penalties because of its FCPA scrutiny.[17] Such predictions were widely speculative and entirely off-base, as the largest FCPA settlement in history is the $800 million action against Siemens.

In 2010, shares of SciClone Pharmaceuticals Inc. (a U.S.-based, China-focused specialty pharmaceutical company) plunged approximately 40 percent and closed down approximately 32 percent from its previous trading day. Such a dramatic decline in a company's stock price is normally associated with a Chief Executive Officer resigning, a declaration of bankruptcy, or other crisis-like events. However, the decline in SciClone's stock price was due to the following disclosure made by the company.

> SciClone was contacted by the SEC and advised that the SEC has initiated a formal, non-public investigation of SciClone. In connection with this investigation, the SEC issued a subpoena to SciClone requesting a variety of documents and other information. The subpoena requests documents relating to a range of matters including interactions with regulators and government-owned entities in China, activities relating to sales in China and documents relating to certain company financial and other disclosures. The Company [also] received a letter from the DOJ indicating that the DOJ was investigating FCPA issues in the pharmaceutical industry generally, and had received information about the Company's practices suggesting possible violations.[18]

The dramatic decline in SciClone's share price was thus merely based on disclosure that the company had received an SEC subpoena and a letter of inquiry from the DOJ as part of an industry-wide investigation of the pharmaceutical industry.

A company's stock price, and thus its market capitalization, can also be negatively impacted by investment analyst downgrades due to FCPA scrutiny. For instance, the shares of technology company NCR Corp. fell approximately 8 percent after an investment analyst downgraded the company's stock to neutral from outperform because of the company's FCPA scrutiny. Among the concerns noted in the analyst report were: a multi-quarter investigation; potential fines and penalties from the single millions to tens of million; much of the company's share gains over the last two years came in emerging markets and such growth may be at risk if an FCPA investigation restricts current business practices; and that companies uninhibited by the FCPA, such as China-based competitors, could gain market share.[19]

Whether FCPA scrutiny will impact a company's market capitalization often depends on the nature of the company (for instance SciClone is a China-focused pharmaceutical company with a substantial portion of its revenue tied to that country, making FCPA scrutiny in China a significant event) or the means by which the FCPA scrutiny is communicated (such as a front-page article in the *New York Times* about Wal-Mart).

Indeed, investor reaction to FCPA scrutiny or enforcement is not often as dramatic as the above examples suggest. For instance, a *Wall Street Journal* analysis sought to measure market reaction to an FCPA investigation by asking 'whether and to what extent shareholders trade on the announcements of FCPA investigations (internal or government) and settlements.' The analysis, based on more than 40 corporate cases since 2004, found 'a lot of shrugging on the part of investors' and that 'the average change in stock price from the day before to the day after the disclosure of an FCPA investigation was a decrease of 1%.'[20] An analysis by Nera Economic Consulting drew a similar conclusion.[21] Using a market model analysis that measured the relationship between stock price movement of companies that resolved FCPA enforcement actions against the S&P 500 index prior to the first apparent announcement of FCPA-related allegations, the analysis found that 'in some instances the implication of an alleged FCPA violation is considered serious by the market,' but for most companies that resolve an FCPA enforcement action 'there was no statistically significant price reaction' by the market upon apparent first announcement of FCPA-related allegations.

Even if the stock of certain companies declines upon news of FCPA scrutiny, business managers may find comfort in the short duration of the FCPA-induced dip. For instance, even SciClone's stock soon recovered its lost value and began trading at a higher price. Likewise, Wal-Mart's stock soon recovered all of its value and outperformed the market after its FCPA-induced dip.

These examples suggest that FCPA-induced dips in stock prices may be the result of misinformed doomsday scenarios and not financial fundamentals. Based upon the above studies, it appears that in most instances of FCPA scrutiny, markets care little and investment professionals may realize how diluted FCPA enforcement has become in this new era. Indeed, commenting on the rapid rise in Wal-Mart's stock price after the *Times*-induced FCPA dip, a Forbes commentator stated: 'My 30 years of experience in the markets has repeatedly shown to me that whenever a company is accused of violations of FCPA, headlines are always scary, but in the end, the downdraft in the stock invariably becomes a buying opportunity.'[22]

Even if a company's FCPA-induced stock dip is short-lived and even if a company's stock price declines on average only 1 percent after disclosure of FCPA scrutiny, one business effect of FCPA enforcement, or merely the mention of FCPA scrutiny, can be a negative impact on a company's market capitalization.

Cost of Capital

FCPA scrutiny can also negatively impact a company's cost of capital, specifically a company's credit rating. A company's credit rating matters for a number of reasons. For instance, a company with a lower credit rating may be faced with a smaller pool of potential investors and thus may have to offer those investors a higher interest rate. Likewise, a company's credit rating will determine the interest rate at which the company can borrow money and certain institutional investors may be barred from owning non-investment grade corporate bonds.

A report titled 'U.S. Foreign Corrupt Practices Act – No Minor Matter' by ratings agency Fitch Ratings highlighted the variety of cost of capital effects that can arise from FCPA scrutiny or enforcement.[23]

The report noted that FCPA scrutiny can have ratings implications for companies with modest free cash flow ('FCF') and/or liquidity constraints. The report further noted 'that it can take years from the discovery of a violation to the time a plea agreement is reached' and stated:

> In the interim, corporate credit profiles, liquidity, and ratings may weaken. The fine that could be easily paid with cash on hand today might not be readily payable years down the road if a company's credit profile has weakened and liquidity becomes constrained.

As to the financial effect of 'deferring the legal consequences' of alleged FCPA violations via NPAs and DPAs, the report noted that prosecutions declined or deferred pursuant to these agreements could be activated if the company fails to adhere to its obligations under the agreements meaning 'that investors and analysts cannot take a deep breath or relax until' the time period in the NPA or DPA has expired.

The Fitch report also highlighted the significant amount of pre-enforcement action professional fees and expenses typically incurred by companies under FCPA scrutiny. Indeed, Avon's bond rating has been downgraded due to 'expenses related to the ongoing investigation under the FCPA.'[24]

Although the Fitch report noted that many FCPA fines are 'imposed on large investment grade corporations whose substantial cash balances easily afforded them the ability to absorb the payments with no or minimal increases in leverage,' the report also noted that 'there have also been [FCPA] violations by non-investment grade companies.'

One instance discussed in the Fitch report focused on Willbros Group Inc., a company that paid approximately $32 million in DOJ and SEC fine and penalty amounts to resolve its FCPA scrutiny.[25] The report noted that Willbros borrowed from banks on a secured basis and that when the company became aware of its FCPA issues, the company's scrutiny and related issues resulted in the restatement of its annual financial statements. The report further noted that the company's FCPA scrutiny required 'several amendments on its bank credit facility,' which was reduced from $150 million to $100 million.

As the above examples indicate, FCPA scrutiny and enforcement can negatively impact a company's cost of capital and set into motion a host of negative financial consequences.

Mergers and Acquisitions

In addition to market capitalization and cost of capital, FCPA scrutiny and enforcement can also negatively impact merger or acquisition activity. Such negative impacts range from terminating planned merger or acquisition activity, to restructuring the terms and conditions of the planned transaction, to reducing the expected financial benefits of the transaction.

Termination

The failed merger between aerospace company Lockheed Martin Corporation and Titan Corporation demonstrates the FCPA's long tentacles. In announcing the planned acquisition, Lockheed's Chairman and CEO stated:

> Titan provides additional presence within the U.S. Government customer base and expands our competencies. Titan is an excellent fit with Lockheed Martin, and its acquisition is consistent with our disciplined growth and cash deployment strategies. Titan's outstanding record of sales growth and the quality of its workforce made this transaction very attractive to us. This workforce, together with our highly skilled people, allows us to provide more cost effective and robust solutions to customers of both companies.[26]

However, soon thereafter Lockheed announced that it 'learned of allegations that improper payments were made, or items of value were provided, by consultants for Titan Corporation or its subsidiaries to foreign officials.' Lockheed stated:

> The allegations were identified as part of a review conducted with Titan of payments to Titan's international consultants in connection with the proposed acquisition of Titan. The alleged payments and provision of items of value, if true, raise questions concerning whether there has been a violation of the FCPA. [...] The review is ongoing. Titan is cooperating with this effort, as well as conducting its own review. Lockheed Martin and Titan have met with the SEC and the DOJ to discuss the allegations of improper payments. [...] Closing of the Titan transaction is subject to approval of Titan's stockholders, the absence of any material adverse change in Titan and other conditions set forth in the merger agreement. [...] Lockheed Martin will need to determine whether the conditions to the merger have been satisfied.[27]

Titan FCPA's scrutiny, which Lockheed could have inherited upon completion of the merger, resulted in a delay of the shareholder vote to approve the merger as well as an amended merger agreement extending the time period for the merger to occur. The amended merger agreement provided that 'as a condition to the closing of the transaction, Titan must obtain written confirmation that the DOJ considers its investigation of these allegations resolved and does not intend to pursue any claims against Titan, or Titan must have entered into a plea agreement with the DOJ and completed the sentencing process.'

Ultimately, Titan's unresolved FCPA scrutiny caused Lockheed to abandon the merger because Titan 'did not satisfy all the closing conditions.' Lockheed stated:

> Under the terms of the amended merger agreement, either party could terminate the merger agreement if Titan either: (i) had not obtained written confirmation from the DOJ that the investigation of alleged FCPA violations was resolved as to Titan and the Department did not intend to pursue any claims against Titan; or (ii) Titan had not entered into a plea agreement [by a certain date] ... Titan did not satisfy either requirement. [...] The corporation declined Titan's request for a further extension.[28]

In announcing termination of the merger, a Lockheed spokesperson said that the company 'made every possible effort to make this happen, but it just reached a point where we didn't want the uncertainty surrounding this to continue indefinitely.'[29]

Termination of the merger had several adverse consequences for Titan. In addition to losing an acquirer, news of the merger termination caused Titan's shares to fall by approximately 20 percent and investment analysts downgraded the company's stock. Titan's FCPA scrutiny of course did not disappear and the company pleaded guilty to FCPA charges for, among other things, making corrupt payments through an agent of more than $2 million to the election campaign of Benin's then-incumbent President. In resolving its FCPA scrutiny, Titan agreed to pay approximately $28 million in combined fine and penalty amounts, the largest FCPA settlement in history at the time.[30]

Termination of the Lockheed–Titan merger has lessons for both an acquiring company and a target company. For an acquiring company, FCPA-related due diligence of a target company should be part of the merger due diligence agenda so that potential FCPA issues can be learned of in advance of closing. For a target company, implementing pro-active FCPA compliance policies and procedures that seek to minimize risk can increase the value of the company and its attractiveness to a potential acquiring company.

Not all instances of FCPA scrutiny have as severe an effect on merger activity as in the Lockheed Martin–Titan example. However, as demonstrated by the below examples, FCPA scrutiny and enforcement actions can also result in restructuring of the terms and conditions of planned transactions and reduce the expected financial benefits of the transaction.

Restructuring

An instructive case study for how FCPA scrutiny can significantly impact the terms and conditions of a planned merger concerns engineering companies PBSJ Corporation and WS Atkins. In 2010, PBSJ disclosed an FCPA internal investigation in connection with certain projects undertaken by its subsidiary.[31] A few months later, PBSJ disclosed that its 'Audit Committee completed the internal investigation [and] the results of that investigation suggest that FCPA violations may have occurred.'

Shortly thereafter, PBSJ announced that it had entered into a definitive merger agreement in which WS Atkins planned to acquire PBSJ in an all-cash transaction. Proxy materials filed by PBSJ in connection with the merger provided an informative insight into how the FCPA issues impacted the terms and conditions by which PBSJ would attempt to sell itself.

Among other things, the proxy materials highlighted how interested purchasers of PBSJ: held meetings with PBSJ's outside counsel and its in-house counsel to discuss the FCPA investigation; requested the opportunity to meet with DOJ representatives regarding the FCPA investigation; and requested access to attorney-client privileged documents regarding the FCPA investigation.[32]

In the end, PBSJ's board approved a merger agreement with Atkins even though PBSJ had received a higher offer from another company. However, the other company sought more stringent closing conditions concerning PBSJ's FCPA scrutiny. In approving Atkin's bid, the PBSJ proxy materials stated:

> Positive factors considered by the [PBSJ] board of directors included: [...] the terms of the merger agreement and the related agreements, including: the limited number and nature of the conditions to Atkins' obligation to consummate the merger, including its willingness not to impose special conditions related to our previously disclosed FCPA investigation beyond those developments that would independently constitute a material adverse effect.[33]

Reduced financial benefits

FCPA scrutiny or an enforcement action can also reduce the full financial benefits expected from a merger by imposing significant post-closing expenses on the acquiring company for the target company's pre-closing FCPA scrutiny.

For instance, facilities services company ABM Industries Inc. disclosed:

> [The] Company [has] began an internal investigation into matters relating to compliance with the FCPA and the Company's internal policies in connection with services provided by a foreign entity affiliated with a Linc joint venture partner. Such services commenced prior to the Company's acquisition of Linc. As a result of the investigation, the Company has caused Linc to terminate its association with the arrangement. The Company [has] contacted the DOJ and the SEC to voluntarily disclose the results of its internal investigation to date. The Company cannot reasonably estimate the potential liability, if any, related to these matters.[34]

As highlighted by the above disclosure, ABM's FCPA scrutiny does not involve anything it did. Rather, ABM's scrutiny is based on a foreign entity affiliated with a joint venture partner of a company ABM acquired. The value of the merger was approximately $300 million and it is already being reduced by the acquired company's FCPA scrutiny as ABM has spent approximately $3.5 million in pre-enforcement action professional fees and expenses.[35] Factoring in ABM's potential exposure based on an

FCPA actual enforcement action, 5 percent of the merger price could easily evaporate due to the acquired company's FCPA issue.

In addition, post-enforcement action professional fees and expenses can further reduce the expected financial benefits of a merger. For instance, Alliance One International resolved an FCPA enforcement action by agreeing to pay $19.5 million in combined fines and penalties.[36] The entire enforcement action was based on the pre-merger conduct of acquired entities and, pursuant to the NPA, Alliance One was required to engage a compliance monitor for three years. Two years into the NPA, Alliance One has disclosed approximately $10 million in post-enforcement action monitoring costs.

Other Effects

FCPA scrutiny or enforcement can also result in several other wide-ranging negative business effects.

For instance, Swiss logistics company Panalpina was under FCPA scrutiny between 2007 and 2010 for business conduct in Nigeria. In 2010, the company agreed to pay approximately $82 million to resolve DOJ and SEC enforcement actions based on the conduct.[37]

In the midst of this scrutiny, during the company's annual meeting a shareholder demanded that someone 'step up and take responsibility' for the company's poor performance. In response, Panalpina's CEO stated, among other things, that 'it is not easy being under investigation for two years, and [the FCPA investigation] is not making the situation any easier.'[38] The company's Chief Operating Officer added:

> You can say the whole FCPA and Nigeria situation reflects badly on the management, but the fact is that as long as we are still involved in the investigation we will continue to lose market share, because our customers have internal regulations which prevent them from doing business with companies which are under investigation by the DOJ. As soon as this investigation is over, we will win some of this business back. Customers have told us 'as soon as you have settled the FCPA, we will do business with you again.'

FCPA scrutiny can also crimp company growth and make general business conditions more difficult as demonstrated by Wal-Mart's scrutiny. According to the *Wall Street Journal*, three years ago Wal-Mart set out to be India's top retailer by 2015. However, the article stated that 'Wal-Mart's advance on India is barely moving' and one of 'biggest reasons has been a compliance crackdown at Wal-Mart' following its FCPA scrutiny discussed in more detail in Chapter 9.[39] The article noted that 'developing and operating stores in India is complicated, even for locals' because 'dozens of permits and licenses are required from various agencies down to the municipal level.' In response to its FCPA scrutiny, the article noted that Wal-Mart has 'enlisted a phalanx of lawyers from a U.S. firm to develop compliance procedures and train employees in India' and that 'the company also has begun requiring its Indian landlords to attest that they haven't greased any government palms.' In short, 'running people through those hoops has slowed' Wal-Mart's expansion plans in India.

FCPA scrutiny can also be distracting for company management forced to focus on FCPA issues instead of other core business issues. For instance, Wal-Mart has disclosed that its FCPA issues 'may require the involvement of certain members of the Company's senior management that could impinge on the time they have available to devote to other matters relating to the business.'[40]

Another instructive example involved gas detection company RAE Systems. The company resolved DOJ and SEC FCPA enforcement actions by agreeing to pay approximately $3 million in combined fines and penalties for payments made by employees of two joint ventures majority owned and controlled by RAE Systems to alleged Chinese officials.[41] In a revealing interview, the CFO at the time of the investigation and enforcement action discussed how the company's FCPA scrutiny came to derail his other job duties and caused him to have a falling out with the company's CEO. Further to the three buckets of FCPA financial exposure discussed in Chapter 5, the former CFO also highlighted how the company's pre-enforcement action professional fees and expenses (approximately $4.2 million) exceeded the combined fine and penalty amount ($2.95 million) in the FCPA enforcement action.

Even companies that employed individuals criminally charged in the manufactured Africa Sting action have suffered negative business effects. Smith & Wesson disclosed as follows a few months after criminal charges were announced against its employee Amaro Goncalves: 'Pistol sales decreased 25.3%, driven by the reduction in consumer demand as well as reduced international shipments related to our investigation of the FCPA matter.'[42]

Even after the DOJ dismissed the case and the judge called the dismissal 'the end of a long and sad chapter in the annals of white collar criminal enforcement,' the manufactured case continues to have negative business effects on companies that employed individuals charged. For instance, in 2011, BlastGard International Inc. acquired HighCom Security Inc. (HighCom's former CEO was charged in the case). In a 2013 disclosure, BlastGard stated that it vendor registration status was suspended by the United Nations because of the individual's criminal charges, and the disclosure stated: 'The Company requested that the U.N. reconsider their decision as HighCom is under new ownership and management and that since their decision the United States District Court of Columbia dismissed all charges against the former CEO. A final decision is still pending the U.N.'s internal review.'[43]

BlastGard also disclosed that another U.N. committee had suspended its registration status 'based on integrity/ethical issues surrounding the former CEO's actions,' and that 'to date we have not been re-instated but we are in communication with the United Nations Procurement Division in an effort of securing re-instatement.'

FCPA scrutiny can also negatively impact an executive's compensation. For instance, security systems company Diebold Inc. disclosed:

> While conducting due diligence in connection with a potential acquisition in Russia, Diebold identified certain transactions and payments by its subsidiary in Russia [...] that potentially implicate the FCPA, particularly the books and records provisions of the FCPA. While the company's current assessment indicates that the transactions and payments in question do not materially impact or alter the company's financial statements, the company continues to collect information and is conducting an internal review of its global FCPA compliance. At this time, Diebold cannot predict the outcome or impact of this global review. In addition, the company has voluntarily self-reported its findings to the DOJ and SEC and intends to fully cooperate with these agencies in their review.[44]

Thereafter, Diebold's Compensation Committee reduced the cash bonus of the company's President and CEO concluding that 'given the CEO's ultimate responsibility for the oversight of the company, as a result of the impact to the company of the global FCPA investigation it was appropriate that [his] cash bonus be reduced.'[45]

Whether it is a negative impact on market capitalization or cost of capital, a variety of effects on merger and acquisition activity, or the ability of FCPA scrutiny to impede or distract a company from achieving other business objectives, as highlighted in this section FCPA scrutiny and enforcement can negatively impact a business in a variety of ways separate and distinct from any enforcement action. Thus, FCPA scrutiny and exposure is not just a legal issue, but a business issue as well that needs to be on the radar screen of business leaders operating in the global marketplace.

The business effects of FCPA scrutiny and enforcement in this new era have become so pronounced that FCPA and associated risks have come to be included in the generic risks (such as loss of key personnel, global economic conditions, and currency fluctuations) companies disclose to investors as required in most SEC filings. The annual report of manufacturer Gardner Denver, Inc. provides a representative example. In its annual report filed with the SEC, the company disclosed, among other risk factors, as follows.

> The risk of non-compliance with U.S. and foreign laws and regulations applicable to our international operations could have a significant impact on our results of operations, financial condition or strategic objectives. Our global operations subject us to regulation by U.S. federal and state laws and multiple foreign laws, regulations and policies, which could result in conflicting legal requirements. These laws and regulations are complex, change frequently, have tended to become more stringent over time and increase our cost of doing business. These laws and regulations include [...] anti-corruption and bribery laws such as the FCPA ... and local laws prohibiting corrupt payments to government officials. We are subject to the risk that we, our employees, our affiliated entities, contractors, agents or their respective officers, directors, employees and agents may take actions determined to be in violation of any of these laws, particularly as we expand our operations geographically through organic growth and acquisitions. An actual or alleged violation could result in substantial fines, sanctions, civil or criminal penalties, debarment from government contracts, curtailment of operations in certain jurisdictions, competitive or reputational harm, litigation or regulatory action and other consequences that might adversely affect our results of operations, financial condition or strategic objectives.[46]

Because of the FCPA's long tentacles and the many negative business effects of FCPA scrutiny and enforcement, it is important that FCPA enforcement be subject to judicial scrutiny and that enforcement actions actually represent instances of provable FCPA violations, not merely settlements entered into for reasons of risk aversion. It is thus debatable whether many of the negative business effects companies often endure in this new era are warranted.

Regardless, this section closes on a positive note by highlighting the silver lining that often results from FCPA scrutiny or enforcement. Yes, FCPA scrutiny and enforcement has many direct and indirect negative effects on a company and is distracting to management.

Yet at the same time, management involved in an FCPA investigation often learn information about a variety of meaningful corporate issues including: the company's business in foreign countries; how the company operates in foreign countries; the personnel who run the business units and make the key decisions in foreign countries; and whether the company has effective internal controls.

During the stress and strain of FCPA scrutiny, company management (assuming they themselves are not culpable) often grow closer and develop a deeper trust of each other. In addition, the company's commitment to FCPA compliance (and compliance in general) often grows stronger. Given the motivation to improve, a company may try new things, such as aligning management compensation more closely to compliance metrics, and/or rewarding employees for compliance-related achievements. Nothing of course prevents company management from learning of these issues or taking these actions in the absence of FCPA scrutiny. However, the realities of the business world often put these issues on the back-burner.

Even Wal-Mart's FCPA scrutiny, likely the most high-profile and expensive instance of FCPA scrutiny in history, has a silver lining. During an investor conference call, the following exchange occurred between an investment analyst and Wal-Mart's CEO.

> *Analyst*: '… I'm going to step into the FCPA issue, if I can … I think the investment community's already voted that it's not really an issue from our standpoint, in terms of financial issues, but it's obviously a big one reputationally and a big one that you had to deal with from a standpoint of the media and all of that … Which really, we think, are probably unfair because of a lot of good things that Wal-Mart has been involved in over the last decade and continues to be involved in. How do you use this opportunity? How do you think about it? I know [Wal-Mart executive vice president, general counsel] has got to think about it from protecting the Company and that's what that outside investigation is. But [CEO], you have to think about it from a standpoint of transparency, and how do you lift this up and then show the entire world how you handle this situation and crisis, which has come to the Company and not at your desire, but from just those events that have transpired?'
>
> *CEO*: 'One thing that's clear is that we will be a better company because of this. Sometimes when there's a situation, like this, you can treat it as a challenge or create an opportunity. And frankly, you can see we're already taking this as an opportunity to be a better company. And so even the focus on doing business the right way, and the initiatives of outreach to communities is something we're just going to be – you might say just doubling the efforts to be a better company in everything that we do. And frankly, I think it will just lead to long-term being a better company serving communities and serving customers. So yes, a short-term challenge; long-term, it creates us a greater opportunity to be even better.'[47]

C. SHAREHOLDER LITIGATION

FCPA scrutiny and enforcement actions can also expose corporate directors and executives to private FCPA-related civil suits. Although courts have held that the FCPA does not provide a private right of action, in this new era plaintiffs' lawyers representing shareholders often target directors and executive officers of companies subject to FCPA scrutiny with civil suits alleging, among other things, breach of fiduciary duty or securities fraud. This section highlights the trend in FCPA-related shareholder litigation and explores whether such suits serve a purpose or are merely parasitic actions which feed off FCPA scrutiny and enforcement in this new era.

Two types of FCPA-related shareholder lawsuits are highlighted: derivative claims alleging director and officer breach of fiduciary duty and securities fraud class action claims. Before analyzing these two types of claims, it is instructive to learn how such claims often follow a predictable pattern. In the days and weeks following an FCPA enforcement action, or even a company disclosing or otherwise being the subject of FCPA scrutiny, purported investigations are launched by plaintiffs' firms representing shareholders and lawsuits often begin to rain down on the company, its board of directors or executive officers.

For instance, as highlighted earlier in this chapter in connection with market capitalization issues, in 2010 shares of SciClone Pharmaceuticals plunged approximately 40 percent and closed down approximately 32 percent from its previous trading day based on the company's disclosure that it had received an SEC subpoena and a letter of inquiry from the DOJ as part of an industry-wide FCPA investigation of the pharmaceutical industry. A feeding frenzy followed, and on the same day four separate plaintiffs' firms announced investigations of SciClone on behalf of shareholders to determine whether securities laws were violated.[48] The next day four additional plaintiffs' firms announced similar investigations. The following days saw numerous other investigations, and within three days of the disclosure the first securities class action lawsuit was filed on behalf of certain SciClone shareholders.

As noted in the law firm's release:

> The Complaint allege[d] that throughout the Class Period, defendants were engaged in illegal and improper sales and marketing activities in China and abroad regarding its products. This ultimately caused the Company to become the focus of a joint investigation by the [SEC and DOJ] for possible violations of the [FCPA]. It was only at the end of the Class Period, however, that investors ultimately learned the truth about the Company's operations after it

> was reported that the SEC and DOJ were investigating the Company for violations of the FCPA. At that time, shares of the Company declined almost 40% in the single trading day, on abnormally large trading volume.[49]

In the following days and weeks, numerous other plaintiffs' firms announced investigations and/or filed lawsuits against the company, its board of directors or executive officers.

A similar feeding frenzy also followed the 2012 *New York Times* front-page article regarding Wal-Mart's alleged conduct in Mexico. Within 48 hours, several plaintiffs' firms announced investigations on behalf of shareholders and within ten days shareholder civil suits tracking the *Times* article began to pour in against the company and its directors and executive officers.[50] Approximately one month after the Times article, Wal-Mart disclosed:

> The Company is a defendant in several recently-filed lawsuits in which the complaints closely track the allegations set forth in a news story that appeared in the *New York Times* […]. One of these is a securities lawsuit […] in which the plaintiff alleges various violations of the [FCPA] beginning in 2005, and asserts violations of [the securities laws] relating to certain prior disclosures of the Company. […] In addition, eleven derivative complaints were filed […] also tracking the allegations of the *Times* story, and naming various current and former officers and directors as additional defendants. The plaintiffs in the derivative suits […] allege, among other things, that the defendants who are or were directors or officers of the Company breached their fiduciary duties in connection with oversight of FCPA compliance.[51]

Chapter 6 previously highlighted FCPA Inc., and in this new era a component of FCPA Inc. includes plaintiffs' firms representing shareholders who frequently pounce on FCPA enforcement actions or instances of FCPA scrutiny by filing derivative actions and securities fraud class actions. Commenting on this trend, a *Forbes* columnist wrote under the title 'Plaintiff Lawyers Join the Bribery Racket' as follows.

> The Justice Department's unprecedented campaign to enforce a once-backwater statute called the [FCPA] has made corporate lawyers and accountants rich as big companies pay big law and accounting firms to investigate and defend potential violations. Plaintiff lawyers have noticed the enormous fees, which are often reaching into the hundreds of millions of dollars, enhanced FCPA enforcement is generating and are moving to extract their own cut. […] The unintended consequences of the Justice Department's FCPA policy simply continue to mount. […] Now the plaintiff lawyers are trying to join the fun. […] What is clear is that the cost of enhanced FCPA enforcement on U.S. corporations keeps going up. And that more lawyers are finding ways to get rich off of it.[52]

Derivative Actions

The internal affairs of a corporation, such as the rights and responsibilities of corporate directors, are governed by state law. State law, including most prominently Delaware law, provides directors broad discretion to manage the corporation subject to their fiduciary duties to the corporation and its shareholders. A director's fiduciary duties include the duty of care and the duty of loyalty, including its subsidiary component, the duty of good faith.

In a notable case in the corporate director context, a court observed:

> The sentinel asleep at his post contributes nothing to the enterprise he is charged to protect [...] Shareholders have a right to expect that directors will exercise reasonable supervision and control over the policies and practices of a corporation. The institutional integrity of a corporation depends upon the proper discharge by directors of those duties.[53]

A corporate director's duty of good faith has evolved over time to include an obligation to attempt in good faith to assure that an adequate corporate information and reporting system exists. In the notable *Caremark* decision by the influential Delaware Court of Chancery, the court held that a director's failure to do so, in certain circumstances, may give rise to individual director liability for breach of fiduciary duty.

In *Stone v. Ritter*, the Delaware Supreme Court provided the following necessary conditions for director oversight liability under the so-called *Caremark* standard: (i) a director utterly failed to implement any reporting or information system or controls; or (ii) having implemented such systems or controls, a director failed to monitor or oversee the corporation's operations.[54] The court held that both situations require a showing that a director knew that they were not discharging their fiduciary obligations, and courts have widely recognized that a director's good faith exercise of oversight responsibility may not necessarily prevent employees from violating criminal laws or from causing the corporation to incur significant financial liability or both.

Before highlighting a derivative case in the FCPA context, it is necessary to first understand the unique pleading requirements associated with derivative claims. Ordinarily, a company's board of directors has the exclusive authority to institute corporate action such as filing a lawsuit on behalf of the corporation when it has been harmed. However, when the harm to the corporation is the result of an alleged breach of fiduciary duty by the directors, the law recognizes that the board of directors is unlikely to sue itself in such a situation. Thus, the law provides a mechanism for shareholders to bring a lawsuit, not in their individual capacity, but on behalf of the corporation to recover monetary damages for the corporation.

Because this derivative action usurps a traditional board of director function and can be subject to harassment and abuse, state law often requires shareholders to first make a demand on the corporation to file suit or to plead with particularity so-called demand futility, meaning that demand on the board would be futile because the board is incapable of making an independent judgment concerning the conduct at issue.

Most derivative actions, including those in the FCPA context, are brought as demand futility cases because if a shareholder makes a demand on the board of directors to bring the claim, it will be assumed that the shareholder views the board of directors as sufficiently independent to analyze the claim and the board's decision will be analyzed under the board-friendly business judgment rule. To survive a motion to dismiss, a shareholder pleading demand futility must allege more than conclusory allegations regarding a breach of fiduciary duty. Rather, the shareholder must allege with particularity facts suggesting that the majority of directors were interested; or that the directors failed to inform themselves; or that the directors failed to exercise due care as to the conduct at issue.

Derivative claims in the FCPA context 'are often based on one or more of the following alleged actions or failures of directors and/or officers:

- participation in, concealment of, or failure to prevent the FCPA violations;
- preparation, review, and/or signing of false and misleading public statements;
- failure to comply with the company's code of business conduct or similar policy requiring FCPA compliance;
- failure to require the company to implement internal controls in compliance with the FCPA's antibribery provisions or books, records, and internal accounting provisions;
- failure to monitor the company's compliance with, or implement mechanisms for enforcement of, the company's anti-corruption policies and procedures;
- failure to implement information and reporting systems to ensure senior management and the board of directors have adequate information about the company's business and operations, material events, and compliance;
- failure to fulfill the responsibilities and duties of membership on committees of the company's board of directors;

- failure to remedy any illegal conduct or direct the company to institute suit against current or former board members and officers for permitting FCPA violations;
- and failure to oversee, manage, and operate the company in a lawful and ethical manner.'[55]

A derivative claim brought against directors and officers of oil and gas services company Tidewater Inc. after the company resolved an FCPA enforcement is representative of the type of derivative claims frequently brought in the FCPA context.[56] In ruling on the motion to dismiss the complaint by the individual directors and the company, the court began by providing the following relevant background.

> Plaintiff alleges that Tidewater, via Tidewater Marine International ('TMI' – a wholly-owned subsidiary of Tidewater) violated the [FCPA] by paying $160,000 in bribes to officials in Azerbaijan to resolve tax audits in Tidewater's favor, while knowing that some or all of the money would be paid to Azeri tax officials. [...] Plaintiff further states that Tidewater paid approximately $1.6 million in bribes to the Nigerian Customs Service to induce Nigerian officials to disregard customs regulations regarding the importation of vessels into Nigerian waters. [...] Further, Plaintiffs note that none of Tidewater's financial statements during the relevant period filed with the SEC described the bribes or the purposes of the reimbursements. In 2010 Tidewater settled with the SEC paying $8,104,362.00 in disgorgement and pre-judgment interest. Also in 2010 Tidewater entered into a DPA with the DOJ. TMI paid a $7.35 million penalty as a part of the DPA. Plaintiff Jonathan Strong ('Strong') brought this shareholder derivative suit [...] arising from these violations of the FCPA and the Securities Exchange Act of 1934 ('Exchange Act'). Strong, a shareholder in Tidewater since 1999, brought this action against the officers and members of the Board of Directors of Tidewater alleging that they breached their fiduciary duties in that they: (1) knew or recklessly disregarded the fact that employees, representatives, agents and/or contractors were paying, had paid and/or had offered to pay bribes to Azerbaijani and Nigerian government officials to obtain favorable treatment for Tidewater; (2) caused Tidewater to pay bribes and to disguise the bribe payments as legitimate expenses in Tidewater's books and financial disclosures; and (3) failed to maintain adequate internal controls to ensure compliance with the FCPA and Exchange Act. As a result of these actions, Plaintiff alleges that, in addition to the multi-million dollar penalties, Tidewater has suffered damages to its goodwill and reputation and has incurred significant expenses in connection with investigating illegal activities.

The court noted that the plaintiff did not make a demand on Tidewater's board to bring the claim and it thus analyzed whether the claim could survive a motion to dismiss because demand on the board would have been futile. To survive a motion to dismiss, the court stated that the shareholder must allege with particularity facts suggesting that directors were interested or that the directors failed to exercise due care as to the conduct at issue. The court concluded:

> First, the Complaint states that the Individual Defendants have and will continue to receive substantial remuneration from Tidewater. The acts complained of herein have resulted in short term economic benefits to Tidewater (as well as to the Individual Defendants through their increased and continued compensation). Second, the Complaint notes that the Individual Defendants did not enforce anti-bribery policies and turned a blind eye to the bribes because the revenues that were derived from the bribery were worth more than the costs of any fines it would have to pay to the DOJ and/or the SEC if Tidewater were to be caught in violation of the FCPA. Lastly, the Complaint asserts that the Individual Defendants course of conduct has demonstrated their unwillingness and/or inability to comply with their fiduciary duties. Even taken as true, these statements do not indicate that any of the board stood on either side of the bribes or benefitted personally and materially from the bribes. [...] Ultimately, this Court finds that the Complaint is completely devoid of any allegations of an interested director. There is no allegation that any director appeared on both sides of a transaction or expected to derive a personal financial benefit from it. Nowhere in the Complaint can it be found that any one of the directors, much the less a majority of them, benefitted from the bribes themselves, benefitted from failing to establish and maintain adequate internal controls, benefitted from enforcing policies and programs designed to prevent violations, benefitted from improperly recorded payment of bribes in Tidewater's books and records or benefitted from inadequately training their employees, agents, representatives and/or contractors with respect to compliance with the FCPA.

The court also examined whether the individual defendants violated their fiduciary duties by failing to exercise oversight or by failing to act and concluded:

> The bulk of Plaintiff's allegations that demand on the board would be futile revolve around the directors supposed substantial likelihood of personal liability. Specifically, Plaintiff alleges that the Individual Defendants face substantial liability: (1) based on their knowledge of Tidewater's FCPA violations; (2) based on their failure to maintain adequate internal controls; (3) due to violations of the Exchange Act. [...] Plaintiff alleges that the Individual Defendants made no effort to enforce anti-bribery policies and turned a willful and blind eye to the bribes funded and paid for by Tidewater. Plaintiff claims that the Individual Defendants did this because paying the bribes were worth more than the costs of any fines by the DOJ or SEC if Tidewater was to be caught. Plaintiff also contends that the Individual Defendants ignored, consciously disregarded and/or were reckless in not

establishing internal controls that were compliant with the FCPA and its underlying directives. Plaintiff alleges that these failures were the result of a conscious decision not to take action by the board. As a result, Plaintiff concludes that the Individual Defendants now face a substantial likelihood of personal liability. The Court finds that these claims are completely conclusory. There is nothing in the Complaint concerning any alleged scheme such that there was a conscious decision among the board members. Generalized allegations of participation, acquiescence, or approval are insufficient to excuse demand. Thus, this Court cannot conclude that Plaintiff has met his burden to show that a substantial likelihood of liability for the Individual Defendants in this situation. [...] In this case much of Plaintiff's allegations stem from the Board's failure to maintain adequate internal controls and compliance systems. As noted earlier, Plaintiff contends that this failure was the result of conscious decision(s) made by the board. [...] Plaintiff fails to allege a single particularized fact detailing knowledge as to any particular director. The Complaint merely recites instances whereby certain Individual Defendants, notably not a majority of them, signed financial forms and that audit committee meetings took place. Even taking these as true, nowhere in these allegations is there any indication of a knowing discharge of their fiduciary duties or a conscious disregard of those duties. To have a substantial likelihood of director liability on an oversight claim, a plaintiff must plead the existence of facts suggesting that the board knew that internal controls were inadequate, that the inadequacies could leave room for illegal or materially harmful behavior, and that the board chose to do nothing about the control deficiencies that it knew existed. The Plaintiff has not alleged any acts to suggest that Tidewater's internal controls were deficient, much the less that the board or the Audit Committee had any reason to suspect that they were so. The conclusory allegation that because illegal behavior occurred, internal controls must have been deficient and the board must have known so has been routinely rejected. Ultimately, the Complaint falls woefully short of pleading facts that are sufficient to show that there was any knowledge or conscious disregard on behalf of the directors. As a result, the Plaintiff has failed to plead its claim with particularity and demand is not excused. [...] While Plaintiff's allegations are sufficient to show that Tidewater was evidently violating both the FCPA and the Exchange Act, nowhere in the Complaint do Plaintiff's allegations meet the specificity to show that the Individual Defendants were acting with the intent to violate these laws. The mere fact that a violation occurred does not demonstrate that the board acted in bad faith. Alleging that 'upon information and belief' the 'Headquarters' made the decision to avoid tax assessments in violation of the FCPA falls woefully short of the pleading requirements. Nowhere can this Court find who made this decision, how this decision was made or that there was an intent to violate any law. Moreover, the Court finds it significant that Tidewater's directors voted and voluntarily initiated an FCPA investigation and advised the federal government of their violations before the government even suspected any violations.

Not only was the Tidewater derivative claim representative of the type of derivative claims frequently brought in the FCPA context, it was also representative of the outcome. According to an analysis, 'the majority of the recent shareholder derivative suits filed in the wake of FCPA actions have been dismissed, a handful have settled, and none have been fully litigated on the merits.'[57]

Securities Fraud Actions

Given how FCPA scrutiny can impact a company's share price, it is not surprising that securities fraud class actions are another frequent form of shareholder litigation in this new era following an instance of FCPA scrutiny.

The securities laws are based on the general premise that issuers must make full and complete disclosure of all material facts relevant to its business. Although materiality is a murky concept, courts have construed this key concept to mean all information, whether positive or negative, that might be relevant to an investor's decision to buy, sell, or hold a security.

The securities laws foundation of full and complete disclosure of all material facts is enforced through, among other provisions, Section 10(b) of the Exchange Act and its associated Rule 10b-5. Section 10(b) generally prohibits the use of 'any manipulative or deceptive device or contrivance in contravention of such rules and regulations as the SEC may prescribe as necessary or appropriate in the public interest or for the protection of investors.' Rule 10b-5 supplements Section 10(b) by making it unlawful for any person, directly or indirectly: (i) to employ any device, scheme or artifice to defraud; (ii) to make any untrue statement of a material fact or to omit to state a material fact necessary in order to make the statements not misleading; or (iii) to engage in any act, practice, or course of business which operates or would operate as a fraud or deceit upon any person – in connection with the purchase or sale of any security. Under the heightened pleading standard in the Private Securities Litigation Reform Act ('PSLRA') investor complaints alleging misrepresentations or omissions under Rule 10b-5 must specify each statement alleged to have been misleading, the reason or reasons why the statement is misleading, and, if an allegation regarding the statement or omission is made on information and belief, the complaint shall state with particularity all facts on which that belief is formed.

Securities fraud claims in the FCPA context generally allege that a company's public disclosures regarding potential FCPA violations and/or the potential settlement with the DOJ or the SEC were misleading in themselves or are proof of material misstatements in the company's prior public statements regarding one or more of the following topics:

- the non-existence of FCPA violations and improper accounting of funds used in illegal activity;
- the quality of the company's internal controls;
- the company's general compliance with corporate policies, the FCPA, and other applicable laws;
- the risks and costs associated with an FCPA investigation, including legal and consulting fees and disruptions to the company's operations;
- predictions regarding the results, effects, or ultimate materiality of a FCPA-related investigation;
- the company's profitability or financial performance following the cessation of illegal activity and/or any decision to suspend certain operations due to illegal conduct; and
- the financial impact of increased monitoring expenses.[58]

Plaintiffs typically assert in such cases that because of the issuer's false statements or omissions '(1) the market price of the company's securities was artificially inflated and maintained, and (2) shareholders suffered losses when the stock price fell following the issuance of corrective disclosures and the materialization of risks previously concealed by the defendants (i.e., then the 'truth' was revealed).'[59]

If an FCPA-related securities fraud class action is fully litigated, plaintiffs face a heightened pleading standard that is often difficult to satisfy. For instance, an institutional investor alleged that InVision Technologies, along with its CEO and CFO, violated section 10(b) of the Exchange Act and Rule 10b-5 promulgated thereunder in connection with alleged misstatements in its merger agreement.[60] The civil action followed InVision's settlement of an FCPA enforcement action based on payments to foreign sales agents in China, the Philippines, and Thailand.[61] The enforcement agencies alleged that InVision knew of the 'high probability' that the payments to the agents would be used to make improper payments to foreign officials and also alleged that InVision failed to maintain proper internal controls and failed to adequately train its foreign third parties.

In the civil action, plaintiff alleged that the merger agreement contained the following misstatements.

> First, [...] the agreement broadly warrants that InVision is 'in compliance in all material respects with all laws ... .' Second, [...] the agreement provides

> that InVision was in compliance with the [FCPA's] books and records provisions. Finally, [...] the agreement provides: 'neither the Company ... nor, to the knowledge of the Company, any director, officer, agent, employee or other person acting on behalf of the Company' has violated the [FCPA's] anti-bribery provisions ... [62]

The court noted the heightened pleading requirements applicable to the securities fraud claim and the requirement that, among other things, the plaintiff state with particularity facts giving rise to a strong inference that the defendants acted with intent to deceive, manipulate, or defraud. A disputed issue was whether the plaintiff 'was required to plead scienter as [to specific individuals], or whether it can rely on a theory of "collective scienter," which would hold the company as a whole responsible for the statements contained in the merger agreement.'

The appellate court held that the plaintiff was required to 'plead scienter with respect to the individuals who actually made the false statements in the merger agreement.' In so holding, the court also observed:

> [Plaintiff] argues that the settlement agreements InVision entered into with the DOJ and SEC are sufficient to create a strong inference of scienter. In those agreements, InVision accepted responsibility for misconduct and admitted that the company 'was aware of the high probability that its foreign sales agents or distributors paid or offered to pay something of value to government officials in order to obtain or retain business for InVision.' The company further admitted that it 'improperly accounted for certain payments ... in its books and records in violation of the FCPA.' The district court correctly held that these agreements were not sufficient to meet the pleading requirements of the PSLRA. First, the admissions in these settlement agreements were largely legal conclusions, rather than particularized facts giving rise to a strong inference of scienter. More importantly, even if InVision accepted the SEC's and DOJ's statements of fact, there is nothing in either settlement agreement that would support the conclusion that [any specific individuals] had actual knowledge of the violations. As discussed earlier, the mere fact that someone at InVision had knowledge of the illegal transactions is not sufficient to satisfy the scienter pleading requirements of the PSLRA, given the context and limited nature of the misrepresentations at issue.

Although plaintiffs face a heightened pleading requirement in an FCPA-related securities fraud action that is often difficult to satisfy, few such cases are actually litigated. Rather, most cases settle and according to an analysis 'a number of FCPA-related securities fraud suits have settled for amounts in excess of the penalty assessed by the DOJ and/or SEC' in the underlying FCPA enforcement action.[63]

However, just because certain FCPA-related securities fraud class actions have settled does not mean that such actions would have succeeded on the merits. Companies often make the business decision to settle shareholder litigation (whether derivative actions or securities fraud class actions in the FCPA context or otherwise) for nuisance value and backed by insurance coverage.

A typical corporate position concerning settlement of FCPA-related shareholder litigation was articulated by the Chief Financial Officer of Maxwell Technologies, a company that resolved an FCPA enforcement action in 2011.[64] During an investor call, the CFO stated:

> As we have disclosed in past public filings in 2010, two shareholders had alleged that certain of our past and current officers and directors failed to prevent us from violating the [FCPA]. [...] [M]ediation was held and a proposed settlement was reached wherein $3 million would be paid to plaintiff's counsel, with $2.7 million to be paid by our insurance carrier, and $290,000 would be paid by the Company. In addition, we would be required to insure that certain corporate governance measures are in place and in force. The agreement is subject to among other things, court approval and notice to our shareholders. Without admitting any wrongdoing, the defendants to this suit are willing to enter into this settlement in order to expedite resolution of the matter, and to relieve the defendants and the Company from further financial burden. We are pleased that this suit is near final settlement, and look forward to putting this matter behind us.[65]

It is difficult to discern what, if anything, is accomplished by much shareholder litigation in the FCPA context. Two recent FCPA-related civil settlements demonstrate this point.

In 2012, Halliburton announced that a Texas state court issued an order approving the proposed settlement of a derivative claim concerning a variety of misconduct, including Nigeria conduct that was the basis of a 2009 FCPA enforcement action against the company and its related entities as previously highlighted.[66] Pursuant to the settlement, Halliburton's board agreed to implement various corporate governance and internal control revisions. However, the revisions most related to FCPA compliance were already required by the settlement of the 2009 FCPA enforcement action. Nevertheless, pursuant to the settlement agreement, plaintiffs' counsel in the derivative action was paid approximately $7 million in fees and expenses.

Likewise, in 2012 Johnson & Johnson (J&J) announced a settlement of a derivative claim concerning a variety of misconduct, including conduct that was the basis of a 2011 FCPA enforcement action previously highlighted.[67] As previously highlighted in Chapter 5, pursuant to the

FCPA enforcement action, J&J agreed to implement a host of FCPA-related compliance enhancements including enhanced compliance obligations. In settling the derivative action, J&J agreed to many of the same compliance enhancements and agreed to reimburse plaintiffs' counsel approximately $10 million and to pay approximately $450,000 for its expenses.

Given the frequency in which shareholder litigation follows an FCPA enforcement action or instance of FCPA scrutiny, and given the largely unsuccessful track record of such cases surviving the motion to dismiss stage, the question ought to be asked: does the majority of shareholder litigation in the FCPA context serve a purpose or are such actions merely parasitic attempts to feed off FCPA scrutiny and enforcement in this new era?

When a company's FCPA violations are the result of board of director or executive officer conduct, or the condoning or encouraging of such conduct by those with fiduciary duties, such civil suits or investigations would seem to be warranted and in the public interest. As previously highlighted, while there have been a few such FCPA enforcement actions, in the vast majority of FCPA enforcement actions the enforcement agencies do not allege any knowledge, participation, or acquiescence in the conduct at issue by the board of directors or executive officers.

Rather, based on *respondeat superior*, a company faces FCPA exposure because of the actions of a single employee or small group of employees whose conduct was often in violation of the company's pre-existing FCPA compliance policies and procedures and the company's good faith efforts to comply with the law. In this typical scenario, shareholder litigation would seem to be merely an attempt by plaintiffs' lawyers to feed off this new era of FCPA enforcement.

Testimony at a 2011 House Judiciary Committee hearing by a witness appearing on behalf of the Chamber of Commerce highlighted the parasitic nature of much shareholder litigation in the FCPA context and its negative effects. At the hearing, the witness highlighted specific areas of 'substantial litigation abuse' including 'private lawsuits that piggyback on government investigations.'[68] As to this issue, the majority of the testimony focused on the FCPA and the witness stated:

> More recently, the piggyback-litigation phenomenon has been most noticeable with respect to [FCPA] enforcement proceedings brought by the [DOJ and SEC]. These piggyback cases tend to fall into two categories: (1) shareholder class actions alleging that a company did not adequately disclose its FCPA exposure; and (2) derivative actions against officers and directors alleging that they failed to prevent a company from bribing foreign officials.

Follow-on FCPA cases target companies at a difficult time. Companies going through DOJ or SEC FCPA enforcement proceedings often spend tens of millions of dollars, if not more, on attorneys and forensic accountants – on top of potentially multimillion-dollar criminal and civil fines and disgorgement – in order to determine whether their employees (often at a relatively low level) acted improperly. Enforcement proceedings also interrupt normal business operations, as companies make employees and documents available to lawyers, and take action against truly culpable employees. The investigations themselves are disclosable events and are almost always 'bad news,' resulting in negative publicity. Shareholder suits against companies involved in enforcement proceedings threaten to further delay the companies' ability to return to normal operations and to further damage shareholder value. These suits serve no purpose but to take money from current shareholders and transfer it to former (or other) shareholders – with a hefty slice cut out for the plaintiffs' lawyers.

Derivative shareholder suits are equally problematic in this arena. These suits tend to target senior officers and directors, not the employees who actually paid any bribes or condoned others paying them. The reason is simple enough: directors and officers are backed by the deep pockets of the company's [Director and Officer's] insurer; culpable employees have little money to pay in private civil damages, especially if they themselves have been the target of an individual enforcement proceeding.

Often, lawyers filing shareholder class actions against companies under investigation or derivative actions against directors and officers of a company under investigation do not even wait until the government investigation is complete. Such tactics are particularly egregious, because they necessarily involve the company and senior management in defending against a private civil suit – and in making strategic judgments regarding such defense – when their focus should be on resolving the government's investigation. Both the DOJ and the SEC have developed leniency policies for companies that actively assist in government investigations. These policies acknowledge that U.S. government resources are limited, and that cooperating companies can materially assist the government in enforcing the law and protecting shareholders. As part of cooperating with the government, companies in FCPA investigations frequently investigate their own potential wrongdoing and self-report misconduct to the government. When companies and their senior officers and directors face personal civil liability in addition to any exposure to the DOJ and SEC, their judgments regarding what issues to investigate and what results to report to the DOJ and SEC necessarily will be affected, possibly to the detriment of the integrity of the government's investigation.[69]

As with many things in this new era of FCPA enforcement, FCPA-related shareholder litigation seems to have spiraled out of control and an FCPA practitioner rightly observed:

Setbacks in court do not appear to have slowed the pace of new cases filed against corporations and their directors after FCPA disclosures. As the DOJ

> and SEC bring more cases, and as more companies voluntarily disclose potential FCPA violations, the trend of related civil litigation is likely to continue. In attempting to satisfy the expectations of the DOJ and SEC, a company's thorough internal investigation may also serve as the roadmap for a civil litigant. Companies negotiating with the DOJ and SEC must therefore balance the government's requests for the results of internal investigations with the risk of waiver of privilege and subsequent production to civil litigants. As a result of these practical considerations, reputational risk, and expenses involved in litigation, companies targeted by civil suits will feel pressure to settle, potentially even before the DOJ or SEC takes action.[70]

Regardless of the substantive merits of much FCPA-related shareholder litigation, the take-away point from this section is that such civil litigation following an FCPA enforcement action or FCPA scrutiny represents yet another instance of the FCPA's long tentacles.

D. OFFENSIVE USE OF THE FCPA

Whether it is a DOJ or SEC FCPA enforcement action, a related foreign law enforcement investigation, or an FCPA-related civil suit brought by plaintiffs' lawyers representing shareholders, companies are ordinarily in a defensive posture when it comes to the FCPA. Even if a company is not involved in an FCPA investigation or related litigation, the FCPA still usually frustrates a business objective such as not acquiring a foreign target or not engaging a foreign agent because of FCPA risk. While such defensive positions continue to dominate, in this new era the FCPA is increasingly being used offensively by companies to achieve a business objective or to further advance a litigating position.

For instance, in 2013 Dish Network and Tokyo-based SoftBank were battling for control of wireless carrier Sprint Nextel. Among the regulatory approvals needed for SoftBank to complete the transaction was Federal Communications Commission ('FCC') approval of a license transfer from Sprint Nextel to SoftBank. In opposing the transfer, Dish Network cited to the FCC a 2009 FCPA enforcement action against UTStarcom, previously discussed in Chapter 3, in which the company agreed to pay $3 million via a DOJ NPA and SEC civil settlement 'for the actions of UTS-China [its wholly-owned subsidiary) and its employees and agents, who arranged and paid for employees of Chinese state-owned telecommunications companies to travel to popular tourist destinations in the United States, including Hawaii, Las Vegas and New York City.'[71]

The link Dish Network made between the FCPA enforcement action and its battle with SoftBank for Sprint Nextel was that Softbank's founder Masayoshi Son was on the board of UTStarcom during certain time periods relevant to the conduct at issue in the FCPA enforcement action.[72] Dish Network asserted that the UTStarcom enforcement action was 'relevant to the public interest analysis of the proposed transaction.' In reply, Softbank stated that the UTStarcom enforcement action was not relevant to its attempt to gain control of Sprint Nextel and asserted:

> [The enforcement action did] not involve SoftBank or Mr. Masayoshi Son, Chairman and CEO of SoftBank. The settlement documents do not name, implicate, or otherwise relate to SoftBank or Mr. Son, and are legally and factually irrelevant to this proceeding.
>
> DISH suggests that these settlements raise a potential issue in this proceeding because Mr. Son at one time served as the Chairman of the Board of UTSI. Neither the DOJ or SEC settlement documents, however, even mention SoftBank or Mr. Son. This is hardly surprising. Mr. Son was not an operating officer of UTStarcom at any time and the alleged violations came to light years after Mr. Son left the Board, which he did in 2004. The FCPA-related misconduct, according to the settlement documents, involved an executive of the company's Chinese subsidiary, UTStarcom China Co., Ltd.[73]

Another example of offensive use of the FCPA in a battle for corporate control involved Central European Distribution Corporation ('CEDC'), a large vodka producer headquartered in the U.S. In 2012, CEDC disclosed:

> There has been a breach of the books and records provisions of the [FCPA] and potentially other breaches of the FCPA. It was determined that payments or gifts were made in a foreign jurisdiction in which the Company operates, and that there was a failure to maintain documentation in respect of certain of these payments or gifts adequate to establish whether there was a valid business purpose in making the payments or gifts. Furthermore, our management also identified a material weakness in our internal control over financial reporting regarding the implementation of our policy on compliance with applicable laws [...]. Our conclusion that this deficiency is a material weakness in our internal control over financial reporting is not based on misstatements in our historical consolidated financial statements or our consolidated financial statements [...], but instead on the determination that we did not design or maintain sufficient policies, procedures, controls, communications or training to deter or prevent the risk of violations of law, including the [FCPA].[74]

Shortly thereafter, Russian billionaire Roustam Tariko, the founder of CEDC rival Russian Standard and CEDC's largest shareholder, claimed that CEDC executives themselves were the subject of an FCPA investigation. The claims of CEDC's largest shareholder caused the company to issue a letter to shareholders that stated:

> As you may be aware … Mr. Roustam Tariko, Chairman of Russian Standard, published a letter to CEDC investors that has created anxiety and confusion in the marketplace. What you may not be aware of is that Mr. Tariko's letter was published less than 48 hours after the CEDC Board voted 5 to 3 (the 3 being Mr. Tariko and his Board designees) against Mr. Tariko's request that he be given total control over CEDC's operations and finance. This request follows repeated attempts by Russian Standard to remove the interim CEO. The purpose of this letter is to provide you with [among other things] correct information regarding FCPA matters … .[75]

The letter then stated that 'despite suggestions in the Russian Standard letter to the contrary, the company is NOT on notice that any of its current executives are under investigation with respect to FCPA violations or otherwise.'

Perhaps the most high-profile instance of offensive use of the FCPA involved the boardroom battle between Wynn Resorts and its board member Kazuo Okada. In early 2012, Wynn Resorts disclosed as follows.

> In May 2011, Wynn Macau, a majority owned subsidiary of Wynn Resorts, Limited (the 'Company'), made a commitment to the University of Macau Development Foundation in support of the new Asia-Pacific Academy of Economics and Management. This contribution consists of a $25 million payment made in May 2011 and a commitment for additional donations of $10 million each year for the calendar years 2012 through 2022 inclusive. The pledge was consistent with the Company's longstanding practice of providing philanthropic support for deserving institutions in the markets in which it operates. The pledge was made following an extensive analysis which concluded that the gift was made in accordance with all applicable laws. The pledge was considered by the Boards of Directors of both the Company and Wynn Macau and approved by 15 of the 16 directors who serve on those boards. The sole dissenting vote was Mr. Kazuo Okada whose stated objection was to the length of time over which the donation would occur, not its propriety. Also as previously disclosed, Mr. Okada commenced litigation […] in Nevada seeking to compel the Company to produce information relating to the donation to the University of Macau, among other things. […] Following Mr. Okada's lawsuit, the Company received a letter from the [SEC] requesting that, in connection with an informal inquiry by the SEC, the Company preserve information relating to the donation to the University of Macau, any donations by the Company to any other educational charitable institutions, including the University of Macau Development Foundation, and the Company's casino or concession gaming licenses or renewals in Macau. The Company intends to fully comply with the SEC's request.[76]

While Wynn's disclosure did not specifically mention the FCPA, given that the company's disclosure of the SEC inquiry appeared to link the donation to the 'Company's casino or concession gaming licenses or renewals in Macau,' the disclosure seemed to implicate the FCPA. As Okada alleged in his complaint 'Wynn Macau's gaming concession expires in June 2022 – the last year of Wynn's donation commitment.' According to Okada's complaint, he objected to the donation, called it unprecedented in university history, and claimed that the Chinese government owned the land on which the university is located.

Shortly thereafter, Wynn accused Okada of separate and distinct conduct that could implicate the FCPA. In a press release, Wynn announced that its 'Compliance Committee has concluded a year-long investigation after receiving an independent report detailing numerous apparent violations of the [FCPA] by Aruze USA, Inc., its parent company Universal Entertainment Corporation, and its principal shareholder, Kazuo Okada.'[77]

In the release, Wynn noted that its Compliance Committee engaged a variety of experts, including Louis Freeh (the former Director of the FBI), who conducted 'a thorough independent investigation' which 'uncovered and documented more than three dozen instances over a three-year period in which Mr. Okada and his associates engaged in improper activities for their own benefit in apparent violation of U.S. anti-corruption laws and gross disregard for the Company's Code of Conduct.' According to the release, 'Mr. Okada and his associates and companies appear to have engaged in a longstanding practice of making payments and gifts to his two chief gaming regulators at the Philippines Amusement and Gaming Corporation, who directly oversee and regulated Mr. Okada's Provisional Licensing Agreement to operate in that country.'

The Wynn releases further stated as follows.

> The Board has requested that Mr. Okada resign as a Director of Wynn Resorts. The Company will immediately inform the Board of Directors of its Hong Kong listed subsidiary, Wynn Macau, Limited, of its actions and will recommend that Mr. Okada be removed from the Wynn Macau Board. [...] The Freeh Report is the culmination of a year-long investigation by the Compliance Committee based on increasing concerns the Board had relating to the activities of Mr. Okada and Aruze USA, Inc. in the Philippines and statements made by Mr. Okada to Wynn Resorts' Directors that gifts to regulators are permissible in Asia. Mr. Okada is the only Director of Wynn Resorts who has continued to refuse to sign the Company's Code of Conduct or participate in mandatory Foreign Corrupt Practices Act training for Directors.

Wynn's FCPA allegations against Okada were used by the company to support its finding that Okada was an 'unsuitable person' under Nevada gaming regulations and thus justified Okada's removal from Wynn's board.[78] The boardroom battle occurred in the context of Wynn's attempt to purchase Okada's 20 percent stake in Wynn at an approximate 30 percent discount. Okada ultimately resigned from Wynn's board and in doing so stated: 'I no longer believe it is appropriate for me to serve on the Board of Directors of a company that is behaving in a manner that I deeply believe to be unethical.'[79]

In addition to the FCPA being used offensively to achieve a business objective, in this new era the FCPA is also being used offensively to advance litigating positions. As previously indicated, while certain courts have held that the FCPA does not contain a private right of action, plaintiffs have nevertheless frequently brought causes of action under the Racketeer Influenced and Corrupt Organizations Act ('RICO') for bribery-related conduct.

To establish a violation of any of the substantive offenses under RICO, a plaintiff must show that defendants engaged in a 'pattern of racketeering,' which requires at least two acts of racketeering activity. A violation of the Travel Act is one of the enumerated predicate offenses under RICO. The Travel Act, enacted prior to the FCPA, is part of the racketeering chapter of the criminal code and prohibits interstate and foreign travel or transportation in aid of racketeering enterprises. Specifically, the Travel Act prohibits travel in interstate or foreign commerce or use of the mail or any facility in interstate or foreign commerce with intent to, among other things, carry on 'any unlawful activity' which is defined to include bribery in violation of state law.

In short, conduct in violation of the FCPA is often in violation of state law, which in turn implicates the Travel Act, which in turn can implicate RICO given that a Travel Act violation is a predicate act under RICO.

For instance, in 2008 Aluminum Bahrain BSC ('Alba') (one of the largest aluminum smelters in the world owned by, among others, the government of Bahrain) filed a civil lawsuit against Alcoa Inc. (the world's leading producer of primary aluminum products) and others alleging RICO violations. The complaint alleged that certain Alcoa entities and their agents engaged in a conspiracy over a 15-year period to defraud Alba and specifically alleged the defendants: (i) illegally bribed officials of the government of Bahrain and (or) officers of Alba in order to force Alba to purchase alumina at excessively high prices; (ii) illegally bribed officials of the government of Bahrain and (or) officers of Alba and issued threats in order to pressure Alba to enter into an agreement by which Alcoa would purchase an equity interest in Alba; and (iii) assigned portions of existing supply contracts between Alcoa and Alba for the sole purpose of facilitating alleged bribes and unlawful commissions.[80]

After the judge denied the defendants' motion to dismiss, Alcoa agreed to settle the case by paying Alba approximately $85 million and the action represented the 'first time that a foreign-owned corporation has successfully sued a U.S. company in a federal court to recover losses suffered due to allegations of corrupt activity.'[81]

While FCPA-related civil litigation often involves RICO claims, such civil cases have also involved other causes of action as well. For instance, after Innospec resolved an FCPA enforcement action, NewMarket Corp., a competitor company, learned of Innospec's conduct from the DOJ and SEC resolution documents. The conduct included allegations that Innospec's bribe payments in Iraq ensured that a field test of a competitor's product failed. Based on Innospec's acknowledgment of this conduct in resolving the FCPA enforcement action, the competitor filed a civil case against Innospec alleging violations of the Robinson-Patman Act, the Virginia Antitrust Act, and the Virginia Business Conspiracy Act. Innospec agreed to resolve the case by agreeing to pay NewMarket approximately $45 million.[82]

The trend of offensive use of the FCPA to advance litigating positions is not just limited to business organizations. In this new era, individuals are also increasingly citing the FCPA to support claims of wrongful termination of employment.

For instance, Khaled Asadi, a former employee of a wholly-owned subsidiary of General Electric Company ('G.E.'), filed a civil complaint alleging that G.E. harassed and pressured him to vacate his position, and ultimately terminated him after he informed his supervisor and G.E.'s Ombudsperson 'regarding potential violations of the FCPA committed by G.E. during negotiations for a lucrative, multi-year deal with the Iraqi Ministry of Electricity.'[83]

Likewise, Stephen Lowe, who was previously employed by Allison Transmission as its Managing Director for operations in China, Japan, and Korea, filed a civil complaint against the company alleging that Allison fired him because he 'refused to engage in violations of the FCPA.'[84] Among other things, Lowe alleged that: (i) he witnessed Allison's Commercial Director of Asia Strategy deliver a cash-filled envelope to Beijing City Bus officials during dinner; (ii) he heard the Commercial Director describe how he purchased silver jewelry for Chinese government officials 'in order to please the officials'; (iii) the Commercial Director bragged about winning a Beijing City Bus Olympics contract by doing 'whatever it took to please the officials' 'including giving gifts, money and prostitutes'; and (iv) the Commercial Director 'deliberately lost' high-stakes card games to 'key Beijing City Bus officials.' According to Lowe's complaint, Allison's Vice President of International Sales and Marketing knew and approved of certain of the Commercial Director's conduct and he further alleged that 'a month before Allison fired him' he disclosed his concerns about the Commercial Director and the Vice President to Allison's Marketing Manager.

Such 'noisy exits' by employees alleging wrongful termination of employment can also be the origins of high-profile FCPA scrutiny of the company involved. For instance, casino company Las Vegas Sands has been the subject of FCPA scrutiny since 2010 when Steven Jacobs, the former President of the company's Macau operations, filed a civil complaint against the company alleging breach of contract and tort-based causes of action.[85] Jacobs alleged, among other things, that the company's 'notoriously bellicose' CEO and majority shareholder made several 'outrageous demands' upon him including 'demands that Sands China continue to use the legal services of a Macau attorney [...] despite concerns that [the individual's] retention posed serious risks' under the FCPA. The civil lawsuit has led to enforcement agency FCPA inquiries concerning the conduct at issue in the civil lawsuit as well as other conduct.

While the FCPA is a law exclusively enforced by the DOJ and SEC, the take-away point from this chapter is that the FCPA has many long tentacles. Whether it is a related foreign law enforcement investigation, the negative business effects of FCPA scrutiny, FCPA-related civil litigation against corporate directors or executives, or offensive use of the FCPA to achieve a business objective or advance litigating positions, actual FCPA enforcement actions brought by the enforcement agencies are often just one consequence of FCPA scrutiny in this new era.

This new reality presents two distinct issues. First, because of the FCPA's long tentacles and the feeding frenzy that often follows FCPA scrutiny or enforcement actions, it is important that FCPA enforcement be subject to judicial scrutiny and that enforcement actions represent legitimate instances of provable FCPA violations, not merely settlements entered into for reasons of risk aversion. Second, the FCPA's long tentacles should make clear to business organizations that there are many reasons to comply with the FCPA in addition to the obvious reason that non-compliance can expose a company and culpable individuals to an FCPA enforcement action.

Avoiding the FCPA's many long tentacles can best be accomplished by managing and mitigating risk, and the next chapter highlights various FCPA compliance best practices.

NOTES

1. Andrew Boutros and Markus Funk, '"Carbon Copy" Prosecutions: A Growing Anticorruption Phenomenon in a Shrinking World,' The University of Chicago Legal Forum (2012).
2. FCPA Professor, 'Friday Roundup' (Apr. 26, 2013).
3. FCPA Professor, 'More on Alliance One and Universal' (Aug. 25, 2010), containing links to original source documents.
4. FCPA Professor, 'Friday Roundup' (Aug. 20, 2010).
5. Halliburton Press Release, 'Halliburton Confirms Agreement to Settle with Federal Government of Nigeria' (Dec. 21, 2010).
6. *Supra* note 1.
7. Dana Hughes, ABC News, 'Exclusive: Nigerian Prosecutor to Dick Cheney: Nobody is above the Law,' (Dec. 15, 2010).
8. Transparency International, '2010 Progress Report of the OECD Anti-Bribery Convention.'
9. Argyle Journal, 'Turning a New Page against Corruption at the Corporate Level: Freshfield's Partner Explains Impact of UK Bribery Act' (Aug. 9, 2012).
10. FCPA Professor, 'SFO Flexing Its Muscle Even without the Bribery Act' (Feb. 17, 2011).
11. FCPA Professor, 'Innospec Gets Hit on Both Sides of the Atlantic' (Mar. 19, 2010), containing links to original source documents.
12. OECD Convention on Combating Bribery of Foreign Public Officials in International Business Transactions.
13. FCPA Professor, 'Lord Justice Thomas's Innospec Sentencing Remarks' (Apr. 6, 2010), containing links to original source documents.
14. FCPA Professor, 'BAE … Inside the SFO' (Apr. 30, 2010), containing links to original source documents.
15. Id.
16. FCPA Professor, 'A Conversation with Richard Alderman Regarding BAE' (Mar. 15, 2011).
17. Eric Platt, Business Insider, 'How a Wal-Mart Bribery Fine Could Spiral up over $13 Billion' (Apr. 23, 2012).
18. SciClone Pharmaceuticals Inc., Form 10-K (filed Aug. 9, 2010).
19. Wall Street Pit, 'NCR Corp (NCR): Downgraded as Potential FCPA Issues Add Meaningful Risk – Wedbush' (Aug. 14, 2012).
20. Joe Palazzolo, Wall Street Journal Corruption Currents, 'Does the FCPA Move Markets' (Oct. 2, 2012).
21. Raymond Wong and Patrick Conroy, Nera Economic Consulting, 'FCPA Settlements: It's a Small World after All' (Jan. 28, 2009).
22. Nigam Arora, Forbes, 'Mexican Bribery Gave Me a Chance to Make Money in Wal-Mart' (May 17, 2012).
23. Fitch Ratings, 'U.S. Foreign Corrupt Practices Act – No Minor Matter' (2010).
24. Reuters, 'S&P cuts Avon Products Inc' (Mar. 16, 2012).
25. Press Release, U.S. Dep't of Justice, 'Willbros Group Inc. Enters Deferred Prosecution Agreement and Agrees to Pay $22 Million Penalty for FCPA Violations' (May 14, 2008).
26. Press Release, 'Lockheed Martin Announces Agreement to Acquire Titan Corporation' (Sept. 15, 2003).
27. Press Release, 'Lockheed Martin Updates Status of Review of Titan's International Consultants' (Mar. 5, 2004).

28. Press Release, 'Lockheed Martin Terminates Merger Agreement with the Titan Corporation' (June 26, 2004).
29. Los Angeles Times, 'Lockheed Drops Titan Merger after Delays by Bribery Probe' (June 26, 2004).
30. Press Release, U.S. Dep't of Justice (Mar. 1, 2005).
31. FCPA Professor, 'The FCPA's Long Tentacles' (Aug. 3, 2010), containing links to original source documents.
32. Id.
33. Id.
34. FCPA Professor, 'ABM Industries Discloses Merger Related Issue' (Dec. 26, 2011), containing links to original source documents.
35. ABM Industries, Inc., Form 10-K (filed Dec. 20, 2012).
36. FCPA Professor, 'FCPA Issues Can Reduce the Value of a Merger' (June 14, 2012), containing links to original source documents.
37. Press Release, U.S. Dep't of Justice, 'Oil Services Companies and a Freight Forwarding Company Agree to Resolve Foreign Bribery Investigations and to Pay More Than $156 Million in Criminal Penalties' (Nov. 4, 2010).
38. FCPA Professor, 'It's Not Easy Being under Investigation for Two Years …' (Mar. 15, 2010).
39. Megha Bahree, 'Wal-Mart's Path to Power in India Hits Its Limits: The Lawyers' (Apr. 1, 2013).
40. FCPA Professor, 'Scrutiny Alerts and Updates' (Apr. 3, 2013).
41. FCPA Professor, 'The Former CFO of RAE Systems Speaks' (Aug. 14, 2012), containing links to original source documents.
42. FCPA Professor, 'A Favor… Plus the Friday Roundup' (Sept. 10, 2010).
43. FCPA Professor, 'Africa Sting Continues to Sting' (May 15, 2013).
44. FCPA Professor, 'Friday Roundup' (July 30, 2010).
45. FCPA Professor, 'Business Effects' (Mar. 21, 2012).
46. GardnerDenver Inc., Form 10-K (filed Feb. 27, 2013).
47. FCPA Professor, 'The Silver Lining' (June 7, 2012).
48. FCPA Professor, 'SciClone – an FCPA Feeding Frenzy' (Oct. 13, 2010).
49. FCPA Professor, 'In the Blink of an Eye … Along Comes a Securities Fraud Suit' (Aug. 19, 2010).
50. FCPA Professor, 'Friday Roundup' (May 4, 2012).
51. FCPA Professor, 'Friday Roundup' (June 8, 2012).
52. Nathan Vardi, Forbes, 'Plaintiff Lawyers Join the Bribery Racket' (Aug. 6, 2012).
53. 432 A.2d 814 (1981).
54. 911 A.2d 362 (2006).
55. Jeffrey Johnston and Erika Tristan, Vinson & Elkins Securities Litigation Insights, 'The Next FCPA Battleground: Private Civil Lawsuits Following Foreign Corrupt Practices Act Settlements with U.S. Government Authorities' (Fall 2010).
56. 877 F.Supp.2d 433 (E.D.La. 2012).
57. Amy Westbrook, 'Double Trouble: Collateral Shareholder Litigation Following Foreign Corrupt Practices Act Investigations,' 73 Ohio State Law Journal 1217 (2012).
58. *Supra* note 55.
59. Id.
60. 549 F.3d 736 (9th Cir. 2008).
61. Press Release, U.S. Dep't of Justice, 'InVision Technologies, Inc. Enters into Agreement with the United States' (Dec. 6, 2004).
62. 549 F.3d 736 (9th Cir. 2008).
63. *Supra* note 57.

64. Press Release, U.S. Dep't of Justice, 'Maxwell Technologies Inc. Resolves Foreign Corrupt Practices Act Investigation and Agrees to Pay $8 Million Criminal Penalty' (Jan. 31, 2011).
65. FCPA Professor, 'Friday Roundup' (Mar. 2, 2012).
66. FCPA Professor, 'Nice Pay Day, but What Did You Accomplish?' (Sept. 20, 2012), containing links to original source documents.
67. Id.
68. Testimony of John H. Beisner, On Behalf of the U.S. Chamber Institute for Legal Reform, before the Subcommittee on the Constitution of the Committee on the Judiciary, United States House of Representatives Hearing, 'Can We Sue Our Way to Prosperity?: Litigation's Effect on America's Global Competitiveness' (May 24, 2011).
69. Id.
70. James Tillen and Lauren Torbett, Bloomberg Law Reports – White Collar Crime, 'Multiplying the Risks: Parallel Civil Litigation in FCPA Investigations' (2010).
71. Press Release, U.S. Dep't of Justice, 'UTStarcom Inc. Agrees to Pay $1.5 Million Penalty for Acts of Foreign Bribery in China' (Dec. 31, 2009).
72. FCPA Professor, 'Offensive Use of the FCPA' (June 6, 2013).
73. Id.
74. FCPA Professor, 'Friday Roundup' (Nov. 30, 2012), containing links to original source documents.
75. Id.
76. FCPA Professor, 'Wynn Resorts $135 Million University of Macau Donation the Subject of SEC Scrutiny' (Feb. 14, 2012).
77. FCPA Professor, 'Wynn's Boardroom Battle Royale' (Feb. 20, 2012), containing links to original source documents.
78. Chris Sieroty, Las Vegas Review-Journal, 'Okada Claims against Wynn Resorts Ruled Baseless,' (Feb. 4, 2013).
79. Chris Sieroty, Las Vegas Review-Journal, 'Kazuo Okada Resigns from Wynn Resorts Board of Directors' (Feb. 23, 2013).
80. FCPA Professor, 'Alcoa Agent Charged in the U.K.' (Oct. 25, 2012), containing links to original source documents.
81. Akin Gump Press Release, 'Akin Gump Secures Settlement Valued at $447 Million in First-Ever RICO Claim by Foreign Company' (Oct. 9, 2012).
82. FCPA Professor, 'Innospec Related News' (Aug. 10, 2010).
83. Christopher Matthews, Wall Street Journal Corruption Currents, 'Former GE Exec Claims He Was Fired for Relaying FCPA Concerns' (Feb. 7, 2012).
84. FCPA Professor, 'Still Yet Another Noisy Exit' (Dec. 23, 2010).
85. FCPA Professor, 'Another Noisy Exit' (Nov. 2, 2010).

8. FCPA compliance and best practices

This chapter is devoted to FCPA compliance. However, before diving into the specifics on this topic, it is important to recognize that FCPA compliance is difficult for even the most well-managed and well-intentioned business organizations. This is due to *respondeat superior*, the realities of doing business in the global marketplace, and the shifting and often conflicting messages of the enforcement agencies. Because of these difficulties, and the fact that rogue employees exist and no compliance program can ever prevent all misconduct, FCPA risk can not be eliminated.

However, FCPA risk can be effectively managed and minimized, and one positive result of the increase in FCPA enforcement in this new era has been the related increase in 'soft' enforcement of the FCPA through compliance policies and procedures. Certain FCPA enforcement actions provide an opportunity to learn, and this chapter will showcase various teachable moments from compliance failures in actual enforcement actions.

FCPA compliance however is not a one-size-fits-all proposition. Rather effective and cost-efficient FCPA compliance is best achieved through conducting a risk assessment, and you will learn the basic fundamentals of conducting an FCPA risk assessment so that compliance can be uniquely tailored to a company's FCPA risk profile.

This chapter also highlights various FCPA best practices – from high-level commitment to third-party due diligence and oversight, to review and monitoring of compliance programs – designed to manage and minimize FCPA risk. A component of FCPA best practices is ensuring that compliance is not viewed strictly as a legal function but rather holistically throughout a business organization. This requires not only active engagement and participation by legal personnel, but also training of other personnel such as finance and audit professionals so that they can approach their job functions with FCPA goggles and recognize FCPA risk and report it to appropriate experts within the organization.

Even though more FCPA compliance is one positive result of this new era, this chapter concludes by examining whether certain aspects of FCPA enforcement have resulted in wasteful overcompliance, and whether too much FCPA compliance and training have resulted in compliance fatigue and its unintended consequence of numbing individuals to the FCPA.

A. THE DIFFICULTIES OF FCPA COMPLIANCE

FCPA compliance is difficult for even the most well-managed and well-intentioned business organizations. As previously highlighted in this book, various courts have found that the FCPA's anti-bribery provisions contain ambiguous terms and the FCPA's books and records and internal controls provisions are qualified by terms such as 'reasonable detail' 'accurately and fairly' and 'reasonable assurances.' In this way, many of the FCPA's prohibitions are principle-based, not rules-based, making compliance difficult in much the same way if the speed limit was to drive 'reasonably' and not a specific speed such as 65 miles per hour.

In addition, as discussed in Chapter 2, the basic question of what the FCPA actually means is often anything but straightforward, and much of what defines this new era of FCPA enforcement is non-binding, non-legal sources of information including prosecutorial common law.

Another reason FCPA compliance is difficult for even the most well-managed and well-intentioned organizations is because of the shifting and often conflicting messages by the enforcement agencies. For instance, the FCPA Guidance states:

> Devoting a disproportionate amount of time policing modest entertainment and gift-giving instead of focusing on large government bids, questionable payments to third-party consultants, or excessive discounts to resellers and distributors may indicate that a company's compliance program is ineffective. A $50 million contract with a government agency in a high-risk country warrants greater scrutiny than modest routine gifts and entertainment. Similarly, performing identical due diligence on all third-party agents, irrespective of risk factors, is often counter-productive, diverting attention and resources away from those third parties that pose the most significant risk.

In connection with the FCPA Guidance, the Assistant Attorney General stated that the DOJ is 'focused on bribes of consequence – ones that have a fundamentally corrosive effect on the way companies do business abroad.'[1] Likewise, the Chief of the SEC Enforcement Division stated that the enforcement agencies 'hope that [the Guidance] will clear up some myths about the type of conduct that gets prosecuted under the FCPA – that it is not the $5 cup of coffee, or the one-off $50 gift to a public official, that companies need to be concerned about, but payments of real and substantial value that clearly represent an unambiguous intent to bribe a foreign official to obtain or retain business.'[2] The SEC official further stated that the SEC was 'interested in companies spending compliance dollars in the most sensible way' and hoped that the Guidance and the hypotheticals provided in it would help companies decide where they can 'minimize investment and where they can maximize it.'[3] The Assistant Attorney General added that the DOJ wants compliance programs 'to address real matters of concern.'[4]

However, notwithstanding the above sensible enforcement agency guidance and statements, recent FCPA enforcement actions have involved allegations about perfume, dresses and handbags; a bottle of wine; a watch; a camera, kitchen appliances and business suits; television sets, laptops and appliances; and tea sets and office furniture.[5] To be sure, these were not the only allegations in the enforcement actions. However, one must assume that the enforcement agencies included such allegations by design and for specific reasons. Because few companies subject to the FCPA have $50 million contracts with government agencies in high-risk countries – or even any business with government agencies – the end result of such cursory and non-determinative allegations in many FCPA enforcement actions is to induce risk-averse business organizations to act contrary to the sensible enforcement agency guidance and statements described above.

FCPA compliance is also difficult for even the most well-managed and well-intentioned organizations because of the inherent realities of doing business in the global marketplace. For starters, doing business in the global marketplace requires hiring local workers who are products of different cultures and experiences, speak different languages, and are located in different time zones from corporate headquarters. While bribery is prohibited by the written laws of every country and while a suitcase full of cash to a government official to obtain or retain a government contract is a universal wrong regardless of culture, language, or experience, this is often where the consensus ends. Even with best practices compliance policies and procedures, the practical reality of monitoring and supervising this vast and diverse network of individuals is difficult and no FCPA compliance program is foolproof.

Even so, in the minds of some, 'good companies don't bribe – period.' Indeed, this was the title of a *Minneapolis StarTribune* business column which assailed those who have criticized various aspects of the FCPA. In support of the position that 'good companies don't bribe – period,' the article stated:

> The [FCPA] has established America's reputation as a strong proponent of ethical business practices abroad. As Microsoft recognizes in its anti-corruption policy: corruption promotes poverty, hunger, disease and crime, and keeps societies and individuals from reaching their full potential. Corruption is one of the leading obstacles to economic and social development. Microsoft is committed to observing the standards of conduct set forth in the [FCPA] and the anti-corruption and anti-money-laundering laws of the countries in which it operates.[6]

The absolutist position that 'good companies don't bribe – period' was undermined a few months later when it was reported that the DOJ and SEC both 'opened preliminary investigations into bribery accusations involving Microsoft in China, Italy and Romania.'[7] A Microsoft executive acknowledged the investigation and stated:

> Like other large companies with operations around the world, we sometimes receive allegations about potential misconduct by employees or business partners, and we investigate them fully regardless of the source. We also invest heavily in proactive training, monitoring and audits to ensure our business operations around the world meet the highest legal and ethical standards. [...] We are a global company with operations in 112 countries, nearly 98,000 employees and 640,000 business partners. [...] We have more than 50 people whose primary role is investigating potential breaches of company policy, and an additional 120 people whose primary role is compliance. In addition, we sometimes retain outside law firms to conduct or assist with investigations. This is a reflection of the size and complexity of our business and the seriousness with which we take meeting our obligations. We also invest in proactive measures including annual training programs for every employee, regular internal audits and multiple levels of approval for contracting and expenditure. In a company of our size, allegations of this nature will be made from time to time. It is also possible there will sometimes be individual employees or business partners who violate our policies and break the law. In a community of 98,000 people and 640,000 partners, it isn't possible to say there will never be wrongdoing.[8]

How is it that Microsoft, a company championed as a leader in ethical and compliant business conduct, became the subject of FCPA scrutiny? For the same reasons that many ethically sound business organizations have resolved FCPA enforcement actions, and for the same reasons that approximately one hundred companies are currently the subject of active FCPA scrutiny (and thousands more would be if each company hired FCPA counsel to do a thorough review of its world-wide operations). These reasons, as discussed in previous chapters, are broad concepts of corporate criminal liability and the inherent realities of doing business in the global marketplace.

Consider a typical multi-national company that employs 10,000 individuals. Even if the company engages leading compliance professionals and spends millions of dollars conducting an FCPA risk assessment and implementing FCPA compliance policies and procedures consistent with the best practices discussed later in this chapter, and even if 99% of the company's employees abide by the policy in all respects on a daily basis, this still means that 100 instances of non-compliance – and thus potential FCPA scrutiny – occur every day.

For instance, in the DOJ's FCPA prosecution of Garth Peterson, a former managing director of Morgan Stanley's real estate business in China, the DOJ stated:

> Morgan Stanley maintained a system of internal controls meant to ensure accountability for its assets and to prevent employees from offering, promising or paying anything of value to foreign government officials. Morgan Stanley's internal policies, which were updated regularly to reflect regulatory developments and specific risks, prohibited bribery and addressed corruption risks associated with the giving of gifts, business entertainment, travel, lodging, meals, charitable contributions and employment. Morgan Stanley frequently trained its employees on its internal policies, the FCPA and other anti-corruption laws. Between 2002 and 2008, Morgan Stanley trained various groups of Asia-based personnel on anti-corruption policies 54 times. During the same period, Morgan Stanley trained Peterson on the FCPA seven times and reminded him to comply with the FCPA at least 35 times. Morgan Stanley's compliance personnel regularly monitored transactions, randomly audited particular employees, transactions and business units, and tested to identify illicit payments. Moreover, Morgan Stanley conducted extensive due diligence on all new business partners and imposed stringent controls on payments made to business partners.[9]

Despite Morgan Stanley's pro-active FCPA compliance policies and procedures, the DOJ alleged that Peterson 'circumvented Morgan Stanley's internal controls in order to transfer a multi-million dollar ownership interest in a Shanghai building to himself and a Chinese public official with whom he had a personal friendship.' The DOJ specifically stated that Peterson 'actively sought to evade Morgan Stanley's internal controls,' that 'he lied and cheated his way to personal profit,' and that 'each of Peterson's [Morgan Stanley required FCPA certifications] was but another lie that lulled his employer into trusting Peterson.'[10]

As the Peterson enforcement action demonstrates, rogue employees do exist and no compliance program can ever prevent all wrongdoing by an organization's employees. Indeed, the DOJ recognizes this as a matter of policy in its U.S. Attorneys' Manual, which states that 'no compliance program can ever prevent all criminal activity by a corporation's employees.'[11] In addition, high-ranking DOJ officials have recognized that 'there will always be employees who decide to take matters into their own hands – they are a fact of life,' and that 'even the best compliance program may not stop fraud or corruption from occurring.'[12] The former Assistant Chief of the DOJ's FCPA Unit candidly stated 'most government attorneys realize that a company can take every reasonable step to prevent wrongdoing but ultimately is powerless if somebody really wants to break the law.'[13]

Consider also the frequency in which companies subject to the FCPA engage, often pursuant to foreign law requirements, various third parties when doing business in the global marketplace. As survey data in Chapter 3 highlighted, approximately 80% of U.S. companies partner with a third party when doing business abroad and the average company works with between 1,000 and 10,000 different third parties. Even if the company engages leading compliance professionals and spends millions of dollars developing and implementing FCPA best practices applicable to third parties, and even if 99% of the company's third parties abide by the policies in all respects on a daily basis, this still means that between 10 and 100 third parties are non-compliant – and thus expose the company to potential FCPA scrutiny – on a daily basis.

Consider also the number of foreign licenses or permits a company may need to secure in a foreign country in order to do business – not with the government, but just in the general sense. For instance, in order to open up a new factory in Russia, John Deere Co. first needs to obtain more than 240 certifications and inspections from Russian authorities.[14] These requirements present 240 distinct points of contact with Russian foreign officials. Even if 99% of the certifications and inspections are secured by company employees or representatives acting consistent with the company's FCPA compliance policies and procedures, this still means that two of the certifications or inspections may expose Deere to FCPA scrutiny based on the enforcement theory that payments in connection with foreign licenses and permits satisfy the FCPA's obtain or retain business element.

An FCPA practitioner stated:

> I think that companies' main frustration is that even with an outstanding compliance program and 99% of the employees maintaining strict adherence to the laws, you can still have violations which expose the entire company to extraordinarily serious penalties. I think the government has, at times, lost track of the main motivations for this statute and has become focused on the amounts of penalties, the imposition of compliance monitors, and exercising

> government control over what are basically private businesses. The vast majority of companies are absolutely committed to following the spirit and the letter of the FCPA, but when a company gets into trouble, the whole enterprise can be put at risk because of the conduct of a few people, and that doesn't seem right.[15]

In short, and as discussed previously in Chapter 2 concerning the 'world's most ethical FCPA violators,' while a certain limited number of companies do business in the global marketplace intent on engaging in bribery as a business strategy and without a commitment to FCPA compliance, the overwhelming majority of business organizations subject to the FCPA do business in the global marketplace with a commitment to FCPA compliance, yet subject to unrealistic legal standards and difficult and complex business conditions. On this issue, the insight of the former DOJ FCPA Unit chief bears repeating.

> In my almost 40 years' of experience, I have rarely seen American companies affirmatively offering bribes in the first instance; rather they are typically reacting to a world not of their making. It is a fact that corruption in government remains endemic worldwide and that is not likely to change. As the world shrinks companies who seek to do the right thing can't help but confront corrupt officials – as customers, regulators, and adjudicators – and confront them often.[16]

Also insightful is the following from FCPA practitioners, including a former DOJ FCPA enforcement attorney.

> The world of business [...] frequently operates in territory that is somewhat grey: a world in which business persons strive to grow the company ethically in situations where the application of the existing rules are not entirely clear. For instance, in the current era of FCPA enforcement, international businesses struggle with their responsibilities to monitor and control the conduct of third parties with whom they do business: distributors and sub-distributors, joint venture partners, dealers, and resellers. Even for companies that are firmly dedicated to compliance with the FCPA, it is not always clear when a third party amounts to an agent whose improper conduct might someday be ascribed to the company and its employees. Good and ethical companies struggle, every day, with the concept of defining an agent of the company as opposed to an independent customer who engages in an arm's-length transaction to purchase the company's products.[17]

Recognizing that the absolutist 'good companies don't bribe – period' position is a fallacy allows one to better understand why FCPA compliance can be difficult for even the most well-managed and well-intentioned business organizations, and why FCPA risk can't be eliminated when doing business in the global marketplace.

B. 'SOFT' ENFORCEMENT AND LEARNING FROM ENFORCEMENT ACTIONS

While FCPA risk can not be eliminated, it can be effectively managed and minimized when doing business in the global marketplace, and one positive result of the increase in FCPA enforcement in this new era has been the related increase in 'soft' enforcement of the FCPA through compliance policies and procedures.

As distinguished from 'hard' enforcement of a law by enforcement agencies, 'soft' enforcement generally refers to a law's ability to facilitate self-policing and compliance to a greater degree than can be accomplished through 'hard' enforcement alone. Those subject to such a law, whether a traffic law or otherwise, comply with the law's prohibitions because they could be found to be in violation of the law, even though the prospect of 'hard' detection and enforcement of the violation is low. Indeed, one of the most notable statements from the FCPA's legislative history was made by the Chairman of Lockheed who stated:

> So it is true that we knew about the practice of payments on some occasions to foreign officials. But so did everyone else who was at all knowledgeable about foreign sales. There were no U.S. rules or laws which banned the practice or made it illegal. [...] If Congress passes laws dealing with commissions and direct or indirect payments to foreign officials in other countries, Lockheed, of course, will fully comply with them.[18]

In passing the FCPA, Congress anticipated that the 'criminalization of foreign corporate bribery will to a significant extent act as a self-enforcing preventative mechanism.'[19] Likewise since the FCPA's earliest days, the DOJ has recognized that the 'most efficient means of implementing the FCPA is voluntary compliance by the American business community.'[20] In this regard, a former DOJ prosecutor responsible for investigating and prosecuting FCPA cases rightly observed that 'this new era of more aggressive [FCPA] prosecution has, in turn, encouraged corporations to pay even greater attention to their internal compliance programs, matching the "hard" enforcement with "soft" enforcement.'[21]

In its 2002 review of U.S. enforcement of the FCPA, the OECD reported 'the commonly-held view among the members of the Bar who met with the examiners was that the reputation for aggressive pursuit that the Fraud Section of the DOJ has developed over the years has been a major factor in deterring companies from bribery.'[22] The OECD report further stated:

> An important effect of the FCPA is that it encourages the development of compliance programs. According to one member of the Bar with a specialist FCPA practice, corporate compliance programs are the single most important measure contributing to prevention and deterrence. [...] Compliance programs are by now well-developed and well-understood among large public companies, especially those operating in risk-averse industry sectors such as defense procurement, and others involved in government contracting for which there are stringent standards of eligibility and the risk of disbarment. The indirect or collateral damage that would be inflicted on such companies by an indictment for violation of the FCPA of itself operates as a powerful incentive to enforce compliance throughout the entire organization.

Likewise, in its 2010 review of U.S. enforcement of the FCPA, the OECD stated:

> In meetings with ... private sector representatives, of which the vast majority were large multi-national companies, it was clear that serious efforts have been taken to ensure effective compliance with the FCPA. These companies have a high level of sensitivity to risk areas, and what needs to be done to address them. Across the board, these companies cited active enforcement by the DOJ and the SEC, in particular recently imposed large financial penalties, as the main thrust for putting into place these measures. [...] Overall, the evaluators believe that the heightened concern has had a very positive impact on the development of corporate controls in the United States, and thereby the prevention and detection of foreign bribery.[23]

Even the failed Africa Sting action – a case with irreversible negative effects on the individuals charged and in the words of the presiding judge 'a long and sad chapter in the annals of white collar criminal enforcement' – had a positive 'soft' enforcement effect. As previously discussed, the enforcement action targeted executives and employees of companies (mostly small- to medium-size enterprises – 'SMEs') in the military and law enforcement products industry. Prior to the enforcement action, FCPA compliance was likely not on the radar screen of many industry participants. However, after the enforcement action, at the industry 'SHOT Show' in Las Vegas (the same event at which the majority of individuals were arrested in 2010), FCPA compliance made the event agenda. Event participants were given the opportunity to take a Global Anti-Corruption Course and the conference sponsor's release stated:

> If your company will be exhibiting at SHOT Show, now is a great time for you and your employees to learn how to steer clear of violating anti-bribery

> and anti-corruption laws when speaking with potential customers. The penalties for violating the FCPA are too great for you and your employees not to take the course or for your business not to have an FCPA compliance program.[24]

The Africa Sting action also had a positive 'soft' enforcement effect beyond the military and law enforcement products industry by causing many SMEs to think more proactively about FCPA compliance and risk assessment. As noted in the OECD's 2010 report, a 'recent "sting operation" involving mid-sized firms was also believed to have had a significant impact, particularly on SMEs, making them more aware of the need for effective compliance.'[25]

The increase in FCPA enforcement has also resulted in more information in the public domain regarding the DOJ and SEC's enforcement theories and compliance expectations including through publicly available NPAs and DPAs. Although, as discussed in Chapter 2, these agreements do not represent precedent, nor in all instances necessarily represent conduct that Congress sought to capture in enacting the FCPA and are thus problematic for many reasons, and although the same objective could be achieved through other charging documents, it is nevertheless true that these agreements do provide insight into the enforcement agencies' enforcement theories and compliance expectations.

Indeed, the DOJ has stated: 'DPAs and NPAs benefit the public and industries by providing guidance on what constitutes improper conduct. […] Because the agreements typically provide a recitation of the improper conduct at issue, the agreements can serve as an educational tool for other companies in a particular industry.'[26]

In this way, certain FCPA enforcement actions provide an opportunity to learn from other compliance failures and represent teachable moments. For instance, the FCPA enforcement action against medical device company Orthofix International concerned conduct by employees of its indirect wholly-owned subsidiary responsible for sales in Latin America and allegations that the employees paid Mexican officials to induce the officials to purchase company product.[27] The resolution documents alleged, under the heading 'Internal Controls,' as follows.

> Orthofix International, which grew its direct distribution footprint in part by purchasing existing companies, often in high-risk markets, failed to engage in any serious form of corruption-related diligence before it purchased [the subsidiary]. Although Orthofix International promulgated its own anti-corruption policy, that policy was neither translated into Spanish nor implemented at [the subsidiary]. Orthofix International failed to provide any

> FCPA-related training to many of its personnel [...] Orthofix also failed to train [subsidiary] personnel for years on the FCPA, to test regularly or audit particular transactions, or to ensure that its subsidiary maintained controls sufficient to detect, deter or prevent illicit payments to government officials.

The compliance message from the Orthofix enforcement action would seem to be clear: (i) FCPA-specific due diligence ought to be a part of merger and acquisition due diligence; (ii) a parent company's FCPA compliance policies and procedures including internal controls ought to be incorporated into acquired companies and implemented throughout the corporate hierarchy; and (iii) such policies and procedures ought to be translated into local languages and employees ought to be trained on them.

The FCPA enforcement action against Halliburton and its affiliated entities concerning Bonny Island, Nigeria conduct likewise provide teachable moments concerning the engagement, monitoring, and supervision of foreign agents. Entities within Halliburton's corporate organization were part of a joint venture that hired agents to assist in winning lucrative contracts and the alleged bribery scheme focused on U.K. and Japanese agents hired by the joint venture. The SEC alleged that Halliburton, as the parent company of the relevant entities, failed to devise adequate FCPA internal controls relating to foreign agents and failed to maintain and enforce even the internal controls it had.[28] The SEC acknowledged that Halliburton's legal department conducted a due diligence investigation of the U.K. agent, but it alleged that the due diligence was inadequate because Halliburton's policies did not require a specific description of the agent's duties and because the agent did not agree to any accounting or audit of fees received. The SEC also alleged that company attorneys never learned the identity of the owners of a consulting company used by the U.K. agent and did not check all of the agent's references, some of which turned out to be false. As to the Japanese agent, the SEC alleged that Halliburton conducted no due diligence and that Halliburton's policies and procedures were deficient because the agreement with the agent was not properly scrutinized.

Although the SEC's complaint made no mention of Halliburton having any knowledge that the agents would use money obtained from the joint venture to bribe Nigerian officials, Halliburton's FCPA books and records and internal controls liability was based on: (i) its control and supervision of the entity participating in the joint venture; and (ii) its insufficient due diligence of the joint venture agents.

The compliance message from the Halliburton enforcement action would likewise seem to be clear: (i) it is not enough to conduct some due diligence on foreign agents operating in high-risk jurisdiction; rather, the due diligence must be thorough, comprehensive, and designed to uncover FCPA issues; and (ii) a parent company should employ best practices due diligence not just to its own agents, but also to agents engaged by all subsidiaries and affiliates over which the parent company exercises control and supervision.

Although the compliance messages from the above Orthofix and Halliburton enforcement actions would seem to be obvious even in the absence of those enforcement actions, sometimes it takes a public airing of a company's alleged compliance failures for competitors or those in the same industry to take notice and make improvements to their own FCPA policies and procedures.

In short, one positive result of the increase in FCPA enforcement in this new era has been the related increase in 'soft' enforcement of the FCPA and the opportunity to learn from alleged compliance shortcomings at other companies.

Indeed, actual FCPA enforcement actions against peer companies have served as the impetus for other companies to conduct FCPA risk assessments and uncover potential issues which have resulted in FCPA scrutiny or enforcement actions. For instance, Wal-Mart's FCPA scrutiny was the result of a pro-active internal review conducted by the company after Wal-Mart's general counsel learned of an FCPA enforcement action against Tyson Foods – like Wal-Mart, a company headquartered in Arkansas.[29] Similarly, an FCPA enforcement action against Watts Water Technologies that focused on alleged payments made by the company's wholly-owned Chinese subsidiary to employees of Chinese design institutes was prompted by a prior similar FCPA enforcement. The SEC's order stated:

> Watts' General Counsel learned of a [SEC] enforcement action against another company that involved unlawful payments to employees of Chinese design institutes. Because Watts' senior management in the U.S. knew that [the subsidiary's] customers included state-owned enterprises, Watts implemented anti-corruption and FCPA training for its Chinese subsidiaries. [...] [F]ollowing FCPA training sessions for certain management of Watts China, Watts China's in-house corporate counsel became aware of potential FCPA violations at [the subsidiary] through conversations with [subsidiary] sales personnel who were participating in the training. Shortly thereafter, the in-house lawyer notified Watts' management in the U.S. of the potential violations. Watts [then] retained outside counsel to conduct an internal investigation of [the subsidiary's] sales practices. Watts' outside counsel subsequently retained forensic accountants to assist with the investigation [and] Watts self-reported its internal investigation to the [SEC].[30]

C. MANAGING AND MINIMIZING FCPA RISK

FCPA compliance of course is not a one-size-fits-all proposition. Rather effective and cost-efficient FCPA compliance is best achieved through conducting a risk assessment. This section highlights the basic fundamentals of conducting a risk assessment so that compliance can be uniquely tailored to a company's FCPA risk profile. From there, this section highlights various best practices designed to manage and minimize FCPA risk. This section concludes by demonstrating that FCPA compliance is best achieved holistically throughout a business organization by training a wide variety of non-legal personnel so that they can approach their job functions with FCPA goggles and recognize FCPA risk and report it to appropriate experts within the organization.

Conducting a Risk Assessment

Prior to implementing FCPA policies or procedures, a business organization should conduct a risk assessment. In fact, conducting a risk assessment is the first step in following FCPA compliance best practices. An FCPA risk assessment should generally focus on the unique circumstances of the company such as the foreign bribery risks facing the company given its geographical footprint; interactions with various types and levels of foreign officials; industrial sectors of operation; degree of governmental oversight and inspection; and volume and importance of goods and personnel clearing through customs and immigration.

Set forth below, in question format, are certain basic fundamentals of conducting an FCPA risk assessment.

- In which countries does the company do business? As to each country, what is the country's reputation for corruption?
- Who are the company's customers or potential customers in each country? Is the customer a government (whether federal, state, or local) or a government department, agency or instrumentality? Does a government department, agency, or instrumentality, or individual associated with such units, have an ownership or equity interest in the customer?
- How does the company do business and/or interact with customers or potential customers in the country? Does the company use third parties in the foreign countries?
- How does the company's product enter and exit the country? Does the company use the services of a customs broker or freight forwarder?

- What licenses, permits, or certifications does the company need to do business in the country? As to each license, permit or certification, how does the company obtain such approvals?
- Is the company subject to other unique forms of government regulation in the country? What other points of contact does the company have with foreign government in the country (such as tax and immigration authorities)?

The answers to these questions will be different for a defense contractor compared to an industrial manufacturer, but will best allow each company to prioritize its FCPA risk areas and thus adopt unique FCPA policies and procedures tailored to its risk.

In addition to the above questions, a useful question that should be asked in connection with an FCPA risk assessment is the following: 'An FCPA violation is occurring today in the company – where do you think it is occurring and why do you think it is occurring?' The answer – whether it focuses on the country and the business conditions in that country, the third party utilized in the country, or the company's personnel in that country – can help a company prioritize its FCPA compliance policies and procedures to the most-needed aspects of its business.

After conducting an FCPA risk assessment, a business organization can best tailor its FCPA policies and procedures to the company's unique FCPA risk profile and in doing so can find guidance in the below best practices.

Compliance Best Practices

The FCPA best practices and benchmarking metrics discussed in this section are primarily derived from five sources: (i) FCPA Guidance issued by the DOJ and SEC; (ii) FCPA NPAs and DPAs; (iii) the DOJ's Principles of Prosecution of Business Organizations; (iv) the U.S. Sentencing Guidelines; and (v) OECD Guidance.

The 2012 FCPA Guidance contains a section titled 'Hallmarks of Effective Compliance Programs.' The DOJ's Principles of Prosecution contain a section titled 'Corporate Compliance Programs.' The 2012 Sentencing Guidelines contain a section titled 'Effective Compliance and Ethics Program.' While the Sentencing Guidelines are not FCPA specific, the section contains metrics relevant to certain corporate governance issues in maintaining an effective compliance and ethics program.[31] The 2010 OECD Good Practice Guidance on Internal Controls, Ethics, and Compliance 'is addressed to companies for establishing and ensuring the effectiveness of internal controls, ethics, and compliance programs or measures for preventing and detecting the bribery of foreign public officials in their international business transactions.'[32]

After providing a comprehensive topical aggregation of these sources (Table 8.1), additional best practices and benchmarking metrics are highlighted relevant to third parties and customer travel and entertainment.

Table 8.1 FCPA best practices

Implementation of a program	Based on the company's risk assessment, a company should: (i) Implement an anti-corruption compliance code, policies, and procedures designed to detect and deter violations of the FCPA and other applicable anti-corruption laws; (ii) Implement a system of internal accounting controls designed to ensure that the company makes and keeps fair and accurate books, records, and accounts. The above policies and procedures should be in a written form, clearly articulated, accessible throughout the company and translated into relevant local languages.
High-level commitment	A company should ensure that its directors and senior managers are knowledgeable about the FCPA policies and procedures and that they provide strong, explicit, and visible support and commitment to the policies and procedures. A company should take appropriate measures to encourage and support observance of the policies and procedures by all individuals at all levels of the company.
Oversight	A company should assign responsibility to one or more senior managers for the implementation and oversight of the FCPA policies and procedures. Such managers should have direct reporting obligations to independent monitoring bodies, including internal audit, the company's Board of Directors, or any appropriate committee of the Board, and should have an adequate level of autonomy from management as well as sufficient resources and authority to maintain such autonomy.
Application	The FCPA policies and procedures should apply to all directors, officers, and employees of the company and where necessary and appropriate, outside parties acting on behalf of the company in a foreign jurisdiction including but not limited to agents and intermediaries, consultants, representatives, teaming partners, contractors and suppliers, consortia, and all joint venture partners (collectively 'third parties').

Specific policies and procedures	Policies and procedures should address: (i) gifts; (ii) hospitality, entertainment, and expenses; (iii) customer travel; (iv) political contributions; (v) charitable donations and sponsorships; (vi) facilitation payments; and (vii) solicitation and extortion. Financial and accounting policies and procedures should be reasonably designed to provide reasonable assurances that: (i) transactions are executed in accordance with management's general or specific authorization; (ii) transactions are recorded as necessary to permit preparation of financial statements in conformity with generally accepted accounting principles and to maintain accountability for assets; (iii) access to assets is permitted only in accordance with management's general or specific authorization; and (iv) the recorded accountability of assets is compared with the existing assets at reasonable intervals and appropriate action is taken with respect to any differences.
Training and guidance	A company should implement mechanisms to ensure that its FCPA policies and procedures are effectively communicated to all directors, officers, employees, and, where necessary and appropriate, third parties. The mechanisms should include: (i) periodic training for all directors and officers, all employees in positions of leadership or trust, positions that require such training (such as internal audit, sales, legal, compliance, finance), or positions that otherwise pose a corruption risk to the company, and, where necessary and appropriate, third parties; (ii) annual certifications by all such directors, officers, employees, and third parties certifying compliance with the training requirements. A company should maintain an effective system for providing guidance and advice to directors, officers, employees, and, where necessary and appropriate, third parties on complying with the FCPA policies and procedures, including when such persons need advice on an urgent basis or in any foreign jurisdiction in which the company operates.

Third parties	A company should institute appropriate due diligence and compliance requirements pertaining to the retention and oversight of all third parties including: (i) properly documented risk-based due diligence pertaining to the hiring and appropriate and regular oversight of third parties; (ii) informing third parties of the company's commitment to FCPA compliance; and (iii) seeking a reciprocal commitment from third parties. Where necessary and appropriate, a company should include standard provisions in third-party agreements, contracts, and renewals that are reasonably calculated to prevent violations of the FCPA. Depending on the circumstances, such provisions should include: (i) representations and undertakings relating to the FCPA; (ii) rights to conduct audits of the books and records of the third party; and (iii) rights to terminate the third party as a result of any breach of the company's FCPA policies and procedures or the representations and undertaking related to such matters.
Mergers and acquisitions	A company should develop specific policies and procedures for mergers and acquisitions requiring that the company conduct appropriate risk-based due diligence on potential new business entities. A company should ensure that its FCPA policies and procedures apply as quickly as practicable to newly acquired businesses or entities merged with the company. A company should also promptly: (i) train the directors, officers, employees, and third parties on the company's FCPA policies and procedures; and (ii) conduct an FCPA-specific audit of all newly acquired or merged businesses as quickly as practicable.
Internal reporting and investigation	A company should maintain an effective system for internal, and where possible, confidential reporting by directors, officers, employees, and where appropriate, third parties concerning violations of the company's FCPA policies and procedures. A company should maintain an effective and reliable process with sufficient resources for responding to, investigating, and documenting allegations of violations of the company's FCPA policies and procedures.

Enforcement and discipline	A company should implement mechanisms designed to effectively enforce its FCPA compliance policies and procedures, including appropriately incentivizing compliance. Such incentives could include personnel evaluations and promotions, rewards for improving and developing a company's policies and procedures, and rewards for ethics and compliance leadership.
	A company should implement appropriate disciplinary procedures to address, among other things, violations of the company's FCPA policies and procedures by the company's directors, officers, and employees. Such procedures should be applied consistently and fairly, regardless of the position held by, or perceived importance of, the director, officer, or employee. The company should implement procedures to ensure that where misconduct is discovered, reasonable steps are taken to remedy the harm resulting from such misconduct and to ensure that appropriate steps are taken to prevent further similar misconduct, including assessing the FCPA policies and procedures and making modifications necessary to ensure that the overall policies and procedures are effective.
Review, monitoring and testing	A company should review its FCPA policies and procedures no less than annually and update them as appropriate to ensure continued effectiveness, taking into account relevant developments in the field and evolving international and industry standards.

The FCPA best practices shown in Table 8.1 will surely not eliminate FCPA risk within a business organization – no compliance program can achieve such an unrealistic result – but implementing the above best practices and monitoring them for effectiveness can effectively manage and minimize FCPA risk.

Although the above best practices are presented as FCPA specific, such policies and procedures can also help reduce other instances of improper conduct within a business organization. As the FCPA Guidance rightly notes, 'good internal controls can prevent not only FCPA violations, but also other illegal or unethical conduct by the company, its subsidiaries, and its employees' such as financial fraud, commercial bribery, export controls violations, and embezzlement or self-dealing by company employees. Likewise, the SEC Chairman has noted:

> Corrupt practices by [an issuer] are generally indicators of larger problems within the business – problems with the potential to harm that business's shareholder-owners. Bribery and other corrupt practices may result in accounting fraud and falsified disclosures where shareholders are not getting

> an accurate picture of a company's finances in their regulatory filings. Bribery means losing control of – or deliberately falsifying – books and records. Often, key executives or board members are kept in the dark, limiting their ability to make informed decisions about the company's business. Obviously, engaging in corrupt practices means weakening or circumventing internal control mechanisms, leaving a company less able to detect and end not just corruption but other questionable practices. A company that has lost its moral compass is in grave danger of losing its competitive roadmap, as well – while shareholders are kept in the dark.[33]

In addition to the above FCPA best practices, it is often necessary for a business organization, depending on its unique FCPA-risk profile, to have additional specific policies and procedures concerning, at a minimum, third parties and travel and entertainment expenses. After all, engagement of third parties and customer travel and entertainment are common in today's business environment and perfectly acceptable and legal in most instances. Yet, as demonstrated by several enforcement actions throughout this book, such business practices often give rise to FCPA scrutiny and liability.

Third parties

As discussed in Chapter 3, companies are most often exposed to FCPA enforcement actions or scrutiny based on the conduct of third parties. The FCPA does not impose absolute liability on a company for the actions of its third parties. However, the FCPA's broad knowledge standard, coupled with the enforcement agencies' aggressive interpretation of the standard, typically make engagement of third parties the greatest source of FCPA risk for any company.

For this reason, it is often necessary for a company to have specific policies and procedures regarding pre-engagement, engagement, and post-engagement of third parties.

Pre-engagement

Prior to engaging a foreign third party, a company should: (i) require the third party to complete a detailed FCPA questionnaire; (ii) have the third party execute an FCPA acknowledgment letter; and (iii) use these materials and other information to assemble a complete and thorough due diligence file on the third party.

The FCPA questionnaire should be designed to illicit information capable of identifying certain FCPA 'red flags.' At a minimum, the third party should provide: (i) contact information for its owners/principals and board of directors, including percentage of ownership by each, and other businesses in which each might have an interest; (ii) information on related companies; (iii) business, banking, and credit references; (iv) a detailed description of its qualifications, experience, and services; and (v) disclosure of any relationships with current or former foreign officials or political parties.

The FCPA acknowledgement letter to the prospective third party should explain the FCPA's requirements and the company's commitment to FCPA compliance. The purpose of the acknowledgment letter is to make clear to the prospective third party during the initial negotiation phase that the company takes FCPA compliance seriously and that it will expect the same from the third party.

In addition to a completed FCPA questionnaire and an executed FCPA acknowledgement letter, an FCPA due diligence file on each third party should be created and maintained. The file should include, at a minimum: (i) a discussion of how the company learned of the third party; (ii) a description of the third party's fee, commission, or payment structure and how the financial terms of the relationship compare to typical terms in the industry and country; (iii) a summary of the company's due diligence efforts; and (iv) a list of company personnel or counsel who performed specific due diligence activities.

The due diligence report should also discuss: (i) why the third party's services are necessary and whether its fees are reasonable; (ii) the third party's business experience and qualifications; (iii) a summary of the third party's business, banking, and credit references; and (iv) identification and resolution of any FCPA red flags.

Common FCPA red flags relevant to third parties may include: (i) the third party places reliance on political/government contacts, as opposed to knowledgeable staff and investment of time, to promote company interests; (ii) the third party is related or otherwise connected to a foreign official; (iii) the third party is unwilling to agree in writing to abide by the FCPA and other relevant laws; (iv) the third party is requesting payment to an account outside its home jurisdiction; (v) the third party is unwilling to agree in writing to subject its books and records to audit by the company; (vi) the third party wants to keep its relationship with the company secret; (vii) the third party has had unexplained or inadequately explained breakups or other relationship problems with other companies; and (viii) the third-party has engaged in other suspicious conduct that would raise questions in the eyes of a reasonable person.

An affirmative answer to any one of these issues does not, in and of itself, suggest that a foreign third party is corrupt or likely to make improper payments to a 'foreign official' on behalf of the company. However, an affirmative answer to any one of these issues should trigger concern and a more thorough review prior to engaging the third party.

Engagement

All relationships with third parties should be memorialized in a written agreement; however, deficient FCPA due diligence is not remedied solely by a written agreement including language prohibiting the third party from violating the FCPA.

At a minimum, a company's written agreement with a third party should specifically describe the services the third party is going to perform. In addition, a company should also consider including the following provisions in its written contract with a third party: (i) third-party representations and warranties that it will abide by the company's FCPA compliance policies and procedures, that it is not owned or controlled by a foreign government department, agency or instrumentality, and that no foreign official holds an ownership interest in it; (ii) the right of the company to audit, at its discretion, the third party's books and records; (iii) the right of the company to terminate the business relationship if it has a good-faith belief that the third party has made improper payments; and (iv) the right of the company to disclose the third party's conduct to U.S. enforcement agencies.

Post-engagement

Monitoring and supervision of a third party should continue while the third party is engaged by the company. At a minimum, a company should have each of its third parties certify, on an annual basis, that it is in compliance and will continue to comply with the company's FCPA policies and procedures. In addition, any red flags that arise during the relationship with the third party should be investigated and the relationship reevaluated based on the results.

Like other aspects of FCPA compliance, the above third-party policies and procedures will not eliminate the FCPA risks of utilizing third parties in foreign countries. However, adherence to the above best practices will best position a company should a third party ever expose it to FCPA scrutiny.

Customer travel and entertainment

Like engagement of third parties, customer travel and entertainment are common in today's business environment and perfectly acceptable and legal in most instances. Yet, as demonstrated by several FCPA enforcement actions, travel and entertainment expenses can easily morph into conduct giving rise to FCPA liability in the eyes of the enforcement agencies. Further, as noted by an FCPA practitioner, even though excessive travel and entertainment expenditures seldom yield high-penalty FCPA enforcements, 'a disproportionate number of enforcement matters ultimately resulting in a high penalty for bribes unrelated to gifts/meals/travel/entertainment had their genesis in marketing/promotion expenses that soon turned out to be the "tip of the iceberg" revealing more extensive and substantial corruption.'[34] The practitioner noted:

> Companies who focus on keeping a clean FCPA house in the gifts/meals/entertainment/travel part of the statute stand a better chance of keeping big problems from occurring elsewhere among the statute's danger zones, both because it sends a strong 'tone from the top' and because it keeps small problems from going undetected until they've morphed into big ones.

Accordingly, it is often prudent for a business organization to have specific policies and procedures concerning payment of customer travel and entertainment expenses. The FCPA Guidance sets forth the following 'non-exhaustive list of safeguards' in evaluating 'whether a particular expenditure is appropriate or may risk violating the FCPA.'

- Do not select the particular officials who will participate in the party's proposed trip or program or else select them based on pre-determined, merit-based criteria.
- Pay all costs directly to travel and lodging vendors and/or reimburse costs only upon presentation of a receipt.
- Do not advance funds or pay for reimbursements in cash.
- Ensure that any stipends are reasonable approximations of costs likely to be incurred and/or that expenses are limited to those that are necessary and reasonable.
- Ensure the expenditures are transparent, both within the company and to the foreign government.
- Do not condition payment of expenses on any action by the foreign official.
- Obtain written confirmation that payment of the expenses is not contrary to local law.
- Provide no additional compensation, stipends, or spending money beyond what is necessary to pay for actual expenses incurred.
- Ensure that costs and expenses on behalf of the foreign officials will be accurately recorded in the company's books and records.

The Importance of FCPA 'Goggles'

As highlighted above, training is an essential component of an FCPA compliance program. However, not all FCPA training is equal, and before plowing ahead with FCPA training a company ought to pause and reflect on the most appropriate way to deliver FCPA training.

The first issue to address is who to include in FCPA training. Officers, directors, employees in high-risk job functions such as sales and marketing, and third parties are obvious candidates for FCPA training. However, because many instances of FCPA scrutiny arise from seemingly mundane corporate tasks such as securing foreign licenses and permits or interacting with customs and immigration officials, it is critical that company employees who perform these routine tasks are also included in FCPA training. In addition, it is important to include administrative assistants in FCPA training. While such individuals may not have direct contact with foreign officials or have decision-making authority in the company, these individuals are often most familiar with corporate channels of communications and can spot and identify FCPA risk at early stages if properly trained.

A second issue to address before conducting FCPA training is how to actually deliver the training. The goal of FCPA training should not be to make each participant an expert on the FCPA's specific elements, but rather to provide each participant a pair of FCPA goggles so that they can approach their specific job function able to recognize FCPA risk and report it to the appropriate experts within the organization.

An FCPA practitioner provided the following insight regarding his experience with business managers:

> Despite sitting through a couple of PowerPoint slides about the FCPA during a compliance training, the managers did not understand how and where bribery occurs. I'd be interviewing the manager of a company's foreign operations in a high risk country and have a stack of documents to go through with him. I'd ask him a series of questions about some fairly run-of-the-mill issues – why certain dinners occurred with some government officials, what the thousand dollars of 'miscellaneous' expenses on a hotel bill were for, whether the manager ever saw any of the holiday gifts he approved a large budget for – and it would often become clear to me that the manager had no idea that I was asking him about possible bribes. It had simply never occurred to him that there could be FCPA risks associated with any of these kinds of expenses. And those kinds of blind spots existed with managers who supposedly had received FCPA training. Numerous times people have told me that they remember the FCPA training they had, but that they never thought the Act applied to the kinds of expenses I'm asking them about.[35]

In this regard, the first few minutes of FCPA training is critical to the success of the training, and the trainer needs to properly set the tone and engage participants at their level. If the trainer starts off an FCPA training session as follows – 'today I will be talking about a U.S. law that makes it a crime to bribe foreign government officials to get business' – the trainer has likely lost a good portion of the audience and, regardless of what is said during the rest of the training session, the training session will not be as successful as it could have been.

Crime? The participant in the second row has a clean record and wouldn't hurt a fly. He coaches his son's soccer team and worships on the weekend and is thinking to himself, 'I have never committed a crime and I don't intend to – what does this FCPA training session have to do with me?'

Government? The job responsibilities of the participant in the first row does not result in any contact or communication with government officials and she is thinking, 'does this company even do business with foreign governments – what does this FCPA training session have to do with me?'

Business? The logistics manager from outside the U.S. who was flown in for the FCPA training session is thinking, 'business – I'm not a sales and marketing guy, I just make sure our product gets into and out of the country and I occasionally help secure various licenses and permits for the company – what does this FCPA training session have to do with me?'

To avoid having the minds of training participants wander this way during the first few minutes of FCPA training, it may be more effective to start an FCPA training session as follows:

> Today, I will be talking about a U.S. law that applies to all of you – regardless of whether you are in the sales and marketing department, the executive office suite, the finance and audit department, or the logistics department. This law can cover a wide range of conduct the company engages in when doing business in the global marketplace. Your understanding of this law and how it may relate to your specific job function will best ensure that the company remains compliant with this law and is able to achieve its business objectives.

In short, not all FCPA training is equal. The most successful way to manage and minimize FCPA risk in a company through training is to provide each participant a pair of FCPA goggles so that they can then use the goggles in their specific job function to recognize FCPA risk. This is best accomplished not through endless and detailed PowerPoint slides, but case studies and role-playing exercises and question and answer sessions. While web-based training is often the most cost- and time-efficient way to reach a company's global work force, such training often fails to capture the beneficial aspects of live in-person FCPA training.

To best manage and minimize FCPA risk, it is also important that a company not view FCPA compliance as strictly a legal function, but rather a function best achieved holistically throughout a company. This requires finance and audit professionals to have FCPA goggles so that they can recognize FCPA risk in their job functions.

It is clear from recent FCPA enforcement actions that the enforcement agencies, and the SEC in particular, expect much from finance and audit professionals when it comes to FCPA compliance including the ability to spot FCPA issues and display a high degree of intellectual curiosity as to many company transactions and expenditures.

For instance, in the York International enforcement action, the SEC alleged:

> (i) 'York International's management had the ability to review or cause internal audit to review [the problematic contracts] and, had this been done, it would have been immediately apparent that the consultancy agreements were a sham'; and (ii) it was 'clear that local finance personnel did not provide an independent internal control function, but rather acquiesced in questionable practices and documentation without critical review.'[36]

In the Eli Lilly enforcement action, the SEC alleged:

> Despite an understanding that certain emerging markets were most vulnerable to FCPA violations, Lilly's audit department … had no procedures specifically designed to assess the FCPA or bribery risks of sales and purchases. Accordingly, transactions with off-shore entities or with government-affiliated entities did not receive specialized or closer review for possible FCPA violations. In assessing these transactions, the auditors relied upon the standard accounting controls which primarily assured the soundness of the paperwork. There was little done to assess whether, despite the existence of facially acceptable paperwork, the surrounding circumstances or terms of a transaction suggested the possibility of an FCPA violation or bribery.[37]

Likewise, in the AGCO enforcement action, the SEC alleged that:

> (i) the 'accrual account [where the kickback payments were recorded] was created by AGCO Ltd.'s marketing staff with virtually no oversight from AGCO Ltd.'s finance department'; (ii) 'no one questioned the existence of the dual accounts'; (iii) 'no one questioned why the [accrual account] contained approximately ten percent of the contract value despite the fact that there was no contract in place requiring that such ten percent be paid to the ministry or anyone else'; and (iv) 'when the finance department authorized payments from the [accrual account], it did not ask for or receive any proof of service to warrant the payments.'[38]
>
> Given the enforcement agencies' expectations, and just as importantly because of the critical role non-legal personnel can play in assisting in FCPA compliance, it is important to specifically train finance and audit professionals

to approach their job functions with FCPA goggles on so that they are able to recognize FCPA risk. At a minimum, finance and audit professionals should:

- Understand the broad interpretations given to the 'anything of value,' 'foreign official,' and 'obtain or retain business' elements of an FCPA anti-bribery violation and clearly understand that conduct other than a 'suitcase full of cash to a government official to get a government contract' is problematic.
- Be aware of the FCPA's third-party payment provisions and be able to spot and follow up on the previously identified FCPA red flags relevant to third parties. Specifically, to look for evidence that the third party actually provided legitimate value-added services before payment is made on the invoice by the company.
- Understand who within the company, the relevant business unit, etc. has the authority to authorize payments that present FCPA risk and make sure those authorizations are scrutinized. Because of title, prestige, and in some countries gender, certain individuals are subjected to less oversight and scrutiny when authorizing payments.
- Pay particular attention to employee reimbursement requests and identify FCPA issues in connection with these requests. For instance, if a specific sales and marketing employee is the designated 'wine and dine' person, is there any heightened scrutiny of that individual's reimbursement requests?
- Pay particular attention to various vague or ambiguous accounts such as the following, all of which have been identified in FCPA enforcement actions to conceal improper payments: 'additional assessments,' 'extra costs,' 'extraordinary expenses,' 'urgent processing,' 'urgent dispatch,' 'customs processing,' 'importation advances.'

Finance and audit professionals clearly have an FCPA-compliance role to play, and the enforcement agencies clearly expect such professionals to play that role. However, finance and audit professionals can only raise FCPA issues if they first know what FCPA issues to look for in their job functions. Thus, providing finance and audit professionals with a pair of FCPA goggles can go a long way in helping to achieve FCPA compliance within a business organization.

As detailed in this section, FCPA compliance can be difficult for even the most well-managed and well-intentioned business organization. The above FCPA best practices will not eliminate FCPA risk within a business organization – no compliance program can achieve such an unrealistic result – but implementing the above best practices and monitoring them for effectiveness can effectively manage and minimize FCPA risk.

A fitting conclusion to this section concerning FCPA compliance and risk assessment is the following advice from Trace International.

> Remember, perfection is neither possible nor necessary. When devising a compliance plan, it's important to remind oneself of the big picture. A company need not break the bank to have a compliance program that follows accepted best practices. [...] [T]here are various ways that good compliance can be affordable. And companies are not responsible for developing full-proof compliance programs; they only need to develop programs proportionate to the risk they face, with the understanding that no program will completely eliminate all risk from the equation. Unlike in other areas of business, when it comes to compliance, being in the middle of the pack is okay.[39]

D. POTENTIAL NEGATIVE EFFECTS OF TOO MUCH FCPA COMPLIANCE

Even though more FCPA compliance is one positive result of this new era, certain aspects of FCPA enforcement have resulted in wasteful overcompliance by companies subject to the FCPA. In addition, a potential negative effect of too much FCPA compliance can be compliance fatigue and its unintended negative consequence of numbing individuals to the FCPA. Both of these issues are examined in this section.

Wasteful Overcompliance

Much has been written how statutes with uncertain terms coupled with sparse judicial interpretation can result in overcompliance. When the statute is a criminal statute, such as the FCPA, the risk of overcompliance is greatest and it has been noted:

> Because the current corporate criminal liability standard is so broad and the collateral consequences of a criminal indictment are so devastating, entities will attempt to avoid formal charges ex ante by investing in 'compliance' products intended to impress prosecutors in the future, even if these programs are more costly than effective.[40]

The FCPA would seem to be 'Exhibit A' for how a criminal law with ambiguous terms, coupled with sparse judicial interpretation, can result in overcompliance and its unintended negative consequence.

As previously noted in Chapter 1 concerning a 1980 Executive Branch report, soon after passage of the FCPA, attorneys were found to be giving cautious guidance 'that their clients simply forego any transactions where the FCPA could possibly become an issue,' and it was found that 'even where a company is totally convinced that a court would find that it had not violated the FCPA, it nonetheless may forego the export opportunity for fear that an enforcement agency could publicly charge it with a violation of the Act.'[41]

Fast forward to this new era, and such concerns remain and are more prominent given the extent of international business activity. For instance, following the Senate's 2010 FCPA hearing, Senators Amy Klobuchar and Christopher Coons stated in a letter to the Attorney General as follows.

> It has become apparent that too many companies are devoting a disproportionate amount of resources to FCPA compliance and internal investigations. To be clear, it is both necessary and desirable that companies pay adequate attention to compliance efforts, and in certain cases, adequate anti-corruption initiatives may require a significant corporate commitment. Over-compliance, however, can have a negative effect on product development, export promotion, and workforce expansion.[42]

In addition to the negative business effects of FCPA scrutiny and enforcement discussed in Chapter 7, an additional, yet seldom discussed negative business effect of this new era of FCPA enforcement is wasteful overcompliance by business organizations.

To be sure, any company competing in the global marketplace should address FCPA risk and implement FCPA policies and procedures specifically tailored to the company's unique FCPA risk profile. Compliance based on the law is wise and cost-effective from the standpoint of potentially reducing legal exposure or its impact.

However, compliance based on enforcement agency interpretations not subjected to any meaningful judicial scrutiny can be wasteful and divert limited corporate resources from other value-added endeavors. This has long been recognized in the FCPA context and, as detailed in Chapter 4 in highlighting the SEC's 1981 FCPA Guidance, it was noted that the public is not well served by 'overly-burdensome compliance systems which extend beyond the requirements of sound management or the policies embodied' in the FCPA.

Yet this is often the end result given the way in which the FCPA is enforced in this new era. NPAs and DPAs, as well as SEC 'neither admit nor deny' settlements, are championed as de facto case law and many risk-averse companies tailor FCPA compliance to these resolution vehicles despite the fact that they do not necessarily reflect the triumph of an enforcement agencies' legal position.

These FCPA resolution vehicles and the supposed compliance messages they evidence are then often aggressively marketed by FCPA Inc. participants to showcase how the enforcement action represents a new trend requiring the need for more FCPA compliance services. Nearly every instance of FCPA scrutiny or enforcement action in this new era is portrayed as a 'sobering reminder,' there is constant speculation as to which industry 'is going to be the next target,' and every company is warned to ask itself will it be prepared when the 'government knocks on the door.'[43]

A candid FCPA practitioner observed:

> The FCPA Paparazzi has done a great disservice to the business community. Call it a complete lack of credibility. Legal marketing has become confused in this day and age – marketing has now been turned into the 'Fear Factor,' meaning that lawyers need to scare potential clients into hiring them. That is flat-out wrong. Each week, new client alerts, client warnings and other cries of impending disaster are transmitted through the Internet to businesses.[44]

Many risk-averse companies, lacking a proper perspective on many things FCPA related including the FCPA enforcement statistics discussed in Chapter 5, have responded to this fear-based marketing by over-spending on FCPA compliance.

On one level, who can blame companies? Despite enforcement agency guidance that it is not effective to devote 'a disproportionate amount of time policing modest entertainment and gift-giving,' and despite enforcement agency statements that they are 'interested in companies spending compliance dollars in the most sensible way,' recent FCPA enforcement actions have involved allegations about perfume, dresses and handbags; a bottle of wine; a watch; a camera, kitchen appliances and business suits; television sets, laptops and appliances; and tea sets and office furniture. These enforcement actions essentially force companies to 'sweat the small stuff' or risk fear of an FCPA enforcement action. The end result is often contrary to the sensible enforcement agency guidance, and business organizations are indeed spending 'thousands of dollars' to 'conserve hundreds.'

In addition, despite 'reasonable' being a prominent concept in the FCPA's books and records and internal controls provisions, despite legislative history instructing that the concept of reasonableness 'contemplates the weighing of a number of relevant factors, including the costs of compliance,' and despite judicial authority that states that the concept of 'reasonable assurances' contained in the internal controls provisions 'recognizes that the costs of internal controls should not exceed the benefits expected to be derived,' the enforcement agencies nevertheless frequently bring enforcement actions against parent companies under a standard that resembles strict liability for any improper payment or misrecording of the payment anywhere in its corporate hierarchy. In the words of an FCPA practitioner, enforcement agencies should be 'true to their word – "do not hold companies to a standard of perfection" and accept common sense compliance judgments, even when things ultimately go wrong.'[45]

The generic allegations included in many FCPA enforcement actions further contribute to the fear of companies and thereby induce over-compliance. For instance, in the Total enforcement action the DOJ alleged, in support of criminal FCPA internal controls violations, as follows:

> Total: (a) failed to implement adequate anti-bribery compliance policies and procedures; (b) failed to maintain an adequate system for the selection and approval of consultants; (c) failed to conduct adequate audits of payments to purported consultants; (d) failed to establish a sufficiently empowered and competent corporate compliance office; (e) failed to take reasonable steps to ensure the company's compliance and ethics program was followed; (f) failed to evaluate regularly the effectiveness of the company's compliance and ethics program; (g) failed to provide appropriate incentives to perform in accordance with the compliance and ethics program; (h) concealed the consulting agreements' true nature and true participants; (i) performed no due diligence concerning the named or unnamed parties to these agreements; and (j) lacked controls sufficient to provide reasonable assurances that the consulting agreements complied with applicable laws.[46]

The DOJ's generic allegations were notable because survey after survey indicates that a significant percentage of companies, including issuers subject to the FCPA's internal controls provisions, fail to maintain an adequate system for selection and approval of consultants, fail to conduct audits of payments to consultants, fail to conduct due diligence of third parties, and fail to regularly evaluate the effectiveness of its compliance and ethics program. The allegations were all the more alarming because during the 1995 to 2004 time period relevant to the Total enforcement action few, if any, issuers engaged in all of the compliance practices identified in the enforcement action.

Seemingly lost in the entire exercise of FCPA enforcement actions being aggressively marketed by FCPA Inc. as representing new trends requiring the need for more FCPA compliance services is the fact that most of the enforcement actions are based merely on enforcement agency theories not subjected to any meaningful judicial scrutiny and not necessarily reflecting the triumph of the enforcement agencies' legal position.

Consider the enforcement agencies' interpretation of the 'foreign official' element to include all employees of SOEs. Even though there is no case law of precedent blessing this theory, companies nevertheless spend significant time and money investigating the ownership structure of foreign customers and potential customers for any trace of foreign government ownership or control. Such a costly investigation, often involving lawyers and other investigative firms, is not motivated by the company's desire to make improper payments to the foreign customer or potential customer to obtain or retain business should the investigation reveal no foreign government ownership or control. Rather, the costly investigation is often motivated for the simple reason that the company wants to treat these foreign customers the same way it treats its other customers. This means hosting such customers at corporate events in which some fun may take place (e.g., golf) or inviting such customers to an industry trade show in a tourist location. Companies fear providing such things of value to a 'foreign official' even though the company is legitimately and legally providing the exact same thing of value to its customers or potential customers that are not 'foreign officials.'

It is unlikely that Congress wanted or anticipated lawyers being involved in the simple corporate decision of whether to invite a particular customer to the company's golf outing or trade show. Yet this is exactly what is occurring in this new era.

Similarly, because of the enforcement agencies' aggressive interpretation of the FCPA's 'obtain or retain business' element to include payments outside the context of foreign government procurement – an interpretation the government has an overall losing record on when subjected to judicial scrutiny – companies spend significant time and resources policing business segments that have little or no contact with foreign government decision makers. These business segments may be involved in paying foreign taxes, helping secure foreign licenses, or simply tasked with moving product into and out of a country. Monitoring the activity of these business segments, if done on a rational risk-basis, makes sense. However, it is wasteful to over-monitor the activity of these business segments based on a paranoia induced by the increase in FCPA enforcement actions involving foreign licenses, permits, and certifications. Yet this is exactly what is occurring in this new era, and risk-averse companies have responded with fear-based, not risk-based, FCPA compliance measures.

Another area in which the FCPA's new era has significantly increased compliance costs is third-party due diligence. As detailed throughout this book, a company can be exposed to FCPA liability indirectly based on the conduct of its foreign third parties under the FCPA's third-party payment provisions. Under these provisions, liability hinges on the company 'knowing' that a thing of value will be given to a foreign official by the third party. Because of the enforcement agencies' aggressive interpretation of this knowledge standard, companies seeking to engage a foreign third party often start from the mind-set that the third party is corrupt and is an FCPA violation waiting to happen. Thus, companies often engage in extensive and expensive due diligence and monitoring of the third party in an attempt to prove the negative so that if the enforcement agencies ever come calling, the company can turn over an extensive due diligence file to negate any 'knowledge' finding. Such paranoia is fear-based not risk-based, yet is facilitated by this new era of FCPA enforcement.

Compliance Fatigue

In addition to how certain aspects of FCPA enforcement have caused wasteful overcompliance by companies subject to the FCPA, another potential negative effect of this new era is that too much compliance may lead to compliance fatigue and its unintended negative consequence of numbing individuals to the FCPA.

It has been noted:

> Rules and controls and training programs are essential in any organization, but at some point, the burdens imposed by intricate matrices of rules, complex reporting and approval processes, and seemingly never-ending training requirements become a net drag on the business. [...] The deleterious effects of too much compliance activity include much more than a drag on productivity. A system that is overly-controlled, that has passed its optimal point of compliance activities, will engender backlash and bewilderment from those who are being controlled. Managers and other employees will balk at a sclerotic network of rules and processes, and they won't – and in many instances may not be able to – comply. Rules and signoffs will be overlooked, and training courses never taken. Such backlash can actually move a program backward down the benefits curve. And when an employee population sees the compliance program as overly burdensome and poorly aligned with business reality, they will undermine the credibility of the entire enterprise.[47]

At a recent compliance industry conference, compliance officers expressed concerns 'about too much compliance' across a wide variety of areas.[48] More to the point, a recent survey found that although 'many companies have intensified their efforts to combat bribery and corruption, especially given the aggressive enforcement environment' many executives 'must overcome a certain degree of institutional fatigue about anti-corruption compliance initiatives.'[49] The survey concluded: 'we found many boards felt increasingly swamped by risk management and control information. Combined with a growing sense of [bribery and corruption] compliance fatigue, this contributes towards a "tick the box" approach to managing risk.'

Annual FCPA training, annual FCPA certifications, databases full of customers with government ownership, an automated process for this and that, periodic FCPA compliance reminders, FCPA compliance as an agenda item on each meeting, etc. – all of these are considered best practices, but the question is asked: is too much FCPA compliance actually a net negative?

Think of a typical television commercial for a new drug. Thirty seconds of the commercial is devoted to describing the benefits of the drug. However, because of regulatory requirements and the company's potential legal liability, 90 seconds of the commercial are devoted to a laundry list of negative side effects associated with the drug. At some point, viewers disengage from the message and the positive attributes of the drug (the reason for the commercial in the first place) are lost.

Applying this dynamic to FCPA compliance, is trying to anticipate and address every potential instance of FCPA risk through training slides and compliance modules diverting attention away from the big picture of FCPA compliance and numbing employees and others who operate on the company's behalf to the underlying objectives of the company's FCPA compliance policies and procedures? In short, when it comes to FCPA compliance, is less more?

A compliance professional observed:

> In response [to this new era of FCPA enforcement], companies have begun to provide more and more accessible (read: web-based) anti-corruption and related regulatory training programs. Predictably, a panoply of vendors have surfaced offering state-of-the-art customizable online training modules, complete with scenarios, live actors, knowledge checks and certifications. Online compliance training has now become a cottage industry serving a wide array of organizations faced with the daunting task of communicating a Western regulatory concept to tens of thousands of employees across multiple languages, cultures and jurisdictions – again, under the watchful eye of various enforcement bodies. [...] [Does] repeated online and other mass training over time actually have the unintended effect of desensitizing employees to, rather than making them more aware and cautious of, bribery and other corrupt activity.[50]

Indeed, one of the ironies of this new era of FCPA enforcement is that the increase in FCPA scrutiny and enforcement is occurring at the same time companies are spending more and devoting more resources to FCPA compliance. The adage that the sun rose, a dog barked, and a company disclosed FCPA scrutiny seems appropriate in this new era. Effective

FCPA compliance policies and procedures would seem not to reduce FCPA scrutiny, but to uncover more potential FCPA issues.

In other words, FCPA compliance policies and procedures may be working, and as the SEC's 1981 Guidance stated 'routine discovery and correction' of FCPA issues evidence 'effective' internal controls. If so, a company that makes good faith efforts to comply with the FCPA through pro-active policies and procedures ought to be rewarded for this investment, not punished through an FCPA enforcement action or being subjected to FCPA scrutiny. The last chapter of this book addresses this issue as well as other FCPA reform issues.

NOTES

1. FCPA Professor, 'The Guidance Press Conference' (Nov. 15, 2012).
2. Id.
3. Id.
4. Id.
5. FCPA Professor, 'Do Lanny Breuer and Robert Khuzami Actually Read FCPA Enforcement Actions?' (Dec. 13, 2012), containing links to original source documents.
6. Charles Denny and David Weissbrodt, Minneapolis StarTribune, 'Business Forum: Good Companies Don't Bribe. Period' (May 29, 2012).
7. Nick Wingfield, New York Times, 'U.S. Said to Look into Microsoft Bribery Allegations' (Mar. 19, 2013).
8. Microsoft Blog, 'Our Commitment to Compliance' (Mar. 19, 2013).
9. Press Release, U.S. Dep't of Justice, 'Former Morgan Stanley Managing Director Pleads Guilty for Role in Evading Internal Controls Required by FCPA' (Apr. 25, 2012).
10. FCPA Professor, 'Judge (Again) Significantly Rejects DOJ's Recommendation in Sentencing Garth Peterson, Peterson Goes on Offense and Says the DOJ is Lying about Morgan Stanley's FCPA Compliance Procedures' (Aug. 20, 2013), containing links to original source documents.
11. DOJ Principles of Federal Prosecution of Business Organizations, 9-28.800, Corporate Compliance Programs.
12. Press Release, U.S. Dep't of Justice, 'Assistant Attorney General Lanny A. Breuer of the Criminal Division Speaks at the Annual Meeting of the Washington Metropolitan Area Corporate Counsel Association' (Jan. 26, 2011); Lanny A. Breuer, Assistant Attorney General, Criminal Division U.S. Department of Justice, Prepared Remarks to Compliance Week 2010 – 5th Annual Conference for Corporate Financial, Legal, Risk, Audit & Compliance Officers (May 26, 2010).
13. The Metropolitan Corporate Counsel, 'Former Chief of DOJ Fraud Unit Discusses Healthcare and FCPA Enforcement' (Sept. 29, 2012).
14. Peter Van Dyk, National Public Radio, 'From Iowa to Russia, Tractors Build Economic Bridge' (May 15, 2012).
15. FCPA Professor, 'Q & A with Martin Weinstein' (May 18, 2010).
16. FCPA Professor, 'Former DOJ FCPA Chief Supports FCPA Compliance Defense' (Oct. 4, 2011).

17. Jones Day Commentary, 'U.S. Department of Justice and Securities and Exchange Commission Guidance on the Foreign Corrupt Practices Act: What to Expect' (Sept. 2012).
18. Lockheed Bribery: Hearings before the S. Comm on Banking, Housing, and Urban Affairs, 94th Cong. (1975).
19. S. Rep. No. 93-114, at 10 (1977).
20. 'Justice Outlines Priorities in Prosecuting Violations of For. Corrupt Practices Act,' The American Banker (Nov. 21, 1979).
21. Philip Urofsky, et al., 'How Should We Measure the Effectiveness of the Foreign Corrupt Practices Act? Don't Break What Isn't Broken – the Fallacies of Reform,' 73 The Ohio Law Journal 1145 (2012).
22. OECD, 'Report on Application of the Convention on Combating Bribery of Foreign Public Officials in International Business Transactions and the 1997 Recommendation on Combating Bribery in International Business Transactions' (Oct. 2002).
23. OECD, 'Phase 3 Report on Implementing the OECD Anti-Bribery Convention in the United States' (Oct. 2010).
24. Professional Outdoor Media Association, 'Free to NSSF Members: Global Anti-Corruption Course' (Jan. 11, 2012).
25. *Supra* note 23.
26. U.S. Government Accountability Office, 'Corporate Crime: DOJ Has Taken Steps to Better Track Its Use of Deferred and Non-Prosecution Agreements, but Should Evaluate Effectiveness' (2009).
27. Information, U.S. v. Orthofix Int'l N.V., No. 4:12-cr-00150 (E.D. Tex., July 12, 2012).
28. Complaint, SEC v. Halliburton Co., No. 4:09-399 (S.D. Tex., Feb. 11, 2009).
29. Stephanie Clifford and David Barstow, New York Times, 'Wal-Mart Inquiry Reflects Alarm on Corruption' (Nov. 15, 2012).
30. In the Matter of Watts Water Technologies, Inc. and Leesen Chang, SEC Release No. 65555 (Oct. 13, 2011).
31. U.S. Sentencing Commission, 2012 Guidelines Manual, Chapter Eight – Sentencing of Organizations, Part B – Remedying Harm from Criminal Conduct, and Effective Compliance and Ethics Program (2012).
32. OECD, 'Good Practice Guidance on Internal Controls, Ethics, and Compliance' (Feb. 18, 2010).
33. SEC Release, 'Opening Remarks at Foreign Bribery and Corruption Training Conference' (Feb. 11, 2013).
34. FCPA Professor, 'Can We Make the Expenditure in the First Place? Practical Advice for Navigating Gift, Travel and Entertainment Issues' (May 22, 2013).
35. FCPA Professor, 'A Practical Resource for Managers and Executives' (Dec. 8, 2010).
36. Complaint, SEC v. York Int'l Corp., No. 1:07-cv-01750 (D.D.C., Oct. 1, 2007).
37. Complaint, SEC v. Eli Lilly and Co., No. 1:12-cv-02045 (D.D.C., Dec. 20, 2012).
38. Complaint, SEC v. AGCO Limited, No. 1:09-cv-01865 (D.D.C., Sept. 30, 2009).
39. Trace Blog, '5 Ways to Fight off Anti-bribery Compliance Fatigue' (Feb. 26, 2013).
40. Miriam Baer, 'Insuring Corporate Crime,' 83 Indiana L.J. 1035 (2008).
41. 'Report of the President on Export Promotion Functions and Potential Export Disincentives: Together with the Review of Executive Branch Export Promotion Functions and Potential Export Disincentives,' Transmitted to the Congress (Sept. 1980).
42. FCPA Professor, 'Friday Roundup' (Feb. 17, 2012), containing links to the original source document.
43. FCPA Professor, 'Marketing the FCPA … the FCPA Risks of … Well, Just about Everything' (May 16, 2013).

44. Corruption Crime & Compliance, 'Five Important Compliance Principles to Prevent FCPA Liability' (Oct. 21, 2012).
45. FCPA Professor, 'Can We Bring Quality FCPA Compliance and Investigative Services to the Underserved Middle Market?' (May 21, 2013).
46. Deferred Prosecution Agreement, U.S. v. Total S.A., No. 1:13-cr-239 (May 29, 2013).
47. LN Corporation, 'Culture & the Optimal Degree of Compliance' (2011).
48. Nichols Elliott, Wall Street Journal Risk & Compliance Report, 'The Morning Risk Report: "There's Too Much Compliance"' (Apr. 5, 2013).
49. Ernst & Young, 'Growing Beyond: A Place for Integrity – 12th Global Fraud Survey' (2012).
50. Gregory Esslinger, 'Anti-Corruption Compliance: Are Employees Becoming "Over-Trained"?' (2011).

9. FCPA reform

This book concludes by returning to an opening thesis – while the FCPA is a fundamentally sound statute, this does not mean that the FCPA could not be improved or that FCPA enforcement is always fundamentally sound. Indeed, one of the greatest challenges in this new era is how to enforce the FCPA consistent with the rule of law, and its demand for transparency and consistency, and in a way that inspires public confidence that enforcement is fair and actually effective in achieving the objectives of the FCPA.

As noted in Chapter 1, FCPA reform is nearly as old as the FCPA itself. However, reforming a law called the 'Foreign *Corrupt* Practices Act' has always been a political hot potato and a substantive, issue-based discussion of the law has always been difficult.

Declaration of the FCPA's new era and wider recognition of the enforcement theories and policies which have come to define this era have resulted in the positive development of greater attention to the FCPA and its enforcement on Capitol Hill and among other policy makers and interested observers.

This chapter focuses on FCPA reform and highlights, among other things, recent reform proposals and related Congressional hearings. As history instructs, the mere discussion of FCPA reform has once again been opposed by some who have advanced the simplistic – either you are against bribery or for bribery – position. The implicit position of those opposing FCPA reform would seem to be that the FCPA is a perfect statute and that the current FCPA enforcement policies are best achieving the laudable objectives of the FCPA.

This is not the position advanced in this concluding chapter. Rather, FCPA reforms are suggested designed to ensure that the FCPA is best achieving the original goals of the law and that FCPA enforcement is transparent and otherwise consistent with rule of law principles. Using the knowledge base acquired throughout this book, you can analyze this new era of FCPA enforcement and determine for yourself whether FCPA reform is warranted.

A. THE CURRENT REFORM ENVIRONMENT

This section highlights various FCPA reform proposals by experienced and knowledgeable individuals, including many former DOJ and SEC enforcement attorneys who helped shape and enforce the FCPA. Next, it discusses recent FCPA Congressional hearings which evidenced bipartisan support for certain aspects of FCPA reform. However, with an actual FCPA reform bill looming on the horizon, this section chronicles how political posturing by the enforcement agencies and a high-profile instance of FCPA scrutiny stalled FCPA reform.

Reform Proposals

In many respects the current FCPA reform environment approximately a decade ago by Stanley Sporkin, the former Director of the SEC's Division of Enforcement in the mid-1970s, who played a key role in addressing the foreign corporate payments issues investigated by Congress and in shaping what would become the FCPA's books and records and internal controls provisions.

In a 2004 speech before an FCPA audience, Sporkin stated:

> We need more than Congress passing a new statute, and the SEC requiring strict compliance with existing legislation. We need a comprehensive assault on the problem [of bribery of foreign officials]. This means we need the assistance of our government and indeed all the countries of the world along with the world business community, to provide a climate which enables our corporations to compete honestly and fairly throughout the world. There is a way to fix this problem if there is a will to do so.[1]

Among other things, Sporkin proposed – no doubt recognizing that most FCPA issues arise from use of foreign agents – the 'establishment of a country-by-country list of agents that have been properly vetted and have agreed to be examined and audited by an independent international auditing group.'

In 2006, Sporkin made another speech before an FCPA audience as the statute neared its 30th anniversary. He stated:

> What I envisioned when the law was enacted was a new corporate regime where bribery of foreign officials would be almost completely extinguished at least as it pertained to major U.S. corporations. As all of us here have observed, the wild-eyed-do-gooder predictions never occurred. Instead statistics indicate that bribery of foreign officials has maintained a steady pace over the years.[2]

In his 2006 speech, Sporkin did not advocate the FCPA's repeal, but he did 'think the DOJ and the SEC can do something forward-looking which would be win-win for both the government and the private sector.'

Sporkin called it the 'FCPA Immunization-Inoculation Program' and stated that the 'quasi-amnesty program' would consist of the following:

- 'agreement by participating firms to conduct a full and complete review [conducted jointly by a major accounting firm or specialized forensic accounting firm and a law firm] of the company's compliance with the FCPA for the previous 3 years';
- the company would agree 'to disclose the results of the legal-accounting audit to the SEC, its investors, and the public';
- 'if any violations turned up in the process of the audit, the participating [company] would agree to take all steps to eliminate the problems and implement the appropriate controls to prevent further violations';
- participating companies 'would agree to subject themselves to a similar audit on an annual basis for at least 5 years to ensure that compliance was being maintained';
- participating companies 'would be required to create the position of FCPA compliance officer, whose sole responsibility would be to ensure the company's compliance with the FCPA' and make an annual certification; and
- 'in exchange … the SEC and DOJ would give qualified assurances that no actions would be brought for violations exposed by the review.'

As envisioned by Sporkin, the 'limited amnesty would not apply if violations rose to flagrant or egregious levels.' According to Sporkin, the 'immunization-inoculation program would serve the dual purpose of: (i) creating suitable incentives to compliance-minded companies to adopt and maintain high ethical standards in the conduct of their business; and (ii) reducing the case load and investigative burden of governmental agencies that enforce the FCPA while reassuring regulators that companies are taking active steps to limit corruption in their foreign contracting and other activities.' Sporkin believed that his proposal 'would provide the right-thinking corporate community with the necessary assurances that it needs to develop a vibrant overseas business without having to defend itself against very costly and time consuming investigations.'

In 2007, James Doty, writing as a private lawyer before being appointed by the SEC as the Chairman of the Public Company Accounting Oversight Board, advocated for FCPA reform in the form of a so-called Regulation FCPA.[3]

According to Doty, the most troubling issues concerning the FCPA enforcement climate were:

> (i) trends in the imposition of civil liability on a parent issuer for acts of a subsidiary's employee or agent in the absence of active complicity of the parent, and in some cases where the actions of employees and agents contravene established, company-wide policies; (ii) prosecution on aggressive legal theories extending beyond traditional bribery (which underscore the need for prospective regulatory clarification of permitted activities); and (iii) the expansive criminalization of vicarious liability under a vague statute, in some cases where there is not certainty that a bribe has been offered or paid by the corporation.

The pressing issue Doty identified was 'whether our law enforcement agencies should be left to devise their own, case-by-case interpretation of the FCPA, without the rigor of greater regulatory clarity and the benefits of more consistent administrative interpretation.'

Doty noted that the enforcement climate reflected 'the confluence of a number of enforcement developments' and identified the following:

> (i) the SEC is increasingly pursuing substantive bribery charges against the corporate parent, in addition to focusing, as usual, on enforcement of the books and records and internal controls provisions of the FCPA; (ii) non-litigated settlement orders are aggressively expanding the range of conduct subject to the statute; (iii) DPAs, which have been used in this context only since 2004, have become virtually commonplace; (iv) linkage of FCPA charges to other Exchange Act charges is becoming more aggressive.

Doty then stated:

> Aggressive enforcement, based on an expansive interpretation of a vague statute, a little-used DOJ opinion process, and the temptation perhaps to assume that more draconian criminal enforcement is better, have all led to a lack of predictability in law enforcement and [...] some incorrect application of the standards. [...] Consistency and predictability are not matters of grace granted to corporate citizens at the government's pleasure; the government owes consistency and predictability to public corporations that are attempting to accomplish complex tasks in difficult foreign venues, and to management and directors who want to know the 'how-to-do-it' of compliance in these circumstances.

Doty likewise did 'not advocate repeal or weakened enforcement of the FCPA,' but stated that 'support for the policies of the FCPA does not require turning a deaf ear to warnings about the increased costs associated with current enforcement practices under the statute.' Absent reform, Doty wrote, 'there is a policy vacuum in which law is developed on an ad hoc basis by Assistant U.S. Attorneys and by the Staff of the SEC and DOJ as they respond to the exigencies of particular factual situations.'

Doty's FCPA proposal – Regulation FCPA – was a permissive filing regime whereby an issuer 'would benefit from a regulatory presumption of compliance' and thus 'protect itself, its senior management and its board of directors from vicarious, general corporate liability' in the FCPA context. Doty wrote that 'for a company to avail itself of the benefits of Reg. FCPA, it would be required to establish an FCPA Compliance Program designed to prevent and detect, insofar as practicable, any violations. The company would also be required to certify that it has, to the best knowledge and belief of its certifying officers, reasonably discharged the duties and obligations under the program, and that the company is not aware of continuing, unremedied violations.' Doty stated that 'as with any regulatory safe harbor, the claimant would have the burden of demonstrating compliance with the conditions' and that 'upon satisfying these conditions, the company would be presumed not to have violated the statute,' a presumption that 'could be rebutted by a preponderance of the evidence.'

As indicated by Sporkin's and Doty's FCPA reform proposals, and as further evidenced by more recent FCPA reform proposals detailed below, a hard-to-ignore feature of the current FCPA reform debate is that experienced and knowledgeable individuals, including many former DOJ and SEC enforcement attorneys who helped shape and enforce the FCPA, share a belief that the current FCPA enforcement environment is in need of reform.

Congressional Hearings

Although there were certain minor FCPA amendments in 1998, Congress had taken little interest in the FCPA or its enforcement since the last major substantive reforms in 1988. In this new era, however, members of Congress began asking pointed questions about certain features of FCPA enforcement. For instance, in 2010 Senator Arlen Specter confronted the DOJ Assistant Attorney General during a Senate Judiciary Committee hearing about the then lack of individual prosecutions in the record-setting Siemens enforcement action.[4] Later that same month, Congressman Edolphus Towns released a letter to the Attorney General expressing concern that settlements of certain civil and criminal cases by the DOJ, including certain FCPA enforcement actions, 'are being used as a shield to foreclose other appropriate remedies, such as suspension and debarment, that protect the government from continuing to do business with contractors who do not have satisfactory records of quality performance and business ethics.'[5]

Congressional interest in the FCPA and its enforcement continued to grow as FCPA enforcement increased, as enforcement agency theories became more aggressive, and as the competitiveness of U.S. business in the global marketplace declined. Between November 2010 and June 2011, the Senate and House both held FCPA hearings.

The impetus for the hearings was likely a white-paper released in 2010 by the Institute for Legal Reform, an affiliate of the U.S. Chamber of Commerce, titled 'Restoring Balance: Proposed Amendments to the Foreign Corrupt Practices Act' ('Restoring Balance').[6] Restoring Balance was far from the first time FCPA reform ideas were proposed, but the paper from the nation's largest business group certainty elevated FCPA reform issues.

The lead author of Restoring Balance was Andrew Weissmann, former Director of the DOJ's Enron Task Force. Restoring Balance stated:

> In spite of this rise in enforcement and investigatory action, judicial oversight and rulings on the meaning of the provisions of the FCPA is still minimal. Commercial organizations are rarely positioned to litigate an FCPA enforcement action to its conclusion, and the risk of serious jail time for individual defendants has led most to seek favorable terms from the government rather than face the expense and uncertainty of a trial. Thus, the primary statutory interpretive function is still being performed almost exclusively by the DOJ Fraud Section and the SEC. Notably, these enforcement agencies have been increasingly aggressive in their reading of the law.

Like prior FCPA reform proposals, Restoring Balance did not advocate repealing the FCPA, but proposed that 'the FCPA should be modified to make clear what is and what is not a violation,' and it recommended the following reforms:

- adding a compliance defense;
- limiting a company's liability for the prior actions of a company it has acquired;
- adding a 'willfulness' requirement for corporate criminal liability;
- limiting a company's liability for acts of a subsidiary; and
- better defining 'foreign official.'

Predictably, and with history as a guide, the Chamber's call for FCPA reform was blasted by some. Within days of the release of Restoring Balance, a popular cable news program assailed the mere mention of FCPA reform as being 'pro-bribery' and akin to paving the way for business to go on a bribery binge.[7] For its part, the DOJ maintained that the FCPA is 'set forth in the terms of the statute' and 'courts are available to companies if they dispute the [DOJ's] interpretation of the law.'[8] Such a simplistic and cavalier response from the DOJ of course ignored the fact that its enforcement policies, such as frequent use of NPAs and DPAs in the FCPA context, have shielded prosecution theories from meaningful judicial scrutiny in all but the rarest of circumstances.

In opening the 2010 Senate hearing, Senator Specter noted that 'oversight is a major function of Congress,' but that Congress does 'not do very much of it.'[9] The hearing focused on DOJ's FCPA enforcement program, the general lack of individual FCPA prosecutions, and FCPA reform.

During the hearing, Senator Amy Klobuchar noted that 'one of the basic principles of due process is that people in companies have to be able to know what the law is in order to comply with it' and she further stated that 'many very good standing companies … do not always know what behavior will trigger an enforcement action.' Senator Christopher Coons stated that he 'would welcome the opportunity' to work on 'potential amendments to the [FCPA] that would allow clarification on the definition of foreign official and the creation of a compliance defense.'

Following the 2010 hearing, Senators Coons and Klobuchar submitted written questions to the DOJ concerning various aspects of FCPA reform and the DOJ's consistent answer was 'no.'[10] As to an FCPA compliance defense, the DOJ stated that it 'opposes the adoption of a formal compliance defense' because it 'already considers a company's compliance efforts in making appropriate prosecutorial decisions, and the United States Sentencing Guidelines also appropriately credits a company's compliance efforts in any sentencing determination.' Among other things, the DOJ stated:

> The creation of such a defense would transform criminal FCPA trials into a battle of experts over whether the company had established a sufficient compliance mechanism. Against this backdrop, companies may feel the need to implement a purely paper compliance program that could be defended by an 'expert,' even if the measures are not effective in stopping bribery. If the FCPA were amended to permit companies to hide behind such programs, it would erect an additional hurdle for prosecutors in what are already difficult and complex cases to prove.

As to whether 'well-meaning businesses are faced with significant uncertainty as to their potential exposure to civil and criminal penalties under the FCPA,' the DOJ stated that 'it provides clear guidance to companies with respect to FCPA enforcement through a variety of means.' The DOJ then listed various charging documents, plea agreements, NPAs and DPAs, and the DOJ's FCPA Opinion Procedure Releases. The DOJ concluded its response as follows. 'In the end, a review of the Department's FCPA enforcement actions makes clear that companies have never been charged for minor or incidental issues. By contrast, the Department's prosecutions involved extensive and often widespread corruption over significant periods of time.'

In 2011, picking up where the Senate left off in 2010 on FCPA reform, the House held an FCPA hearing focused on a wide range of issues including the DOJ's FCPA enforcement program and FCPA reform.[11]

Predictably, some blasted the very existence of the hearing and one organization called the hearing a 'fight to make bribery easier for big business.'[12] Regarding calls for further clarity as to certain FCPA elements, the organization stated: 'Greater certainty of what? Greater certainty of who they are permitted to bribe and who they are not permitted to bribe.'[13] As to a potential compliance defense, the organization stated, in contrast to even prior enforcement agency statements that no compliance program can ever prevent all criminal activity, as follows: 'If a company is found to be in violation of the FCPA, then the existence of a company's compliance program must not have prevented the acts of bribery. So why should the existence of their compliance program be a defense to the charge of bribery?'

In many respects, the 2011 House FCPA hearing was similar to FCPA reform hearings in the 1980s in that a common theme was whether the current FCPA enforcement environment is harming U.S. business. In opening the hearing, Chairman James Sensenbrenner noted that 'the world was a very different place' when the FCPA was passed in 1977, but since then 'the world has turned upside down … China has become a global manufacturing power, and the nature of overseas business has changed.' Placing FCPA enforcement in the context of the then economic downturn, Chairman Sensenbrenner stated that 'FCPA prosecutions should be effective and fair,' yet at the same time 'predictable' so that the 'rules of the road … are clear' so that 'business can start moving again.' Representative Robert Scott also commented on the necessity of periodically reviewing laws to make sure they 'remain fair and just.'

During the hearing bipartisan support for certain aspects of FCPA reform was evident. Representative John Conyers, who appeared most supportive of the current state of FCPA enforcement, even stated he would support certain FCPA reform proposals. For instance, Representative Conyers supported clarification of 'foreign official' because it can create a problem when those subject to the FCPA do not have a clear understanding of who a 'foreign official' is, and he also supported the addition of a compliance defense so that companies can fight imposition of criminal liability if individual employees and agents circumvent compliance measures.

At the hearing the DOJ once again rejected calls for FCPA reform including a compliance defense. The DOJ witness stated that an FCPA compliance defense could 'create a loophole' and allow for some bribery to occur. He called such a potential defense 'novel and risky' and said that the 'time is not right to consider it.'

Although an SEC representative did not testify at either the 2010 or 2011 FCPA hearings, the FCPA's other enforcement agency soon made its views known regarding FCPA reform. Responding to a Senator letter requesting answers to a number of FCPA-related questions, the SEC Chairman stated:

> Continued strong enforcement of the FCPA sends the message that American companies operating abroad will not pay bribes as a 'cost of doing business.' The deterrence message of the Commission's FCPA enforcement program incentivizes companies to self-assess and update their compliance and internal controls – all of which benefits companies' operations overall and provides greater transparency to investors. While I certainly appreciate and share your concerns about the costs of FCPA compliance in certain circumstances, I believe that the risks to investors and costs to companies posed by outdated or weak FCPA compliance measures are equally significant.[14]

As to an FCPA compliance defense, the Chairman stated: 'The Commission, in deciding whether to approve the filing of an FCPA enforcement action against a public company, already considers as one mitigating factor whether the company's compliance program was reasonably designed and operated in a manner to detect and prevent FCPA violations.'

'Similarly,' the Chairman stated, 'companies facing FCPA inquiries can obtain credit for cooperation under the Commission's new Cooperative Initiative, in which cooperation is defined to include, among other factors, having reasonable internal controls and compliance measures.' The Chairman stated that 'it seems unnecessary – and even counterproductive – to recognize a formal affirmative defense for having such a [compliance] program, given that there are at least three significant costs associated with such a defense.' The Chairman then identified the following three issues.

> First, the reasonableness of a compliance program is best measured not by how it exists on paper, but by how it operates in practice. Consequently, the ease with which an employee was able to circumvent anti-corruption controls is some evidence – not sufficient evidence, but some evidence – that internal controls were insufficient. The Commission would not want to be foreclosed from bringing FCPA charges under those circumstances, since holding companies accountable for weak internal controls incentivizes companies to create a robust FCPA compliance environment.
>
> Second, providing an affirmative defense for reasonably designed compliance programs could allow companies to retain ill-gotten gains. A company could engage in bribery or other corrupt behavior, obtain a benefit from such conduct (i.e. securing lucrative contracts), and yet not disgorge its ill-gotten gains. Enabling companies to retain proceeds generated from the payment of bribes would disincentivize those companies from adopting rigorous anti-corruption programs.
>
> Third, sanctioning corrupt behavior sends a strong message of general deterrence to all similarly situated companies that there is a high financial and reputational cost to be paid if they bribe foreign officials. There is often no substitute for the deterrent impact of financial and reputational sanctions, which prevent improper behavior from becoming ingrained as just another 'cost of doing business.' That deterrence message likely would be diluted if such an affirmative defense was adopted.

The 2011 House hearing was much more contentious than the Senate's 2010 FCPA hearing and reflected the growing divide between the legitimate concerns of many as to this new era of FCPA enforcement and the enforcement agencies' seemingly 'circle the wagons' approach when it comes to FCPA reform or critique of its FCPA enforcement program. For instance, in closing the hearing, Chairman Sensenbrenner sternly told the DOJ witness that it 'would behoove the [DOJ] to realize that this statute needs updating' because the current enforcement climate has caused U.S. business not to pursue legitimate business activity, thereby putting U.S. business at a significant disadvantage to foreign companies. During the hearing, Chairman Sensenbrenner said that his Committee would be drafting an FCPA reform bill.

With the prospect of a reform bill on the horizon, a wide variety of groups made their voices heard on FCPA issues. For instance, the Open Society Foundations released a professor-authored white-paper titled 'Busting Bribery: Sustaining the Global Momentum of the Foreign Corrupt Practices Act' ('Busting Bribery') as a direct response to the Chamber's Restoring Balance white-paper.[15] Busting Bribery asserted, among other things, that the Chamber's FCPA reform proposals: (i) 'would substantially undermine the possibility for successful enforcement of America's anti-bribery commitments;' and (ii) 'also set back decades of progress in the global struggle against corruption.' Busting Bribery stated that 'FCPA prosecutorial overreach by the DOJ is a myth' and that the 'Chamber's proposals would needlessly hamstring what has been a judicious and increasingly effective use of prosecutorial discretion to encourage compliance and isolate the most egregious violations.'

As to an FCPA compliance defense, Busting Bribery stated:

> Often seen as the least concerning of the Chamber's proposals, the creation of an affirmative defense of 'compliance' to FCPA corporate criminal liability is actually potentially very dangerous. Compliance is already taken into account at every stage in the investigation and resolution of FCPA violations. [...] A defense of 'adequate' or 'good faith' compliance makes no sense when, as under the current FCPA, corporate criminal liability requires proof beyond a reasonable doubt that the company acted with actual knowledge and corrupt intent to influence a foreign government to gain an improper business advantage. Creating a compliance defense to knowing and intentional violations of the FCPA would amount to eliminating criminal liability under the Act all together by permitting a 'fig leaf' compliance program to insulate companies from their knowing and intentional wrongdoing.

In conclusion, Busting Bribery asserted that 'the FCPA is working as Congress intended and new legislation is neither necessary nor advisable.'

However, Busting Bribery was off-target in many respects and caused an FCPA practitioner to ask in a Tweet 'why are professors with no apparent experience actually investigating corruption used as experts?'[16] For instance, Busting Bribery exhibited a poor understanding of the basic *respondeat superior* principle of corporate criminal liability discussed in Chapter 2. It stated that an FCPA compliance defense 'makes no sense when, as under the current FCPA, corporate criminal liability requires proof beyond a reasonable doubt that the company acted with actual knowledge and corrupt intent to influence a foreign government to gain an improper business advantage.' While it is true that the corrupt intent element of the FCPA must be met in order to convict a company of an FCPA offense, that corrupt intent element can be satisfied, and often is, by singular and isolated acts of any employee, even if the employee's conduct is contrary to pre-existing compliance policies and procedures. Busting Bribery simply glossed over this fundamental concept in its compliance defense rebuttal and the term (or general concept) *respondeat superior* does not even appear in the lengthy white-paper.

Moreover, an FCPA compliance defense along the lines suggested in the below section would not, as Busting Bribery suggested, create a wholesale corporate defense to 'knowing and intentional violations of the

FCPA.' If the board of directors, executive officers, or other senior personnel were involved in the knowing and intentional conduct at issue, a company could not rely on the compliance defense suggested below. Likewise, if an employee at any level engaged in knowing and intentional conduct in violating of the FCPA, a company could not rely on a compliance defense unless it had in place pre-existing compliance policies and procedures reasonably designed and implemented to prevent and detect, insofar as practicable, the conduct at issue. The notion that creating an FCPA compliance defense 'would amount to eliminating [corporate] criminal liability under the Act all together' is simply false and off-target.

Finally, Busting Bribery's assertion that 'FCPA prosecutorial overreach by the DOJ is a myth' seems, in retrospect, comical given subsequent developments when the DOJ was put to its burden of proof in the Africa Sting, Lindsey Manufacturing and O'Shea cases previously highlighted in Chapter 5.

What is most striking about many of the opposition pieces written about FCPA reform is that while opponents of FCPA reform warn of a U.S. retreat on bribery and corruption issues should the FCPA be amended, opponents fail to address the fact that an amended FCPA, or revisions to FCPA enforcement policy, would actually align the FCPA with many FCPA-like laws or enforcement policies of peer nations. For instance, and as discussed in more detail below as to a compliance defense, many OECD Convention countries have compliance-like defenses in their FCPA-like law.[17] In addition, the U.S. is believed to be the only OECD Convention country that uses NPAs and DPAs to resolve instances of alleged corporate bribery.

That the U.S. enforces the FCPA out-of-step with its OECD Convention peer countries was the focus of a white paper released by the International Business Transactions Committee of the Bar Association of New York City.[18] The New York Bar Report analyzed the FCPA and FCPA enforcement from an economic perspective and stated:

> There are three elements to the current approach to FCPA enforcement that are helpful in understanding the costs, risks and other constraints that the FCPA places on U.S.-regulated companies vis-à-vis their non-U.S. regulated competitors: (1) the U.S. enforcement agencies' expansive reading of the scope of the FCPA (both in terms of conduct and jurisdiction), (2) the limited checks on FCPA enforcement (whether judicial or otherwise) and (3) the massive size of the potential direct costs (e.g., fines, sanctions and defense and compliance costs) and indirect costs (e.g., reputational effects and 'debarment' from current or future government business) of avoiding or defending an actual or threatened enforcement action.

Noting the rise in FCPA enforcement and the 'asymmetric approach to enforcement' between the U.S. and other OECD Convention countries, the New York Bar Report stated:

> (1) the United States has pursued, and is currently pursuing, a virtually stand-alone approach to deterring foreign corruption, … (2) this approach places significant costs on companies that are subject to the FCPA as compared to their competitors that are not, … and, (3) if these circumstances are unlikely to change, … the United States should reevaluate its approach to the problem of foreign corruption.

The New York Bar Report stated that the 'continued unilateral and zealous enforcement of the FCPA by the United States may not be the most effective means to combat corruption globally – in fact, in some circumstances it may exacerbate the problem of overseas corruption.' The report concluded as follows: 'While the task is daunting and the discomfort of admitting that the current approach has significant flaws is unavoidable, that does not mean that action should not be taken.'

On the opposite end of the spectrum from many civil society groups who opposed any aspect of FCPA reform, some used the ongoing FCPA reform debate to advocate for repeal of the FCPA. Writing at the Cato Institute's blog, a commentator stated that FCPA 'clarification is not enough' and that the FCPA 'is a feel-good piece of overcriminalization that oversteps the proper bounds of federal lawmaking …'.[19] Another commentator stated:

> At its core, the FCPA is our government's way of pretending to be the mean old school marm, telling all the nasty children of the world how to behave. If it doesn't appeal to the school marm's sensibilities, then it's a crime, and demands a hard smack across the knuckles. A very expensive hard smack. […] We may hate corporations, but we need them, and we need them to be productive around the globe. To tie them down because of vague, child-like notions of fairness that conflict with cultural norms everywhere else is just foolish and counterproductive. Surviving and competing in foreign cultures isn't wrong, and it shouldn't be a crime. The FCPA has got to go.[20]

Repealing the FCPA is not a position advanced in this book. Rather, as explained below in more detail, while the FCPA and certain enforcement agency policies ought to be reformed and while FCPA enforcement has in many cases become unhinged, the FCPA remains a fundamentally sound statute that was passed by Congress for valid and legitimate reasons that remain true today.

Reform Stalls

The force with which Representative Sensenbrenner stated at the 2011 House FCPA hearing that an FCPA reform bill would be introduced left one with the impression that an actual reform bill would soon follow.

Guidance Promised

However, in late 2011 the DOJ announced that it would issue FCPA guidance in 2012.[21] This development stalled FCPA reform and those on Capitol Hill who were inclined to introduce an FCPA reform bill said they would await the promised guidance before introducing such a bill.[22]

The timing of the DOJ's announcement – at the height of the FCPA reform debate – was curious and likely designed to forestall actual FCPA reform. In this regard, it is important to understand the following background information.

As part of the FCPA's 1988 amendments, Congress encouraged the DOJ to issue FCPA guidance. A relevant House report stated: 'In order to enhance compliance with the provisions of the FCPA [the FCPA amendment] establishes a procedure for the [DOJ] to issue guidance describing examples of activities that would or would not conform with the [DOJ's] present enforcement policy regarding FCPA violations.'[23]

Despite Congress's suggestion, the DOJ determined in 1990 that 'no [FCPA] guidelines are necessary.'[24]

In its 2002 review of FCPA enforcement, the OECD encouraged the U.S. to issue FCPA guidance. The OECD report stated:

> Despite the abundance of articles and commentaries on [the FCPA], there is only limited amount of authoritative or official guidance available on compliance with the [FCPA]. ... Much of the authority or guidance regarding the Act comes from speeches from DOJ and SEC officials, DOJ opinions, DOJ and SEC complaints, settlements that have been filed, and informal discussions of issues between companies' counsel and the DOJ or the SEC. ... The status of these various sources of information is however not always clear: there could be merit in regrouping and consolidating them in a single guidance document.[25]

The OECD report concluded:

> In the view of the lead examiners, the time has come to explore the need for further forms of guidance, mainly to assist new players ... on the international scene, and to provide a valuable risk management tool to guide companies through some of the pitfalls which might arise in structuring international transactions involving potential exposures.

Likewise, in its 2010 review of FCPA enforcement the OECD stated: 'The evaluators recommend that the United States consider consolidating and summarizing [all relevant sources of FCPA information] to ensure easy accessibility, especially for [companies] which face limited resources.'[26]

Despite Congress suggesting FCPA guidance in 1988, and repeated OECD recommendations for guidance in 2002 and 2010, the DOJ refused to issue guidance. For instance, in the aftermath of the 2010 Senate FCPA hearing, the DOJ was asked 'do you believe companies could comply with more certainty with the FCPA if they were provided with more generally applicable guidance from the Department in regards to situations covered by the FCPA that are not clear cut or fall into gray areas?' The DOJ stated that it 'believes it provides clear guidance with respect to FCPA enforcement through a variety of means,' and it then listed the same general categories of information the OECD identified in 2002 as being deficient.[27] Likewise in the aftermath of the 2011 House FCPA hearing, the SEC suggested that specific FCPA guidance was not necessary and stated:

> Both the Commission and the DOJ have numerous mechanisms for providing guidance on FCPA matters. Perhaps the most important guidance comes from the enforcement actions that are brought by the Commission and the DOJ. The Commission uses its pleadings and accompanying public news releases to highlight and reinforce the key elements of each case. Additionally, senior staff in the Division of Enforcement speak regularly at industry conferences and provide guidance on the FCPA program.[28]

In short, after consistently refusing to do so for nearly twenty-five years, the DOJ announcement in late 2011 – at the height of the FCPA reform debate – that it would issue FCPA guidance in 2012 was likely a political maneuver designed to forestall actual FCPA reform.

Regardless of the DOJ's motivation in announcing its intention to release FCPA guidance in 2012, the announcement did not silence the many voices calling for FCPA reform. Nor should it have, as non-binding enforcement agency guidance will not cure many of the issues being debated in good faith during this new era of FCPA enforcement.

For instance, former Attorney General Michael Mukasey, an individual active in the FCPA reform debate on behalf of the Chamber of Commerce, co-authored an article that stated:

> The unobjectionable vision [of the FCPA] has virtually disappeared in a miasma of aggressive prosecutions by the Justice Department … The FCPA is almost never litigated in court. Public companies are the typical FCPA target,

> and such defendants are rarely positioned to litigate criminal charges, or even risk indictment, given (among other things) the substantial risk of federal contract debarment in many industries. The same is often true for individuals, most of whom face substantial prison time if convicted and who are thus unwilling to hang their hopes on uncertain interpretive arguments. As a result, the FCPA has had almost no judicial oversight, with the result that corporations trying to comply with its mandates find they are fighting corruption in the dark, their quest for standards confined to making mitigation arguments in prosecutors' offices. This has enabled the FCPA's enforcers, the Justice Department, and the SEC, to 'win' most FCPA cases through plea bargains or settlements, in which regulators set the terms, and into which regulators import their capacious constructions of the FCPA. This regulatory latitude has, in turn, transformed the FCPA into a catch-all for illicit conduct abroad, no matter how removed the target of the enforcement action is from the underlying offense. As Professor Mike Koehler has put it, 'the FCPA means what the enforcement agencies say it means.'[29]

The article argued that 'because the FCPA will never be heavily litigated – thus depriving the courts of the opportunity to clarify its murky text – Congress must speak clearly about what conduct does and does not violate the FCPA' and it largely restated the FCPA reform proposals originally set forth in Restoring Balance.

Yet another former high-ranking DOJ official joined the growing chorus arguing for FCPA reform as William Jacobson (a former assistant chief for DOJ FCPA enforcement) authored an article that did not advocate any changes to the FCPA but stated:

> Instead, the DOJ could, and should, exercise its prosecutorial discretion and commit to not bringing FCPA-related criminal charges against companies that have done all they could to curb corruption within their midst and to cooperate with the government when corruption is discovered. Such a policy would serve both government and corporate interests by, among other things, bringing more cases to the attention of the government, facilitating more prosecutions of individuals, and deterring future violations while at the same time bringing predictability to the prosecutorial process and rewarding responsible companies.[30]

Jacobson's five-part test was as follows.

> (i) the company must voluntarily disclose the violation; (ii) the potential breach did not include illegal conduct by senior leaders within the company; (iii) the company must cooperate fully with the government, including providing evidence and information against employees, officers, directors, and agents of the company; (iv) the company must agree to implement appropriate remedial measures to mitigate the chances for future violations; and (v) prior

to discovering the misconduct, the company must have implemented a robust compliance program.

Jacobson stated that 'if a company meets each element of this test, DOJ policy should state that the company will not be charged (including by DPA or NPA).'

In conclusion, Jacobson stated:

> Current FCPA enforcement policy punishes rather than rewards companies that do all they can reasonably be expected to do to deter corruption and to cooperate with the government. This had led to an FCPA legislative reform movement that has gained considerable momentum over the past 18 months. DOJ can blunt most of these efforts with a shift in its prosecution policy that rewards responsible companies while at the same time serves important government interests and continues DOJ's fight against international corruption.

Wal-Mart's FCPA scrutiny

High-profile instances of FCPA scrutiny focus attention on the law and its enforcement across a broad spectrum. In 2012, arguably the most high-profile instance of scrutiny in the FCPA's thirty-five year history occurred as Wal-Mart's alleged conduct in Mexico dominated the news cycle. In addition to the enforcement agencies political posturing on FCPA Guidance, Wal-Mart's FCPA scrutiny likely further stalled FCPA reform.

Even though Wal-Mart disclosed FCPA scrutiny in a late 2011 SEC filing, attention to its FCPA scrutiny exploded in 2012 when the *New York Times* ran a front-page article titled 'Vast Mexico Bribery Case Hushed Up by Wal-Mart after Top-Level Struggle.'[31] The *Times* article was both unremarkable and remarkable.

The unremarkable portion of the *Times* article was that a foreign subsidiary of a multi-national company operating in an FCPA high-risk jurisdiction allegedly made payments in approximately 2005 to 'foreign officials' to facilitate the issuance of certain licenses or permits. The *Times* article focused on Wal-Mart's largest foreign subsidiary, Wal-Mart de Mexico, and suggested that Wal-Mart Mexico 'orchestrated a campaign of bribery to win market dominance' and 'paid bribes to obtain permits in virtually every corner' of Mexico. According to the article, the alleged payments: 'bought zoning approvals, reductions in environmental impact fees and allegiance of neighborhood leaders'; the idea behind the payments 'was to build hundreds of new stores so fast that competitors would not have time to react'; and the payments 'accelerated growth … got zoning maps changed … made environmental objections vanish' and that 'permits that typically took months to process magically materialized in days.' According to the *Times*, Wal-Mart Mexico 'had taken steps to conceal [the payments] from Wal-Mart's headquarters in Bentonville, Ark.' and Wal-Mart Mexico's chief auditor altered reports sent to Bentonville discussing various problematic payments.

The above portions of the *Times* article were unremarkable and not just because, as highlighted in Chapter 3, the government has an overall losing record when put to its burden of proof as to non-foreign government procurement-type payments at issue in Wal-Mart. In addition, as noted in a subsequent *Times* article, Wal-Mart's investigation 'was uncovering the kinds of problems and oversights that plague many global corporations.'[32]

Nevertheless, the 2012 *Times* article clearly heightened Wal-Mart's FCPA scrutiny and the company quickly became one of the most high-profile instances of FCPA scrutiny ever.

The remarkable aspects of the *Times* article included the conduct (or lack thereof) of Wal-Mart and its top executives upon learning of the conduct of its Mexican subsidiary. Even in 2005 and continuing today most business leaders, audit committees, and boards tend to overreact to potential FCPA issues and often reflexibly launch broad internal investigations.

However, the payment issues at Wal-Mart Mexico apparently resulted in the opposite at Wal-Mart's corporate headquarters. The *Times* article stated as to events in 2005:

> Wal-Mart dispatched investigators to Mexico City, and within days they unearthed evidence of widespread bribery. They found a paper trail of hundreds of suspected payments totaling more than $24 million. They also found documents showing that Wal-Mart de Mexico's top executives not only knew about the payments, but had taken steps to conceal them from Wal-Mart's headquarters in Bentonville, Arkansas.

According to the *Times*, Wal-Mart's lead investigator, a former FBI agent, 'recommended that Wal-Mart expand the investigation,' but its own examination found that 'Wal-Mart's leaders shut it down.' The article stated that 'in one meeting where the bribery case was discussed, [Wal-Mart's then chief executive] rebuked internal investigators for being overly aggressive.' The *Times* article also suggested that instead of following outside legal advice to set up a 'spare-no-expenses investigation major corporations routinely undertake when confronted with allegations of serious wrongdoing,' Wal-Mart's leaders rejected this approach. Instead, Wal-Mart's lawyers supervised 'a far more limited preliminary inquiry by in-house investigators.' According to the *Times*, Wal-Mart again considered a full investigation of the conduct in Mexico, but in the end, the company largely delegated responsibility for the investigation to Wal-Mart Mexico.

In short, Wal-Mart dominated the news cycle in 2012 not because it joined a list of approximately one hundred companies the subject of FCPA scrutiny, but rather because of the conduct (or lack thereof) of Wal-Mart and its top executives upon learning of potential FCPA issues. Against this backdrop, it is useful to view the Wal-Mart story as a corporate governance sandwich with the FCPA merely a condiment.

Nevertheless, Wal-Mart's high-profile FCPA scrutiny instantly became linked to FCPA reform efforts. Representatives Elijah Cummings and Henry Waxman soon sent letters to the Chairman of the Board of Directors of the Retail Industry Leaders Association and the President of the U.S. Chamber of Commerce that stated:

> We are concerned about the role that Wal-Mart officials may have played in the Chamber's Institute for Legal Reform. It would appear to be a conflict of interest for Wal-Mart officials to advise on ways to weaken the FCPA at a time when the leadership of the company was apparently aware of corporate conduct that may have violated the law.[33]

A *New York Times* columnist observed:

> The investigation of Wal-Mart has brought the FCPA to the attention of the public in a way not seen since the 1970s scandals that led to its adoption. Congress may find it politically impossible to adopt changes to the statute that would arguably make it more difficult to pursue cases as long as the allegations of foreign bribery by a leading American company remain in the headlines.[34]

Even though an aide to Senator Christopher Coons (who was emerging as a leader of the FCPA reform movement on Capitol Hill) said that legislative policy would not be decided based on a news story,[35] that is exactly what happened as news of Wal-Mart's high-profile scrutiny further stalled FCPA reform. Indeed, the Chief Counsel to the House Energy and Commerce Committee said that the *New York Times* Wal-Mart article 'changed the tide and mood entirely' on Capitol Hill regarding FCPA reform.[36] The Congressional Aide stated that as 'practical matter, public opinion matters, what happens in the real world matters' and that the atmosphere surrounding FCPA reform after the Wal-Mart article has made it 'harder for different groups to advocate' for FCPA reform. He further acknowledged that this perception 'does not have a whole lot to do with the underlying facts' of the Wal-Mart matter, but that 'public perception and pressure on government institutions' matters.

History had indeed repeated itself and a substantive, issue-based discussion of the FCPA and its enforcement proved elusive. Attention and focus thus turned to the FCPA Guidance, and predicting its release turned into an amusing FCPA Inc. parlor game. Despite both the DOJ and SEC having specific FCPA units, and despite both enforcement agencies indicating in the past, in various ways and in various settings, that the FCPA is a clear and unambiguous statute, it took one year for the Guidance to be released. In a further sign of political maneuvering, the FCPA Guidance was released approximately one week after the November 2012 presidential election and during a lame duck Congress.

Despite the Guidance and despite the belief of certain civil society organizations long opposed to any FCPA reform that the Guidance 'renders moot' reform,[37] FCPA reform remains a viable issue.

Why should the non-binding FCPA Guidance be the end to FCPA reform discussions? As both DOJ and SEC officials acknowledged at the press conference, the Guidance 'does not represent a change in policy.'[38] Further, the FCPA Guidance was not the result of a policy debate whether the current FCPA and its enforcement represent the best approach. In fact and as detailed above, it is likely that one of the purposes of the Guidance was to prevent such a policy debate from going forward.

Post-FCPA Guidance many have continued to call for FCPA reform. For instance, in early 2013, the Manhattan Institute for Policy Research released an issue brief that stated:

> There is a strong case for reforming the FCPA through legislation, in order to continue to uphold the statute's historical commitment to maintain the integrity of American businesses' dealings abroad while limiting the ability of federal enforcement agencies to police business conduct worldwide and gain broad, quasi-regulatory powers over global businesses absent judicial oversight.[39]

Likewise, in early 2013, the Chamber of Commerce and a broad coalition of business groups sent a letter to the enforcement agencies expressing appreciation for the FCPA Guidance, but also identifying 'several areas of continuing concern for businesses seeking in good faith to comply with the FCPA' including many of the same issues first identified in Restoring Balance.[40]

What the FCPA and FCPA enforcement needs at this critical juncture is not non-binding enforcement agency guidance, but reform. The final section of this book suggests FCPA reforms.

B. SUGGESTED FCPA REFORM

The implicit position of those opposing FCPA reform would seem to be that the FCPA is a perfect statute and that current FCPA enforcement policies are best achieving the laudable objectives of the law. This is not the position advanced in this book and the insightful words of the U.S. Trade Representative from a prior era of FCPA reform bear repeating.

> Just because the FCPA spotlights a sensitive subject, some people wish to turn a 'blind eye' to its shortcomings rather than risk being accused of being 'soft on bribery.' That is too easy a way out. Retreating from controversy will not cure the law's deficiencies. […] Is there any U.S. law that ought to be above such review and clarification – especially one as complex as the FCPA.[41]

After addressing the shortcomings of certain FCPA reform proposals discussed above, this section suggests FCPA reforms designed to ensure that the FCPA is best achieving the original goals of the law and that FCPA enforcement is transparent and otherwise consistent with rule of law principles.

The FCPA reform proposals discussed above all have certain limitations or deficiencies. The Chamber's FCPA reform proposals are in large part a plea for judicial scrutiny and application of black-letter legal principles to FCPA enforcement. However, the remedy for enforcement of a law that largely takes place in the absence of meaningful judicial scrutiny and is often inconsistent with black-letter legal principles is not to amend the law, but to inject judicial scrutiny into the enforcement process so that legal issues can be vetted and decided upon by someone other than the enforcement agencies.

So-called 'Regulation FCPA', a permissive filing regime whereby an issuer 'would benefit from a regulatory presumption of compliance' and thus 'protect itself, its senior management and its board of directors from vicarious, general corporate liability' in the FCPA context focuses only on issuers and thus would not apply to most business organizations subject to the FCPA's anti-bribery provisions.

The 'FCPA Immunization-Inoculation Program,' in which the enforcement agencies would give a qualified assurance that no enforcement action would be brought against participating companies under certain conditions, would only be triggered after expensive and lengthy engagements of accounting firms and law firms and disclosure of accounting-legal audit results to government agencies.

The proposal that the DOJ change its internal policy and commit to not bringing FCPA-related criminal charges against companies that have done all they could to curb corruption and cooperate with the DOJ when corruption is discovered merely calls for a change to non-binding DOJ policy.

What the FCPA and FCPA enforcement need at this critical juncture is not simply revisions to non-binding policy, pleas for judicial scrutiny, reform applicable to just issuers, or reform dependent on disclosure to the enforcement agencies. Rather, the best forward-looking solution to FCPA reform is two-fold: first, amend the FCPA to include a compliance defense; and second, abolish NPAs and DPAs in the FCPA context. As explained in more detail below, the end result of such reforms would be to better incentivize more robust corporate compliance – and thus reduce improper conduct and best advance the FCPA's objectives of reducing bribery – as well as increase the transparency of FCPA enforcement and better align it with rule of law principles.

The reform proposals set forth below are in addition to those previously mentioned in Chapter 5 (remove the SEC from enforcing the FCPA's anti-bribery provisions) and Chapter 6 (prohibit DOJ or SEC FCPA enforcement attorneys who have supervisory and discretionary authority from providing FCPA defense or compliance services in the private sector for five years upon leaving government service).

Compliance Defense

A compliance defense recognizes the unique aspects and challenges of complying with the FCPA in the global marketplace as highlighted throughout this book. A compliance defense would mean that a company's pre-existing compliance policies and procedures, and its good-faith efforts to comply with the FCPA, would be relevant *as a matter of law* when a non-executive employee or agent acts contrary to those policies and procedures and in violation of the FCPA. Such a compliance defense would not eliminate corporate criminal liability under the FCPA or reward 'fig leaf' or 'purely paper' compliance programs. For instance, a compliance defense would not apply to corrupt business organizations, activity engaged in or condoned by directors or executive officers, or activity by any employee or agent if it occurred in the absence of pre-existing compliance policies and procedures.

A compliance defense amendment is best incorporated into the FCPA as an additional element of an anti-bribery offense, meaning that to charge a business organization with such an offense, the DOJ will have the burden of establishing, as an additional element, that the company failed to have pre-existing policies and procedures reasonably designed to detect and prevent the improper conduct by non-executive employees or agents. As highlighted below, incorporating a compliance defense into the FCPA in this way is consistent with the FCPA-like laws of several peer nations.

A compliance defense is not a new or novel idea

Contrary to the DOJ's claims that an FCPA compliance defense is 'risky and novel,' a compliance defense is not a new or novel idea. Rather it has been around for nearly as long as the FCPA itself. The first apparent reference to a compliance-like defense in the FCPA's legislative history was in 1983 during a House hearing regarding a bill to amend the FCPA. A former SEC enforcement official testified at the hearing and stated:

> I would also support some type of affirmative due diligence defense that a corporation would be able to prove to avoid criminal responsibility on a reckless disregard theory. Since 1933, in the Securities Act of 1933, there has been a due diligence defense for issuers and their officers and directors with respect to whether or not a registration statement is false. I think comparable language could be placed in the bill so that corporations would have an affirmative due diligence defense.[42]

The first FCPA reform bill to include a compliance defense was introduced in 1986 and the relevant portion of the bill stated:

> Due Diligence. – An issuer [or domestic concern] may not be held vicariously liable, either civilly or criminally, for a violation [of the FCPA's anti-bribery provisions] by its employee, who is not an officer or director, if – (1) such issuer [or domestic concern] has established procedures, which would reasonably be expected to prevent and detect, insofar as practicable, any such violation by such employee, and (2) the officer and employee of the issuer [or domestic concern] with supervisory responsibility for the conduct of the employee used due diligence to prevent the commission of the offense by that employee. Such issuer [or domestic concern] shall have the burden of proving by a preponderance of the evidence that it meets the requirements set forth in paragraphs (1) and (2).[43]

The House Report summarizing the bill stated that if 'a corporation has set up internal controls to avoid illicit payments or has otherwise acted to keep within the law, its "due diligence" can be used as a defense against both civil and criminal liability in cases where its employees have nonetheless engaged in bribery.'[44] Elsewhere, the House Report stated that 'a company may not be held vicariously liable if it can show that it had established procedures to prevent its employees from making bribes and that its supervisory employees had used "due diligence" to prevent employees or third parties from making bribes.'

Other FCPA reforms bills in the 1980s also incorporated a compliance defense, including a bill introduced in 1987 that ultimately passed the House. The House Report summarizing the bill stated: 'The bill also provides incentives for self-policing by business, by setting forth standards of due diligence to prevent and detect violations of the law by employee and agents.'[45] Elsewhere, the House Report stated:

> The bill establishes … a new, 'due diligence' defense for civil and criminal liability of issuers and domestic concerns for violations of the FCPA by employees and agents. It provides that if the issuer or domestic concern has established procedures for detecting violations, and if the officers and employees with supervisory responsibility for the employees or agent violating the law have exercised due diligence to prevent the violation, then no vicarious liability will apply. Of course, supervisory responsibility for the actions of a particular employee or agent may be exercised by many officials in an organization and can include, for example, the general supervisory authority of high level corporate officials. The requirements must be established by a preponderance of the evidence.
>
> Although 'due diligence' is a familiar concept under the Federal securities laws, the bill does not specifically define the term. It is intended that what would constitute 'due diligence' would be factual determination by the trier of fact and would vary depending upon the particular circumstances of the transaction at issue.
>
> In meeting the defense under this section, it must be shown that reasonable steps were taken. It is perhaps most important that firms create an environment which fosters good business practice and compliance with the law. In this connection, employees and agents should be encouraged to comply with the law and to report factors that may indicate improper behavior.

While the bill passed the House, a different bill containing FCPA provisions without a compliance defense passed the Senate. In conference, the House receded to the Senate and the FCPA reform that did occur in 1988 did not include a compliance defense.

The legislative history of an FCPA compliance defense is instructive and should inform the current debate on the issue. Far from a 'dangerous' or 'risky' proposal, amending the FCPA to include a compliance defense was recognized long ago as the best way to encourage and reward self-policing by companies doing business in the difficult and challenging global marketplace. What is most revealing from the legislative history is that an FCPA compliance defense reached its zenith during a period when relatively few companies engaged in substantial business beyond U.S. borders and during an era of little FCPA enforcement.

In short, the justification and rationale for an FCPA compliance defense in the 1980s pale in comparison to now as most business organizations, large and small and in a variety of industry sectors, operate in the difficult and challenging global marketplace during an era of increased FCPA enforcement.

Reforming the FCPA to include a compliance defense is also not a novel idea. As discussed above, the first reference to a compliance-like defense in the FCPA's legislative history recognized the FCPA as part of the securities laws and that other securities laws contained good-faith compliance concepts. Indeed, the FCPA is part of the Securities Exchange Act and other provisions excuse legal liability based on good-faith compliance efforts. As highlighted in Chapter 4, even the FCPA's internal controls provisions contain good-faith compliance concepts. In short, amending the FCPA's antibribery provisions to incorporate good-faith compliance concepts is not a novel idea given that the FCPA's internal controls provisions, as well as other securities law provisions, already recognize good-faith compliance efforts as being relevant as a matter of law.

Reforming the FCPA to include a compliance defense is also not a novel idea, given that several peer countries have a compliance-like defense relevant to their 'FCPA-like' law.

As previously highlighted, the U.S. is not the only country with a law prohibiting bribery of foreign officials for a business purpose. Approximately 40 other countries have adopted, like the U.S., the OECD Convention and several countries have a compliance-like defense relevant to their 'FCPA-like' law, including the United Kingdom's recently enacted Bribery Act.[46]

The U.K. Bribery Act came into force in 2011, and under the law 'a commercial organization will be liable to prosecution if a person associated with it bribes another person intending to obtain or retain business or an advantage in the conduct of business for that organization.' However, the Bribery Act also states that a 'commercial organization will have a full defense if it can show that despite a particular case of bribery it nevertheless had adequate procedures in place to prevent persons associated with it from bribing.' According to the U.K. Ministry of Justice ('MoJ'), the adequate-procedures defense is included in the Bribery Act 'to encourage commercial organizations to put procedures in place to prevent bribery by persons associated with them.'

The MoJ recognized, as the U.S. enforcement agencies have, that 'no policies or procedures are capable of detecting and preventing all bribery' and that 'no bribery prevention regime will be capable of preventing bribery at all times.' According to the MoJ, 'the objective of the Bribery Act is not to bring the full force of the criminal law to bear upon well run commercial organizations that experience an isolated incident of bribery on their behalf.' In this regard, the U.K. has taken a different approach than the U.S. and in the view of many, the U.K. approach in the Bribery Act is 'better crafted' and thus a smarter law.[47]

In addition to the United Kingdom, the following OECD Convention signatory countries also have a compliance-like defense relevant to their 'FCPA-like' laws: Australia, Chile, Germany, Hungary, Italy, Japan, Korea, Poland, Portugal, Sweden, and Switzerland.[48]

As to the type of compliance defense suggested (i.e., the DOJ would have the burden of establishing, as an addition element of an anti-bribery violation, that the company failed to have policies and procedures reasonably designed to detect and prevent improper conduct), the laws of Chile, Italy, Korea, Portugal, and Switzerland are most noteworthy.

Under Chilean law, in order for a legal person to be held responsible for a foreign bribery offence, the following element, among others, must be satisfied.

> The offence must have been made possible as a consequence of a failure of the legal entity to comply with its duties of management and supervision. An entity will have failed to comply with its duties if it violates the obligation to implement a model for the prevention of offences, or when having implemented the model, it was insufficient.[49]

Under Chilean law:

> The failure to comply with duties of management and supervision is an element of the offence rather than a defense. Therefore the burden of proof lies on prosecutors, i.e. it will be up to prosecutors to prove that the entity failed to comply with its duties of management and supervision.

Under Italian law, 'criminal liability cannot be attributed to legal persons,' but 'administrative liability may be attributed to legal persons for certain criminal offences including foreign bribery committed by a natural person.'[50] The relevant administrative decree 'provides a "defense of organizational models" to a corporate body which makes reasonable efforts to prevent the commission of an offence.' Under Italian law, 'the defense of organization models operates as a full defense which completely exculpates a legal person.'

Korean law establishes the criminal responsibility of legal persons for the bribery of a foreign public official. However, a legal person is exempt from liability 'where it has paid "due attention" or exercised "proper supervision" to prevent the offence.'[51]

Under Portuguese law, legal persons can be liable for conduct 'committed on their behalf and in the collective interest by natural persons occupying a leadership position within the legal personal structure; or by whoever acts under the authority of the natural persons.' However, 'the liability of legal persons and equivalent entities is excluded when the actor has acted against the orders or express instructions of the person responsible.'[52]

Under Swiss law, a 'defective organization is a condition for corporate criminal liability.' In order to incur criminal liability, 'the enterprise must not have taken all reasonable and necessary organizational measures to prevent the individual from committing the offence.' Under Swiss law, the burden is on the prosecutor to furnish proof of defective organization.[53]

As the above summaries highlight, a compliance-like defense is not novel, risky, or dangerous. That numerous peer countries have adopted a compliance-like defense relevant to their 'FCPA-like' laws demonstrates, among other things, that amending the FCPA to include a compliance defense would not conflict with OECD Convention obligations.

As noted above, at recent Congressional hearings the DOJ has called an FCPA compliance defense 'novel and risky' and has stated that the 'time is not right to consider it.' The DOJ Assistant Attorney General flatly rejected the need for an FCPA compliance defense and stated: 'We can't engage in some sort of formalistic solution from a script that says if you check the following six boxes you're guaranteed this outcome.'[54] Likewise, at the FCPA Guidance press conference, the Assistant Attorney General called an FCPA compliance 'dangerous' and a 'race to the bottom.'

It is difficult to understand how an FCPA compliance program consistent with the best practices set forth in Chapter 8 could ever be viewed as a purely paper compliance program or a check-a-box exercise that a company can hide behind. It is further difficult to understand how an FCPA compliance defense is 'novel and risky,' given that several other peer countries have a compliance-like defense relevant to their FCPA-like law.

The DOJ already recognizes a *de facto* compliance defense

It is even more difficult to distill the logic of the DOJ's institutional opposition to an FCPA compliance defense, given the DOJ's current recognition of a *de facto* compliance defense in its declination decisions.

For instance, in connection with the 2011 House FCPA hearing, the DOJ was requested to provide 'information on cases that had been brought to the attention of DOJ, but [the DOJ] decided, for one reason or another, not to investigate or pursue prosecution within the last year along with the rationale for those decisions.' The DOJ responded by generally referring to the Principles of Prosecution and also stated:

> During the previous two years, the DOJ declined matters in which some or all of the following circumstances existed: a corporation voluntarily and fully self-disclosed potential misconduct; corporate principals voluntarily engaged in interviews with the Department and provided truthful and complete information about their conduct; a parent corporation voluntarily and fully self-disclosed information to the Department regarding alleged conduct by subsidiaries; a parent company conducted extensive pre-acquisition due diligence of potentially liable subsidiaries, and engaged in significant remediation efforts after acquiring the relevant subsidiaries; a company provided information to the Department about the parent's extensive compliance policies, procedures, and internal controls, which the parent had implemented at the relevant subsidiaries; a company agreed to a civil resolution with the SEC, while also demonstrating that a declination was appropriate for additional reasons; a single employee, and no other employee, was involved in the provision of improper payments; and the improper payments involved minimal funds compared to the overall business revenues.[55]

Likewise, in the FCPA Guidance the enforcement agencies stated that they had declined to bring an FCPA enforcement action based on, among other factors: 'the total amount of the improper payments was relatively small, and the activity appeared to be an isolated incident by a single employee at the subsidiary' and the 'payments were detected by the company's existing internal controls.'

Thus, the DOJ already may decline to prosecute business organizations for FCPA violations under strict *respondeat superior* principles when, among other reasons, the organization had pre-existing compliance policies and procedures, only a rogue employee was involved in the improper conduct, or the improper conduct was limited in scope. Again, it is difficult to comprehend how an FCPA compliance defense is novel and risky when it would include factors the DOJ already considers in making its internal prosecutorial decisions.

In short, even though the DOJ opposes an FCPA compliance defense, it already recognizes a *de facto* compliance defense in certain instances, even if only in the opaque and unpredictable world of DOJ decision making. Thus, an FCPA compliance-defense amendment would accomplish, among other things, the policy goal of removing factors relevant to corporate criminal liability away from this world towards a more transparent and predictable model.

Former DOJ officials support a compliance defense

The DOJ's institutional opposition to an FCPA compliance defense sharply contrasts with the growing chorus of former DOJ officials who support a compliance defense. This group of former officials include, among others, two former Attorney Generals, a former Deputy Attorney General, a former Chief of the DOJ's FCPA Unit, and a former high-profile DOJ prosecutor.

For instance, former Attorney General Michael Mukasey testified at the House FCPA hearing on behalf of the Chamber of Commerce and stated:

> It is true that the DOJ or SEC may look more favorably on a company with a strong FCPA compliance program when determining whether to charge the company or what settlement terms to offer, and such compliance programs may be taken into account by a court at the sentencing of a corporation convicted of an FCPA violation. However, such benefits are subject to unlimited prosecutorial discretion, are available only after the liability phase of a prosecution, or both. There is also no guarantee that a strong compliance program will be given the weight it deserves.[56]

In advocating for a compliance defense, Mukasey noted that 'responsible companies implement and enforce strong compliance measures designed to avoid and promptly address infractions,' but that 'the absence of a compliance defense tells corporate America, in effect, no compliance effort can be good enough – even if you did everything the DOJ required, the DOJ still retains the right to prosecute purely as a matter of its discretion.' Mukasey questioned 'whether that is the appropriate signal to send to the business community and to American shareholders.'

Former Attorney General Alberto Gonzales has stated:

> I think that companies have an obligation of due diligence and should have in place a strong compliance program – particularly when doing business in countries where corruption is routine and expected. Companies cannot purposefully remain ignorant. The question is how much do they have to do? I think if the company follows the DOJ Principles of Prosecution: (1) makes a voluntary disclosure of wrongdoing, (2) if there was no participation in the illegal conduct by senior management, (3) if there is full cooperation with the government, including providing evidence and information against employees,

> officers, directors, and agents of the company, (4) if the company implements remedial measures to prevent future violations, including disciplining culpable employees, implementing internal controls, and improving anticorruption training, and (5) if the company has in place a strong compliance program before the alleged behavior happened, then I question the fairness in going after the company for the unknown violations by an agent in a foreign land.[57]

Larry Thompson, a former Deputy Attorney General and current general counsel at a large multinational company, stated:

> The FCPA serves the important goal of discouraging bribery by U.S. companies overseas. But by making firms criminally responsible for even the most uncontrollable acts of low-level employees and agents – and ignoring any efforts to create a culture of ethics and compliance – many U.S. companies withdraw rather than face limitless exposure. As a result, less-scrupulous foreign competitors often step in, harming America's economic vitality and, ironically, fueling the very misconduct the act was intended to reduce. The solution: make the act apply only to material misconduct and allow companies to assert a 'best efforts' defense if they have effective compliance and ethics programs.[58]

Joseph Covington, a former head of the DOJ's FCPA Unit, has called consideration of an FCPA compliance defense 'manifestly reasonable' and observed that a compliance defense 'would recognize and reward strong compliance programs; provide a powerful incentive for companies to develop and enforce such programs; may encourage more companies to come forward with voluntary disclosures; and yet still enable prosecution of the culpable individuals.'[59]

Andrew Weissmann, the former Director of the DOJ's Enron Task Force, has long advocated 'rethinking criminal corporate liability'[60] and stated at the 2010 Senate FCPA hearing on behalf of the Chamber of Commerce:

> The FCPA should incentivize the company to establish compliance systems that will actively discourage and detect bribery, but should also permit companies that maintain such effective systems to avail themselves of an affirmative defense to charges of FCPA violations. This is so because in such countries even if companies have strong compliance systems in place, a third-party vendor or errant employee may be tempted to engage in unauthorized acts that violate the business's explicit anti-bribery policies.[61]

Weissmann observed that 'it is unfair to hold a business criminally liable for behavior that was neither sanctioned by nor known to the business' and that 'the imposition of criminal liability in such a situation does nothing to further the goals of the FCPA; it merely creates the illusion that the problem of bribery is being addressed, while the parties that actually engaged in bribery often continue on, undeterred and unpunished.' Weissmann further stated that an FCPA compliance defense 'will give corporations some measure of protection from aggressive or misinformed prosecutors, who can exploit the power imbalance inherent in the current FCPA statute – which permits indictment of a corporation even for the acts of a single, low-level rogue employee – to force corporations into DPAs.'

Against the backdrop of a growing chorus of former DOJ officials who support an FCPA compliance defense, there seems little principled basis for the DOJ's institutional opposition to such a defense. Rather, the DOJ's opposition to a compliance defense seems motivated by its desire to protect its lucrative FCPA enforcement program which provides maximum leverage against business organizations when a non-executive employee or agent acts contrary to pre-existing FCPA compliance policies and procedures.

Policy objectives advanced by an FCPA compliance defense

In addition to removing factors relevant to corporate criminal liability away from the opaque and unpredictable world of DOJ decision making towards a more transparent and predictable model, an FCPA compliance defense would also advance certain other important policy objectives.

An FCPA compliance defense would better incentivize more robust corporate compliance, reduce improper conduct, and thus best advance the FCPA's objective of reducing bribery. An FCPA compliance defense would also increase public confidence in FCPA enforcement and allow the enforcement agencies to better allocate their limited prosecutorial resources to cases involving corrupt business organizations and the individuals who actually engaged in the improper conduct.

The goal of the FCPA is to prevent bribery of foreign officials. That goal is best accomplished not solely through *ad hoc* enforcement actions, but also by better incentivizing corporate compliance designed to prevent improper payments. This has long been recognized by Congress, the DOJ, and others. For instance, in passing the FCPA, Congress anticipated that the 'criminalization of foreign corporate bribery will to a significant extent act as a self-enforcing preventative mechanism.' Likewise, since the FCPA's earliest days the DOJ has recognized that the 'most efficient means of implementing the FCPA is voluntary compliance by the American business community.'

As highlighted in Chapter 2, business organizations currently have at least two incentives to implement FCPA compliance policies and procedures. First, a factor the DOJ considers under its Principles of Prosecution in deciding whether to bring criminal charges against an organization is 'the existence and effectiveness of the corporation's pre-existing compliance program.' An organization with pre-existing FCPA compliance policies and procedures facing FCPA scrutiny because of *respondeat superior* principles is likely to be treated less harshly by the DOJ than an organization without pre-existing policies and procedures. Second, a factor determining organization fine and penalty amounts under the Sentencing Guidelines is the existence of 'an effective compliance and ethics program.' An organization with pre-existing FCPA compliance policies and procedures will likely face a lower fine amount when resolving an FCPA enforcement action than an organization without pre-existing policies and procedures.

The above incentives however are not well known by a meaningful segment of the business community and there are likely few business leaders well versed in the details of these incentives. In addition, despite these incentives, business organizations operating in a world of finite resources are not sufficiently implementing comprehensive FCPA policies and procedures.

Survey after survey indicates that a significant percentage of business organizations subject to the FCPA fail to maintain an adequate system for selection and approval of consultants, fail to conduct audits of payments to consultants, fail to conduct due diligence of third parties, and fail to regularly evaluate the effectiveness of their compliance and ethics programs. Even the enforcement agencies acknowledged in the FCPA Guidance that '64% of general counsel whose companies are subject to the FCPA say there is room for improvement in their FCPA training and compliance programs.'

Compliance is a cost center within a business organization and expenditure of finite resources on FCPA compliance is an investment best sold if it can reduce legal exposure, not merely lessen the impact of legal exposure. For instance, in reference to the U.K.'s adequate procedures defense, a former DOJ prosecutor stated: '[The Bribery Act has a] wonderful feature to it, which is that a corporation is legally not responsible if it had adopted adequate procedures. It's a great argument that we can take to the business about why they ought to invest in an appropriate compliance program.'[62]

The incentives business organizations currently have to adopt FCPA compliance policies and procedures are solely to lessen the impact of legal exposure. These incentives thus represent 'baby carrots' when what is needed to better incentivize more robust FCPA compliance are real 'carrots.' As the enforcement agencies acknowledge in the FCPA Guidance, 'positive incentives' can drive compliant behavior and an FCPA compliance defense is the best 'positive incentive' as it represents a real 'carrot' that will better incentivize compliance across the business landscape. Organizations with existing FCPA compliance policies and procedures will be incentivized to make existing programs better. Likewise, organizations currently without stand-alone FCPA policies and procedures – and statistics indicate there are many – will be incentivized to spend finite resources to implement FCPA compliance policies and procedures.

In short, an FCPA compliance defense can increase 'soft enforcement' of the FCPA by better incentivizing organizations to implement more robust FCPA policies and procedure. More robust FCPA compliance policies and procedures can reduce instances of improper conduct and thereby advance the FCPA's objectives.

The root causes of several FCPA enforcement actions have been inadequate training of employees and inadequate due diligence of foreign third parties. While the answer will never be known, the question can nevertheless be asked: if there were an FCPA compliance defense that better incentivized companies to implement more robust FCPA compliance policies and procedures, would more companies properly train their employees on FCPA risk and properly scrutinize foreign third parties?

An FCPA compliance defense surely will not result in 100 percent compliance in all business organizations subject to the FCPA. However, it is reasonable to conclude that an FCPA compliance defense will better incentivize more robust FCPA compliance policies and procedures, reduce improper conduct, and thus best advance the FCPA's objective of reducing bribery.

A compliance defense will also increase public confidence in FCPA enforcement actions and allow the DOJ to better allocate its limited enforcement resources. As previously highlighted in Chapter 2, several companies have resolved FCPA enforcement actions or have otherwise been the subject of FCPA scrutiny during the same general time period as being recognized as one of the 'world's most ethical companies.' As previously explained, this is illogical yet possible because of *respondeat superior* principles under which an employee or agent can expose a business organization to FCPA liability even if such payments were contrary to the company's pre-existing compliance policies and procedures and even if the company in good faith engaged in all reasonable steps to prevent such conduct.

Given the number of companies under FCPA scrutiny and given the many FCPA industry sweeps currently underway, it should be asked whether misconduct is so rampant among business organizations or, as a former prosecutor noted in the non-FCPA context, whether the enforcement and scrutiny have 'more to do with the leverage the government enjoys than the merits of what the company did or didn't do.'[63] The same observation can be made in this new era of FCPA enforcement. Yet because of *respondeat superior* and the 'carrots' and 'sticks' relevant to resolving an FCPA enforcement action, the enforcement agencies have tremendous leverage against good corporate citizens doing business in difficult and challenging global markets when a non-executive employee or agent acts contrary to the company's pre-existing FCPA compliance policies and procedures.

The rule of law is best advanced and public confidence in a law is best achieved when law enforcement agencies make transparent and predictable decisions. On a number of issues, the enforcement agencies' FCPA decisions are opaque and unpredictable. As the DOJ's own words demonstrate, sometimes the DOJ declines to prosecute an organization if: (i) it has 'extensive compliance policies, procedures, and internal controls'; (ii) 'a single employee, and no other employee, was involved in the provision of improper payments'; or (iii) the 'improper payments involved minimal funds compared to the overall business revenues.' Yet, as FCPA enforcement actions demonstrate, sometimes the DOJ decides to proceed with an FCPA enforcement in similar situations.

An FCPA compliance defense would also allow the enforcement agencies to better allocate its limited prosecutorial resources to cases involving corrupt business organizations and the individuals who actually engaged in the improper conduct. As highlighted in Chapter 5, key to achieving deterrence in the FCPA context is individual prosecutions, and during this new era of FCPA enforcement the DOJ has consistently stated that 'prosecution of individuals is a cornerstone of its FCPA enforcement strategy.'

An FCPA compliance defense will better facilitate the DOJ's prosecution of culpable individuals and advance the objectives of its FCPA enforcement program. Even though, as highlighted in Chapter 5, voluntary disclosures are the single largest source of corporate FCPA enforcement actions, many business organizations that learn through internal reporting mechanisms of rogue employee conduct implicating the FCPA are nevertheless hesitant to report such conduct to the enforcement authorities. In such situations, business organizations are rightfully concerned to submit to the DOJ's opaque and unpredictable decision-making process and are rightfully concerned that its pre-existing FCPA compliance policies and procedures and its good faith compliance efforts will not be properly recognized. The end result is that the enforcement agencies often do not become aware of individuals who make improper payments in violation of the FCPA and the individuals are thus not held legally accountable for their actions.

An FCPA compliance defense surely will not cause every business organization that learns of rogue employee conduct to disclose such conduct to the enforcement agencies. However, it is reasonable to conclude that an FCPA compliance defense will cause more organizations with robust FCPA compliance policies and procedures to disclose rogue employee conduct to the enforcement agencies. Thus, an FCPA compliance defense can better facilitate DOJ prosecution of culpable individuals and increase the deterrent effect of FCPA enforcement actions.

Amending the FCPA to include a compliance defense is just one component of suggested FCPA reform. An FCPA compliance defense also needs to be coupled with abolishing NPAs and DPAs in the FCPA context.

Abolition of Non-Prosecution and Deferred Prosecution Agreements

An FCPA compliance defense will better incentize more robust corporate compliance, reduce improper conduct and thus best advance the FCPA's objectives of reducing bribery. The second prong of FCPA reform – abolishing NPAs and DPAs – will increase the transparency of FCPA enforcement and better align FCPA enforcement with rule of law principles.

The proposal to abolish NPAs and DPAs in the FCPA context does not seek to abolish a long-standing feature of the U.S. criminal justice system. Rather, as noted in Chapter 2, these resolution vehicles are new inventions that were introduced to FCPA enforcement in 2004. In this way, abolishing NPAs and DPAs merely seeks a return to the 'prosecute or do not prosecute' criminal justice system that has served our country well since its founding.

It is clear that the DOJ feels constrained by this traditional two-choice system, and the Assistant Attorney General has maintained that it presents prosecutors a 'stark choice when they encounter a corporation that had engaged in misconduct – either indict, or walk away.'[64] However, there is absolutely nothing wrong with this choice. Bringing criminal charges against a business organization or individual should not be easy. It should be difficult. Our founding fathers recognized this as a necessary bulwark against an all-powerful government and there is no legal or policy reason warranting a change from such a fundamental and long-lasting principle.

To justify its extensive use of NPAs and DPAs, the DOJ has constructed the policy argument that actually criminally prosecuting a business organization will cause its demise. In support, the DOJ frequently references how the 2002 indictment and conviction of accounting firm Arthur Andersen led to its demise even though the criminal conviction was ultimately reversed by the Supreme Court. For instance, the Assistant Attorney General stated:

> I personally feel that it's my duty to consider whether individual employees with no responsibility for, or knowledge of, misconduct committed by others in the same company are going to lose their livelihood if we indict the corporation. In large multi-national companies, the jobs of tens of thousands of employees can be at stake.[65]

However, the so-called 'Arthur Anderson effect' that serves as the DOJ's primary policy justification for using NPAs and DPAs is a fallacy and has been effectively debunked.[66] Relying on actual enforcement action data, a study found that 'much in opposition to the warnings of extreme collateral consequences that are continually repeated in both the popular and academic literature –no publicly traded company went out of business as the result of a federal criminal conviction in the years 2001 to 2010.' Indeed, in 2013 the DOJ Deputy Assistant Attorney General acknowledged that there is a very small chance that a company would be put out of business as a result of actual DOJ criminal charges.[67]

The DOJ also justifies its extensive use of NPAs and DPAs to resolve alleged instances of corporate crime by maintaining that such agreements 'have had a truly transformative effect on particular companies and, more generally, on corporate culture across the globe.' The Assistant Attorney General stated:

> The result has been, unequivocally, far greater accountability for corporate wrongdoing – and a sea change in corporate compliance efforts. [...] One of the reasons why DPAs are such a powerful tool is that, in many ways, a DPA has the same punitive, deterrent, and rehabilitative effect as a guilty plea.[68]

Here again however, the DOJ's policy justification rings hollow as there is no data to suggest that resolving alleged instances of corporate criminal liability via NPAs or DPAs achieves any deterrent effect. For instance, the GAO study on NPAs and DPAs found:

> DOJ cannot evaluate and demonstrate the extent to which DPAs and NPAs – in addition to other tools, such as prosecution – contribute to the department's efforts to combat corporate crime because it has no measures to assess their effectiveness. Specifically, DOJ intends for these agreements to promote

> corporate reform; however, DOJ does not have performance measures in place to assess whether this goal has been met. [...] While DOJ has stated that DPAs and NPAs are useful tools for combating and deterring corporate crime, without performance measures, it will be difficult for DOJ to demonstrate that these agreements are effective at helping the department achieve this goal.[69]

Likewise, the OECD report on FCPA enforcement observed that the 'actual deterrent effect [of NPAs and DPAs] has not been quantified' and it requested that the U.S. 'make public any information about the impact of NPAs and DPAs on deterring the bribery of foreign public officials.'[70] The DOJ's response to this request stated:

> Scholars have recognized that quantifying deterrence is extremely difficult. This is equally true for the deterrent effect of DPAs and NPAs. Thus [...] measuring 'the impact of NPAs and DPAs in deterring the bribery of foreign public officials' would be a difficult task, save providing certain anecdotal and other circumstantial evidence. One of the best sources of anecdotal evidence demonstrating that DPAs and NPAs have a deterrent effect comes from the companies themselves. The companies against which DPAs and NPAs have been brought have often undergone dramatic changes.[71]

Despite the DOJ's statement that companies resolving FCPA enforcement actions via NPAs or DPAs have 'undergone dramatic changes,' several companies that resolved FCPA enforcement actions through NPAs or DPAs have subsequently resolved additional FCPA enforcement actions or been the subject of additional FCPA scrutiny.

For instance, in 2008 Aibel Group Ltd. pleaded guilty to violating the FCPA's anti-bribery provisions and 'admitted that it was not in compliance with a DPA it had entered into with the DOJ in 2007 regarding the same underlying conduct.' The DOJ release stated: 'This is the third time since July 2004 that entities affiliated with Aibel Group have pleaded guilty to violating the FCPA.'[72] Likewise, Ingersoll-Rand, fresh off its exit of a DPA in 2011, soon disclosed other potential violations of the FCPA.[73] Further, the DPA that the DOJ used to resolve Daimler's egregious conduct in violation of the FCPA was extended.[74] Although the reasons for the extension were not made public, the DPA provided that it could be extended if Daimler 'knowingly violated any provision of the Agreement.'

In short, the policy justifications the DOJ has advanced in support of its frequent use of NPAs and DPAs are either based on a fallacy or ring hollow, and it has been stated that the DOJ's justifications are a 'policy is search of a rationale.'[75]

What is clear from the DOJ's frequent use of NPAs and DPAs, as well as public statements by high-ranking DOJ officials, is that the DOJ is clearly troubled, and with good reason, by traditional notions of corporate criminal liability. However, rather than seek substantive solutions to this issue either on a statute-by-statute basis, such as an FCPA compliance defense as suggested above, or more comprehensively, the DOJ has instead defended an alternate reality that is equally problematic for the reasons stated above as well as in Chapter 2 which detailed the many controversial aspects of NPAs and DPAs.

Simply put, the extensive use of NPAs and DPAs to resolve alleged corporate criminal liability in the FCPA context presents two distinct, yet equally problematic public policy issues. The first is that such vehicles, because they do not result in any actual charges filed against a company – and thus do not require the company to plead guilty to any charges – allow egregious instances of corporate conduct to be resolved too lightly without adequate sanctions and without achieving maximum deterrence. The second is that such vehicles, because of the same factors discussed above, nudge companies to agree to the vehicles for reasons of risk aversion and efficiency and not necessarily because the conduct at issue actually violates the FCPA. Thus NPAs and DPAs both facilitate the under-prosecution of egregious instances of business bribery as well as the over-prosecution of business conduct.

The FCPA enforcement action against BizJet/Lufthansa is instructive as to both of these issues.[76] As to under-prosecution, the BizJet criminal information alleged misconduct by several senior executives. The information further alleged that

> at a Board of Directors meeting [the executives] discussed with the Board that the decision of where an aircraft is sent for maintenance work is generally made by the potential customer's director of maintenance or chief pilot, that these individuals are demanding $30,000 to $40,000 in commissions, and that BizJet would pay referral fees in order to gain market share.

The DOJ further alleged that at the Board meeting, in response to a question by a director about how BizJet would survive the next six months without 'burning cash,' a senior executive stated that BizJet expected to gain market share by paying 'referral fees' just as the competition was doing. Despite senior executive misconduct and apparent knowing acquiescence by the board of directors, BizJet was allowed to resolve its FCPA scrutiny via a DPA and, should it abide by the terms and conditions of the agreement, the company will never be required to plead guilty to anything.

As to 'over-prosecution,' the DOJ also announced that BizJet's 'indirect parent company, Lufthansa Technik AG' entered into an NPA with the DOJ 'in connection with the unlawful payments by BizJet and its directors, officers, employees and agents.' The release stated: 'The DOJ has agreed not to prosecute Lufthansa Technik provided that Lufthansa Technik satisfies its obligations under the agreement for a period of three years.' The open question is on what basis the DOJ could prosecute Lufthansa as there was no factual basis in the Lufthansa Technik NPA for any charges. The NPA was likely the most opaque, bare-bones NPA in the history of the FCPA. It merely stated that the DOJ will 'not criminally prosecute' the entity 'for any crimes' related to violations of the FCPA's anti-bribery provisions arising from or related to the conduct described in the BizJet criminal information and DPA even though there is no mention of Lufthansa in these documents. All that was apparent from the DOJ's resolution documents was that BizJet was an indirect subsidiary of Lufthansa.

As previously highlighted, in analyzing whether NPAs or DPAs represent over-prosecution of the FCPA, a suitable proxy is comparing the number of individual prosecutions that follow corporate NPAs or DPAs compared to individual prosecutions that follow actual criminal charges against a company. The hypothesis is that the latter represents a higher-quality FCPA enforcement action whereas the former represents a lower-quality FCPA enforcement action. A compelling data point is that since NPAs and DPAs were first introduced to the FCPA context, only 6.5 percent of corporate enforcement actions resolved solely with an NPA or DPA have resulted in related criminal charges of company employees.[77] In stark contrast, 83 percent of corporate enforcement actions that were the result of a criminal indictment or resulted in a guilty plea by the corporate entity have resulted in related criminal charges of company employees.

It is easy to see why the DOJ favors the use of NPAs and DPAs to resolve FCPA enforcement actions. The use of such resolution vehicles insulates the DOJ's FCPA enforcement theories from judicial scrutiny in all but the rarest of circumstances and places the DOJ in the role of prosecutor, judge, and jury all at the same time. Think of the judicial process as a river where legal issues are allowed to flow into the proper channel. NPAs and DPAs are the logs and rubbish blocking the flow of issues into the proper channel and instead of judicial decisions framing the law, prosecutorial common law flourishes.

The use of NPAs and DPAs also allows the DOJ to feed its lucrative FCPA enforcement program. In the words of the OECD 'it seems quite clear that the use of these agreements is one of the reasons for the impressive FCPA enforcement record in the U.S.,' and in the words of the DOJ's former DOJ FCPA Unit chief, if the DOJ did not have NPAs and DPAs, it 'would certainly bring fewer cases.'

However, more FCPA enforcement – while politically popular with civil society groups and FCPA Inc. – is not an inherent good, particularly when the reason for the high levels of enforcement conflict with accepted rule of law principles.

The enforcement agencies often speak of the rule of law in connection with FCPA enforcement, but it is usually the U.S. as the preacher and the rest of the world as the congregation. For instance, the DOJ Assistant Attorney General delivered a speech before the Council on Foreign Relations titled 'International Criminal Law Enforcement: Rule of Law, Anti-Corruption and Beyond,' and how the increase in FCPA enforcement was consistent with U.S.'s global approach to promote the rule of law.[78] The Assistant Attorney General began his speech by asking two rhetorical questions: is the rule of law 'more than just a catch phrase' and 'does the rule of law have any real meaning,' and concluded his speech by saying that there is nothing 'more critical, both to our country and to other nations, than establishing true rule of law.'

The same could be asked as to various aspects of FCPA enforcement in this new era, including the extensive use of NPAs and DPAs. Is the rule of law 'more than just a catch phrase' and 'does the rule of law have any real meaning?'

A commonly accepted rule of law principle includes limited government powers. The World Justice Project defines this factor as a 'system of checks and balances to limit the reach of excessive government power' and 'the distribution of authority in a manner that ensures that no single organ of government has the practical ability to exercise unchecked power.'[79]

The prevalent use of NPAs and DPAs to resolve FCPA enforcement actions falls short of this rule of law principle. As previously highlighted: 'Prosecutors' virtually unchecked powers under DPAs and NPAs threaten our constitutional framework. [...] Federal prosecutors are ... assuming the role of judge (interpreting the law) and of legislature (setting broad policy choices about industry conduct), substantially eroding the separation of powers.'

Likewise, former Attorney General Mukasey stated:

> The primary statutory interpretive function is performed almost exclusively by the DOJ. [...] By negotiating resolutions [...] before an indictment or enforcement action is filed, the agencies effectively control the disposition of

> FCPA cases they initiate. […] We are left with a circumstance in which […] the FCPA means what the enforcement agencies say it means.[80]

In short, NPAs and DPAs are a new experiment in enforcing the FCPA. However, the policy rationales justifying the experiment are based on a fallacy or ring hollow, and the alternative resolution vehicles are otherwise controversial in many respects. NPAs and DPAs in the FCPA context both facilitate the under-prosecution of egregious instances of corporate conduct as well as the over-prosecution of business conduct. In both instances, the DOJ has the practical ability to exercise unchecked power and an important rule of law principle is violated.

For these reasons, NPAs and DPAs in the FCPA context ought to be abolished and this reform proposal will increase the transparency of FCPA enforcement and better align FCPA enforcement with rule of law principles.

The two-fold FCPA reform proposal suggested above will result in the following enforcement landscape. If a payment is made in violation of the FCPA's anti-bribery provisions within a business organization, two issues will be relevant. First, if the payment was made, authorized or condoned by a director or executive officer, the business organization will not be able to avail itself of an FCPA compliance defense. Second, if the payment was made by any employee or agent in the absence of pre-existing FCPA compliance policies consistent with the best practices discussed in Chapter 8, the business organization will not be able to avail itself of an FCPA compliance defense.

In these scenarios involving corrupt directors or executive officers or business organizations without a commitment to FCPA compliance, the enforcement agencies will have two choices: do not prosecute or prosecute the business organization for violating the FCPA. This is a just and reasonable result and the third option of an NPA or DPA is not needed in such a scenario. As even the DOJ has acknowledged and empirical research has demonstrated, it is extremely unlikely that actual criminal prosecution of such a business organization will result in its demise.

Conversely, if the payment at issue is made by a non-executive employee or agent contrary to the business organization's pre-existing FCPA compliance policies, the organization will be able to avail itself of an FCPA compliance. Thus, as a matter of law, no FCPA prosecution of the organization will be able to proceed. This too is a just and reasonable result and aligns FCPA enforcement with enforcement regimes in several other peer countries.

The above FCPA reforms will take courage, both by Congress in amending the FCPA and by the enforcement agencies in abolishing the resolution vehicles they created. The reform proposals may indeed result in fewer FCPA enforcement actions as certain business organizations will be able to avail themselves of the compliance defense, and as enforcement agencies are once again mindful of their burdens of proof in prosecuting alleged FCPA violations. However, more FCPA enforcement is not necessarily an inherent good and ought not be the singular goal. The goal ought to be constructing an enforcement regime that best promotes compliance, reduces improper conduct, best advances the FCPA's objective of reducing bribery, increases transparency, and better aligns FCPA enforcement with rule of law principles.

The above FCPA reforms will accomplish these goals as well as increase public confidence in FCPA enforcement. The proposals will also rein in many of the FCPA's long tentacles and allow the enforcement agencies to better allocate limited prosecutorial resources to cases involving corrupt business organizations and the individuals who actually engage in the improper conduct.

The FCPA has witnessed courageous moments before. In 1977 Congress passed the pioneering law and the FCPA became the first law in the world governing business conduct with foreign government officials in foreign markets. Likewise, in the mid-1980s Congress and the enforcement agencies alike recognized that the FCPA, while fundamentally sound, could be improved upon and made a better statute. Despite misguided rhetoric that amending the FCPA was pro-bribery, sensible FCPA reform occurred.

A courageous moment is once again presented.

NOTES

1. 'The Foreign Corrupt Practices Act – Then and Now,' 12th Annual Foreign Corrupt Practices Act Conference (Nov. 15–16, 2004).
2. 'Origins of the FCPA,' Address at the ABA National Institute on the Foreign Corrupt Practices Act (Oct. 16, 2006).
3. James Doty, 'Toward a Reg. FCPA: A Modest Proposal for Change in Administering the Foreign Corrupt Practices Act,' 62 Business Lawyer 1233 (2007).
4. FCPA Professor, 'Breuer – Siemens Investigation (As to Individuals) Remains Open' (May 10, 2010).
5. FCPA Professor, 'Congressman Towns is Asking the Right Questions' (May 24, 2010).
6. U.S. Chamber Institute for Legal Reform, 'Restoring Balance: Proposed Amendments to the Foreign Corrupt Practices Act' (Oct. 27, 2010).
7. Keith Olbermann, MSNBC Countdown (NBC television broadcast Oct. 27, 2010).
8. Compliance Report, 'What? No Case Law? FCPA Enforcement Faces Attack,' (Jan. 17, 2011); Bloomberg, 'Swiss Shipper Finds Resistance Futile in U.S. Bribery Probe,' (Nov. 13, 2010).

9. Examining Enforcement of the Foreign Corrupt Practices Act, Hearing before the Subcommittee on Crime and Drugs of the Committee on the Judiciary, Senate (Nov. 30, 2010).
10. FCPA Professor, 'No – the Consistent Answer in DOJ Responses to Senator Questions Regarding FCPA Reform' (Apr. 14, 2011), containing links to original source documents.
11. 'Foreign Corrupt Practices Act,' Hearing before the Subcommittee on Crime, Terrorism, and Homeland Security of the Committee on the Judiciary, House of Representatives (June 14, 2011).
12. Brian Powell, Political Correction, 'Rep. Lamar Smith's Fight to Make Bribery Easier for Big Business' (June 9, 2011).
13. FCPA Professor, 'House Hearing – Pregame' (June 14, 2011), containing links to original source documents.
14. FCPA Professor, 'SEC Chairman Schapiro's FCPA Responses' (Oct. 7, 2011), containing links to original source documents.
15. Open Society Foundations, 'Busting Bribery: Sustaining the Global Momentum of the Foreign Corrupt Practices Act' (Sept. 2011).
16. FCPA Professor, 'Off Target' (Oct. 17, 2011).
17. FCPA Professor, 'The Compliance Defense around the World' (June 28, 2011).
18. New York City Bar Association, Committee on International Business Transactions, 'The FCPA and Its Impact on International Business Transactions – Should Anything Be Done to Minimize the Consequences of the U.S.'s Unique Position on Combating Offshore Corruption?' (Dec. 2011).
19. Walter Olson, Cato at Liberty, 'The Foreign Corrupt Practices Act: Clarification Is Not Enough' (Nov. 11, 2011).
20. Simple Justice, 'A Criminal Culture, The FCPA' (Nov. 13, 2011).
21. Press Release, U.S. Dep't of Justice, 'Assistant Attorney General Lanny A. Breuer Speaks at the 26th National Conference on the Foreign Corrupt Practices Act' (Nov. 8, 2011).
22. Wall Street Journal Law Blog, 'Rep. Scott Hopeful for FCPA Guidance' (Feb. 8, 2012).
23. House Rep. No. 100-40, Part 2 (April 6, 1987).
24. 55 Fed. Reg. 28,694 (July 12, 1990).
25. OECD, 'Report on Application of the Convention on Combating Bribery of Foreign Public Officials in International Business Transactions and the 1997 Recommendation on Combating Bribery in International Business Transactions' (Oct. 2002).
26. OECD, 'Phase 3 Report on Implementing the OECD Anti-Bribery Convention in the United States' (Oct. 2010).
27. *Supra* note 10.
28. *Supra* note 14.
29. Michael Mukasey and James Dunlop, Engage Vol. 13, Issue 1, 'Can Someone Please Turn on the Lights? Bringing Transparency to the Foreign Corrupt Practices Act' (March 2012).
30. William Jacobson, BNA Bloomberg Criminal Law Reporter, 'No Legislation Necessary: A Five-Part Test to Negate Corporate Criminal Liability in FCPA Cases' (Apr. 11, 2012).
31. David Bartsow, New York Times, 'Vast Mexico Bribery Case Hushed up by Wal-Mart after Top-Level Struggle' (Apr. 21, 2012).
32. Stephanie Clifford and David Barstow, New York Times, 'Wal-Mart Inquiry Reflects Alarm on Corruption' (Nov. 15, 2012).
33. FCPA Professor, 'Wal-Mart and FCPA Reform' (May 8, 2012).
34. Peter Henning, New York Times DealBook, 'Taking Aim at the Foreign Corrupt Practices Act' (Apr. 30, 2012).

35. Samuel Rubenfeld, Wall Street Journal Corruption Currents, 'Wal-Mart Bribery Allegations Stir up FCPA Debate Anew' (Apr. 24, 2012).
36. FCPA Professor, 'The FCPA – a View from the Hill' (June 28, 2012).
37. Press Release, Financial Transparency Coalition, 'Civil Society Organizations Welcome Justice Department and SEC's Anti-Corruption Guidance' (Nov. 14, 2012).
38. FCPA Professor, 'Guidance Press Conference' (Nov. 15, 2012).
39. Paul Enzinna, Manhattan Institute for Policy Research, 'The Foreign Corrupt Practices Act: Aggressive Enforcement and Lack of Judicial Review Create Uncertain Terrain for Businesses' (Jan. 2013).
40. FCPA Professor, 'Broad Coalition Of Business Groups Seek Real FCPA Reform' (Feb. 22, 2013).
41. Joint Hearings before the Subcommittee on Securities and the Subcommittee on International Finance and Monetary Policy of the Committee on Banking, Housing, and Urban Affairs, U.S. Senate, 97th Cong. (May 20, 1981).
42. The Foreign Trade Practices Act: Hearings on H.R. 2157 before the Subcomm. on Int'l Econ. Policy & Trade of the H. Comm. on Foreign Affairs, 98th Cong. (1983).
43. H.R. Rep. No. 99-580, pt. 1 (1986).
44. Id.
45. H.R. Rep. No. 100-40, pt. 2 (1987).
46. U.K. Ministry of Justice, The Bribery Act 2010: Guidance (2011).
47. The Economist, 'Bribery Abroad – a Tale of Two Laws' (Sept. 17, 2011).
48. *Supra* note 17.
49. OECD Working Group on Bribery in Int'l Business Transactions, Chile: Phase 1: Review of Implementation of the Convention and 1997 Recommendation (2009).
50. OECD Working Group on Bribery in Int'l Business Transactions, Italy: Phase 2: Report on the Application of the Convention on Combating Bribery of Foreign Public Officials in International Business Transactions and the 1997 Revised Recommendation on Combating Bribery in Int'l Business Transactions (2004).
51. OECD Working Group on Bribery in Int'l Business Transactions, Korea: Phase 2: Report on the Application of the Convention on Combating Bribery of Foreign Public Officials in International Business Transactions and the 1997 Revised Recommendation on Combating Bribery in Int'l Business Transactions (2004).
52. OECD Working Group on Bribery in Int'l Business Transactions, Portugal: Phase 2: Report on the Application of the Convention on Combating Bribery of Foreign Public Officials in International Business Transactions and the 1997 Revised Recommendation on Combating Bribery in Int'l Business Transactions (2009).
53. OECD Working Group on Bribery in Int'l Business Transactions, Switzerland: Phase 2: Report on the Application of the Convention on Combating Bribery of Foreign Public Officials in International Business Transactions and the 1997 Revised Recommendation on Combating Bribery in Int'l Business Transactions (2005).
54. Joe Palazzalo, Wall Street Journal Law Blog, 'An FCPA Compliance Defense? No Way Breuer Says' (Apr. 1, 2011).
55. FCPA Professor, 'DOJ Declines to Get Specific in Declination Responses' (Oct. 12, 2011), containing links to original source documents.
56. *Supra* note 11.
57. FCPA Professor, 'Former Attorney General Alberto Gonzales Criticizes Various Aspects of DOJ FCPA Enforcement' (April 4, 2013).
58. Philip K. Howard, Newsweek, 'Government Is Broken. These Guys Can Fix It' (Apr. 10, 2011).
59. FCPA Professor, 'Former DOJ FCPA Chief Supports FCPA Compliance Defense' (Oct. 4, 2011).
60. Andrew Weissmann and David Newman, 'Rethinking Criminal Corporate Liability,' 82 Indiana Law Journal 411 (2007).

61. *Supra* note 9.
62. Argyle Journal, 'Turning a New Page against Corruption at the Corporate Level: Freshfield's Partner Explains Impact of UK Bribery Act' (Aug. 9, 2012).
63. FCPA Professor, 'On Point' (Jan. 14, 2011).
64. Press Release, U.S. Dep't of Justice, 'Assistant Attorney General Lanny A. Breuer Speaks at the New York City Bar Association' (Sept. 13, 2012).
65. Id.
66. Gabriel Markoff, 'Arthur Andersen and the Myth of the Corporate Death Penalty: Corporate Criminal Convictions in the Twenty-First Century,' 15 Univ. of Pennsylvania Journal of Business Law 797 (2013).
67. FCPA Professor, 'Our Stellar FCPA Unit Continues to Go Gangbusters, Bringing Case after Case,' (May 6, 2013).
68. Press Release, U.S. Dep't of Justice, 'Assistant Attorney General Lanny A. Breuer Speaks at the New York City Bar Association' (Sept. 13, 2012).
69. U.S. Government Accountability Office, 'Corporate Crime: DOJ Has Taken Steps to Better Track Its Use of Deferred and Non-Prosecution Agreements, But Should Evaluate Effectiveness' (2009).
70. *Supra* note 26.
71. OECD, United States: Follow-Up to the Phase 3 Report & Recommendations (Dec. 2012).
72. Press Release, U.S. Dep't of Justice, 'Aibel Group Ltd. Pleads Guilty to Foreign Bribery and Agrees to Pay $4.2 Million in Criminal Fines' (Nov. 21, 2008).
73. Joe Palazzolo, Wall Street Journal Corruption Currents, 'Ingersoll-Rand Exits DPA Gracefully, Despite New FCPA Issues' (Feb. 23, 2011).
74. Christopher Matthews, 'Daimler not out of the Woods in Bribery Case' (Apr. 5, 2012).
75. FCPA Professor, 'Our Stellar FCPA Unit Continues to Go Gangbusters, Bringing Case after Case,' (May 6, 2013).
76. FCPA Professor, 'The Problem with FCPA Enforcement? Look No Further Than BizJet/Lufthansa Technik' (Apr. 12, 2012), containing links to original source documents.
77. FCPA Professor, 'DOJ Prosecution of Individuals – Are Other Factors at Play?' (Jan. 29, 2013).
78. 'International Criminal Law Enforcement: Rule of Law, Anti-Corruption and Beyond,' Remarks of Lanny A. Breuer, Assistant Attorney General for the Criminal Division, U.S. Department of Justice, Council on Foreign Relations (May 4, 2010).
79. The World Justice Project, Rule of Law Index (2012–2013).
80. *Supra* note 11.

Conclusion

From a pioneering law that many originally viewed as unenforceable and nothing more than a 'policy assertion,' to the most important and feared law when conducting business in the global marketplace, the Foreign Corrupt Practices Act has indeed come a long way. However, many of the same difficult and complex issues confronted decades ago remain the same in the FCPA's new era.

What is bribery? Who decides what bribery is? Are all attempts to punish and deter bribery good? You now know how an entire book can be devoted to these topics and why the answers to these questions are not the simple, safe answers they appeared to be at first blush.

In dissecting the FCPA's new era, you have encountered the FCPA's statutory text, legislative history, judicial decisions, enforcement agency guidance, and FCPA enforcement actions. This legal authority and other information has provided you a pair of FCPA goggles and thus a fundamental skill-set that will serve you well in the global marketplace.

Your FCPA goggles provide insight into the FCPA's new era and the many legal and policy issues associated with FCPA enforcement. With your FCPA goggles you can now better understand the FCPA's provisions, appreciate the 'three buckets' of FCPA financial exposure and the FCPA's other long tentacles, and best manage and minimize FCPA risk. And most importantly, with your FCPA goggles you now have a sharper focus to critically analyze various aspects of this new era, including whether the current FCPA and its enforcement best advance the laudable objectives of the FCPA.

Conclusion

Index